THE AMAZING BOOK OF HISTORY

Extraordinary Facts and Stories

D0089552

WEST
SIDE
PUBLISHING

Contributing Writers: Mark K. Anderson, Robert Bullington, William W. David, Tom DeMichael, Eric Ethier, R.G.W. Griffin, Peter Haugen, Jonathan W. Jordan, J. K. Kelly, David Lesjak, J. David Markham, Bill Martin, Michael Martin, Mark McLaughlin, Ed Moser, Peter Muggeridge, Eric D. Nelson, Jean L. S. Patrick, Bill Sasser, Chuck Wills

Cover Illustrator: Peter Siu

Contributing Illustrator: Linda Bittner

Fact-checkers: Donna Halper; Regina Montgomery; Katrina O'Brien; Marilyn Perlberg, Ph.D.; Betsy Rossen Elliot

CONTENTS

A JOURNEY THROUGH TIME

In the words of Aldous Huxley, "The charm of history and its enigmatic lesson consist in the fact that, from age to age, nothing changes and yet everything is completely different."

With those words in mind, we began to create *Armchair Reader™: The Amazing Book of History.* We wanted this new Reader to have information that would be thought-provoking and enjoyable for both the novice and the expert. You never know—a relaxing browse for one reader could become the stepping-off point to a journey of information-seeking for another.

Most important, we wanted to make this journey entertaining, enlightening, and captivating.

Reviewing historical events can be so many things: exciting, moving, mystifying, horrifying, confounding, inspiring—it's the panorama of human interaction set against the backdrop of time. We definitely had our work cut out for us as we sought the most unusual and intriguing topics. This process began with topic selection, an exhaustive search for writers, editing, art selection, cover selection, production, more editing, fact-checking, indexing, more editing (I think you get the picture), and finally—with a deep sigh—reflection. That reflection is focused on our wish and hope that you enjoy this book as much as we have enjoyed putting it together for you.

Please enjoy,

Allen Orso

Publisher

P.S. If you have any questions, concerns, or ideas pertaining to this book, or if you would like more information about other West Side Publishing titles, please contact us at: **www.armchairreader.com.**

DON'T TOUCH THAT DIAL! THE BIRTH OF RADIO

At the turn of the 20th century, no one could have imagined today's world of shock-jocks, satellite radio, or streaming Internet audio. The idea of wireless communications was as foreign as the thought that humans would one day fly to the moon.

IN THE BEGINNING

In the 1800s, discoveries by the German-born Heinrich Hertz and Scottish James Clerk Maxwell set the stage for Guglielmo Marconi's notable invention: the wireless telegraph. But his home country of Italy offered no support for his work, so Marconi sought and received aid from the British government. Soon the dots and dashes of Morse code were spanning the English Channel via radio signals. In 1897, Marconi founded the Wireless Telegraph & Signal Company Limited. A few year later, Morse code for the letter "S" was sent from the shores of England and received in Newfoundland, Canada. Marconi's radio signal had reached across the Atlantic Ocean.

ENTER LEE DE FOREST

Inventor Lee De Forest took wireless communications a step further. The brilliant De Forest labored with many types of wireless telegraphs in the 1900s, building some for Western Electric and the U.S. Navy. In 1906, he invented the Audion, a three-element electron tube that amplified audio signals (the Audion was an improvement of the two-element device patented by Sir John Ambrose Fleming in 1904). The Audion was capable of transmitting Morse code and, more importantly, voice farther than ever before.

Initially, wireless transmissions were used strictly as communication for business or military operations. However, De Forest thought the new medium had greater potential. From 1907 to

1912, he invited members of the press to listen at receiving sets during several demonstrations in which he broadcast opera performances. These "broadcasts," were done using arc radiotelephones, which were less sophisticated but more popular than the Audion at the time. Still, they showed that the wireless system could have much broader applications than its inventors had previously thought.

MOVING DOWN THE DIAL

By 1913, De Forest had sold his patent for the Audion to AT&T, which used the device to boost voice signals across the continent. In 1916, the Audion tube became an essential part of commercial transmitters.

De Forest's work was not limited to radio. In 1920, he developed the first sound-on-film process (Phonofilm) for the motion-picture industry. He received Hollywood's highest honor—an honorary Oscar in 1959—for his "Pioneer Invention which brought sound to the Motion Picture." His process is still used today for analogue film audio.

- *Some say the beginning of broadcasting was January 12, 1908. The* USS Ohio *had previously played music for its own troops, but on that date, the ship broadcast band tunes to nearby ships—and even took requests from their sailors.*

- *Live from New York: In 1916, Lee De Forest became the first person to broadcast election results to an audience. From the High Bridge in New York, he shared the results of the Hughes-Wilson presidential election.*

"The wireless music box has no imaginable commercial value. Who would pay for a message sent to nobody in particular?"
—DAVID SARNOFF, AMERICAN RADIO PIONEER, 1921

ONE HECK OF A HOAX? THE MYSTERIOUS VOYNICH MANUSCRIPT

Dubbed the "World's Most Mysterious Book," the Voynich manuscript contains more than 200 vellum pages of vivid, colorful illustrations and handwritten prose. There's only one small problem: No one knows what any of it means. Or whether it means anything at all.

It was "discovered" in 1912 after being hidden from the world for almost 250 years. An American antique book dealer named Wilfried Voynich came across the medieval manuscript at an Italian Jesuit College. Approximately nine inches by six inches in size, the manuscript bore a soft, light-brown vellum cover, which was unmarked, untitled, and gave no indication as to when it had been written or by whom.

Bound inside were approximately 230 yellow parchment pages, most of which contained richly colored drawings of strange plants, celestial bodies, and other scientific matter. Many of the pages were adorned by naked nymphs bathing in odd-looking plumbing and personal-size washtubs. Handwritten text written in flowing script accompanied the illustrations.

Although Voynich was an expert antiquarian, he was baffled by the book's contents. And today—nearly a century later—the manuscript that came to bear his name remains a mystery.

WEIRD SCIENCE

The mystery surrounding the Voynich Manuscript begins with its content, which reads (so to speak) like a work of weird science presented in six identifiable "sections":

- a botanical section, containing drawings of plants that no botanist has ever been able to identify

- an astronomical section, with illustrations of the sun, moon, stars, and zodiac symbols surrounded by naked nymphs bathing in individual washtubs

  - a "biological" section, showing perplexing anatomical drawings of chambers or organs connected by tubes—and which also features more nymphs swimming in their inner liquids

- a cosmological section, consisting mostly of unexplained circular drawings

- a pharmaceutical section, depicting drawings of plant parts (leaves, roots) placed next to containers

- a recipe section, featuring short paragraphs "bulleted" by stars in the margin

Weirder still are the ubiquitous nymphs—a nice touch perhaps, but how they relate to the subject matter is anyone's guess.

MANY MYSTERIES, STILL NO ANSWERS

And then there's the manuscript's enigmatic text. The world's greatest cryptologists have failed to unravel its meaning. Even the American and British code breakers who cracked the Japanese and German codes in World War II were stumped. To this day, not a single word of the Voynich manuscript has been deciphered.

This, of course, has led to key unsolved questions, namely:

- Who wrote it? A letter found with the manuscript, dated 1666, credits Roger Bacon, a Franciscan friar who lived from 1214 to 1294. This has since been discredited because the manuscript's date of origin is generally considered to be between 1450 and 1500. There are as many theories about who wrote it as there are nymphs among its pages. In fact, some believe Voynich forged the whole thing.

- What is it? It was first thought to be a coded description of Bacon's early scientific discoveries. Since then, other theories ranging from an ancient prayer book written in a pidgin Germanic language to one big, elaborate hoax (aside from that supposedly perpetrated by Voynich) have been posited.

• Is it real writing? Is the script composed in a variation of a known language, a lost language, an encrypted language, an artificial language? Or is it just plain gibberish?

WHAT DO WE KNOW?

Despite the aura of mystery surrounding the manuscript, it has been possible to trace its travels over the past 400 years. The earliest known owner was Holy Roman Emperor Rudolph II, who purchased it in 1586. By 1666, the manuscript had passed through a series of owners to Athanasius Kircher, a Jesuit scholar who hid it in the college where Voynich found it 250 years later.

After being passed down to various members of Voynich's estate, the manuscript was sold in 1961 to a rare-book collector who sought to resell it for a fortune. After failing to find a buyer, he donated it to Yale University, where it currently resides—still shrouded in mystery—in the Beinecke Rare Book and Manuscript Library.

THE SEARCH FOR MEANING CONTINUES...

To this day, efforts to translate the Voynich manuscript continue. And still, the manuscript refuses to yield its secrets, leading experts to conclude that it's either an ingenious hoax or the ultimate unbreakable code. The hoax theory gained some ground in 2004 when Dr. Gordon Rugg, a computer-science lecturer at Keele University, announced that he had replicated the Voynich Manuscript using a low-tech device called a Cardan grille. According to Rugg, this proved that the manuscript was likely a fraud—a volume of jibberish created, perhaps, in an attempt to con money out of Emperor Rudolph II. Mystery solved? Well, it's not quite as simple as that. Many researchers remain unconvinced. Sure, Rugg may have proven that the manuscript might be a hoax. But the possibility that it is *not* a hoax remains. And thus, the search for meaning continues....

MILLIONS OF MUMMIES

It sounds like the premise of a horror movie—
millions of excess mummies just piling up. But for the Egyptians,
this was simply an excuse to get a little creative.

The ancient Egyptians took death seriously. Their culture believed that the afterlife was a dark and tumultuous place where departed souls *(ka)* needed protection throughout eternity. By preserving their bodies as mummies, Egyptians provided their souls with a resting place—without which they would wander the afterlife forever.

Starting roughly around 3000 B.C., Egyptian morticians began making a healthy business on the mummy trade. On receiving a corpse, they would first remove the brain and internal organs and store them in canopic jars. Next, they would stuff the body with straw to maintain its shape, cover it in salt and oils to preserve it from rotting, and then wrap it in linens—a process that could take up to 70 days. Finally, the finished mummies would be placed in a decorated sarcophagus, now ready to face eternity.

Mummies have always been a source of great mystery and fascination. The tales of mummy curses were wildly popular in their time, and people still flock to horror movies involving vengeful mummies. Museum displays, especially King Tut or Ramses II, remain a sure-fire draw, allowing patrons the chance for a remarkably preserved glimpse of ancient Egypt.

At first, mummification was so costly it remained the exclusive domain of the wealthy, usually royalty. However, when the middle class began adopting the procedure, the mummy population exploded. Soon people were mummifying everything—even crocodiles. The practice of mummifying the family cat was also common; the owners saw it as an offering to the cat goddess Bast.

Even those who could not afford to properly mummify their loved ones unknowingly contributed to the growing number of mummies. These folks buried their deceased in the Egyptian desert, where the hot, arid conditions dried out the bodies, creating natural mummies. When you consider that this burial art was in use for more than 3,000 years, it's not surprising that over time the bodies began piling up—literally.

So, with millions of mummies lying around, local entrepreneurs began looking for ways to cash in on these buried treasures. To them, mummies were a natural resource, not unlike oil, which could be extracted from the ground and sold at a heavy profit to eager buyers around the world.

MUMMY MEDICINE

In medieval times, Egyptians began touting mummies for their secret medicinal qualities. European doctors began importing mummies, boiling off their oils and prescribing it to patients. The oil was used to treat a variety of disorders, including sore throats, coughs, epilepsy, poisoning, and skin disorders. Contemporary apothecaries also got into the act, marketing pulverized mummies to noblemen as a cure for nausea.

The medical establishment wasn't completely sold on the beneficial aspects of mummy medicine, however. Several doctors voiced their opinions against the practice, one writing that: "It ought to be rejected as loathsome and offensive," and another claiming: "This wicked kind of drugge doth nothing to help the diseased." A cholera epidemic, which broke out in Europe, was blamed on mummy bandages, and the use of mummy medicine was soon abandoned.

MUMMY MERCHANTS

Grave robbers, a common feature of 19th-century Egypt, made a huge profit from mummies. Arab traders would raid ancient tombs, sometimes making off with hundreds of bodies. These would be sold to visiting English merchants who, on returning to England, could resell them to wealthy buyers. Victorian socialites would buy mummies and hold fashionable parties, inviting friends over to view the unwrapping of their Egyptian prize.

MUMMIES IN MUSEUMS

By the mid-19th century, museums were becoming common in Europe, and mummies were prized exhibits. Curators, hoping to make a name for their museums, would travel to Egypt and purchase a mummy to display back home. This provided a steady stream of revenue for the unscrupulous mummy merchants. In the 1850s, the Egyptian government finally stopped the looting of their priceless heritage. Laws were passed allowing only certified archaeologists access to mummy tombs, effectively putting the grave robbers out of business.

MUMMY MYTHS

There are so many stories regarding the uses of mummies that it's often hard to separate fact from fiction. Some historians suggest the linens that comprised mummy wrappings were used by 19th-century American and Canadian industrialists to manufacture paper. At the time, there was a huge demand for paper, and suppliers often ran short of cotton rags—a key ingredient in the paper-making process. Although there's no concrete proof, some historians claim that when paper manufacturers ran out of rags, they imported mummies to use in their place.

Another curious claim comes courtesy of Mark Twain. In his popular 1869 travelogue *The Innocents Abroad,* Twain wrote: "The fuel [Egyptian train operators] use for the locomotive is composed of mummies three thousand years old, purchased by the ton or by the graveyard for that purpose." This item, almost assuredly meant as satire, was taken as fact by readers and survives to this day. However, there is no historical record of Egyptian trains running on burnt mummies. Besides, the mischievous Twain was never one to let a few facts get in the way of a good story. Perhaps those who believe the humorist's outlandish claim might offset it with another of his famous quotes: "A lie can travel halfway around the world while the truth is putting on its shoes."

Fast Facts

- Your kitchen contains the materials needed to make the starting element for mummification (though please don't try it at home): natron. This is a naturally occurring combination of sodium bicarbonate and sodium chloride—baking soda and salt—dissolved in water. The body soaked in this stuff for 40 days.

- Egyptian embalmers were like modern funeral homes—they'd show you sample statues until you found a process that fit your price range.

- An "el cheapo" mummification consisted of cleaning out the intestines, then soaking the body in natron for ten weeks. After that, the family got the body back to do with as they wished.

- Near the mummy, embalmers set canopic jars (often made of ornate alabaster) supposed to contain the mummy's entrails. However, some lazy or unscrupulous embalmers just filled the jars with mud and cedar pitch. It was probably easy to get away with. The only people inspecting the jars were looters, who didn't care.

- The long era of Egyptian mummification ended soon after A.D. 392 when Theodosius II, emperor of Rome, banned the practice.

- By studying mummies, historians learned that it wasn't odd for an Egyptian to have parasites almost large enough to merit separate mummification. Many had Guinea worms, a horrible pest that can grow to three feet long.

- No cancerous tumor has yet been identified in the soft tissue of any Egyptian mummy. Bone tumors, yes; internal organ cancers, no.

- By the 1800s, mummy unwrappings rivaled garden parties and fox hunts as highlights of the English social season. Lords would send out printed invitations to their friends: "A Mummy from Thebes to be unrolled at half past two, 10th June 1850."

- It's possible to isolate and clone DNA from Egyptian mummies.

THE VANISHING TREASURE ROOM

In the Age of Enlightenment, kings and emperors built immense palaces to outdo one another—each one bigger and more gilded and bejeweled than the last. But one of Russia's greatest 18th-century treasures became one of the 20th century's greatest unsolved mysteries.

The storied history of the Amber Room begins in 1701, when it was commissioned by Frederick I of Prussia. Considered by admirers and artists alike to be the "Eighth Wonder of the World," the sparkling, honey-gold room consisted of wall panels inlaid with prehistoric amber, finely carved and illuminated by candles and mirrors. In 1716, Prussian King Freidrich Wilhelm I gifted the panels to then-ally Russian Tsar Peter the Great to ornament the imperial palace at his new capital, St. Petersburg.

After sitting at the Winter Palace for four decades, the Amber Room was moved to Tsarskoye Selo, the Romanov palace just south of St. Petersburg. During the mid-18th century, Prussia's King Frederick the Great sent Russia's Empress Elizabeth more of the amber material from his Baltic holdings, and Elizabeth ordered her court's great Italian architect, Bartolomeo Rastrelli, to expand the Amber Room into an 11-foot-square masterpiece.

The golden room was not finished until 1770, under the reign of Catherine the Great. Incorporating more than six tons of amber and accented with semiprecious stones, the fabled room became not only a prized jewel of the Russian empire, but a symbol of the long-standing alliance between Prussia and Russia.

FROM PEACE TO WAR

Two centuries after the Amber Room was removed to the Catherine Palace, the world was a much darker place. Prussia and Russia, formerly faithful allies, were locked in a deadly struggle that would bring down both imperial houses. By 1941, the former dominions of Frederick and Peter were ruled by Adolf Hitler and Joseph Stalin.

In a surprise attack, Hitler's armies drove across the Soviet border in June 1941 to launch the most destructive war in history. German panzers drove from the Polish frontier to the gates of Moscow in an epic six-month campaign, devouring some of the most fertile, productive territory in Eastern Europe.

One of the unfortunate cities in the path of the Nazi onslaught was St. Petersburg, renamed Leningrad by its communist masters. Frantic palace curators desperately tried to remove the Amber Room's antique panels, but the brittle prehistoric resin began to crumble as the panels were detached. Faced with probable destruction of one of Russia's greatest treasures or its abandonment to the Nazis, the curators attempted to hide the room's precious panels by covering them with gauze and wallpaper.

Although Leningrad withstood a long, bloody siege, German troops swept through the city's suburbs, capturing Tsarskoye Selo intact in October 1941. Soldiers discovered the treasure hidden behind the wallpaper, and German troops disassembled the room's panels over a 36-hour period, packed them in 27 crates, and shipped them back to Königsberg, in East Prussia.

The fabled Amber Room panels were put on display in Königsberg's castle museum. They remained there for two years—until the Third Reich began to crumble before the weight of Soviet and Anglo-American miltary forces. Sometime in 1944, the room's valuable panels were allegedly dismantled and packed into crates, to prevent damage by British and Soviet bombers. In January 1945, Hitler permitted the westward movement of cultural treasures, including the Italo-Russo-German masterpiece.

And from there, the Amber Room was lost to history.

THE GREAT TREASURE HUNT

The world was left to speculate about the fate of the famous imperial room, and dozens of theories have been spawned about the room's whereabouts. Some claim the Amber Room was lost—sunk aboard a submarine, bombed to pieces, or perhaps burned in Königsberg. This last conclusion was accepted by Alexander Brusov, a Soviet investigator sent to find the Amber Room shortly after the war's end. Referring to the destruction of Königsberg Castle by Red Army forces on April 9, 1945, he concluded: "Summarizing all the facts, we can say that the Amber Room was destroyed between 9 and 11 April 1945." An in-depth hunt by two British investigative journalists pieced together the last days of the Amber Room and concluded that its fate was sealed when Soviet troops accidentally set fire to the castle compound during the last month of combat, destroying the brittle jewels and obscuring their location.

Other treasure hunters, however, claim the room still sits in an abandoned mine shaft or some long-forgotten Nazi bunker beneath the outskirts of Königsberg. One German investigator claimed former SS officers told him the room's panels were packed up and hidden in an abandoned silver mine near Berlin; a Lithuanian official claimed witnesses saw SS troops hiding the panels in a local swamp. Neither has been able to prove his claims.

THE TRAIL GOES COLD

The hunt for the Amber Room has been made more difficult because its last witnesses are gone—several under mysterious circumstances. The Nazi curator in charge of the room died of typhus the day before he was scheduled to be interviewed by the KGB, and a Soviet intelligence officer who spoke to a journalist about the room's whereabouts died the following day in a car crash. In 1987, Georg Stein, a former German soldier who had devoted his life to searching for the Amber Room, was found murdered in a forest, his stomach slit open by a scalpel.

In 1997, the world got a tantalizing glimpse of the long-lost treasure when German police raided the office of a Bremen lawyer who was attempting to sell an amber mosaic worth $2.5 million on behalf of one of his clients, the son of a former German lieutenant. The small mosaic—inlaid with jade and onyx as well as amber—had been stolen from the Amber Room by a German officer and was separated from the main panels. After its seizure, this last true remnant of the legendary tsarist treasure made its way back to Russia in April 2000.

Decades of searches by German and Soviet investigators have come up empty. The fate of the fabled room—worth an estimated $142 million to $250 million in today's currency—has remained an elusive ghost for treasure seekers, mystery writers, and investigators looking for the Holy Grail of Russian baroque artwork.

PICKING UP THE PIECES

In 1979, the Soviet government, with help from a donation made by a German gas firm in 1999, began amassing old photographs of the Amber Room and pieces of the rare amber to create a reconstructed room worthy of its predecessor. Carefully rebuilt at a cost exceeding $7 million, the reconstructed room was dedicated by the Russian president and German chancellor at a ceremony in 2003, marking the tricentennial of St. Petersburg's founding. The dazzling Amber Room is now on display for the thousands of tourists who come to Tsarskoye Selo to view the playground of one of Europe's great dynasties.

- *Amber is an orange gem that comes from the dried resin of prehistoric trees.*

- *Of all gems, amber is the lightest. In fact, genuine amber is so light that it floats in saltwater.*

- *When rubbed, amber can acquire an electric charge. Thus, the Greek word for amber is* electrum, *which is the origin of the word* electricity.

Misconceptions of History
THERE'S NO PLACE
LIKE HOME

Every now and then, conventional wisdom turns out to be dead wrong. Throughout history, humankind's big leaps forward have often come only when some bright thinker was willing to challenge generally accepted wisdom. At other times, long-cherished myths, such as "baths are unhealthy" or "the world is flat," simply wither and die over many years by mutual consent.

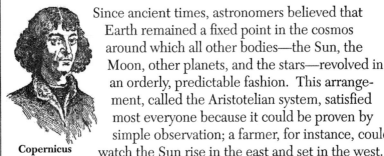

Since ancient times, astronomers believed that Earth remained a fixed point in the cosmos around which all other bodies—the Sun, the Moon, other planets, and the stars—revolved in an orderly, predictable fashion. This arrangement, called the Aristotelian system, satisfied most everyone because it could be proven by simple observation; a farmer, for instance, could watch the Sun rise in the east and set in the west.

Copernicus

It was not until 1514 that Polish astronomer Nicolaus Copernicus began popularizing a theory of *heliocentrism,* which claims that Earth revolves around the Sun and not the other way around. The astronomer's theory was soundly criticized in his day (mostly by fellow scientists, and not so much by clergymen, as is often thought). But subsequent studies showed Copernicus to be right, and the accepted wisdom of the previous 2,000 years went out the window. That is, until 1905, when Albert Einstein concluded that one could never truly say whether the Sun revolved around Earth or vice-versa; all you can say is that they move relative to each other. Beyond that, it's just a matter of your perspective.

PLIGHT OF THE PILGRIMS: JOURNEY TO THE NEW WORLD

When the Pilgrims began their voyage to the New World, they didn't expect to sail on the Mayflower, *nor did they plan to land at Plymouth Rock.*

DESTINATION: HOLLAND

The story of the Pilgrims begins back in 1606—14 years before they set sail on the *Mayflower.*

A band of worshippers from Scrooby Manor, who belonged to the Church of England, decided that they would rather worship God according to the Bible than indulge in the extra prayers and hymns imposed by the church. However, separating from the church was easier said than done. In England, it was illegal to be a Separatist. Risking imprisonment, the worshippers escaped to Holland, a land of religious tolerance. But their time in Holland was a mixed blessing. Although they worshipped freely, they feared their children were becoming more Dutch than English.

DESTINATION: HUDSON RIVER

Meanwhile, English noblemen were seeking brave, industrious people to sail to America and establish colonies in Virginia (which extended far beyond the Virginia we know today). They offered the Separatists a contract for land at the mouth of the Hudson River, near present-day New York City.

Led by William Brewster and William Bradford, the Separatists accepted the offer and began preparing for their voyage. They even bought their own boat: the *Speedwell.* In July 1620, they sailed to England to meet 52 more passengers who rode in their own ship, the *Mayflower.* The Separatists, who called themselves "Saints," referred to these new people as "Strangers."

DESTINATION: UNKNOWN

The *Speedwell* should have been called the *Leakwell*. After two disastrous starts, the Saints abandoned hope of her sailing again. On September 6, they joined the Strangers on the *Mayflower*.

The *Mayflower* was just 30 yards long—about the length of three school buses. The 50 Saints rode in the "tween" deck, an area between the two decks that was actually the gun deck. Its ceilings were only about five feet high.

Accommodations in the rest of the boat were hardly better. Cramped into close quarters were 52 Strangers, 30 crewmen (who laughed at the seasick landlubbers), 2 dogs (a spaniel and a mastiff), barley, oats, shovels, hammers, tools, beer, cheese, cooking pots, and chamber pots. There may have been pigs on board, too.

As they journeyed across the Atlantic, storms and rough waters pushed them off course. After 65 days on the high seas, they realized they were nowhere near the Hudson River. Instead, they sighted the finger of Cape Cod—more than 220 miles away from their destination.

Though they were far from the land contracted for the English colony, the settlers saw their arrival in the New World as an opportunity to build a better life. In November 1620, 41 free men (Saints and Strangers alike) signed the *Mayflower Compact*. They agreed to work together for the good of the colony and to elect leaders to create a "civil body politic."

BUT WHAT ABOUT PLYMOUTH ROCK?

After anchoring in a harbor (which is now Provincetown), the Saints formed three expeditions to locate a suitable place to live. One expedition ventured 30 miles west to a place called "Plimouth," which had been mapped several years earlier by explorer John Smith.

The settlers first noticed a giant rock, probably weighing 200 tons, near the shore. The land nearby had already been cleared. Likely, more than a thousand Native people had lived there before being wiped out by an epidemic. Some remaining bones were still visible.

In December 1620, the group decided to make Plymouth its settlement. According to legend, each passenger stepped on Plymouth Rock upon landing. If this actually happened, leader William Bradford did not record it.

By springtime, half of the *Mayflower's* passengers would be dead. Yet the first steps on land—no matter where they took place— remain important. Helped by Native people, the Saints and Strangers would live and work together to form one of the first British settlements in North America.

- *How do we know all of this? William Bradford kept a detailed journal, now known as* Of Plymouth Plantation. *In it, he detailed the history of the Plymouth colony between the years of 1630 and 1647.*

- *The "First Thanksgiving" was little more than a harvest feast. Thanksgiving was not an official holiday until Abraham Lincoln proclaimed a national day for giving thanks in 1863.*

- *The journey to America left the pilgrims deeply in debt to English merchants who had financed the trip. The early fruits of pilgrim labor were sent back to England to repay the debt.*

- *Pieces of Plymouth Rock can be seen today at Pilgrim Hall Museum, as well as at the Smithsonian.*

- *According to estimates, Plymouth Rock is now only about ⅓ its original size. Over the years, the rock has been broken during attempts to move it, and people have chipped off pieces to take as souvenirs.*

- *The first historical references to "Plymouth Rock" appeared more than 100 years after the pilgrims' landing.*

HOLLYWOOD VERSUS HISTORY

You may not be surprised to learn that Hollywood doesn't always get history right.

Don't ask us how we know this

American Psycho (2000)—Though the action takes place in 1992, the porn film glimpsed on Christian Bale's TV set while he chats on the phone with his fiancée is *Red Vibe Diaries: Object of Desire,* which was released in 1997.

The Millard Fillmore monument is so much more camera friendly

The Color of Friendship (2000)—In this story set in 1977, scaffolding used during the 2000 renovation of the Washington Monument is seen.

Say, man, check out that Mathew Brady dude

Glory (1989)—In this Civil War drama about black Union troops, the soldiers speak in the idiom of the 1980s.

But you had to crank it

O Brother, Where art Thou? (2000)—This film, set in the 1930s, includes the song "You Are My Sunshine," which was not released until 1940.

On his feet and his hands

Tarzan (1999)—One of the apes wears sneakers.

Boy, somebody deserves to be executed for this one

Factory Girl (2006)—Andy Warhol watches an episode of *I Dream of Jeannie* a month before the show's premiere.

Dead silence might have been nice

Dirty Dancing (1987)—Sound track music alternates between period-appropriate pop tunes from the early '60s and synth-rock.

Göring noticed that, too

They Saved Hitler's Brain (1963)—When Hitler speaks in German, the words are actually gibberish.

Thou shalt not covet thy neighbor's Bulova

The Ten Commandments (1956)—An old man who holds up a "graven image" is wearing a wristwatch.

Mention it and he'll punch your lights out

The Big Brawl (1980)—Although set in the 1930s, the film includes a character wearing a disco-style suit.

No, I'm not wearing earrings, those are my eyeballs

The Aviator (2004)—Howard Hughes flies his 1935 open-cockpit H-1 at 350 mph without goggles.

I guess that means the air bags have to go, too

Driving Miss Daisy (1989)—Styrofoam shows up in more than one scene, years before it was marketed commercially.

And a Wonderbra

Geronimo (1962)—Geronimo's Indian wife wears false eyelashes and eyeshadow.

Don't miss the Elvis mummy

The Mummy (1999)—An early shot of the ancient city of Thebes includes the Pyramids of Giza and the Great Sphinx, which are actually at the old city of Memphis, near Cairo.

We kid because we love you

Kelly's Heroes (1970)—Don Rickles has a box full of Almond Joy candy bars—which weren't introduced until after the war, in 1946.

When you're a pirate, *every* day is casual Friday

Pirates of the Caribbean: Curse of the Black Pearl (2003)—When Jack yells, "On deck, you scabrous dogs!," a member of the film crew—wearing a cowboy hat and sunglasses—is visible in the background.

BOMBING THE ROYAL WEDDING

It is traditional for wedding guests to throw birdseed or rose petals to celebrate a newly married couple. But the king of Spain had something different thrown at his wedding—a bomb hidden in a bouquet of flowers.

Proclaimed king of Spain upon his birth on May 17, 1886 (his father Alfonso XII died before he was born), Alfonso XIII inherited a nation long past its imperial prime.

As a member of European royalty, Alfonso inherited status as a high-profile target for anarchist radicals, who had been terrorizing Europe since the mid-19th century. His father had survived an assassination attempt in 1878, the same year that Kaiser Wilhelm I weathered two attempts on his life. Czar Alexander II of Russia was killed in a bombing in 1881, after narrowly escaping assassination attempts in 1866 and 1879.

Throughout the continent, royalty and heads of state were targeted by anarchists under their doctrine of "propaganda of the deed," a violent form of direct action that targeted prominent figures with the goal of gaining notoriety and support for the anarchists' cause. The turn of the 20th century saw a new spate of attacks. In 1894, French President Sadi Carnot was stabbed to death. In 1900, Umberto I of Italy was shot dead. In 1901, anarchist Leon Czolgosz killed U.S. President William McKinley. In 1902, Leopold II of Belgium survived an assassination attempt. In 1905, a bomb killed Duke Sergei Alexandrovich, fifth son of Czar Alexander II.

In Spain, Prime Minister Antonio Cánovas del Castillo had been assassinated by Italian anarchist Michele Angiolillo in 1897. Alfonso XIII's marriage to Princess Victoria Eugénie of Battenberg (a niece of King Edward VII of Britain and granddaughter of

Queen Victoria) offered another tempt-
ing opportunity for propaganda by deed.
After their wedding in Madrid on May
31, 1906, Alfonso and Queen Ena, as she
was known, were proceeding down Calle
Mayor when anarchist Mateu Morral
threw a bomb concealed in a flower
bouquet toward their carriage. Several
bystanders and horses were killed; the
royal couple escaped with only blood spatters on the queen's wed-
ding dress. A Catalan who had quit his family's textile business
to work as a librarian for anarchist educational reformer Francisco Ferrer Guardia, Morral was aided by radical journalist José
Nakens. He fled the assassination attempt and committed suicide
after killing a policeman as he pretended to surrender.

Unrest continued in Spain. In 1909, a general strike and five days
of mob rule were followed by martial law and brutal military sup-
pression as anarchist assassinations continued throughout Europe.
In 1912, Spanish Prime Minister José Canalejas was assassinated
in Madrid. Two years later, the killing of Archduke Franz Ferdinand of Austria in Sarajevo triggered the First World War.
Alfonso maintained his rule and kept Spanish neutrality. WWI
saw the decline of the anarchist movement, as the Russian revolution swept the communists into power and Western nations took
severe measures to suppress radicalism.

Alfonso's reign would last until April 1931, when leftists won
elections throughout Spain and proclaimed the Second Republic. The royal family went into voluntary exile in France in hopes
of avoiding a civil war, but war broke out in 1936 between the
Republicans (allied with anarchist factions) and the right-wing
Nationalists. During the civil war, the Republican government of
Madrid renamed Calle Mayor as Calle Mateu Morral. However,
the Nationalist victory led by General Francisco Franco served as
a prelude to WWII. Upon Franco's death in 1975, Alfonso XIII's
grandson, Juan Carlos I, was restored to the throne.

Fast Facts

- In 499 B.C., Histiaeus, tyrant of Miletus, sent a secret military dispatch by tattooing it on the head of his most trusted slave. The recipient would then shave the slave's head to read the message.

- George Washington's final military promotion, to general of the armies of the United States, didn't occur until 1976—177 years after his death.

- The diary of King George III of England carried this entry on July 4, 1776: "Nothing of importance happened today."

- Before the outbreak of World War II, Winston Churchill was informed that the Italians intended to fight on the side of Germany. After consideration, Churchill responded: "That's fair; we had them last time."

- In 1830, Louis XIX became king of France when his father abdicated the throne. He held the title for a full 20 minutes before he abdicated as well.

- When the practice of smoking tobacco was first introduced to Europe, King James I of England foreshadowed attitudes 400 years later by describing it as "lothsome to the eye, hatefull to the Nose, harmefull to the braine, [and] dangerous to the Lungs...."

- Pope Formosus died in 896, but that didn't stop him from standing trial for perjury in 897. His corpse was disinterred, dressed in papal robes, tried, found guilty, and thrown in the Tiber river.

- As he was being burned at the stake for heresy in 1314, Jacques de Molay reportedly demanded that Pope Clement V and King Philippe le Bel of France meet him before God to answer for their accusations. Both died within the year.

- After losing a congressional election in 1835, Davey Crockett told his constituents: "You may all go to hell, and I will go to Texas."

LUDWIG II:
KING OF CASTLES

*His desire to build fantasy castles and his patronage of, and
infatuation with, famed composer Richard Wagner led many to
refer to Bavarian King Ludwig II as the Dream King,
the Swan King, the Fairytale King—even the Mad King.*

Some say an insular childhood shaped Ludwig II into the eccentric he became. Peculiarities surrounded him from the moment he was born—his own birth announcement was delayed so the date could be moved one day forward to coincide with his grandfather's birthdate.

Ludwig was crowned king at age 18. That same year, Ludwig held his first meeting with composer Richard Wagner. His infatuation with Wagner eventually led Ludwig to pay the composer a stipend and fund construction of a theatre where Wagner's operas were performed.

After Bavaria's absorption into the new German Empire, Ludwig retreated into seclusion. From his mountain retreat in the Bavarian Alps, the king launched several grand construction projects that became the trademark of his reign.

FANTASIES IN STONE

One of Ludwig's most bizarre building projects included an underground lake—complete with electrical lights—at Linderhorf Castle. Ludwig often rowed about the lake in a shell-shape boat while shore-side singers performed operas. The castle's architecture was influenced by French King Louis XIV and was the king's only castle project to be completed.

The most famous of Ludwig's castles is New Castle Hohenschwangau. Several swan motifs were incorporated into the castle's design, leading the edifice to be renamed *Neuschwanstein,* or "New Swan Stone," after his death. Built high above Pollat Gorge,

Neuschwanstein is a mix of Byzantine and Gothic design elements that rate it as one of the most recognized castles in the world. In fact, Disney used it as inspiration when designing the Sleeping Beauty castle featured at Disneyland.

Despite a 22-year construction period, only 14 rooms of Neuschwanstein were ever completed. The castle's interior features several wall paintings, which depict scenes from Wagner's operas. Never one to forgo the modern trappings of life, Ludwig built this castle with several state-of-the-art features, including a forced-air heating system and a flush toilet.

Ludwig's third castle, Herrenchiemsee, was located on an island in Lake Chiemsee. It was modeled after the central section of the Palace of Versailles and contained a reproduction of the palace's ambassador's staircase. Unfortunately, Ludwig died during its construction, and Herrenchiemsee was never completed.

A WORLD OF DREAMS

On June 8, 1886, Ludwig was declared "mentally disordered" by a psychiatrist who hadn't even examined him. On June 10, the king was declared insane and was deposed by his uncle. Two days later, Ludwig was arrested and taken to Castle Berg, south of Munich. After taking a walk along Lake Starnberg with the doctor who had declared him unfit to rule, Ludwig was discovered floating in the shallow water. The doctor's body was found in the water as well. The king's death was ruled a suicide despite the fact that autopsy results showed no water in Ludwig's lungs. This finding has led some to speculate that the king was murdered. On June 19, Ludwig's remains were interred in the crypt of Saint Michael's. In accordance with tradition, his heart was placed in a silver urn and interred in the Chapel of the Miraculous Image.

THEN AND NOW:
ANCIENT CITIES

*In the ancient world, it took far fewer people to make
a great city. Some didn't survive; some have flourished;
and others have exploded. With the understanding that ancient
population estimates are necessarily approximate,
here are the fates of some great metropolises:*

Memphis (now the ruins of Memphis, Egypt): By 3100 B.C.,
this Pharaonic capital bustled with an estimated 30,000 people.
Today it has none—but modern Cairo, 12 miles north, houses
7,786,640 people.

Ur (now the ruins of Ur, Iraq): Sumer's great ancient city once
stood near the Euphrates with a peak population of 65,000 around
2030 B.C. Now its population is zero, and the Euphrates has
meandered about ten miles northeast.

Alexandria (now El-Iskandariya, Egypt): Built on an ancient
Egyptian village site near the Nile Delta's west end, Alexander the
Great's city once held a tremendous library. In its heyday, it may
have held 250,000 people; today more than 3,300,000 people call
it home.

Babylon (now the ruins of Babylon, Iraq): Babylon may have
twice been the largest city in the world, in about 1700 B.C. and
500 B.C.—perhaps with up to 200,000 people in the latter case.
Now, it's windblown dust and faded splendor.

Athens (Greece): In classical times, this powerful city-state
stood miles from the coast but was never a big place—something
like 30,000 residents during the 300s B.C. It now reaches the sea
with nearly 3,000,000 residents.

Rome (Italy): With the rise of its empire, ancient Rome
became a city of more than 500,000 and the center of Western

civilization. Though that mantle moved on to other cities, Rome now has 3,000,000 people.

Xi'an (China): This longtime dynastic capital, famed for its terra-cotta warriors but home to numerous other antiquities, reached 400,000 people by A.D. 637. Its nearly 8,000,000 people make it as important a city now as then.

Constantinople (now Istanbul, Turkey): First colonized by Greeks in the 1200s B.C., this city of fame was made Emperor Constantine the Great's eastern imperial Roman capital with 300,000 people. As Byzantium, it bobbed and wove through the tides of faith and conquest. Today, it is Turkey's largest city with 10,000,000 people.

Baghdad (Iraq): Founded around A.D. 762, this center of Islamic culture and faith was perhaps the first city to house more than 1,000,000 people. It has sometimes faded but never fallen. Today it has a population of 4,500,000.

Tenochtitlán (now Mexico City, Mexico): Founded in A.D. 1325, this island-built Aztec capital had more than 200,000 inhabitants within a century. Most of the surrounding lake has been drained over the years. A staggering 19,000,000 souls call modern Mexico City home.

Carthage (now the ruins of Carthage, Tunisia): Phoenician seafarers from the Levant founded this great trade city in 814 B.C. Before the Romans obliterated it in 146 B.C., its population may have reached 700,000. Today, it sits in empty silence ten miles from modern Tunis—population 2,000,000.

- *Memphis was something of an Egyptian New Orleans, with dikes built to keep out Nile floods. When the city declined, the dikes failed and the unwanted site silted up.*

- *Ur is famed for its great ziggurat, thought by many to be the Biblical Tower of Babel. Only the lower base remains today.*

VANISHED:
THE LOST COLONY OF ROANOKE ISLAND

Twenty years before England established its first successful colony in the New World, an entire village of English colonists disappeared in what would later be known as North Carolina. Did these pioneers all perish? Did Native Americans capture them? Did they join a friendly tribe? Could they have left descendents who live among us today?

TIMING IS EVERYTHING

Talk about bad timing. As far as John White was concerned, England couldn't have picked a worse time to go to war. It was November 1587, and White had just arrived in England from the New World. He intended to gather relief supplies and immediately sail back to Roanoke Island, where he had left more than 100 colonists who were running short of food. Unfortunately, the English were gearing up to fight Spain. Every seaworthy ship, including White's, was pressed into naval service. Not a one could be spared for his return voyage to America.

NOBODY HOME

When John White finally returned to North America three years later, he was dismayed to discover that the colonists he had left behind were nowhere to be found. Instead, he stumbled upon a mystery—one that has never been solved.

The village that White and company had founded in 1587 on Roanoke Island lay completely deserted. Houses had been dismantled (as if someone planned to move them), but the pieces lay in the long grass along with iron tools and farming equipment. A stout stockade made of logs stood empty.

White found no sign of his daughter Eleanor, her husband Ananias, or their daughter Virginia Dare—the first English child born in America. None of the 87 men, 17 women, and 11 children remained. No bodies or obvious gravesites offered clues to their fate. The only clues—if they *were* clues—that White could find were the letters CRO carved into a tree trunk and the word CROATOAN carved into a log of the abandoned fort.

NO FORWARDING ADDRESS

All White could do was hope that the colonists had been taken in by friendly natives.

Croatoan—also spelled "Croatan"—was the name of a barrier island to the south and also the name of a tribe of Native Americans that lived on that island. Unlike other area tribes, the Croatoans had been friendly to English newcomers, and one of them, Manteo, had traveled to England with earlier explorers and returned to act as interpreter for the Roanoke colony. Had the colonists, with Manteo's help, moved to Croatoan? Were they safe among friends?

White tried to find out, but his timing was rotten once again. He had arrived on the Carolina coast as a hurricane bore down on the region. The storm hit before he could mount a search. His ship was blown past Croatoan Island and out to sea. Although the ship and crew survived the storm and made it back to England, White was stuck again. He tried repeatedly but failed to raise money for another search party.

No one has ever learned the fate of the Roanoke Island colonists, but there are no shortage of theories as to what happened to them. A small sailing vessel and other boats that White had left with them were gone when he returned. It's possible that the colonists used the vessels to travel to another island or to the mainland. White had talked with others before he left about possibly moving the settlement to a more secure location inland. It's even possible that the colonists tired of waiting for White's return and tried to sail back to England. If so, they would have perished at sea. Yet there are at least a few shreds of hearsay evidence that the colonists survived in America.

RUMORS OF SURVIVORS

In 1607, Captain John Smith and company established the first successful English settlement in North America at Jamestown, Virginia. The colony's secretary, William Strachey, wrote four years later about hearing a report of four English men, two boys, and one young woman who had been sighted south of Jamestown at a settlement of the Eno tribe, where they were being used as slaves. If the report was true, who else could these English have been but Roanoke survivors?

For more than a century after the colonists' disappearance, stories emerged of gray-eyed Native Americans and English-speaking villages in North Carolina and Virginia. In 1709, an English surveyor said members of the Hatteras tribe living on North Carolina's Outer Banks—some of them with light-colored eyes—claimed to be descendents of white people. It's possible that the Hatteras were the same people that the 1607 colonists called Croatoan.

In the intervening centuries, many of the individual tribes of the region have disappeared. Some died out. Others were absorbed into larger groups such as the Tuscarora. One surviving group, the Lumbee, has also been called Croatoan. The Lumbee, who still live in North Carolina, often have Caucasian features. Could they be descendents of Roanoke colonists? Many among the Lumbee dismiss the notion as fanciful, but the tribe has long been thought to be of mixed heritage and has been speaking English so long that none among them know what language preceded it.

• *According to a popular legend, Virginia Dare was turned into a white doe by an Indian witch doctor whose affections she spurned. To this day, sightings of the ghostly figure of a white doe are reported near Roanoke Island.*

SANDSTONE GATEWAY TO HEAVEN

For hundreds of years, rumors of the lost city of Angkor spread among Cambodian peasants. On a stifling day in 1860, Henri Mahout and his porters discovered that the ancient city was more than mere legend.

French botanist and explorer Henri Mahout wiped his spectacles as he pushed into the Cambodian jungle clearing. Gasping for breath in the rain forest's thick mists, he gazed down weed-ridden avenues at massive towers and stone temples wreathed with carvings of gods, kings, and battles. The ruins before him were none other than the temples of Angkor Wat.

Although often credited with the discovery of Angkor Wat, Mahout was not the first Westerner to encounter the site. He did, however, bring the "lost" city to the attention of the European public when his travel journals were published in 1868. He wrote: "One of these temples—a rival to that of Solomon, and erected by some ancient Michelangelo—might take an honorable place beside our most beautiful buildings."

Mahout's descriptions of this "new," massive, unexplored Hindu temple sent a jolt of lightning through Western academic circles. Explorers from western Europe combed the jungles of northern Cambodia in an attempt to explain the meaning and origin of the mysterious lost shrine.

THE RISE OF THE KHMER

Scholars first theorized that Angkor Wat and other ancient temples in present-day Cambodia were about 2,000 years old. However, as they began to decipher the Sanskrit inscriptions, they found that the temples had been erected during the 9th through 12th centuries. While Europe languished in the Dark Ages, the Khmer Empire of Indochina was reaching its zenith.

The earliest records of the Khmer people date back to the middle of the 6th century. They migrated from southern China and Tibet and settled in what is now Cambodia. The early Khmer retained many Indian influences from the West—they were Hindus, and their architecture evolved from Indian methods of building.

In the early 9th century, King Jayavarman II laid claim to an independent kingdom called Kambuja. He established his capital in the Angkor area some 190 miles north of the modern Cambodian capital of Phnom Penh. Jayavarman II also introduced the cult of *devaraja,* which claimed that the Khmer king was a representative of Shiva, the Hindu god of chaos, destruction, and rebirth. As such, in addition to the temples built to honor the Hindu gods, temples were also constructed to serve as tombs when kings died.

The Khmer built more than 100 stone temples spread out over about 40 miles. The temples were made from laterite (a material similar to clay that forms in tropical climates) and sandstone. The sandstone provided an open canvas for the statues and reliefs celebrating the Hindu gods that decorate the temples.

HOME OF THE GODS

During the first half of the 12th century, Kambuja's King Suryavarman II decided to raise an enormous temple dedicated to the Hindu god Vishnu, a religious monument that would subdue the surrounding jungle and illustrate the power of the Khmer king. His masterpiece—the largest temple complex in the world—would be known to history by its Sanskrit name, "Angkor Wat," or "City of Temple."

Pilgrims visiting Angkor Wat in the 12th century would enter the temple complex by crossing a square 600-foot-wide square moat that ran some four miles in perimeter around the temple grounds. Approaching from the west, visitors would tread the moat's causeway to the main gateway. From there, they would follow a spiritual journey representing the path from the outside world through the Hindu universe and into Mount Meru, the home of the gods. They would pass a giant statue of an eight-armed Vishnu as they entered the western *gopura,* or gatehouse, known as the

"Entrance of the Elephants." They would then follow a stone walkway decorated with *nagas* (mythical serpents) past sunken pools and column-studded buildings once believed to house sacred temple documents.

At the end of the stone walkway, a pilgrim would step up to a rectangular platform surrounded with galleries featuring six-foot-high bas-reliefs of gods and kings. One depicts the Churning of the Ocean of Milk, a Hindu story in which gods and demons churn a serpent in an ocean of milk to extract the elixir of life. Another illustrates the epic battle of monkey warriors against demons whose sovereign had kidnapped Sita, Rama's beautiful wife. Others depict the gruesome fates awaiting the wicked in the afterlife.

A visitor to King Suryavarman's kingdom would next ascend the dangerously steep steps to the temple's second level, an enclosed area boasting a courtyard decorated with hundreds of dancing *apsaras,* female images ornamented with jewelry and elaborately dressed hair.

For kings and high priests, the journey would continue with a climb up more steep steps to a 126-foot-high central temple, the pinnacle of Khmer society. Spreading out some 145 feet on each side, the square temple includes a courtyard cornered by four high conical towers shaped to look like lotus buds. The center of the temple is dominated by a fifth conical tower soaring 180 feet above the main causeway; inside it holds a golden statue of the Khmer patron, Vishnu, riding a half-man, half-bird creature in the image of King Suryavarman.

DISUSE AND DESTRUCTION

With the decline of the Khmer Empire and the resurgence of Buddhism, Angkor Wat was occupied by Buddhist monks, who claimed it as their own for many years. A cruciform gallery leading to the temple's second level was decorated with 1,000 Buddhas; the Vishnu statue in the central tower was replaced by an image of Buddha. The temple fell into various states of disrepair over the centuries and is now the focus of international restoration efforts.

A Day in the Life
RURAL 1920s AMERICA

*The mechanization of American agriculture during
the Roaring Twenties created a good news-bad news scenario for
small farmers. The following account explores what
"a day in the life" might have been like.*

It's shortly after sunrise on a July day in Nebraska. Hollis stands by the roadside watching a billowing dust cloud rumble its way toward his 30-acre family farm.

It's 1925, and the cloud is bringing another dose of modernity to Hollis's farm in the form of a big, noisy, steam-driven threshing machine.

Modernity first arrived last year when Hollis partnered with four fellow farmers to buy a gasoline-powered tractor. The tractor was a godsend. It plows an acre three times faster than his five horses did. Now the ten acres of land he previously used to grow horse feed yield cash crops instead. The tractor pulls the seeder, manure spreader, and binder (which cuts and bundles wheat stalks)—other machines that have reduced Hollis's dependence on paid labor.

Today, the thresher will separate wheat kernels from their stalks in a fraction of the time it takes a gang of workers to do it by hand.

A SOCIAL GATHERING HARD AT WORK

Threshing season is as much a social gathering as it is work. Area farmers band together to work each other's farms using the same thresher. Meanwhile, the women prepare home-cooked feasts.

Hollis and the men gravitate to the thresher as it chugs into the field. Clad in ubiquitous denim overalls, short-sleeved shirts, and wide-brimmed hats, they feed bundles of dried wheat into the thresher. The machine spits out straw collected for livestock bedding and shoots grain through a spout into a wagon hitched to Hollis's tractor.

Meanwhile, the women butcher chickens, cook, and set up tables and chairs. Kids tote sandwiches and cold well water to the men.

The women will lay out gigantic spreads at mid-morning, noon, and late afternoon. Platters of fried chicken, ham, homemade bread and biscuits, butter, jams and preserves, mashed potatoes, vegetables, pies, cakes, iced tea, and lemonade are gobbled up.

At 7 P.M. the works stops, and everyone heads home. The pattern will be repeated on Hollis's farm over the next several days.

MORE SIGNS OF THE TIMES

Exhausted, Hollis leans against another machine transforming American rural life: his 1920 Ford Model T pickup truck. The vehicle enables his family to make daily visits to town, whether it's to sell produce at the market, visit friends, attend a baseball game or church social, or see a movie at the brand-new movie house. The car has ended their isolation from the outside world.

Tonight, however, Hollis is too tired for any of that, choosing to stay home and listen to his battery-powered radio. Sandwiched between music programs is a broadcast from the U.S. Department of Agriculture offering weather and market reports.

Hollis grimaces as the crackling radio voice warns of lower wheat, oat, and corn prices this fall.

EARNING LESS FOR MORE

Although technology is helping Hollis produce more than ever, he's finding this is not necessarily a good thing.

Food production in the United States is now outpacing demand, causing steadily declining commodity prices. Hollis is producing more but earning less. He's swimming in debt from buying new machines. He's hoping to eke out a profit this year—*hoping*.

Many small farmers have already succumbed to this cruel irony and have sold their farms, joining the exodus of people leaving rural America for the cities during the 1920s. But Hollis doesn't want to leave. As upbeat ragtime music blares from the radio, he somberly wonders how much longer he can hold out.

Fast Facts

- Isaac Newton is famous for his explanation of gravity, but he also had other jobs. As Warden of the Mint, Newton disguised himself and made the rounds of London's taverns in search of counterfeiters.

- Shakespeare's original Globe Theatre (built in 1599) was destroyed in 1613 when a real cannon used for special effects during a production of Henry VIII set fire to the thatched roof, burning the building to the ground.

- When King Richard the Lionhearted's (1157–1159) horse was killed under him in a battle with Saladin's forces, Saladin sent Richard a replacement horse, with a note saying: "It is not right that so brave a warrior should have to fight on foot."

- The Spartan warrior Isadas, hearing the sounds of battle outside his city, ran naked from his home to join the fight, killing many enemies. After the battle, the Greeks presented him with a laurel for his bravery, then fined him for going into battle without his armor.

- During the First Crusade (1096–1099), so many horses died in the desert that the Crusaders were reduced to carrying their supplies on the backs of goats and dogs.

- The terms "log house" and "log cabin" actually denoted two distinct types of dwellings. Log cabin timbers were left round while log houses were made from notched, square-hewn logs.

- Early matches were called "Lucifers" because they would burst into flame when jostled.

- Cupboards originated with pioneers and were truly "cup boards"—a shelf built from a single board to hold cups and dishes. It was only later that they acquired sides and fronts.

- Queen Anne Boleyn's head and body were wrapped in sheets and buried in an arrow chest because the king had not ordered her a coffin.

AFRICAN EXPLORATION BECOMES EUROPE'S HEART OF DARKNESS

The improbable meeting of Dr. David Livingston and Henry Morton Stanley in 1871 was perhaps the greatest celebrity interview of all time, a high point in African exploration that would leave as its legacy one of the most brutal colonial empires in history.

It had been five years since Scottish missionary David Livingston disappeared into central Africa to find the source of the Nile, and he was presumed dead by his sponsor, Britain's Royal Geographical Society. New York newspaper magnate James Gordon Bennett, Jr., saw the potential for a great story in Livingston's disappearance. He dispatched young war correspondent Henry Morton Stanley to find him.

DR. LIVINGSTON, I PRESUME?

Stanley led a large party of guards and porters into uncharted territory in March 1871. Within a few days, his stallion was dead from tsetse flies, and dozens of his carriers were deserting with valuable supplies. Over the months that followed, his party was decimated by tropical disease. They endured encounters with hostile tribes—and at one point were pursued by cannibals chanting, "Meat! Meat!" Finally, on November 10, 1871, Stanley found the ailing Livingston at a settlement on Lake Tanganyika in present-day Tanzania, supposedly greeting him with "Dr. Livingston, I presume?"

Though most of his party had perished and he had won only a handful of converts to Christianity, Livingston had become the first European to see Victoria Falls. Stanley's dispatches to the *New York Herald*, which told the world of Livingston's discoveries as well as Stanley's own adventures, were the media sensation of the age.

FAME AND MISFORTUNE

Upon his return to Great Britain, Stanley was met with public ridicule by scientists and the press, who doubted his claim that he found Livingston and questioned the veracity of his other accounts as well. Though his book, *How I Found Livingston*, was a best seller, Stanley was deeply wounded by his detractors.

Indeed, Stanley was an unlikely hero. Born John Rowland, he was a bastard child whose mother gave him up to a workhouse. He left Britain at the age of 17 to work as a deckhand on a merchant vessel. However, he jumped ship in New Orleans and took the name of an English planter, who he claimed had adopted him. Contemporary historians doubt that Stanley ever met the man.

Stanley's adult life was an improbable series of adventures and lies. He served, unremarkably, on both sides during the Civil War and worked unsuccessfully at a variety of trades before trying his hand at journalism, reporting on the Indian wars in the West and the Colorado gold rush. Stanley came to the attention of newspaper magnate Bennett while reporting for the *New York Herald* on a British military expedition into Abyssinia. His colorful writing won him the assignment to find Livingston.

THE GREATEST AFRICAN EXPLORER

Stanley may have found in Livingston the father figure he never had. His accounts of the missionary created a portrait of a saintly doctor who, inspired by his opposition to Africa's brutal slave trade, had opened the continent to Western civilization and Christianity. When Livingston died in 1873, Stanley served as a pallbearer at his funeral in Westminster Abbey. A year later, he set out on another epic expedition to complete Livingston's work. Over the next three years, Stanley established Lake Victoria as the source of the Nile and led his party down the uncharted Congo River—a 2,900-mile course that transversed the continent.

Though acclaimed as the greatest of African explorers, Stanley's accounts of his brutal methods—such as whipping African porters and gunning down tribespeople with modern weaponry—brought public outrage in Britain. After examining his original notes and letters, however, some contemporary historians believe that he often exaggerated his exploits, including the numbers of Africans supposedly killed, to elevate his own legend.

"THE HORROR!"

Unable to persuade the British government to employ him, Stanley undertook a third journey in 1879 under the sponsorship of Belgium's King Leopold II. He established 22 trading posts along the Congo River, laying the foundation for a vast colonial empire that would exploit the rubber and ivory trades at the expense of millions of African lives. Stanley earned the African nickname Bula Matari, or "breaker of rocks," on account of his ruthless determination to build roads linking the Congo's waterways. Natives were beaten, tortured, and killed under his command. This third expedition led to the scramble for Africa among European nations, culminating in the Berlin Conference of 1885, which divided the continent among colonial powers. Leopold II established his rights to the so-called Congo Free State, his private enterprise encompassing most of the Congo Basin. Historians estimate that as many as 13 million Congolese were murdered or died from disease or overwork under Leopold's regime, inspiring Joseph Conrad's novel *Heart of Darkness*.

A final African expedition between 1887 and 1889 further tarnished Stanley's name. Sent to rescue a dubious ally in southern Sudan, he left behind a rear column whose leaders—former British army officers and aristocrats—degenerated into sadism. Though most of his party perished and much more African blood was shed, Stanley helped establish British territorial claims in East Africa and opened a path to further colonization.

Finally marrying and adopting the bastard grandchild of a Welsh nun, Stanley retired from exploration to write books and conduct lecture tours. He won a seat in Parliament in 1895 and was knighted by Queen Victoria in 1899. He died in 1904 at the age of 63. Although he was considered a national hero, he was denied burial next to Livingston at Westminster Abbey due to his mixed reputation.

QUIRKY INVENTOR'S EXPLOSIVE CAREER LEADS TO NOBLE TESTAMENT

He created the Nobel Peace Prize. He also invented dynamite.
When Alfred Nobel wrote his legendary will, was it to atone for
his devastating invention? Or was it simply the final good deed
of a man dedicated to peace?

PROTECTING A SECRET PRIZE

In December 1896, Ragnar Sohlman rode nervously in a carriage through Paris, sitting atop a box containing one of the world's great fortunes. Sohlman was the main executor for the will of Alfred Nobel, the Swedish-born industrialist—and inventor of dynamite—who had just died at an Italian villa, after years of residing in the French capital.

Sohlman had his hands full. Nobel's will consisted of one long, vague paragraph, directing that the then-huge amount of $4.2 million be awarded to those "who during the preceding year shall have conferred the greatest benefit to mankind" in the fields of medicine, chemistry, physics, literature, and peace.

Nobel had named the organizations he wanted to dispense the awards but hadn't bothered to tell them. Nor had he set up a foundation.

Nobel had lived in Italy, Russia, Germany, the United States, and other lands. Thus, many different nations could claim his wealth.

SETTING UP A FAMOUS AWARD

After secreting the treasure with Swedish authorities, Sohlman undertook drawn-out negotiations with the awarding bodies Nobel had chosen. These were the Swedish Academy of Sciences (for chemistry and physics), the Stockholm-based Caroline Institute (medicine), the Swedish Academy (literature), and the

Norwegian Parliament (peace). The first Nobel Prizes were finally granted on December 10, 1901—the fifth anniversary of Nobel's death.

A POLYMATH'S POLYGLOT INTERESTS

Born in 1833, Alfred Nobel had science and technology in his blood. He was a descendant of medical professor Olof Rudbeck the Elder, who discovered the lymphatic system. Alfred's father Immanuel, an architect and engineer, was the inventor of plywood. His brothers founded Russia's oil industry.

Apart from ancestry, Nobel's interest in medicine derived from his chronically bad health. He endured awful migraines and black depression. He said of himself: "Alfred Nobel—a pitiful half-life which ought to have been extinguished by some compassionate doctor as the infant yelled its way into the world." He also suffered from angina. The popularizer of the explosive as well as the medicine known as nitroglycerin wrote: "Isn't it the irony of fate that I have been prescribed nitroglycerin to be taken internally?" He became an amateur authority on blood transfusions. He even underwrote early experiments in physiology, funding the work of Ivan Pavlov.

As for literature, Nobel was a poet and authored the play *Nemesis*. It concerned a terrified family who bludgeoned a violent father to death. His family had 97 of the 100 copies destroyed because the play was considered blasphemous.

One subject Nobel wasn't interested in was law. He wrote: "Lawyers have to make a living, and can only do so by inducing people to believe that a straight line is crooked." It's little wonder he penned his own will.

It's often thought that Nobel's interest in peace was due to guilt over his invention of dynamite. An 1888 French obituary that mistakenly reported his death called him the "merchant of death." It read, "Dr. Alfred Nobel, who became rich by finding ways to kill more people faster than ever before, died yesterday."

However, evidence regarding his feelings of guilt (or lack thereof) is mixed. Recently revealed correspondence with his mistress Sophie, an Austrian flower clerk half his age, indicates he did harbor doubts about his work. However, since he lived in a time of relative peace, almost none of his inventions were used in battle. Indeed, he long believed the destructive power of creations such as dynamite would deter war. Anticipating atomic weapons, he once told a peace activist, "When two armies of equal strength can annihilate each other in an instant, then all civilized nations will retreat and disband their troops."

DEVISING A DOUBLE-EDGED SWORD

Nobel's family was among the leading explosives and armaments manufacturers of the time. His father established a factory in Russia to build naval mines. During the Crimean War, the family business prospered but went belly-up when peace arrived in 1856.

This spurred Alfred into a rabid search for new products. He and his brothers experimented with volatile nitroglycerin, invented by Ascanio Sobrero decades before. In 1864, his youngest brother Emil died when the Nobel nitro factory near Stockholm blew up. Two years later, another accident destroyed a Nobel nitro plant outside Hamburg, Germany.

Undeterred, that same year Alfred tested the substance in a safer place—a raft on the German river Elbe. Finally, at a demonstration in Manhattan, he proved nitro could be used safely.

His famous breakthrough came the next year. He added an inert substance, silicon-laden soil, to nitro, which yielded dynamite, a material that could be handled and transported safely.

Next came blasting caps, patents for 355 inventions, and profitable businesses in many lands. Most of Nobel's explosives were employed for constructing mine shafts, dams, canals, and buildings.

Taken at his word, Nobel's quirky idealism was the reason for his eventual interest in peace: "I've got a mass of screws loose and am a superidealist who can digest philosophy better than food."

THE PLOT TO ASSASSINATE PRESIDENT TRUMAN

Puerto Ricans have sought independence from the United States for decades. In 1950, two ardent nationalists took matters into their own hands as part of a campaign to win independence through violent means. Their target? President Harry Truman.

Members of the Puerto Rican Nationalist Party were spoiling for a fight. They had tried—and failed—to reach their goal of independence through electoral participation. By the 1930s, party leader Dr. Pedro Albuzu Campos was advocating a campaign of violent revolution. Throughout the 1930s and 1940s, the Nationalist Party was involved in one confrontation after another. In 1936, Albuzu was charged with conspiring to overthrow the government and was incarcerated. He spent the next six years in jail in New York. When he finally returned to Puerto Rico in 1947, the tinder of *nacionalismo puertorriqueño* was bone-dry and smoldering.

THE MATCH IS LIT

On October 30, 1950, Nationalists seized the town of Jayuya. With air support, the Puerto Rico National Guard crushed the rebellion. Griselio Torresola and Oscar Collazo, two *nacionalistas*, decided to retaliate at the highest level: the president of the United States.

They had help from natural wastage. The White House, which looks majestic from the outside, has been quite the wretched dump at many points in its history. By 1948, it was physically unsound, so the Truman family moved to Blair House. It would be a lot easier to whack a president there than it would have been at the White House.

THE ATTEMPT

At 2:20 P.M. on November 1, 1950, Torresola approached the Pennsylvania Avenue entrance from the west with a 9mm Luger pistol. Collazo came from the east carrying the Luger's cheaper successor, the Walther P38. White House police guarded the entrance. Truman was upstairs taking a nap.

Collazo approached the Blair House steps, facing the turned back of Officer Donald Birdzell, and fired, shattering Birdzell's knee. Nearby Officers Floyd Boring and Joseph Davidson fired at Collazo through a wrought-iron fence but without immediate effect. Birdzell dragged himself after Collazo, firing his pistol. Then bullets from Boring and Davidson grazed Collazo in the scalp and chest—seemingly minor wounds. Out of ammo, Collazo sat down to reload his weapon.

Officer Leslie Coffelt staffed a guard booth at the west corner as Torresola took him unaware. Coffelt fell with a chest full of holes. Next, Torresola fired on Officer Joseph Downs, who had just stopped to chat with Coffelt. Downs took bullets to the hip, then the back and neck. He staggered to the basement door and locked it, hoping to deny the assassins entry. Torresola advanced on Birdzell from behind as the officer engaged Collazo and fired, hitting his other knee. Birdzell lost consciousness as Torresola reloaded.

Weapon recharged, Oscar Collazo stood, then collapsed from his wounds. At that moment, a startled Truman came to the window to see what was the matter. Torresola was 31 feet away. If he had looked up at precisely the right moment, the Puerto Rican nationalist would have achieved his mission.

Officer Coffelt had one final police duty in life. Despite three chest wounds, he forced himself to his feet, took careful aim, and fired. A bullet splattered the brain matter of Griselio Torresola all over the street. Coffelt staggered back to the guard shack and crumpled.

Collazo survived and was sentenced to death. Before leaving office, President Truman commuted Collazo's sentence to life imprisonment.

Officers Downs and Birdzell recovered. Officer Leslie Coffelt died four hours later. The Secret Service's day room at Blair House is now named the Leslie W. Coffelt Memorial Room.

THE NAZCA LINES—
PICTURES AIMED AT AN EYE
IN THE SKY?

*Ancient artwork etched into a desert floor in South America have
inspired wild theories about who created them and why.
Did space aliens leave them on long-ago visits? Decades of
scientific research reject the popular notion, showing that
the lines were the work of mere Earthlings.*

Flying above the rocky plains northwest of Nazca, Peru, in 1927,
aviator Toribio Mejía Xesspe was surprised to see gigantic eyes
looking up at him. Then the pilot noticed that the orbs stared
out of a bulbous head upon a cartoonish line drawing of a man,
etched over hundreds of square feet of the landscape below.

The huge drawing—later called "owl man" for its staring eyes—
turned out to be just one of scores of huge, 2,000-year-old images
scratched into the earth over almost 200 square miles of the
parched Peruvian landscape.

There is a 360-foot-long monkey with a whimsically spiraled
tail, along with a 150-foot-long spider, and a 935-foot pelican.
Other figures range from hummingbird to killer whale. Unless
the viewer knows what to look for, they're almost invisible from
ground level. There are also geometric shapes and straight lines
that stretch for miles across the stony ground.

THE THEORY OF ANCIENT ASTRONAUTS

The drawings have been dated to a period between 200 B.C. and
A.D. 600. Obviously, there were no airplanes from which to view
them back then. So why were they made? And for whose benefit?

In his 1968 book *Chariots of the Gods?*, Swiss author Erich Von
Däniken popularized the idea that the drawings and lines were
landing signals and runways for starships that visited southern
Peru long before the modern era. In his interpretation, the owl

man is instead an astronaut in a helmet. Von Däniken's theory caught on among UFO enthusiasts. Many science-fiction novels and films make reference to this desert in Peru's Pampa Colorado region as a site with special significance to space travelers.

COMING DOWN TO EARTH

Examined up close, the drawings consist of cleared paths—areas where someone removed reddish surface rocks to expose the soft soil beneath. In the stable desert climate—averaging less than an inch of rain per year—the paths have survived through many centuries largely intact.

Scientists believe the Nazca culture—a civilization that came before the Incas—drew the lines. The style of the artwork is similar to that featured on Nazca pottery. German-born researcher Maria Reiche (1903–1998) showed how the Nazca could have laid out the figures using simple surveying tools such as ropes and posts. In the 1980s, American researcher Joe Nickell duplicated one of the drawings, a condor, showing that the Nazca could have rendered parts of the figures "freehand"—that is, without special tools or even scale models. Nickell also demonstrated that despite their great size, the figures can be identified as drawings even from ground level. No alien technology would have been required to make them.

STILL MYSTERIOUS

As for why the Nazca drew giant doodles across the desert, no one is sure. Reiche noted that some of the lines have astronomical relevance. For example, one points to where the sun sets at the winter solstice. Some lines may also have pointed toward underground water sources—crucially important to desert people.

Most scholars think that the marks were part of the Nazca religion. They may have been footpaths followed during ritual processions. And although it's extremely unlikely that they were intended for extraterrestrials, many experts think it likely that the lines were oriented toward Nazca gods—perhaps a monkey god, a spider god, and so on, who could be imagined gazing down from the heavens upon likenesses of themselves.

Fast Facts

- In 1917, the German government sent a telegram to Mexico, promising the return of Texas, New Mexico, and Arizona in exchange for Mexico entering World War I against the United States.

- Franz Ferdinand, whose assassination would precipitate World War I, survived the first attempt on his life. Unfortunately, later that same day, his chauffeur took a wrong turn, driving the archduke past a cafe where one of the failed conspirators, Gavrilo Princip, was waiting to buy a sandwich. Pricip fired two shots, killing both Ferdinand and his wife.

- Some historians believe one contributing factor to Napoleon's defeat at Waterloo was his strange failure to survey the battle from his customary seat on horseback. His reluctance was brought about by a particularly bad flare-up of his chronic hemorrhoids.

- Franklin Delano Roosevelt was an avid poker player, once rushing from a game directly to the microphone to give one of his signature Fireside Chats. As he delivered the address, he absent mindedly shuffled some poker chips, rendering portions of his speech inaudible.

- In the 11th century, an English monk named Eilmer of Malmesbury built and launched himself in a glider, flying for about 220 feet before crashing and breaking both legs. His abbot forbade any further attempts.

- During World War II, British pilot and double amputee Douglas Bader was forced to bail out of his aircraft, leaving one of his artificial legs behind. Under a special temporary truce agreed to by his German captors, the RAF delivered a replacement leg by parachute.

- After being killed at Trafalgar in 1805, Horatio Nelson's body was preserved in a cask of French brandy that, according to legend, had been captured during the battle.

THE MYSTERY OF THE 700-YEAR-OLD PIPER

It's an intriguing story about a mysterious piper and more than 100 missing children. Made famous by the eponymous Brothers Grimm, this popular fairy tale has captivated generations of boys and girls. But is it actually more fact than fiction?

The legend of *The Pied Piper of Hameln* documents the story of a mysterious musician who rid a town of rats by enchanting the rodents with music from his flute. The musician led the mesmerized rats to a nearby river, where they drowned. When the townsfolk refused to settle their debt, the rat catcher returned several weeks later, charmed a group of 130 children with the same flute, and led them out of town. They disappeared—never to be seen again.

It's a story that dates back to approximately A.D. 1300 and has its roots in a small German town called Hameln. Several accounts written between the 14th and 17th centuries tell of a stained-glass window in the town's main church. The window pictured the Pied Piper with hands clasped, standing over a group of youngsters. Encircling the window was the following verse (this is a rough translation): "In the year 1284, on John's and Paul's day was the 26th of June. By a piper, dressed in all kinds of colors, 130 children born in Hameln were seduced and lost at the calvarie near the koppen."

The verse is quite specific: precise month and year, exact number of children involved in the incident, and detailed place names. Because of this, some scholars believe this window, which was removed in 1660 and either accidentally destroyed or lost, was created in memory of an actual event. Yet, the verse makes no mention of the circumstances regarding the departure of the children or their specific fate. What exactly happened in Hameln, Germany, in 1284? The truth is, no one actually knows—at least not for certain.

THEORIES ABOUND

Gernot Hüsam, the current chairman of the Coppenbrügge Castle Museum, believes the word "koppen" in the inscription may reference a rocky outcrop on a hill in nearby Coppenbrügge, a small town previously known as Koppanberg. Hüsam also believes the use of the word "calvarie" is in reference to either the medieval connotation of the gates of hell—or since the Crusades—a place of execution.

One theory put forward is that Coppenbrügge resident Nikolaus von Spiegelberg recruited Hameln youth to emigrate to areas in Pomerania near the Baltic Sea. This theory suggests the youngsters were either murdered, because they took part in summertime pagan rituals, or drowned in a tragic accident while in transit to the new colonies.

But this is not the only theory. In fact, theories concerning the fate of the children abound. Here are some ideas about what really happened:

• They suffered from the Black Plague or a similar disease and were led from the town to spare the rest of the population.

• They were part of a crusade to the Holy Land.

• They were lost in the 1260 Battle of Sedemünder.

• They died in a bridge collapse over the Weser River or a landslide on Ith Mountain.

• They emigrated to settle in other parts of Europe, including Maehren, Oelmutz, Transylvania, or Uckermark.

• They were actually young adults who were led away and murdered for performing pagan rituals on a local mountain.

Historians believe that emigration, bridge collapse/natural disaster, disease, or murder are the most plausible explanations.

TRACING THE PIPER'S PATH

Regardless of what actually happened in Hameln hundreds of years ago, the legend of the Pied Piper has endured. First accounts of the Piper had roots to the actual incident, but as time passed, the story took on a life of its own.

Earliest accounts of the legend date back to 1384, at which time a Hameln church leader, Deacon von Lude, was said to be in possession of a chorus book with a Latin verse related to the legend written on the front cover by his grandmother. The book was misplaced in the late 17th century and has never been found.

The oldest surviving account—according to amateur Pied Piper historian Jonas Kuhn—appears as an addition to a 14th-century manuscript from Luneburg. Written in Latin, the note is almost identical to the verse on the stained-glass window and translates roughly to:

"In the year of 1284, on the day of Saints John and Paul on the 26th of June 130 children born in Hamelin were seduced By a piper, dressed in all kinds of colors, and lost at the place of execution near the koppen."

Sixteenth-century physician and philosopher Jobus Fincelius believed the Pied Piper was the devil. In his 1556 book, *Concerning the Wonders of His Times*, Fincelius wrote: "It came about in Hameln in Saxony on the River Weser... the Devil visibly in human form walked the lanes of Hameln and by playing a pipe lured after him many children... to a mountain. Once there, he with the children... could no longer be found."

In 1557, Count Froben Christoph von Zimmern wrote a chronicle detailing his family's lineage. Sprinkled throughout the book were several folklore tales including one that referenced the Pied Piper. For some unknown reason, the count introduced rats into his version of the story: "He passed through the streets of the town with his small pipe... immediately all the rats... collected outside the houses and followed his footsteps." This first insertion of rodents into the legend led other writers to follow suit.

In 1802, Johan Wolfgang Goethe wrote "Der Rattenfanger," a poem based on the legend. The monologue was told in the first person through the eyes of the rat catcher. Goethe's poem made no direct reference to the town of Hameln, and in Goethe's version the Piper played a stringed instrument instead of a pipe. The Piper also made an appearance in Goethe's literary work *Faust*.

Jacob and Wilhelm Grimm began collecting European folktales in the early 1800s. Best known for a series of books that documented 211 fairy tales, the brothers also published two volumes between 1816 and 1818 detailing almost 600 German folklore legends. One of the volumes contained the story of *Der Rattenfanger von Hameln*.

The Grimm brothers' research for *The Pied Piper* drew on 11 different sources, from which they deduced two children were left behind (a blind child and a mute child); the piper led the children through a cave to Transylvania; and a street in Hameln was named after the event.

NO END IN SIGHT

While the details of the historical event surrounding the legend of *The Piped Piper* have been lost to time, the mystique of the story endures. Different versions of the legend have even appeared in literature outside of Germany: A rat catcher from Vienna helped rid the nearby town of Korneuburg of rats. When he wasn't paid, he stole off with the town's children and sold them as slaves in Constantinople. A vagabond rid the English town of Newton on the Isle of Wight of their rats, and when he wasn't paid, led the town's children into an ancient oak forest where they were never seen again. A Chinese version had a Hangchow district official use magic to convince the rats to leave his city.

The legend's plot has been adapted over time to fit whichever media is currently popular and has been used as a story line in children's books, ballet, theatre, and even a radio drama. The intriguing story of the mysterious piper will continue to interest people as long as there is mystery surrounding the original event.

HOLLYWOOD VERSUS HISTORY

You may not be surprised to learn that Hollywood doesn't always get history right.

Does this mean their career is already over?

The Mambo Kings (1992)—When the musical group watches their appearance on *I Love Lucy*, the show opens with the later syndicated-run title sequence, not the first-run original.

And it still sounded just as awful

Air America (1990)—Although the movie is set in the late 1960s, singers in a restaurant scene perform "A Horse with No Name," which wasn't written until 1974.

You'll love his duets with his imaginary friend

The Adventures of Robin Hood (1938)—While Robin and Little John battle on the footbridge, Will Scarlett begins to strum a stringless lute.

But he could have been in a drunk tank somewhere

The Doors (1991)—A background tableau shows a billboard advertising a film starring Nick Nolte, who was not yet in movies in 1971.

Sacré bleu!

Moulin Rouge! (2001)—The Sacré-Coeur Catholic basilica seen in the Paris background wasn't completed until 1914, more than a dozen years after the time period of this story.

We loved the peanut sauce

Good Morning, Vietnam (1987)—Although set in Vietnam, the film opens with a shot of the Thai Parliament Building.

We just dig cars, OK?

Quadrophenia (1979)—Rockers in this film set in 1965 wear Motorhead T-shirts a decade before that band emerged.

THE MAKINGS OF A ROCK STAR

Although the musical form had yet to be invented, Niccolò Paganini was perhaps the first rock star in history. Born in Genoa in 1782, Paganini toured the world, taking in vast sums of money, making women swoon, and living the high life.

A mere mortal simply couldn't play the way Niccolò Paganini did. At least, that was the popular opinion; the rumor was that the Italian virtuoso had sold his soul to the devil in exchange for his extraordinary talent. According to reports, at least one audience member had seen a mysterious goatlike creature standing behind the violinist on stage, guiding his hands as he played. Another account told of a mysterious black coach, pulled by horses whose eyes were made of fire, disappearing into the night after a concert. Indeed, Paganini's very name translated to "the little pagan." And, to top it all off, he had refused the Last Rites when on his death bed. Could there be any doubt that he was in league with Satan? The fact that these outlandish claims found support during the great Age of Enlightenment only reinforces the legend that was Paganini.

GENUINE GENIUS

There is, of course, a more prosaic explanation for Paganini's skill: mere genius. And it was fortunate for young Niccolò that he was just that. His father, Antonio Paganini, an 18th-century version of a show-business parent, saw a business opportunity in his son. He constantly reminded the boy that Mozart had composed his first works at the age of five and allegedly forced Niccolò to practice the violin for hours a day, locking him in a room and withholding food—but not withholding the strap.

This method of encouragement may have been abusive, but it did produce results. Niccolò composed his first sonata when he was 8 and was performing for aristocracy by age 11. He was sent to study under the renowned teachers of the day and undertook a tour of Italy at 15 years old. The young musician caused something of a sensation, but the money from the concerts went to his father. Niccolò took full advantage of his growing fame, going to parties, drinking, spending time in the company of a succession of young ladies, and gambling—even, at times, wagering his violin. Eventually tiring of the lifestyle, he left home and kept company with a Tuscan woman whose identity is still a mystery, disappearing for nearly three years while enjoying her companionship and spending his time with the guitar rather than the violin.

BACK IN THE SPOTLIGHT

When Paganini appeared in public again, he took a job in Lucca as composer for Napoleon's sister Elise; according to rumor, he was also her lover and had similar relationships with other ladies of the court. While in her employ, he was charged with playing two concerts a week; he would often put them together in as little as two hours, writing out an accompanying piece and leaving it to himself to improvise his own performance. Improvisation would always be Paganini's favored element. When touring, he would rehearse his accompanying orchestra, requiring the professional musicians to demonstrate mastery of their parts, but when his turn came, he would scrape a few notes on his Guarnerius violin before waving his hand and dismissing the orchestra with an "Et cetera, Signori"—much to their frustration. His time with Elise also produced one of Paganini's famous tricks: She challenged him to play an entire performance on one string of his violin; he complied, sometimes walking out on stage and breaking the other strings in full view of his audience.

Paganini undertook tours of Europe to great initial success. Wherever he went, crowds reached out to touch him; portraits of him went on sale; and ladies abandoned their embroidery and other crafts to take up the violin. Other musicians would attend concert after concert in hopes of learning his technique; one even followed him on tour, renting adjacent hotel rooms and peeking through the keyhole in Paganini's door, but he was not rewarded. People rarely saw Paganini practice; in his view, he had practiced enough for one lifetime. Always nervous before a performance, he was rumored to lie motionless across his bed for hours—whether sleeping or mentally running though his music—perhaps occasionally rising to silently try a fingering on his violin before springing up at the last minute and racing out to his concert.

TWO THUMBS DOWN?

Paganini's career was not without controversy. His love for improvisation was such that other musicians accused him, incorrectly, of being unable to play anything else. In fact, he was quite familiar with Beethoven and other masters and would play them in private, but for public performances he preferred his own compositions. Some critics saw his stage antics—playing on one string, drawing forth animal noises from his instrument, and even at one point playing on a wooden shoe that had been strung—as mere parlor tricks hiding a serious musician. Others complained that he was a moneygrubber due to the enormous increase in ticket prices his appearances were able to command. For his part, Paganini did not go out of his way to appease his critics. At one point, he told a royal patron who had complained about Paganini's requested fee that he ought to pay for admission to a public concert instead.

ARTIST TO THE END

Still, when all was said and done, Paganini's reputation overcame all criticism. While most of his music was never written down, he did leave behind six concertos, an equal number of sonatas, and a variety of other works that continue to challenge the top virtuosos of today. Paganini died on May 27, 1840. Those present say that in his final days, he found the strength to play one last piece, an improvisational music poem that lasted for hours; listeners claim it was the finest the master had ever played. Following that performance, he retired to his bed and died three days later, clutching his violin.

"Where our reason ends, there Paganini begins."

—GIACOMO MEYERBEER, OPERA COMPOSER

EPITAPHS OF THE FAMOUS

ABIGAIL ADAMS (FIRST LADY):
As daughter, wife and mother
a model of domestic worth
Her letters are an American classic

ETHAN ALLEN (REVOLUTIONARY OFFICER):
The mortal remains of Ethan Allen, fighter, writer, statesman,
and philosopher, lie in this cemetery beneath the marble statue.
His spirit is in Vermont now.

SUSAN B. ANTHONY (WOMEN'S RIGHTS ACTIVIST):
Liberty, Humanity, Justice, Equality

MEL BLANC (LOONEY TUNES VOICE):
Man of 1000 Voices
Beloved Husband and Father

WILLIAM BLIGH (AS IN MUTINY ON THE *Bounty*):
Vice Admiral Of The Blue
The Celebrated Navigator Who First Transplanted
The Breadfruit Tree From Otahette To The West Indies
Bravely fought The Battles Of His Country And Died Beloved,
Respected, And Lamented

WILLIAM H. BONNEY (AKA BILLY THE KID):
Truth and History.
21 Men.
The Boy Bandit King
He Died As He Lived.

AL CAPONE:
My Jesus Mercy

WINSTON CHURCHILL (BRITISH LEADER):
I am ready to meet my Maker.
Whether my Maker is prepared for the great ordeal
of meeting me is another matter.

WILLIAM CLARK (AMERICAN EXPLORER):
Soldier, explorer, statesman and patriot.
His life is written in the history of his country.

BETTE DAVIS (ACTRESS):
She did it the hard way.

JEFFERSON DAVIS (PRESIDENT OF THE CONFEDERACY):
At Rest
An American Soldier
And Defender of the Constitution

JACK DEMPSEY (BOXER):
A gentle man and a gentleman

EMILY DICKINSON (POET):
Called Back

SIR ARTHUR CONAN DOYLE (*SHERLOCK HOLMES* AUTHOR):
Steel True, Blade Straight

ALEXANDER HAMILTON (U.S. FOUNDING FATHER):
In testimony of their Respect
For
The Patriot of incorruptible Integrity,
The Soldier of approved Valour
The Statesman of consummate Wisdom;
Whose Talents and Virtues will be admired by
Grateful Posterity
Long after this Marble shall have mouldered into Dust

Timeline

3.85 billion B.C.
Signs of Life! Carbon evidence of life dates back to 3.85 billion years ago as single-cell bacteria begin forming in Earth's oceans.

1.8 billion B.C.
Multicellular organisms form, die, and are preserved for future pale-ontologists in fossil form. For the next one and a half billion years, life evolves into complex forms such as fish, reptiles, and reptilian proto-mammals. Earth's land is collected in one supercontinent named Rodinia.

540 million B.C.
Call Orkin! Segmented bugs develop legs and outer shells. The Cambrian Era bursts with genetic creativity as sponges, trilobites, snails, and more complex animals appear on the scene.

450 million B.C.
Rodinia breaks into large frag-ments, including the huge southern landmass Gondwana.

280 million B.C.
The supercontinent Pangaea forms from a collision of Earth's major landmasses, putting most land animals on the same mass. In a span of 10,000 years, about 90 percent of all life on Earth is snuffed out in the planet's greatest wave of extinctions.

248 million–
65 million B.C.
Age of Dinosaurs. The Mesozoic Era puts dinosaurs in the evolution-ary driver's seat. Pangaea begins breaking into separate continents.

Early birds and mammals evolve on land. Cataclysmic extinctions at the end of the era put an end to dino-dominance and give mammals an opportunity to become the new rulers of Earth.

65 million–
33 million B.C.
Earth warms; tropics extend to the poles; and mammals, birds, and small reptiles dominate Earth's surface. Europe, Asia, and North American make up a loose north-ern continent, while Antarctica, Africa, India, South America, and Australia hang together in the south. Sea levels drop, land bridges are exposed, and plants and animals spread over conti-nents. Lemurlike primates make their first appearance; whales evolve from land mammals; and global cooling kills off as many as 90 percent of animal species.

33 million–
24 million B.C.
Going Ape. Grasslands proliferate and hoofed animals spread— including a 20-foot-tall Asian rhi-noceros. During this period, called the "Oligocene Epoch," apes make their debut, and Antarctica splits from South America and Australia.

24 million–
5 million B.C.
Temperatures rise and drop; ice caps reform; and land bridges appear, encouraging migration among species. Mountain ranges, such as the Cascades, Andes, and Himalayas, form as giant tectonic plates collide. Chimpanzees and

Timeline

early hominoids (proto-humans) coexist.

5 million B.C.
Happy Hunting. The Pliocene Epoch kicks off as woolly mammoths, saber-toothed cats, giant armadillos, and giant flightless birds roam Earth. Mammals grow in size and number as the planet cools off again. North and South America connect.

4.4 million B.C.
Let's go for a walk. Hominoid *Ardipithecus ramidus* walks on two legs around northeastern Africa. A short 300,000 years later, *Australopithecus anamensis* strolls around Lake Turkana, Kenya.

3.2 million B.C.
I Love Lucy: The original "Lucy," a hominoid *(Australopithecus afarensis)* inhabits Ethiopia; her kin spread throughout east Africa.

2.5 million B.C.
The Stone Age begins with *homo habilis,* an apelike biped, using stone tools in Africa. In Canada, Greenland, and northern Europe, huge ice sheets cover the land.

1.6 million B.C.
Homo habilis wanders into central Asia, but the big brains of the planet are found in Africa's *homo erectus.* In another hundred thousand years, *homo erectus* walks out of Africa to begin inhabiting the world.

200,000 B.C.
Neanderthal man, a close relative of modern humans, makes his appearance on the Eurasian landmass. During the next 100,000 years, *homo sapiens* appear in Africa.

100,000 B.C.
Regional characteristics begin to emerge among *homo sapiens* in Australia, Asia, Africa, and Europe.

50,000 B.C.
Homo sapiens show up in the Near East and spread into Asia. Human development heats up: Man tames fire, but the rest of the world takes the news coolly as the last great Ice Age begins. Humans migrate into Europe, and large mammals such as woolly mammoths and giant ground sloths die out.

35,000–15,000 B.C.
Move over—Cro-Magnon man, a true *homo sapien,* begins displacing his smaller-brained Neanderthal neighbor in Europe. Bows and arrows are in vogue for hunting, and cave paintings show up in France's Chauvet and Lascaux Caves. Painted rocks appear in southern Africa. Nomads cross the Bering Straits into the Americas. Before long, the "New World" supports civilizations from Alaska to South America's Tierra del Fuego.

15,000–10,000 B.C.
Dogs are domesticated in east Asia. Hunter-gatherers start building semipermanent settlements. Early Japanese settlers produce pottery.

Wondering what happened next?
Turn to page 114 to find out!

HISTORY'S GRIM PLACES OF QUARANTINE

Life has never been easy for lepers. Throughout history, they've been stigmatized, feared, and outcast by society. Such reactions—though undeniably heartless—were perhaps understandable because the disease was thought to be rampantly contagious. Anyone suspected of leprosy was forced into quarantine and left to die.

Leprosy has affected humanity since at least 600 B.C. This miserable disease, now known as Hansen's disease, attacks the nervous system primarily in the hands, feet, and face and causes disfiguring skin sores, nerve damage, and progressive debilitation. Medical science had no understanding of leprosy until the late 1800s and no effective treatment for it until the 1940s. Prior to that point, lepers faced a slow, painful, and certain demise.

Misinterpretations of Biblical references to leprosy in Leviticus 13:45–46, which labeled lepers as "unclean" and dictated that sufferers must "dwell apart... outside the camp," didn't help matters. (The "leprosy" cited in Leviticus referred to several skin conditions, but Hansen's disease was not one of them.) It's really no surprise that society's less-than-compassionate response to the disease was the leper colony.

CAST OUT IN MISERY AND DESPAIR

The first leper colonies were isolated spots in the wilderness where the afflicted were driven, forgotten, and left to die.

The practice of exiling lepers continued well into the 20th century. In Crete, for instance, lepers were banished to mountainside caves, where they survived by eating scraps left by wolves. More humane measures were adopted in 1903 when lepers were corralled into the Spinalonga Island leper colony and given food and shelter and cared for by priests and nuns. However, once you entered, you never left, and it remained that way until the colony's last resident died in 1957.

Still, joining a leper colony sometimes beat living among the healthy. It wasn't much fun wandering from town to town while wearing signs or ringing bells to warn of one's affliction. And you were always susceptible to violence from townsfolk gripped by irrational fear—as when lepers were blamed for epidemic outbreaks and thrown into bonfires as punishment.

LIFE IN THE AMERICAN COLONY

American attitudes toward lepers weren't any more enlightened. One of modern time's most notorious leper colonies was on the Hawaiian island of Molokai, which was established in 1866.

Hawaiian kings and American officials banished sufferers to this remote peninsula ringed by jagged lava rock and towering sea cliffs. Molokai became one of the world's largest leper colonies—its population peaked in 1890 at 1,174—and more than 8,000 people were forcibly confined there before the practice was finally ended in 1969.

The early days of Molokai were horrible. The banished were abandoned in a lawless place where they received minimal care and had to fight with others for food, water, blankets, and shelter. Public condemnation led to improved conditions on Molokai, but residents later became freaks on display as Hollywood celebrities flocked to the colony on macabre sightseeing tours.

A LEPER HAVEN IN LOUISIANA

While sufferers of leprosy were being humiliated in Hawaii, they were being helped in Louisiana.

In 1894, the Louisiana Leper House, which billed itself as "a place of treatment and research, not detention," opened in Carville. In 1920, it was transferred to federal authority and renamed the National Leprosarium of the United States. Known today as the National Hansen's Disease (leprosy) Program (NHDP), the facility became a leading research and rehabilitation center, pioneering treatments that form the basis of multidrug therapies currently prescribed by the World Health Organization (WHO) for the treatment of Hansen's disease.

It was here that researchers enlisted a common Louisiana critter—the armadillo—in the fight against the disease. It had always been difficult to study Hansen's disease. Human nerves are seldom biopsied, so direct data on nerve damage from Hansen's was minimal. But in the 1960s, NHDP researchers theorized that armadillos might be susceptible to the germ because of their low body temperature. They began inoculating armadillos with it and discovered that the animals could develop the disease systemically. Now the armadillo is used to develop infected nerves for research worldwide.

A THING OF THE PAST?

In 1985, leprosy was still considered a public health problem in 122 countries. In fact, the last remaining leper colony, located in Croatia, didn't close until 2002. However, WHO has made great strides toward eradicating the disease and indicated in 2000 that the rate of infection had dropped by 90 percent. The multidrug therapies currently prescribed for the treatment of leprosy are available to all patients for free via WHO. Approximately four million patients have been cured since 2000.

- *Approximately 95 percent of humans are not susceptible to the bacteria that causes Hansen's.*

- *In 2005, 166 new cases of Hansen's disease were reported in the United States.*

- *Besides humans and armadillos, the only other animals that have been shown to contract leprosy are chimpanzees, sooty mangabeys (a type of monkey), and crab-eating macaques.*

- *The word leprosy comes from ancient Greek words meaning "to scale" and "to peel."*

MERCURY 13: THE MISSION THAT NEVER WENT

In 1961, a group of highly qualified women were selected for astronaut flight training. They passed every test and endured every poke, prod, and simulation. In some cases, they actually fared better than their male counterparts. But was America really ready to send women into space? Apparently not.

The Soviets fired the starter's gun in the space race by launching the *Sputnik* satellite on October 4, 1957. Threatened by the Soviets ability to beat them to the punch, the United States accelerated their own space initiatives, including the formation of the National Aeronautics and Space Administration (NASA). Next time, the United States would be first.

There was much yet to learn about space. What could humans tolerate? Jet pilots required pressure suits; what of weightless space? What of the confinement? Military test pilots—fit, brave, and calm during flight crises—seemed logical candidates. Of course, since women weren't allowed to be military test pilots, they weren't considered for astronaut training. At least, not at first.

SECRET EXPERIMENTS

Freethinking researcher Dr. Randy Lovelace II helped screen the first seven male astronauts as part of the Mercury 7 program. Then Lovelace had a flash of inspiration, thinking: *A space rocket needs every joule of energy. Every gram of weight counts. Women are lighter; they use less oxygen and food. We know for sure they can fly; heck, Jackie Cochran helped me start my research foundation. Maybe they're actually better suited! Let's explore this!*

Cochran herself was well over the age limit of 35, but Oklahoman Geraldyn "Jerrie" Cobb wasn't. A record-setting aviator, Cobb had earned her private pilot's license when she was just 17 years old. Between 1957 and 1960, she set four aviation world records for speed, distance, and absolute altitude.

When Jerrie received an invitation from Dr. Lovelace to train for space flight, she dropped everything for what seemed like the opportunity of a lifetime. She arrived in Albuquerque in 1960 and began the torture tests. She underwent barium enemas and had all her body fluids sampled. Supercooled water was squirted into her ear canal to test her reaction to vertigo. She endured the infamous "Vomit Comet" spin simulator—and many more tests besides.

Cobb blew the trials away. When Lovelace announced this to the media, they fiended over the "astronette." Cobb was the first of 25 women tested for astronaut potential. Only some of the women met one another in person, but Cobb was involved in their recruitment and knew them all. Thirteen passed all the tests to become FLATs: Fellow Lady Astronaut Trainees, an acronym taken from Cobb's written salutation to them.

During this phase, Soviet cosmonaut Yuri Gagarin orbited the planet, lapping NASA once again in the space race.

The women's next planned step was testing at navy facilities in Pensacola. Each went home to wait. But when Lovelace asked to use Pensacola, the navy called NASA. The organization was less than enthused about the female astronauts, so the navy pushed the training overboard.

In September 1961, each FLAT got a telegram: *Sorry, program cancelled. You may now resume your normal lives.*

"LET'S STOP THIS NOW!"

The women couldn't have been more dismayed. All that work—for nothing! They didn't give up, but they also didn't coordinate their lobbying. Cobb, the FLATs' self-appointed spokesperson, didn't get along well with Cochran—who in turn had her own ideas. Cobb's appeals up the national chain of command were honest, impassioned, and naive. Cochran, with personal contacts ranging from Chuck Yeager to VP Lyndon Johnson, preferred to work gradually within the sexist system rather than have an open challenge slapped down. One FLAT, Jane Hart, was the wife of a U.S. senator and was arguably the savviest political spokesperson available. Hart fumed as Cochran testified to Congress that she was against a "special program for women."

WAS IT EVER POSSIBLE?

What if all the Mercury 13 women and Cochran had spoken to Congress and to the country in a unified voice? We can guess the outcome based on LBJ's reaction to the memo across his desk concerning the female astronauts. He scrawled: "LET'S STOP THIS NOW!" If President Kennedy's space tsar had that attitude, there had never been any real hope. The men leading the nation weren't ready to send women into space. Period.

Was Lovelace deluded? Give him credit for trying, but he also didn't clue NASA in until news of the Pensacola plans blindsided them, resulting in a reflex "no way." On the other hand, had he sought advance permission, odds of NASA giving it were... astronomical.

On June 16, 1963, about a year after Cobb, Hart, and Cochran spoke before Congress, cosmonaut Valentina Tereshkova of the Soviet Union flew in space. She was not a test pilot but a parachute hobbyist and textile worker. It would be 20 more years before the first American woman, Sally Ride, made it into space.

- *No exaggeration: Techs took 100 X-rays of each bone in Jerrie Cobb's body.*

- *For Jerrie Cobb, perhaps the worst part was the initial media barrage. She had to field important technical questions: Was she scared; could she cook; what were her measurements?*

- *As unfortunate an acronym as FLATs may be, posterity has tried to filch it from Jerrie Cobb's purse. Most chroniclers spell it out as "First Lady Astronaut Trainees," as though it were an official term conferred by NASA. The women themselves have never embraced it, preferring Mercury 13.*

Fast Facts

- The Chinese emperor Shen-Nung was the first to use acupuncture as a medical treatment in 2700 B.C.

- Christmas wasn't declared a national holiday in the United States until 1890.

- When Grover Cleveland beat incumbent Benjamin Harrison in 1892, he became the first (and, so far, only) person to win nonconsecutive terms as president.

- Of all the people who eventually signed the Declaration of Independence, only John Hancock and Charles Thomson actually signed it on July 4. Most of the others didn't sign until August 2, with the last signature added five years later.

- John Adams was the first person to lose a U.S. presidential election (he was defeated by Thomas Jefferson). George Washington was elected to his two terms unopposed.

- William Henry Harrison was the first U.S. president to die in office (in 1841). He also holds the record for the shortest term in office—32 days.

- The phrase "wear your heart on your sleeve" originated in the Middle Ages when young men and women drew names to see who their valentine would be. They would then wear these names on their sleeves for one week.

- The phrase "second string," which today means replacement or backup, originated in the Middle Ages, when an archer carried a second string in case the one on his bow broke.

- Although officially the seventeenth state in the Union, Congress forgot to vote on the resolution to make Ohio a state until August 7, 1953, which technically makes it the 47th state.

- James Buchanan was the only president to remain a bachelor while in office.

AMERICA'S FIRST FEMALE PRESIDENT

When President Woodrow Wilson suffered a stroke on October 2, 1919, the White House became shrouded in secrecy. His wife, Edith, controlled all access to the president. Many wondered whether she actually controlled the White House too.

EARLY LIFE

Born on October 15, 1872, Edith Bolling was a direct descendent of Pocahontas and John Rolfe. She was raised in Wytheville, Virginia, and married Norman Galt, a Washington jeweler. They lived happily together for 12 years, but Norman died unexpectedly in 1908, leaving Edith a widow at age 35.

One of Edith's close friends, Helen Bones, was a cousin of and hostess for Woodrow Wilson. In March 1915, Edith and Helen stepped out of a White House elevator, both of them muddy from a walk. By chance, they met the recently widowed President Wilson and his friend and physician, Dr. Cary Grayson. On that soggy afternoon, Edith joined President Wilson for tea. Almost immediately, Wilson was drawn to Edith's charm and intellect, and by the end of April, she was dining at the White House on a nightly basis, enjoying intimate conversations about politics and world concerns. On May 4, 1915—a shocking two months after they met—Wilson proposed.

MARRIAGE AND WAR

Following their marriage on December 18, 1915, Edith's political partnership with Wilson continued—perhaps beyond the lines of propriety. In fact, as the United States became involved in the Great War, Edith coded and decoded confidential messages, enjoying direct access to classified information.

After World War I ended on November 11, 1918, Edith shared Wilson's enthusiasm for the Treaty of Versailles and his proposed League of Nations to maintain world peace. However, the Senate refused to ratify the Treaty without several changes.

Wilson refused to compromise. In September 1919, he embarked on a 10,000-mile whistle-stop tour of the country to promote the League, but extreme exhaustion debilitated him between Pueblo, Colorado, and Wichita, Kansas. Edith (along with Doctor Grayson and secretary Joseph Tumulty) cancelled the rest of the tour and rushed Wilson back to Washington.

On October 2, Edith found Wilson on the White House bathroom floor. He'd suffered a debilitating stroke that left the left side of his body paralyzed.

THE SHROUD OF SECRECY

Late that afternoon, Wilson lay nearly lifeless on the large Lincoln bed. But according to Edith's memoir, the words of Dr. Francis Dercum offered assurance. Although Wilson's body was maimed, his mind was "clear as crystal." While Dercum recommended that Wilson not resign from office, he warned Edith that Wilson must be guarded from stress and unnecessary decisions.

So, Edith became Wilson's gatekeeper and spokesperson. Very few people besides Grayson or Tumulty were allowed in Wilson's room. Meanwhile, Grayson told the public that the president was suffering from "nervous exhaustion."

Rumors began to fly as the public demanded answers. Had the president become a drooling, babbling infant? Was he actually suffering from venereal disease? Political enemies accused Edith of running a "petticoat government"; other critics called her the "Presidentress."

RUNNING THE NATION?

While Edith took over many routine duties of government, she maintained that Wilson was in control of major decisions. She defined herself as a steward. In *My Memoir*, she stated: "I, myself, never made a single decision regarding the disposition of public affairs. The only decision that was mine was what was important and what was not, and the very important decision of when to present matters to my husband."

According to some, this was equivalent to running the country, but there is no evidence that she contradicted Wilson. Even when the Treaty was heading for defeat in November 1919, she obeyed her husband's emphatic murmurs that compromise would be dishonorable.

In December 1919, the shroud was lifted: Edith allowed Albert Fall (a Republican senator and political foe) to enter Wilson's room to discuss a crisis in Mexico. Carefully covering his weakened left side, Edith helped present the bedridden Wilson in his best form. Wilson's appearance, intelligence, and wit convinced the senator and other leaders that he was still capable of leading the nation.

Wilson finished his term in 1921 and retired in Washington, D.C. He died on February 3, 1924. During her long widowhood, Edith promoted the legacy of her husband by publishing *My Memoir* (1939) and releasing *Wilson* (1944), a film biography over which she held full control of the script. Edith died on December 28, 1961, the 105th anniversary of her husband's birthday.

WHAT REALLY HAPPENED?

The truth of Edith Wilson's finely crafted memoir was questioned when documents revealed that Doctors Dercum and Grayson were fully aware of the severity of Wilson's stroke and his immediate mental impairment. Furthermore, Grayson's private correspondence indicated that Edith would not allow those details to be released to the nation. If Wilson's true condition had been revealed in the weeks following the stroke, Wilson likely would have been replaced by Vice President Thomas Marshall. Edith's harshest critics believe her secrecy may have changed the course of history, speculating that if Marshall had become president, he may have chosen to negotiate a modified version of the League of Nations that included the United States.

A DAY IN THE LIFE
DAYS CONSUMED BY WAR

*The Civil War cast a long shadow over the lives of all
Philadelphians, especially as victorious rebel yells echoed
through the Pennsylvania countryside in June 1863.
The following is an account of what a day in the life of
a Civil War woman might have been like.*

It's 7:30 A.M. on a late June morning in Philadelphia. Rebecca
looks in the mirror at her outfit. It's modest but fashionable
1863 attire: A navy blue ankle-length gown tapered at the waist to
create a full pleated skirt (sans the hoop—she needs something
functional, not fancy) and accentuated with long wide sleeves and
a jewel neckline covered with a white collar. Satisfied with her
appearance, the 20-year-old patriot leaves her family's working-
class home in the Spring Garden District to do her part for the
Union war effort against the Confederates.

VOLUNTEERING AT THE SALOON

Rebecca takes a horse-drawn cab through a city fully engaged
in war. The factories near her home continuously pump out war
goods. The Baldwin Locomotive Works once employed all the
men in her family—her two older brothers quit to join the Union
army, leaving her father and younger brother behind. The streets
crawl with soldiers, some heading to the fight, others returning.
They congregate in Philadelphia, now threatened by General
Lee's Army of Northern Virginia standing 140 miles to the west.

By 8:00 A.M., she reaches the Union Volunteer Refreshment
Saloon on Swanson Street. Here, weary soldiers passing through
Philadelphia to and from the front wash up, eat a hearty meal, and
rest a bit. It's run by the city's Volunteer Relief Association, and
Rebecca donates her time there most days of the week.

Rebecca eats the Saloon's breakfast of the day—cold ham,
bread and butter, tomatoes, and coffee—then begins serving and

charming the men. She puts in eight hours at the Saloon then has a bit of supper—broiled beef, cheese, fruit, and coffee.

REBECCA, THE NEWS JUNKIE

Throughout the day, Rebecca seeks out the latest news from the front. The news in the *Philadelphia Inquirer* isn't good. Lee's 70,000-strong rebel army continues to advance northward unabated. The Rebs occupied Gettysburg four days ago on June 26 and took York two days later. Harrisburg looks to fall next.

She also scans the paper's daily casualty list and sees the name of a boy from her neighborhood. She thinks back to the day last September when she saw her oldest brother's name on the list; he died at Antietam halting Lee's first invasion of the North.

The Saloon rumor mill produces worse news. One colleague tells Rebecca that the Rebs are pillaging Pennsylvania towns and farms. Another claims that President Lincoln is secretly negotiating an armistice with Jefferson Davis.

There is one bit of good news though. The Union Army of the Potomac, now led by Philly's own Major General George Meade, is *finally* marching to stop Lee.

SOLDIERING ON INTO THE EVENING

After departing the Saloon, Rebecca's personal war effort continues. She and some friends attend an early evening rally organized by the Union League Club at Independence Hall.

After, she returns home and helps her mother and younger sister assemble a care package for her brother at the front. Inside is a pair of newly knitted socks, a deck of playing cards, back issues of the *Inquirer,* and some sweets.

She reads his letter, which arrived earlier in the day, and then pens a reply. Her eyes well up as she writes. The war is going terribly for the North, and she worries about him.

In a few days, in fields near Gettysburg, the situation will change dramatically. Prospects for a Union victory, and her brother's safe return home, will suddenly brighten.

GREAT OBSCURE QUOTES

"If I could save the Union without freeing any slave I would do it; and if I could save it by freeing all the slaves, I would do it; and if I could save it by freeing some and leaving others alone I would also do that."

—ABRAHAM LINCOLN, THE GREAT EMANCIPATOR

"It is apparent to me that the possibilities of the aeroplane . . . have been exhausted."

—THOMAS EDISON, 1895

"It's too bad, but the way American people are, now that they have all this capability, instead of taking advantage of it, they'll probably just piss it all away."

—LYNDON BAINES JOHNSON, 1967, WITH REGARDS TO THE *APOLLO* PROGRAM

"Beer is proof that God loves us and wants us to be happy."

—BENJAMIN FRANKLIN

"Justice is incidental to law and order."

—J. EDGAR HOOVER

MUSE OF THE NURSERY

There was an old lady,
With the name Mother Goose.
She told children stories,
Could she just be a ruse?

Did she really exist?
That legend of old.
The elderly storyteller,
Of whom we were told.

You'll have to read on,
To discover the truth.
To tell you right here,
Would be rather uncouth.

Whether it's the muffin man, the farmer in the dell, or Humpty Dumpty, Mother Goose has rhymes for them all. While collections of these nursery rhymes bear the name Mother Goose and the illustration of an old peasant woman, most of the so-called Mother Goose tales originated centuries ago as folktales and legends handed down from generation to generation. Mothers would comfort their young children by singing rhyming verses to the tunes of ballads and folk songs.

Many have tried to track down the identity of the real Mother Goose, but she is, in fact, a mythical character. The earliest written reference to Mother Goose appeared in a poem titled *La Muse Historique* in a 1660s issue of French critic Jean Loret's monthly periodical. Loret wrote, "...*comme un conte de la Mère Oye*," which translated means "...like a Mother Goose story."

Charles Perrault, who served on the staff of King Louis XIV, was the first author to use the name Mother Goose in the title of a book. In 1697, Perrault published a collection of children's stories titled *Histoires ou Contes du temps passe* ("Histories or Tales from the Past with Morals"). The frontispiece carried the subtitle, *Contes de ma mère l'Oye* ("Tales from My Mother Goose"). On the book's cover was an illustration of an old woman telling stories to a group of children. The book contained a compilation of eight folktales, including Sleeping Beauty, Cinderella, Little Red Riding Hood, and Puss in Boots.

It took more than 30 years for Mother Goose to make her debut in English. In 1729, writer Robert Samber translated Perrault's book into English under the title, *Histories or Tales of Past Times, Told by Mother Goose.*

London bookseller John Newbery had published a collection of nursery rhymes in 1744. In 1765, he incorporated the name Mother Goose when he published *Mother Goose's Melody, or Sonnets for the Cradle.* Newbery's book contained more than 50 rhymes and songs and marked a shift in the subject of children's books from fairy tales to nursery rhymes.

Mother Goose made her first appearance in America in 1786, when Massachusetts printer Isaiah Thomas reprinted Robert Samber's book using the same title. Over the course of 14 years, Thomas's version of the book was reprinted three times.

It was in America that Mother Goose would take hold as the keeper of nursery rhymes. In the early 19th century, she became even more popular when Boston-based Munroe & Francis began printing inexpensive and lavish Mother Goose editions. Since then, numerous collections and editions of Mother Goose stories have been published.

Regardless of whether the original Mother Goose was an actual person, she is real in the minds of many infants and young children. The rhythms, alliteration, and silly stories found in the Mother Goose tales have entranced children for centuries; and as long as there are babies to sing to, they will no doubt continue to do so. As the old storyteller said in the preface of the 1843 edition of the book *The Only True Mother Goose Melodies*:

"My Melodies will never die,
While nurses sing, or babies cry."

Fast Facts

- In 1865, Mary Walker, a Civil War surgeon, became the first (and so far, only) woman to receive the Congressional Medal of Honor.

- In 1916, Jeanette Rankin became the first woman elected to the U.S. Congress. She is also the only person who voted against both World Wars I and II.

- The phrase "mad as a hatter" referred to 19th-century hatmakers who were poisoned by the mercury they used to treat the felt in their hats. Mercury poisoning often causes neurological problems such as excitable or irrational behavior, trembling, and the jumbling of words when speaking.

- Three of the first five presidents died on Independence Day. John Adams and Thomas Jefferson died on the same day— July 4, 1826. James Monroe died on July 4, 1831.

- Each king in a deck of playing cards is meant to represent a king from history: the king of spades is for King David, the king of clubs represents Alexander the Great, the king of hearts depicts Charlemagne, and the king of diamonds is reserved for Julius Caesar.

- Napoleon Bonaparte suffered from ailurophobia, which is the fear of cats.

- In 1920, Florence Harding became the first First Lady to vote in a presidential election.

- You didn't want to be naked on deck in the U.S. navy in the 1840s; it would get you nine lashes. More severe was filthiness (twelve lashes), but less severe was throwing a spittoon lid overboard (six lashes).

- In 1969, Native American activists took over Alcatraz. They claimed that since the island was inhospitable, lacking in any facilities or means of support, and a former prison, it fit the past reservation traditions perfectly.

THE SEVEN WONDERS OF THE ANCIENT WORLD

*It was the ultimate destination guide—seven of the most
spectacular hand-built wonders of the world.
In fact, the Greek referred to these wonders as* theamati,
which translates roughly to "must-sees."

THE SEVEN WONDERS OF THE ANCIENT WORLD

The first comprehensive listing of the Seven Wonders has been attributed to Herodotus, a Greek historian dating back to the 5th century B.C. Other versions soon followed—each reflecting the writer's opinion of what was worth mentioning, and often naming many more than seven sights. Most of the earliest lists were lost; the oldest existing version known today was compiled by Antipater of Sidon in 140 B.C. The items on his list, with a few revisions, are the ones that came to forever be known as the Seven Wonders of the Ancient World. Unfortunately, only one of the seven still exists today; all that remains of the other six are descriptions from writers over the centuries.

SO WHAT'S THE BIG DEAL?

What makes the seven wonders of the world so wonderful? It's a combination of factors: the intricacies of the architecture, the scale of engineering, and the beauty of each project—not to mention the construction technology and available materials in use at the time.

Religion often played a big role in the significance of these structures. Some were built to honor certain gods. Others were built to showcase important rulers, a number of whom had achieved a godlike following.

AND THE SEVEN WONDERS ARE...

1. The Great Pyramid of Giza

Located on the west bank of the Nile river near Cairo, Egypt, this is the largest of ten pyramids built between 2600 and 2500 B.C. Built for King Khufu, the Great Pyramid was constructed by thousands of workers toiling over the span of decades (2609 B.C.–2584 B.C.).

The structure consists of more than two million 2.5-ton stones. If the stones were piled on top of each other, the resulting tower would be close to 50 stories high. The base covers an astonishing 13 acres. It's not known exactly how the blocks were lifted. Theories include mud-and water-coated ramps or an intricate system of levers. Not only did the blocks have to be lifted, but they also had to be transported from the quarries. Even the experts can't say exactly how that was done. The mystery is part of the fascination.

The pyramid originally stood 481 feet high but has been weathered down to about 450 feet. It was considered the tallest structure on the planet for 43 centuries. The Great Pyramid is the only Wonder of the Ancient World still standing—a testament to one of the mightiest civilizations in history.

2. The Hanging Gardens of Babylon

Legend has it the Gardens were built by King Nebuchadnezzar II, ruler of Babylon (near modern Baghdad, Iraq), around 600 B.C. as a present for his wife, Amytis of Media. The gardens consisted of a series of terraces holding trees, exotic plants, and shady pools—all fed by water piped in from the Euphrates River and rising about 60 feet high. References to the Gardens appear as late as the first century B.C., after which they disappear from contemporary accounts. There has been some speculation over whether or not the Gardens ever actually existed.

3. The Temple of Artemis at Ephesus

Constructed around 550 B.C. in what is now Turkey, the Temple was built in honor of Artemis (Diana), goddess of hunting and nature. The marble temple measured 377 by 180 feet and had a tile-covered roof held up by at least 106 columns between 40 and 60 feet high. The temple held priceless art and also functioned as the treasury of the city. It stood until 356 B.C. when it was purposely destroyed by an artist, known in infamy as Herostratus, who burned the Temple merely so his name would be remembered for ages. The outraged Ephesians rebuilt the temple, this time entirely of stone, but the new building was destroyed by invading Goths in A.D. 262. A few surviving sculptures are displayed at the British Museum.

4. The Statue of Zeus at Olympia

Even contemporary historians and archaeologists consider the Statue of Zeus at Olympia to be one of the best-known statues in the ancient world. The image, standing 40 feet high with a 20-foot base, was constructed by Phidias around 435 B.C. to honor Zeus, king of the gods. The statue depicted a seated Zeus (made of ivory, though his robes and sandals were made of gold) holding a golden figure of the goddess of victory in one hand and a staff topped with an eagle in the other. Atop his head was a wreath of olive branches.

In the flickering lamplight of the temple, the statue seemed almost alive and attracted pilgrims from all over Greece for eight centuries. After the old gods were outlawed by Christian emperor Theodosius, the statue was taken as a prize to Constantinople, where it was destroyed in a fire around A.D. 462.

5. The Mausoleum of Maussollos

This white marble tomb, built in what is today southwestern Turkey, was built around 353 B.C. for Maussollos, a Persian king. Around 45 stories tall, the building was covered in relief sculpture depicting scenes from mythology; gaps were filled in with bigger-than-life statues of famous heroes and gods. The very top was capped with a marble statue of Maussollos, pulled in a chariot by four horses. The structure was so impressive that the king's name has been lent to the present-day word *mausoleum,* now used to refer to an impressive burial place.

The tomb remained largely intact until the 13th century, when it was severely damaged by a series of earthquakes. In 1494, the Knights of Saint John raided its stonework to use as building materials for a castle being constructed nearby, and thus the Mausoleum was lost to history.

6. The Colossus of Rhodes

Standing nearly 110 feet tall—rivaling the modern Statue of Liberty, which tops out at 151 feet—the Colossus of Rhodes was a sight to behold. The bronze statue was built near the harbor of Rhodes in the Aegean Sea in honor of the sun god Helios. Construction took 12 years—from approximately 292 B.C. to 280 B.C. The exact pose of the statue is a matter of debate; records say that one arm was raised but are maddeningly silent on other details. The statue stood for only 56 years before it was toppled by an earthquake. It lay on the ground for another 800 years, still a tourist attraction. Accounts say a popular tourist game was to see if a person could encircle one of the fallen statue's thumbs with their arms. Finally, in A.D. 654, Rhodes was captured by Arab invaders who broke up the statue and melted it down for its bronze.

7. The Lighthouse of Alexandria

The youngest of the ancient wonders was a building with a civic, rather than a spiritual, purpose. The famed lighthouse of Alexandria was built around 250 B.C. to aid ships making the journey into that city's harbor. At 380 feet tall, it was a marvel of ancient engineering. Overshadowed only by two of the tallest Egyptian pyramids, a tower of greater height wouldn't be constructed for centuries. An interior ramp led up to a platform supporting a series of polished bronze mirrors, which would reflect sunlight during the day and firelight at night. The fuel source is uncertain but may have been oil or even animal dung. Some accounts claim the lighthouse could be seen 300 miles from the shore; this is almost certainly exaggerated, but more reasonable claims of 35 miles are impressive enough. It continued to impress travelers into the 1300s, when it was destroyed by an earthquake.

LEGACY

It is a tribute to our ancestors that they were able to create works of architecture that capture our imagination even thousands of years after the structures themselves were destroyed. Several efforts are underway to name a definitive list of modern wonders, with such candidates as the Eiffel Tower and the Golden Gate Bridge. One such effort elicited votes from people all over the world via the Internet. The resulting list of the "New 7 Wonders of the World" was released in July 2007. The finalists, in no particular order, are: Petra, Jordan; the Great Wall of China; the Christ Redeemer, Brazil; the Taj Majal, India; Chichen Itza, Mexico; the Colosseum, Italy; and Machu Picchu, Peru. Given the method of collecting votes, the validity of this list is disputed.

- *Proof that the famed Hanging Gardens may be mythical: Herodotus, a very cosmopolitan fellow, visited Babylon but never mentioned them. Indeed, no archaelogical evidence of the Gardens has been found to this day.*

- *In addition to the Seven Ancient Wonders of the World and the New Seven Wonders of the World, there is also a list for natural world wonders. It includes Mount Everest, Ayers Rock, the Matterhorn, the Grand Canyon, the Meteor Crater, the Great Barrier Reef, and Victoria Falls.*

Fast Facts

- *Every male Roman child remained under his father's authority until that father's death.* Pater *could sentence* filum *to death; disinherit him; block him from legal action on his own behalf; even prevent him from borrowing money.*

- *Pay up,* chumpus: *In Rome, if someone got behind on a debt, the creditor might hire a* convicium *(escort) to serenade the deadbeat with ridicule. As long as the song wasn't obscene, this was legal.*

- *A 4th-century survey of Rome counted more than 45,000 tenements, nearly 1,800 villas, 850 bathhouses, 1,300 swimming pools, and a dozen each of libraries and toilet complexes. Of course, by then, Rome had receded from its peak glories.*

- *Before going on a long journey, Romans would bargain with the gods for safety by promising some act of devotion upon arrival. If the gods finked and the trip went sour, the pious supplicant would kick the god's statue on his or her return.*

- *The Bay of Neapolis (now Naples) was Rome's Padre Island or Cabo San Lucas. It was where one went—not for rest and relaxation—but for intercourse and intoxication. Not that genteel Roman society was shy about either to begin with.*

- *Pirates captured a twentysomething Julius Caesar at sea. The brassy kid took offense at the low ransom, ordering the captors to quadruple their demand. While waiting for the ransom to arrive, he made them listen to his oratory and scoffed when the pirates didn't appreciate his clever wit. After his release, he raised a fleet, hunted them down, and crucified them all.*

- *Great Roman women: Fulvia (77–40 B.C.). This patrician wife of Mark Antony was a capable general who led eight legions in a rebellion against land confiscation, fighting to the bitter end before going into exile.*

Great Museums
A NATION'S INHERITANCE

Perhaps no American museum is as well-known, and as beloved, as the Smithsonian Institution's complex of art, science, history, and zoological museums in Washington, D.C.

In 1835, an unknown, illegitimate English-man named James Smithson died, child-less but not penniless. He had inherited a substantial estate from his parents—one of royal blood and the other a duke, and in death he left the world a magnificent gift: an endowment for an American institution "for the increase and diffusion of knowledge among men"—the *Smithson*ian Institution.

Smithson's motives behind his unusual bequest remain a mystery. He never visited the United States, and there is little evidence that he ever even wrote to any American. Bastard son of the Duke of Northumberland, he may have felt slighted by a British society that deprived him of the privileges of a "legitimate" ducal heir. Or he may have taken a far-off interest in the bustling new democ-racy in which ideas and industry appeared to rule the day.

Whatever his motives, Smithson's offer of 100,000 gold sovereigns was too enticing for the young republic to refuse. U.S. President Andrew Jackson urged Congress to accept Smithson's gift, and upon congressional approval, the British gold was recast into 508,318 Yankee dollars.

NOW WHAT?

Having accepted the money, the nation faced an important ques-tion: "What do we do with it?"

Initially, Congress leaned toward using Smithson's gold to estab-lish a national university. Plans for an institution specializing in the classics, science, or teaching skills were all proposed and rejected in turn. Other ideas—a national observatory, a laboratory, a museum, or a library—drew both support and opposition from the divided legislature. So the deadlocked Congress settled the matter by avoiding the issue entirely, leaving it to the Smithsonian's board of directors to determine the direction of the new institution.

AMERICA'S ATTIC

The first proceeds were used for a building that would house the many tasks assigned to the new institution—teaching, experimenting, exhibiting to the public. The building, located on the National Mall and now known as "the Castle," was designed in the medieval revival style, reminiscent of the ancient universities of Smithson's homeland.

While the research and scientific functions of the Smithsonian grew steadily after the 1855 completion of the Castle, it was the national collection of odds and ends that captured the public's mind and earned the Smithsonian its reputation as "America's attic." Fueled by the great American explorations of the Arctic, Antarctic, and interior regions of the United States, the Smithsonian's holdings grew from a small collection of pressed flora and preserved animal specimens to an assemblage that required the construction of a new building, the United States National Museum, in 1881.

Today, more than 170 years after Smithson died, the institute that bears his name comprises 19 museums, 4 research centers, a zoo, and a library research system and is the largest single museum complex on the globe. From the fabled Hope Diamond to the historic Wright Flyer, from George Washington's dress sword to the original Kermit the Frog, the Smithsonian Institution pulls together the best of America's history and many relics of the world in which we live. Its collection, an astounding *136.9 million* objects, and its museums are graced by 23 million visitors per year. With assets worth $2.2 billion today, James Smithson's bequest has grown into the world's biggest museum.

History of the Weird
IN MUSHROOMS WE TRUST

John Allegro: linguist, showman, and certifiable eccentric

It's not often that the world of academia produces a character like John Marco Allegro. Born in 1923, Allegro first studied for the Methodist ministry but later became a brilliant scholar of Hebrew dialects. This latter course of study made him a perfect fit for the international team assembled to decipher the Dead Sea Scrolls, the earliest surviving manuscripts of the Bible.

Because Allegro was part scholar and part showman, he became a star in the otherwise sober world of biblical scholarship. At the time, the historical importance of the scrolls was a cause for controversy, and Allegro gleefully submerged himself into the debate.

Suddenly, however, Allegro took the debate in an absurd direction with his infamous book: *The Sacred Mushroom and the Cross*. In it, he argued that Biblical figures like Moses and Christ were actually literary inventions. In fact, he contended that the Jewish and Christian scriptures were allegories, written to promote an ancient fertility cult. To Allegro, Jesus represented a hallucinogenic mushroom, which followers ingested to enhance their perception of God.

Allegro tried to prove that the Bible was actually a coded text written to preserve the secrets of this drug-worshipping cult. When the writers of these "folktales" died, he argued, their original meaning was forever lost. Subsequent followers—early Christians—began taking scripture literally and interpreted as factual what Allegro maintained had always been meant as fable.

This peculiar thesis was roundly panned by the academic community. Allegro's reputation was destroyed. Though he died in disrepute, Allegro did inspire a group of supporters who, even to this day, still try to defend the man and his zany thesis.

ONLY DEATH IS SURER: CREATIVE TAXATION THROUGHOUT HISTORY

They cursed it in ancient Mesopotamia just as we do today, but as a means of supporting public efforts, tax is as ancient as humanity. One may tax property, transactions, shipments . . . anything humans do. This has led to some interesting ideas.

EGYPT

Income tax varied based on your line of work. Lie and expect a whipping—or worse. They taxed cooking oil, with tax enforcers running around to make sure you bought new oil and didn't reuse the old gross stuff. By the Greek period, Egyptians had introduced "tax farming," a genteel term for organized crime: "In return for a lump sum of 100,000 drachmas, we'll grant you taxing rights." How often do you think tax farmers took a net loss?

CHINA

With thousands of years of sophisticated ruling infrastructure, the Chinese have paid tax on everything imaginable. Local officials had to raise a given amount of tax; how they did so was their problem (especially if they failed). China also had poll taxes (tax per person) for most of its history. Sometimes only males paid. Other times, the imperial leadership decided equality should reign.

GREECE

Like the Egyptians, the Greeks used tax farming. They also imposed poll taxes on foreigners—twice as much for males as females, a reflection of ancient Greek views of women accepted everywhere except Sparta. One creative Greek taxation method was to insinuate the state into all phases of the olive oil industry. From cultivation to extraction to marketing, Uncle Samnos took his due.

INDIA

India has had income taxes, business taxes, and so on, but where India set itself apart was foreign trade. Foreign goods and their merchants got soaked in a big way, which hints at what a great import market India must have been. India also had progressive taxation, which is tax-speak for milking the rich.

ROME

Republican Rome used tax farmers as well; the Bible knew them as the hated publicans, from whom the poor took a major hosing. Augustus replaced this with a combination poll tax and wealth tax, in which the poor again took a hosing. Sense a trend? As the empire went on, though, taxes became more progressive. By Diocletian and Constantine's era (c. A.D. 300), taxes on the wealthy began to strangle the economy. By A.D. 410, Alaric the Goth sacked Rome mainly because no one could be bothered to stop him from doing so.

BRITAIN

Romans brought taxation to Britain, but in the Viking Age, the British had a special tax called Danegeld. The Vikings functioned like a seagoing street gang. If you paid the Dane his gold, the Dane went away for however long it took him to spend the gold. When he was broke, he'd come get more. This tax fell heavily on the wealthy, mainly because only the wealthy had anything worthwhile for Vikings to steal.

✧✧✧

- *You'll like this (unless you work for the government): Egyptian government officials owed tax on the money they took in.*

- *When the American colonies became the young United States, a hatred of British taxation led to strict rules about how the new republic could tax itself. Soon the founding fathers realized they'd have to get creative, so they taxed whiskey. That was a hot button in a relatively drunken nation and led to the Whiskey Rebellion.*

Fast Facts

- Wild Bill Hickok was shot dead at a poker game in 1876 while holding aces and eights—a hand now known as a "Dead Man's Hand."

- American mustangs were introduced to the Americas by the Spanish; Christopher Columbus brought the first horses on his second journey to the New World.

- Old West outlaw Billy the Kid was born in New York City.

- The famed Pony Express only ran for 19 months. But in that time, its riders carried nearly 35,000 pieces of mail more than 650,000 miles!

- For two decades, Judge Roy Bean, the "Only Law West of the Pecos," dispensed justice from a saloon called "The Jersey Lilly," named for a British actress he admired but never met.

- During the peak of the western cattle drives, as many as one in four cowboys was African-American.

- Judge Isaac Parker, the "Hanging Judge" of Fort Smith, Arkansas, sentenced 156 men and 4 women to hang during his 31-year tenure. Of the number sentenced, fewer than half were actually hanged.

- The term "Red Light District" owes its origin to the colored glass in the front door of Dodge City's Red Light Bordello.

- The leaders of the famed Dalton Gang—Grat, Emmett, and Bob—were lawmen before they became bank robbers.

- Spanish guns, crossbows, and swords were not nearly as deadly to Native Americans as the diseases the conquistadores brought; measles, smallpox, cholera, and other diseases cut the population of the Aztec Empire from around 20 million to about 1.6 million in 100 years.

- The famed gunfight at the O.K. Corral was actually fought in a vacant lot off Tombstone, Arizona's Fremont Street.

COUNTDOWN TO DOOMSDAY

Making some long-term plans? Well, forget about it. According to the Doomsday Clock, you don't have much time left.

You've probably seen it before... a street corner prophet orating a chilling warning that the end of the world is nigh. History has been full of such doomsayers, running the gamut from spiritualists, shamans, and clairvoyants to philosophers, scholars, and crackpots. Like the prophet on the corner, they were laughed at by most people (and, fortunately, were mistaken). But there is one contemporary group of apocalypse prognosticators that may not be so easy to laugh off.

This would be the board of directors of the *Bulletin of the Atomic Scientists* seated at the University of Chicago. Since 1947, this learned group of scientists and academics has maintained the infamous Doomsday Clock, the figurative timepiece that appears on the cover of every issue of the *Bulletin* and serves as a constant reminder of how close humankind is to destroying itself.

WHAT IS THE DOOMSDAY CLOCK?

The Doomsday Clock is a symbolic clock face that shows the hour hand positioned at midnight and the minute hand variably positioned minutes before midnight. In effect, the time shown on the Doomsday Clock is always a certain number of minutes to midnight.

The clock face and positioning of the hands are metaphors relating to humankind and its nearness to obliteration:

• The clock itself represents the human race.

• Midnight represents the cataclysmic moment marking the end of the human race—doomsday.

- The minutes before midnight represent the threat humankind poses to itself through nuclear war, environmental degradation, and emerging technologies.

The positioning of the hands on the clock represents the degree of that threat to humankind. The closer the minute hand is to midnight, the nearer our self-destruction. The farther away it is from midnight, the smaller the threat.

The positioning of hands—or time displayed—is determined by the board of directors of the *Bulletin of the Atomic Scientists*. The board periodically adjusts the minute hand forward or backward in response to the current state of world affairs. The more perilous the world seems, the closer to midnight the board sets the Doomsday Clock.

THE PERILS FACING HUMANKIND

According to the board, humankind has excelled in creating perils that threaten to do it in, the most prominent of these being nuclear weapons. The Doomsday Clock was originally conceived in response to the emergence of the nuclear age after World War II. The spectre of war between the two nuclear superpowers, the United States and the Soviet Union, and the apocalyptic doctrine of mutually assured destruction was the primary threat manifested in the minutes before midnight. The periodic settings of the clock were prompted by developments in superpower relations and specific world events that brought the two countries either closer to or further from the brink of war.

Even in the post–Cold War world, the board still considers the possibility of nuclear holocaust to be the number-one threat to humankind. The board cites the thousands of nuclear weapons that the United States and Russia still have aimed at each other—ready for launch at a moment's notice. Though it's unlikely either of the two countries would unleash an attack, the sheer number of warheads in position guarantees annihilation in the event of a nuclear exchange caused by accident or error.

The nuclear danger is further compounded by the development of nuclear weapons programs by other nations in defiance of nuclear nonproliferation treaties. India and Pakistan now threaten each other with nuclear warheads, and other nations either have—or are moving toward—nuclear capability. Added to that is the menace of nuclear terrorism as critical materials required for making nuclear weapons remain unsecured and in danger of falling into the hands of groups seeking to cause mass destruction.

The board also identifies two other perils peculiar to the modern age. One is environmental degradation, more specifically, potentially disastrous climate change due to the widespread use of fossil-fuel technologies. The other is emerging technologies such as advances in genetics, biology, and nanotechnology that—if placed in the wrong hands—could be used for destruction.

Humankind, it seems, has made its own world a dangerous place. The Doomsday Clock is intended to remind us just how dangerous it has become.

EIGHTEEN TIME CHANGES SINCE 1947

The initial time setting on the Doomsday Clock in 1947 was seven minutes to midnight. Since then, the time on the Clock has changed 18 times.

The most optimistic setting of the Clock thus far occurred in 1993. The board set the Clock to 17 minutes before midnight in response to the end of the Cold War and the Strategic Arms Reduction Treaty signed by the United States and Russia, which greatly reduced stores of deployed nuclear weapons.

The gloomiest time setting occurred in 1953. After the United States and the Soviet Union successfully tested thermonuclear devices within eight months of each other, the board set the Clock to two minutes before midnight.

In January 2007, the Clock was set at five minutes to midnight— its most pessimistic setting since 1984. As justification for the move, the board cited the coming of a second nuclear age as more nations moved to acquire the bomb, as well as the continued damage of the planet by global climate.

The Clock is ticking.

What's in a Name?
AWESOME OTTOMAN

Suleiman the Magnificent was a warrior-scholar who lived up to his billing. A Turkish Sultan who reigned from 1520–1566, Suleiman led the Ottoman Empire to its greatest heights.

Not only was Suleiman a brilliant military strategist, he was also a great legislator, a fair ruler, and a devotee of the arts. During his rule, he expanded the country's military empire and brought cultural and architectural projects to new heights. For all this and more, Suleiman is considered one of the finest leaders of 16th-century Europe.

Under Suleiman's leadership, his forces conquered Mesopotamia (now Iraq), fending off the Safavid's Iran. The Ottomans would then successfully occupy Iraq until the First World War. Suleiman annexed or made allies of the Barbary Pirate states of North Africa, who remained a thorn in Europe's underbelly until the 1800s. He also led an army that went deep into Europe itself, crushing the Hungarian King Louis II at the great Battle of Mohács in 1526, which led to the Siege of Vienna.

An accomplished poet, Suleiman was gracious in victory, saying of the young Louis: "It was not my wish that he should be thus cut off while he scarcely tasted the sweets of life and royalty." To his favorite wife Hurrem, a harem woman and daughter of a Ukrainian Orthodox priest, he wrote: "My springtime, my merry faced love, my daytime, my sweetheart, laughing leaf... My woman of the beautiful hair, my love of the slanted brow, my love of eyes full of mischief..."

While Shari'ah, or sacred law, ruled his farflung land's religious life, Suleiman reformed the Ottomans' civil law code. In fact, the Ottomans called him Kanuni, or "The Lawgiver." The final form of Suleiman's legal code would remain in place for more than 300 years.

BUILT TO DEFEND, THE GREAT WALL NOW BECKONS

The Great Wall of China was built and rebuilt over a span of 2,000 years by millions of forced laborers. Each year, sections of the wall draw crowds of tourists, who marvel at the world's largest artificial structure.

For curious extraterrestrials who swing their spacecraft close to Earth, the Great Wall of China provides a particularly dramatic notion of what human beings are all about: cleverness, grandeur, self-preservation, even paranoia.

Portions of the Wall stretch from Gansu Province in the west of China to Shanhai Pass near the Bohai Sea in the east. Because no modern-day survey has ever been completed, the combined length of the various walls that comprise the Great Wall has never been accurately calculated. The most common estimate is 4,000 miles.

The Wall's oldest portions date back more than 2,000 years. In 221 B.C., First Emperor Qin Shi Huangdi unified several feudal Chinese states. At the same time, he transformed the many walls that once separated the warring nations into a single defensive barrier meant to repel nomadic, barbarian invaders. Due to the organic nature of the construction material (much of it earth, wood, and even reeds), most of this first "Great Wall" has eroded and is no longer visible.

Rulers of the Ming Dynasty (A.D. 1368–1644) used brick and stone to transform the wall into the structure we know today.

Upper-floor watchtowers were rebuilt with lookouts, and lower floors were fitted with cannons.

Through the centuries, some sections of the Wall were built in desolate areas, where they acted less as parts of a defensive structure and more as signaling outposts. Thousands of towers along the wall alerted other stations with smoke signals during the day and bonfires at night, calling reinforcements to the area being attacked.

Popular wisdom claims the Great Wall is the only artificial object visible to the naked eye from the moon. That's a neat claim but, alas, it's false. While the Wall can be seen by astronauts in low Earth orbit, the structure cannot be seen outside of Earth's orbit and certainly not from the moon, where even the continents are barely visible.

The Wall's magnificence, however, has never been disputed. Today, the Great Wall of China—designed to repel barbarian invaders—is swarmed by wide-eyed tourists. Despite years of restoration work, many sections of the Wall still lie in ruins, destroyed by the elements and by locals who steal brick and stone for use in their own construction projects.

Significant sections of the Great Wall are located near the Chinese capital of Beijing. When you visit, make time for:

BADALING

Built in 1571, Badaling was the first area of the Wall to be opened to tourists. In 1987, it was declared a United Nations Educational, Scientific, and Cultural Organization (UNESCO) World Heritage Site. It is now heavily visited and has become an unabashed tourist draw, with hundreds of booths that sell souvenir kitsch.

JUYONG GUAN

An attack in A.D. 1213 by Mongol warrior Genghis Khan was repulsed along this section when defenders poured molten iron on the fortress gates. However, a Mongol emissary in the Chinese capital told a Khan general, Tsabar, about a little-known path through Juyong Pass. Tsabar quickly bypassed the Wall and pounced on the defenders from the rear, causing some disruption. When the Mongols retreated in 1368, Ming General Xuda built five defensive walls in and around the pass.

MUTIANYU

Tourists have been invited to this portion since 1986. For those unable to climb the Wall, Mutianyu sports a cable car that whisks visitors to the top.

SIMATAI

Stretches of this portion have crumbled into disrepair. Nevertheless, a trek up to Wangjinglou Tower gives an impressive view of distant Beijing. To reach this summit, however, visitors must climb a 70-degree slope nicknamed the "Stairway to Heaven." Even hardy visitors sometimes find it necessary to complete the climb on all fours.

JINSHANLING

Starting in A.D. 1386, and for nearly 200 years thereafter, this section of the Wall was built and subsequently reconstructed. Jinshanling has 150 battle platforms and obstacle walls with peepholes and shooting holes incorporated into the design. Despite a lack of recent repairs, this is the Wall's second most complete section, after Badaling.

HUANGHUACHENG

Bad luck dogged the builder of this portion, Ming General Kai, who was so methodical he was beheaded under false charges of inefficiency.

GUBEIKOU

This rugged location in the Yanshan Mountain Range was breached in 1549 by Mongol leader Altan Khan, who pillaged Beijing's suburbs before returning home. During World War II, parts of Gubeikou were hit by Japanese artillery fire.

Fast Facts

- Talk about staying power—China's Zhou Dynasty (approximately 1100 B.C. to 221 B.C.) was the longest-running dynasty in history.

- Egypt's most famous queen, Cleopatra, was actually Greek.

- The mad Roman emperor Caligula planned to promote his horse, Incitatus, to the rank of consul—the Roman equivalent of prime minister—before his bodyguard got fed up and assassinated him.

- Mongol emperor Kublai Khan kept 5,000 astrologers busy working for him.

- King Louis XIV, France's "Sun King," owned 413 beds.

- Ancient Egypt's Queen Hatshepsut declared herself pharaoh around 1438 B.C. To look the part, she reportedly wore men's clothes and a fake beard while conducting official business.

- King Otto of Bavaria frequently believed he was a sheep, goat, or stork. He was known to stand on one leg in a pond and attempt to pluck fish out of the water while flapping his arms.

- After she was crowned, the first act of Britain's Queen Victoria was to move her bed out of her mother's bedroom and into a room of her own.

- In 1890, Emperor Menelik II of Abyssinia became so enthralled with stories of the new "electric chair" from America that he ordered three of them, even though his country didn't have any electricity. (He kept one unplugged death chair as his throne.)

- Britain's King George V kept the clocks at his Sandringham estate running 30 minutes fast, so he would never be late.

- Happy Father's Day! Sultan Murad III of the Ottoman Empire had a harem of several hundred women and sired 103 children. Only 20 of his sons outlived him. (To keep things simple, after taking power, Murad's heir put his 19 brothers to death.)

Misconceptions of History
BATHING IS BAD FOR YOU

Regular bathing is now a matter of course. Yet as late as 1920, barely one out of a hundred American homes had bathtubs. The lack of bathing facilities wasn't due to inferior technology and premodern sanitation, but to prevailing attitudes. From the time of the Renaissance, most Europeans were wary of bathing— deeming it unhealthy.

The terrible plagues of the late Middle Ages may have contributed to hydrophobia. Along with bubonic plague, disseminated by fleas and rats, diseases such as cholera and typhoid were spread by filthy water. The people of the time didn't know about germs but may have intuited the link between bad water and ill health. The phrase "catch your death of cold" arose during an era when there was no hot running water for bathing during cold spells.

By the time of America's colonization, the fear of water had taken firm root. When John Smith and his fellow settlers moved to Jamestown, Virginia, the native Powhatans, who bathed every day, literally held their noses when downwind of the colonists.

But it wasn't always so.

LIGHT IN DARKNESS

Contrary to myth, folks in the "Dark Ages" were relatively enlightened about cleanliness. According to the book, *A History of Private Life*, medieval *fabliaux*—tall tales like those of Chaucer—are replete with lovers taking hot baths before lovemaking. Ladies and lords of the manor soaked on stools placed in wooden vats filled with hot water. They also scrubbed their hands and faces before meals and washed their mouths out after, according to the etiquette guides of the time. The more common folk soaked in urban public baths called "stews," the opening of which were heralded by the sound of trumpet and drum each morning. Doughty burghers marched to the stews naked to stop thieves from picking their pockets. Inside, the two sexes bathed together, sometimes clothed.

The Catholic Church frowned on the mixed-gender aspect, especially when it led to prostitution. Some orders of monks prescribed bathing only for Christmas and Easter, with the private parts covered during these sacred ablutions. But the clergy wasn't totally doctrinaire. The founder of the modern papacy, Pope Gregory I, advised taking a bath each Sunday. And monasteries featured *lavabos*, fountains for hand washing.

A noted early scientist, Hildegard of Bingen (1098–1179), offered these prescriptions for good health: "If a person's head has an ailment, it should be washed frequently in this water and it will be healed... If your lord wishes to bathe and wash his body clean... have a basin full of hot fresh herbs and wash his body with a soft sponge." Along with roses, herbs added to bath water included hollyhock, brown fennel, danewort, camomile, and green oats. (At times, the Middle Ages sound positively New Age.)

Hildegard also offered this advice for overly randy fellows: "A man who has an overabundance in his loins should cook wild lettuce in water and pour that water over himself in a sauna bath."

BATHING'S BAD RAP

By the 1400s, however, public opinion had swung the other way. Fires were common in the public baths, where water was heated by the burning of wood. Wood itself was hard to find as growing prosperity led to the leveling of forests. Moreover, peasants often fell ill from the custom of the entire family washing from the same dirty barrel of water.

Furthermore, it was believed that disease spread by way of vapors that passed into the skin through pores that opened during bathing. (This is where the term *malaria*, which means "bad air," comes from.) No less an authority than English philosopher Francis Bacon advised: "After Bathing, wrap the Body in a seare-cloth made of Masticke, Myrrh, Pomander, and Saffron, for staying the perspiration or breathing of the pores." If body odor lingered, courtiers—male and female—cloaked their smell with copious applications of cologne.

Yet, attitudes were never monolithic. In the spring of 1511, the diary of one Lucas Rem of Germany reports that he took 127 baths. Thinking was slowly turning back in the direction of sanitary health.

BACK TO CLEANLINESS

In the United States, bathing bounced back in the mid-19th century. Millions of the "unwashed masses" were forsaking farms for crowded, filthy cities, and millions more were arriving on immigrant ships. In response, the healthier, better-educated natives crusaded for better health. Healthy living—physical and spiritual—became all the rage.

One fad among the wealthy was "taking the waters" at spas such as Saratoga Springs, New York, and Warm Springs, Georgia, the latter of which was frequented by Franklin Roose-velt.

In the 1880s, the Standard Sanitary Manufacturing Company made cast-iron bathtubs available to the public. These were actually advertised as horse troughs/bathtubs; few thought anyone would buy a tub only for bathing.

In the boom of the Roaring Twenties, middle-class folk, envious of mansions trendily outfitted with indoor plumbing, began putting sinks, toilets, and tubs into separate rooms called bathrooms.

Today, Americans are famous for their incessant showering. Sir John Harington, inventor of the water closet, would be pleased.

FAMOUS LAST WORDS

"Everything is a miracle. It is a miracle that one does not dissolve in one's bath like a lump of sugar."

—Pablo Picasso

THE TRAGIC TALE OF *THE CONQUEROR*

Despite its marquee cast, The Conqueror *flopped like a beached garfish. As if that weren't bad enough, the cast learned a hard (and for some, fatal) lesson: You should never film a movie just downwind of a nuclear test site.*

A Hollywood studio once known for classy black-and-white films starring the Katharine Hepburns and Cary Grants of cinema, RKO became a Howard Hughes property in 1948. Soon, RKO was turning out money-losing, sensationalistic clunkers: *Vendetta* (1950, featuring Faith Domergue's breasts), *Underwater!* (1955, starring Jane Russell's breasts), and *Jet Pilot* (made 1949, released 1957 after eight years in cans, starring John Wayne) are examples. After *Underwater!* sank deep beneath the financial waves, Hughes—perhaps inspired by his own business style—decided that the time was ripe for a Genghis Khan movie.

CASTING CALL

Who would play the dreaded Mongol emperor? John Wayne, the most bankable actor of his day, stepped forward. No one had the spine to ask the Duke how his Western drawl was going to make for a convincing Asian warlord, nor was anyone going to turn away such a big name. Susan Hayward was cast as Khan's Tartar love interest/sexual assault victim, Bortai. Dick Powell would direct. Pedro Armendáriz, Agnes Moorehead, John Hoyt, and William Conrad were among the brighter lights in the cast.

ST. GEORGE, AND WE'RE DRAGGIN'

Filming began in 1955, near St. George, Utah. The location's inherent flaws surfaced immediately. With temperatures reaching 120°F, the faux-Asianizing makeup melted on the actors' faces. Hughes sent a number of exotic animals to Utah for use in the film; after the black panther tried to maul Hayward, producers rented a tame mountain lion and painted the poor creature black. The animal licked itself, liked the flavor, and began to slurp off most of the paint.

The dialogue and action were comically bad. Picture John Wayne, drawling in an imagined Mongol accent, sporting a German World War I spiked helmet with French Foreign Legion flaps. One horseback battle scene showed a series of repetitive, isolated flops by vanquished horsemen into the Utah dust. Women's rights lost a decade on the spot when Princess Bortai flailed feebly at the rapist Khan's back, then suffered Hollywood's old version of Stockholm Syndrome as her hatred turned to love.

By 1956 standards, Hughes spent a mint on *The Conqueror*, including $1.4 million pimping its supreme artistry to the great unwashed. He must have been chagrined when audiences viewed it as a comedy—a campy, amusing work of cinema that left them laughing (a better option than clawing out their eyes). *The Conqueror* was a multi-million-dollar clunker at the box office.

TRAGEDY

St. George, Utah, is near Yucca Flat, Nevada, where the U.S. government tested nuclear weapons in 1953. A lot of the fallout collected in Snow Canyon, a natural basin where most of the filming occurred. Everyone inhaled the windblown, radioactive dust throughout months of filming. Cast members played with Geiger counters and joked over the results.

In the end, it wasn't funny. Dick Powell died in 1963 of lymphoma. Pedro Armendáriz passed away later in 1963: suicide, inspired by terminal kidney cancer. Wayne survived lung cancer in 1964, succumbing to it in 1979 (though his heavy smoking muddied the causal waters). Others also died of cancer: Agnes Moorehead, uterine cancer in 1974; Susan Hayward, brain cancer in 1975; John Hoyt, lung cancer, 1991. A total of 220 Hollywood actors and crew worked on location. At last report, 91 have contracted cancer, and 46 have died.

GREAT OBSCURE QUOTES

"The crowd, which follows me with admiration, would run with the same eagerness were I marching to the Guillotine."
—NAPOLEON

"The Pope! How many divisions has he got?"
—JOSEPH STALIN, 1935, ON BEING ASKED TO SUPPORT CATHOLICISM IN RUSSIA

"There is no room in this country for hyphenated Americanism."
—THEODORE ROOSEVELT

"But who prays for Satan? Who, in eighteen centuries, has had the common humanity to pray for the one sinner that needed it most?"
—MARK TWAIN

"My toast would be, may our country be always successful, but whether successful or otherwise, always right."
—JOHN QUINCY ADAMS

"The man who dies rich... dies disgraced."
—ANDREW CARNEGIE

MS. PRESIDENT?

*When Victoria Woodhull ran for president in 1872,
some called her a witch, others said she was a prostitute.
In fact, the very idea of a woman casting a vote for president was
considered scandalous—which may explain
why Woodhull spent election night in jail.*

Known for her passionate speeches and fearless attitude, Victoria
Woodhull became a trailblazer for women's
rights. But some say she was about 100 years
before her time. Woodhull advocated revolutionary ideas, including gender equality
and women's right to vote. "Women are the
equals of men before the law and are equal in
all their rights," she said. America, however,
wasn't ready to accept her radical ideas.

Woodhull was born in 1838 in Homer, Ohio, the seventh child of
Annie and Buck Claflin. Her deeply spiritual mother often took
little Victoria along to revival camps where people would speak in
tongues. Her mother also dabbled in clairvoyance, and Victoria
and her younger sister Tennessee believed they had a gift for it as
well. With so many chores to do at home (washing, ironing, chip-
ping wood, and cooking), Victoria only attended school sporadi-
cally and was primarily self-educated.

Soon after the family left Homer, a 28-year-old doctor named
Canning Woodhull asked the 15-year-old Victoria for her hand
in marriage. But the marriage was no paradise for Victoria—she
soon realized her husband was an alcoholic. She experienced
more heartbreak when her son, Byron, was born with a mental
disability. While she remained married to Canning, Victoria spent
the next few years touring as a clairvoyant with her sister Tennessee. At that time, it was difficult for a woman to pursue divorce,
but Victoria finally succeeded in divorcing her husband in 1864.

Two years later she married Colonel James Blood, a Civil War veteran who believed in free love.

In 1866, Victoria and James moved to New York City. Spiritualism was then in vogue, and Victoria and Tennessee established a salon where they acted as clairvoyants and discussed social and political hypocrisies with their clientele. Among their first customers was Cornelius Vanderbilt, the wealthiest man in America.

A close relationship sprang up between Vanderbilt and the two attractive and intelligent young women. He advised them on business matters and gave them stock tips. When the stock market crashed in September 1869, Woodhull made a bundle buying instead of selling during the ensuing panic. That winter, she and Tennessee opened their own brokerage business. They were the first female stockbrokers in American history, and they did so well that, two years after arriving in New York, Woodhull told a newspaper she had made $700,000.

Woodhull had more far-reaching ambitions, however. On April 2, 1870, she announced that she was running for president. In conjunction with her presidential bid, Woodhull and her sister started a newspaper, *Woodhull & Claflin's Weekly,* which highlighted women's issues including voting and labor rights. It was another breakthrough for the two since they were the first women to ever publish a weekly newspaper.

That was followed by another milestone: On January 11, 1871, Woodhull became the first woman ever to speak before a congressional committee. As she spoke before the House Judiciary Committee, she asked that Congress change its stance on whether women could vote. Woodhull's reasoning was elegant in its simplicity. She was not advocating a new constitutional amendment granting woman the right to vote. Instead, she reasoned, women already had that right. The Fourteenth Amendment says that, "All persons born or naturalized in the United States . . . are citizens of the Unites States." Since voting is part of the definition of being a citizen, Woodhull argued, women, in fact, already possessed the right to vote. Woodhull, a persuasive speaker, actually swayed some congressmen to her point of view, but the committee chairman remained hostile to the idea of women's rights and made sure the issue never came to a floor vote.

Woodhull had better luck with the suffragists. In May 1872, before 668 delegates from 22 states, Woodhull was chosen as the presidential candidate of the Equal Rights Party; she was the first woman ever chosen by a political party to run for president. But her presidential bid soon foundered. Woodhull was on record as an advocate of free love, which opponents argued was an attack on the institution of marriage (for Woodhull it had more to do with the right to have a relationship with anyone she wanted). Rather than debate her publicly, her opponents made personal attacks.

That year, Woodhull caused an uproar when her newspaper ran an exposé about the infidelities of Reverend Henry Ward Beecher. Woodhull and her sister were thrown in jail and accused of publishing libel and promoting obscenity. They would spend election night of 1872 behind bars as Ulysses Grant defeated Horace Greeley for the presidency.

Woodhull was eventually cleared of the charges against her (the claims against Beecher were proven true), but hefty legal bills and a downturn in the stock market left her embittered and impoverished. She moved to England in 1877, shortly after divorcing Colonel Blood. By the turn of the century she had become wealthy once more, this time by marriage to a British banker. Fascinated by technology, she joined the Ladies Automobile Club, where her passion for automobiles led Woodhull to one last milestone: In her sixties, she and her daughter Zula became the first women to drive through the English countryside.

• *The Equal Rights Party was also the first to nominate a black man for vice president. They selected Frederick Douglass, but he declined the offer.*

Timeline

Continued from page 68.

10,000–6,000 B.C.
Neolithic (New Stone Age) Period.
The "Cradle of Civilization" springs up as primitive agriculture develops in the Fertile Crescent (Syria, Jordan, Iraq, and Turkey) and spreads to southern Europe and Asia. Cereals such as wheat and barley are cultivated in the Fertile Crescent, while rice and millet are grown in China and India. Sheep, cats, goats, pigs, and cows are domesticated in western Asia and the Middle East. Farmers in Mesopotamia begin using tokens to keep track of farm products. Fishing villages spring up in coastal Africa. Middle Easterners make early attempts at metallurgy.

6,000–5,500 B.C.
Early agricultural settlements crop up in China, the Americas, and sub-Saharan Africa; soon these settlements become real cities. In Peru, settlers raise guinea pigs; domesticated chickens are raised in Thailand. The wheel, pottery, and systematic farming methods develop in Mesopotamia and slowly spread throughout most of the world. In China, an early form of symbol-writing appears on tortoise shells, and pottery makes its appearance.

5,500–4,500 B.C.
Fertile river valleys give birth to clusters of towns as agricultural communities appear along the Tigris-Euphrates Valley (Iraq), the Nile Delta (Egypt), the Indus River (northern India), and the Yellow River (northern China). In fact, farming communities appear everywhere except Antarctica and Australia. Staple crops include corn (Mexico), chilies (Central and South America), mangoes (southeast Asia), and wheat (Egypt). Husbandry and planting allow fewer residents to feed greater populations—giving the non-farming residents a chance to specialize in linguistics, theology, navigation, medicine, astronomy, metallurgy, and politico-military arts.

4,500–3,500 B.C.
Primitive Spanish tribes begin migrating to Britain. In Mesopotamia, copper is smelted for use in tools, pots, and weapons. Egyptians begin using oared boats for river and coastal travel; the invention of cotton sails soon follows. Animal domestication gallops along smoothly as horses are domesticated on the central Asian steppes and silkworms are raised in China. Indo-Europeans in the Caucasus worship multiple gods, perform burial rituals, farm, and drink fermented beverages.

3,500–3,000 B.C.
Bronze Age begins. Mesopotamians develop primitive accounting systems, and further south, Sumerians pioneer the city-state at Ur and develop cuneiform writing. From Egypt to Iraq, copper and other metals are used in production and for trade. Ancient Britons begin first-stage construction of Stonehenge. Indo-Europeans migrate from the Caucasus to

Timeline

Europe and India. The ox-drawn plow stimulates farming and makes larger settlements possible. Pottery-making begins in Mesoamerica. Memphis, Egypt, is the world's largest city with more than 30,000 residents.

3,000–2,500 B.C.

In Mesopotamia, the wheel is used for making pottery before it is turned upright and used for transportation. King Menes unites Upper and Lower Egypt, and his successors build the first "step" pyramid, the Great Pyramid at Giza, and the Great Sphinx. There, mummification, hieroglyphs, papyrus, ink, trade, and 365-day calendars appear, and meals are sweetened with honey from domesticated bees. Phoenician settlements appear in Lebanon and Syria. Minoan civilization in the Aegean takes root when settlers from Asia Minor sail over and decide to stay. Mathematics and serious astronomy are taken up in China, India, Babylon, and Egypt. Peruvians tame the llama as a food source and beast of burden. China develops an early form of the abacus. Large, permanent communities form in Japan.

2,500–2,000 B.C.

Indo-European peoples begin spreading into Europe. The *Gilgamesh Epic* tells listeners (and later, readers) about legendary deeds of an ancient Sumerian king. Mesopotamian mathematicians prepare multiplication tables. Akkadian King Sargon carves out an empire from Syria to the Persian Gulf, but the fractious land splinters into a patchwork of competing city-states 200 years later. Ur becomes the world's largest city, with a population of around 65,000.

2,000–1,500 B.C.

Technology Boom. War erupts as the Hyksos invade Lower Egypt but are driven out two centuries later by King Amosis I. Surgery in Egypt reaches a very sophisticated level, with medical texts prescribing treatments for a variety of neurological, orthopedic, and internal ailments. Writing flourishes as the Hittites use cuneiform and the Minoans on Crete develop the earliest form of written Greek. Stone anchors are used to steady ships in Cyprus, and the Minoans dominate trade in the eastern Mediterranean and invent indoor plumbing. Babylonian mathematicians perform multiplication, fractions, squares, and square roots. Babylon's King Hammurabi puts writing to good use by developing a code of laws, and his subjects use an early abacus for calculating numbers. On the Indian subcontinent, metalsmiths begin smelting iron, a metal weaker than bronze but much cheaper to produce. In the Far East, Tibetans domesticate the yak. The Xia Dynasty rises in China but falls to Shang rebels. Under the Shang Dynasty, Chinese develop a writing system, bound books, fireworks, and sophisticated bronze metallurgy methods.

Wondering what happened next? Turn to page 161 to find out!

COMING TO AMERICA

This land is your land, this land is my land....
But who was here "first"? Although the Vikings (A.D. 1000) and
15th- and 16th-century Europeans claimed to be among
the first to inhabit North America, this legacy actually belongs to
the Native Americans. But where did THEY come from?

NORTHEAST ASIA?

Native Americans and Eastern Asians have several strong similarities—hair and skin color, little or no facial and body hair, and extremely distinctive dental shapes. Even sophisticated DNA studies show common links between the two groups. This evidence lends credence to the theory that a migration from Eastern Asia into North America (what is now Alaska and Canada) occurred via a land bridge. At the time of the last Ice Age—about 10,000 to 12,000 years ago—a large glacier formed across much of North America. The ice drew from the waters between Siberia and Alaska. The result was a dry ocean bed nearly 1,000 miles wide called *Beringia*. Small, nomadic bands of Asians—known as "hunter-gatherers"—began moving across Beringia in a constant search for food, such as small game animals, nuts, berries, and roots. Seasonal changes continued to push these visitors down the Pacific Coast and inland to what are now the Rocky Mountain states. As the ice melted, Beringia slowly began to shrink, returning to its watery origins within about 4,000 years.

According to anthropologist Paul Martin, the migration across the Americas continued at a rate of about eight miles per year. It took nearly 1,000 years to reach the southern tip of South America.

JAPAN OR SOUTHEAST ASIA?

Another theory of migration suggests that a small group of Japanese fishermen or sailors were caught in a mighty sea current some 3,000 to 4,000 years ago. They followed the tides from mainland Japan to the western coast of Ecuador in South America called Valdivia. Sound impossible? Consider the anthropological evidence: Ecuadorian pottery was found to be identical to the Jomon styles that existed in Japan at the very same time. Yet many experts suggest it is merely coincidence, and the source of the pottery is more likely Columbia than the Far East.

The famous finds of arrowheads near Clovis, New Mexico, in the 1930s showed that these Americans may have lived nearly 14,000 years ago—2,000 years earlier than those who crossed Beringia. More recent finds show that the early inhabitants from that area (and south, all the way to Brazil) resemble ancient Australian Aborigines. Other skeletal finds in contemporary times point to possible origins in Polynesia.

EUROPE OR AFRICA?

Long before 1492, when Columbus sailed the ocean blue, plant forms known to be native to Europe and Africa somehow made their way onto North American soil. Cotton and the bottle gourd were already here in America when Columbus hit the beach in the Bahamas. What's more, the Topper archeological site in South Carolina offered artifacts that predate Clovis by as much as 35,000 years!

Though little hard evidence exists to suggest the origin of the Topper inhabitants, many doubt any connection to Asia or South America—leaving Europe and/or Africa as the possible homes of these early travelers to the New World.

"The American Indian is of the soil, whether it be the region of forests, plains, pueblos, or mesas. He fits into the landscape, for the hand that fashioned the continent also fashioned the man for his surroundings. He once grew as naturally as the wild sunflowers, he belongs just as the buffalo belonged...."
— LUTHER STANDING BEAR, OGLALA SIOUX CHIEF

BLOOMING BUST IN THE DUTCH REPUBLIC

One of the most unlikely of all dramas began in 17th-century Holland, when a French botanist planted a Turkish bulb in a university garden. The resulting flower mesmerized a nation and eventually became a major export and mainstay of the Dutch economy.

Can a mere flower incite great nationalist passion? Well, if it's a tulip, it can. What might be dubbed "Tulipmania" swept what is now Holland in 1636 and 1637. The flowers' popularity turned the pretty plants into serious money spinners and encouraged a competitive fad among the *nouveau riche*. Suddenly, the tulip was a coveted status symbol.

The instigator of all this was a French-born botanist named Carolus Clusius, who lived and died before the craze hit. Born in 1526 and originally educated as a lawyer, Clusius was encouraged by a professor to switch his studies to botany. He subsequently traveled the world gathering plant specimens and became one of Europe's leading botanists. His reputation was so sterling that Austrian Emperor Maximilian II appointed him court physician and overseer of the royal medicinal garden.

In 1593, Clusius settled in the Netherlands, where he was appointed prefect for the newly established horticulture academy at the University of Leiden. That fall, Clusius planted a teaching garden and a private plot that showcased hundreds of varieties of plants, including several hundred tulip bulbs given to him by his friend, Ogier Ghiselin de Busbecq, Austrian Ambassador to the Ottoman Empire.

Prior to Clusius, no Dutch person had ever seen a tulip bulb or blossom. The rarity and beauty of the new flower caused a national sensation. Members of the aristocracy clamored to add tulips to their private gardens. When Clusius declined to sell any of his private stock, many were stolen from his garden. One nighttime raid netted thieves more than 100 bulbs.

BIG MONEY IN THE DUTCH REPUBLIC

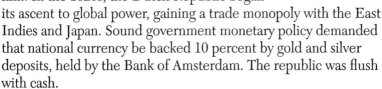

Carolus Clusius died in 1609, but the engine he had set in motion continued to chug without him. In the 1620s, the Dutch Republic began its ascent to global power, gaining a trade monopoly with the East Indies and Japan. Sound government monetary policy demanded that national currency be backed 10 percent by gold and silver deposits, held by the Bank of Amsterdam. The republic was flush with cash.

Money supply in the Dutch Republic was increased further by an influx of precious metals, which were traded for paper currency, as well as by the Dutch East India Company's seizure of Portuguese ships laden with gold, silver, and jewels. At the height of Tulipmania, the Bank of Amsterdam's deposits increased by more than 40 percent. People had more money to spend than ever before, and they became bold in an atmosphere that was ripe for speculation.

MY KINGDOM FOR A TULIP

The tulip quickly became a status symbol. Members of the upper-class spent huge amounts of money to acquire rare bulbs. Some sums were utterly ridiculous. Consider that during the 1600s, the average Dutch worker earned 150 florins per year. In 1623, one particularly rare tulip bulb sold for 1,000 florins. In another famous sale, an extraordinary *Semper Augustsus* bulb sold for 6,000 florins. The price per pound of some bulbs reached the equivalent price of a modest house.

By 1636, a structured, but unregulated, futures market had developed for the tulip trade. Most of the trading occurred in local taverns, where bulbs were bought and resold many times before actual delivery. The Dutch referred to this practice as *windhandel*, or *wind trade*, because payment for the bulbs occurred only when they were dug from the ground in the summer, after the plant had bloomed and died back. Local-government legislation designed to curtail speculation did little to affect the trade.

THE FLOWER ECONOMY CRASHES

In February 1637, the Dutch guild of florists, which had been marginalized by the wildcat trading, decreed that all futures contracts were now mere options contracts. With a futures contract, both parties must fulfill the contract's terms. With an options contract, the holder has the right, *but is not obligated*, to exercise the contract. The florist guild's decision allowed buyers to break their contracts for a fraction of actual value.

On April 27, 1637, the Dutch government canceled all tulip contracts with a decree stating that tulips were a product, not an investment. Between this and an oversupply of bulbs, the value of tulips plummeted and the market crashed. Buyers refused to honor their contracts and simply walked away from their deals. Growers were not only unable to sell their stock, they suddenly had no hope of collecting any of the money owed to them.

Between 1635 and 1637, the number of bankruptcies in Amsterdam doubled. Prices for bulbs stabilized at reasonable levels shortly after the collapse, but many Dutch were so discouraged they never entered the tulip market again.

LOVE AFFAIR CONTINUES

Today, almost 400 years after the crash, the Dutch love affair with tulips is still going strong. Holland's flower bulb farms currently produce about three billion bulbs every year, with approximately two billion of those exported to other countries.

Fast Facts

- The Olympics were first recorded in 776 B.C. Until the early 8th century B.C., there was only one event—the 200-yard dash.

- The ancient Egyptians loved playing a checkerboard game called senets. Players moved pieces around a board determined by tossing numbered throwing sticks.

- Mary Queen of Scots, an avid golfer, was reportedly seen playing a round on the links just two days after the murder of her second husband, Lord Darnley.

- Chess originated in India, where it was first played with four players. The Persians, then Arabs, modified this fine board game before passing the practice down to Europe.

- Chinese acrobatics were performed at least as far back as the Han Dynasty, around 200 B.C.

- Central American Mayans developed their own team sports similar to lacrosse, football, and soccer.

- Ancient Egypt had its own version of the Olympics, featuring gymnastics, javelin, running, swimming, and other events.

- In 1457, the Scottish parliament outlawed golf and football (soccer) because they were dangerous, time-wasting nuisances that detracted from more important pursuits—like archery.

- Native American tribes had many versions of, and names for, the modern sport of lacrosse. The Cherokee called it "Little Brother of War," because it was good training for combat.

- The Roman game of quoits, where a ring is tossed at a stake in the ground, is the forerunner of modern horseshoes.

- The modern marathon owes its name to the story of an ancient Greek messenger who ran nearly 26 miles from the battlefield of Marathon to Athens, to proclaim the Greek victory. The story is almost certainly untrue, but the name stuck.

THE LIBRARY OF THE MUSES

By far the most famous library in history, the Library of Alexandria held an untold number of ancient works. Its fiery destruction meant the irrecoverable loss of a substantial part of the world's intellectual history.

THE LIBRARY'S BEGINNINGS

The cities of ancient Mesopotamia (e.g., Uruk, Nineveh, Babylon) and Egypt (e.g., Thebes, Memphis) had cultivated archives and libraries since the Bronze Age, but the idea for a library as grand as Alexandria did not occur in Greek culture until the Hellenistic Age, when Alexander the Great's conquests brought both Greece and these former civilizations under Macedonian rule. Previous Greek libraries were owned by individuals; the largest belonged to Aristotle (384–322 B.C.), whose work and school (the Lyceum) in Athens were supported by Alexander.

When Alexander died suddenly in 323 B.C., his generals carved his empire into regional dynasties. The Hellenistic dynasties competed with each other for three centuries (until each was in turn conquered by either Rome or Parthia). Each dynasty desired cultural dominance, so they invited famous artists, authors, and intellectuals to live and work in their capital cities. Alexander's general Ptolemy, who controlled Egypt, decided to develop a collection of the world's learning (the Library) and a research center, the *Mouseion* (the Museum, or "Temple of the Muses"), where scholars on subsidy could study and add their research to the collection. This idea may well have come from Demetrius of Phaleron (350–280 B.C.), Ptolemy's advisor and the former governor of Athens, who had been a pupil at the Lyceum, but the grand project became one of the hallmarks of the Ptolemaic dynasty. Under the first three Ptolemies, the Museum, a royal library, and a smaller "daughter" library at the Temple of Serapis (the Serapeum) were built and grew as Alexandria became the intellectual, as well as commercial, capital of the Hellenistic world.

Egypt and Alexandria offered the Ptolemies distinct advantages for accomplishing their goals. Egypt was not only immensely rich, which gave it the wealth to purchase materials and to bring scholars to Alexandria, but it was the major producer of papyrus, a marsh reed that was beaten into a flat surface and made into scrolls for writing and copying. Alexandria was also the commercial hub of the Mediterranean, and goods and information from all over the world passed through its port.

BIBLIOMANIA: SO MANY SCROLLS, SO LITTLE TIME

Acquiring materials for the libraries and Museum became somewhat of an obsession for the Ptolemies. Although primarily focused on Greek and Egyptian works, their interests included translating other traditions into Greek. Among the most important of these efforts was the production of the *Septuagint*, a Greek version of the Jewish scriptures. Besides employing agents to scour major book markets and to search out copies of works not yet in the library, boats coming into Alexandria were required to declare any scrolls on board. If they were of interest, the scrolls were confiscated and copied, and the owners were given the copies and some compensation. Ptolemy III (285–222 B.C.) may have acquired Athens' official state collection of the plays of Aeschylus, Sophocles, and Euripides in a similar way—putting up 15 talents of silver as a guarantee while he had the plays copied, then foregoing the treasure in favor of keeping the originals. Whether or not this is true, it speaks to the value he placed on getting important works and the resources he had at his disposal to do so.

Alexandria's efforts were fueled by a fierce competition with the Hellenistic kingdom of Pergamum (modern Bergamo, Turkey), which created its own library. Each library sought to claim new finds and to produce new editions, leading at times to the acquisition of forgeries and occasional embarrassment. Alexandria finally tried to undercut its rival by cutting off papyrus exports, but Pergamum perfected a method for making writing material out of animal skins (now called "parchment" from the Latin *pergamina*) and continued to build its holdings. Eventually, however, Alexandria got the upper hand when the Roman general Marcus Antonius (Mark Anthony) conquered Pergamum and made a present of its library to his lover, the Ptolemaic Queen Cleopatra.

Estimates as to the number of volumes in the Alexandrian library ranged wildly even in antiquity, generally between 200,000 and 700,000. Estimates are complicated by the fact that it isn't clear whether the numbers originate from works or scrolls: Some scrolls contained one work, some multiple works, and long works like the *Iliad* took multiple scrolls. Over time, a complex cataloguing system evolved, which culminated in a bibliographic survey of the library's holdings called the *Pinakes*. The survey was put together by the great Hellenistic scholar and poet Callimachus of Cyrene (305–240 B.C.). Unfortunately, this important work only exists in fragments today.

BURNING DOWN THE HOUSE

The Royal Library and its holdings were accidentally set aflame in 48 B.C. when Caesar (who had taken Cleopatra's side in her claim to the throne against her brother) tried to burn his way out of being trapped in the port by opposing forces. Further losses probably occurred in A.D. 271 when Emperor Aurelian destroyed part of the Museum while recapturing Alexandria from Queen Zenobia's forces. The "daughter" library of the Serapeum was finally destroyed by Christians under Emperor Theodosius near the end of the 4th century. But by then, much of the contents (like the contents of other great civic libraries of antiquity) had decayed or found their way into other hands, leaving the classical heritage scattered and fragmented for centuries. Much later, Christians dramatically blamed the burning of the library holdings on Muslim conquerors. Although this made for a good story, the legendary contents of the library were already long gone.

A Day in the Life
NEANDERTHAL MAN

*Daily life for Neanderthal man was no picnic, but it wasn't all
about clubbing and bludgeoning thy neighbor either.
Europe's Ice Age residents were social creatures by nature,
which helped make their stark existence tolerable until their
disappearance 30,000 years ago. The following depicts what was
likely a typical day in the life of a Neanderthal.*

Dawn breaks, and a cave on the edge of a forest in prehistoric
Europe begins to stir with life. Inside the dark chamber, Neanderthal man rises along with his family and the rest of the communal
group of cave dwellers that form the basis of his world.

Shucking aside the animal skins that kept him warm during the
night, Neanderthal man readies himself for the one everyday
activity most critical for the group's survival—the hunt for food.

BRINGING HOME THE BACON

Neanderthal man gathers with other men and women from the
group to embark on the day's hunt. If it's a cold day or if inclem-
ent weather looms, he will clad himself in animal skins—being
no more hairy than humans are today, he needs to protect himself from the elements. If it's hot and sunny, he'll go completely
naked. Modesty is not one of his strong suits.

The hunting party heads into the woods in search of their daily
bread, or more accurately, meat. A voracious carnivore, Neanderthal man will eat almost nothing but meat, and in a typical day
he'll devour twice the amount of food that his present-day counterpart normally consumes.

Neanderthal man brings with him a short wooden thrusting spear
tipped with a sharp-edge stone. As he and his colleagues stalk
bears, wolves, deer, wild horses, or cattle, he keeps an eye open
for obsidian stones suitable for making highly effective cutting

tools. Neanderthal man is an expert tool maker, though not a very innovative one: The stone and wooden tools he has forged will remain basically unchanged throughout 250,000 years of existence.

TAKING ONE FOR THE TEAM

Today the hunt goes well for Neanderthal man. He and the others have strategically trapped a small herd of deer in a natural enclosure. Together they carry out an ambush-style attack against their quarry, thrusting their spears into the animals' flesh at close range.

Ideally, they would have driven the herd over a cliff or steep embankment to lessen the risk of injury. But Neanderthal man has to get his food while the getting is good, so he braces himself for the blows often accompanying close-quarter hunting—a stiff kick of a hoof, a painful bite, or an unpleasant goring from a pointed antler.

After a brief but frenzied flurry, the animals are subdued. Neanderthal man emerges from the kill bloodied, but the pain from his wounds is tempered by the thrill of a successful hunt and the promise of a full belly tonight.

AN EVENING OF FRIVOLITY

Tired and sore but happy nonetheless, Neanderthal man returns with the hunting party to the communal caves with the evening meal for the group.

The fresh meat is cooked over an open fire, and Neanderthal man and the group dig in. Later, his hunger sated and his spirits soaring, he joins the group in an evening of frivolity and social bonding that includes singing, clapping, dancing, body slapping, and stick banging. The songs mimic birdsongs or other sounds of nature. The melody is nothing like anything we know today, but it's music to his ears.

Before finally falling asleep, Neanderthal man contemplates a way of life that is often harsh, but considerably less brutish than modern stereotypes suggest.

THE MOUND BUILDERS: MYTHMAKING IN EARLY AMERICA

The search for an improbable past, or,
how to make a mountain out of a molehill.

In the early 1840s, the fledgling United States was gripped by a controversy that spilled from the parlors of the educated men in Boston and Philadelphia—the core of the nation's intellectual elite—onto the pages of the newspapers printed for mass edification. In the tiny farming village of Grave Creek, Virginia (now West Virginia), on the banks of the Ohio River stood one of the largest earthen mounds discovered during white man's progress westward. The existence of these mounds, spread liberally throughout the Mississippi Valley, Ohio River Valley, and much of the southeast, was commonly known and had caused a great deal of speculative excitement since Europeans had first arrived on the continent. Hernando de Soto, for one, had mentioned the mounds of the Southeast during his wandering in that region.

MONEY WELL SPENT

The colonists who settled the East Coast noticed that the mounds, which came in a variety of sizes and shapes, were typically placed near excellent sites for villages and farms. The Grave Creek mound was among the first of the major earthworks discovered by white men in their westward expansion. By 1838, the property was owned and farmed by the Tomlinson family. Abelard B. Tomlinson took an interest in the mound on his family's land and decided to open a vertical shaft from its summit, 70 feet high, to the center. He discovered skeletal remains at various levels and a timbered vault at the base containing the remains of two individuals. More importantly, he discovered a sandstone tablet inscribed with three lines of characters of unknown origin.

WHO WERE THE MOUND BUILDERS?

Owing to the general belief that the aborigines were lazy and incapable of such large, earth-moving operations and the fact that none of the tribes who dwelt near the mounds claimed any knowledge of who had built them, many 19th-century Americans believed that the mound builders could not have been the ancestors of the Native American tribes they encountered. Wild and fantastic stories arose, and by the early 19th century, the average American assumed that the mound builders had been a pre-Columbian expedition from the Old World—Vikings, Israelites, refugees from Atlantis—all these and more had their champions. Most agreed, however, that the New World had once hosted and given rise to a civilization as advanced as that of the Aztecs and Incas who had then fallen into disarray or been conquered by the savage barbarians that now inhabited the land. Speculation on the history of the mound builders led many, including Thomas Jefferson, to visit mounds and conduct their own studies.

MORMONS AND THE MOUNDS

Meanwhile, the Grave Creek tablet fanned the flames of a controversy that was roaring over the newly established, and widely despised, Church of Jesus Christ of Latter Day Saints, founded by Joseph Smith. The Mormon religion is based upon the belief that the American continent was once inhabited by lost tribes of Israel who divided into warring factions and fought each other to near extinction. The last surviving prophet of these people, Mormon, inscribed his people's history upon gold tablets, which were interred in a mound near present-day Palmyra, New York, until they were revealed to fifteen-year-old Joseph Smith in 1823. Though many Americans were ready to believe that the mounds represented the remains of a nonaboriginal culture, they were less ready to believe in Smith's new religion. Smith and his adherents were persecuted horribly, and Smith was killed by an angry mob while leading his followers west. Critics of the Saints (as the Mormons prefer to be called) point to the early 19th-century publication of several popular books purporting that the earthen mounds of North America were the remains of lost tribes of Israel. These texts claimed that evidence would eventually be discovered to support their author's assertions. That the young Smith should have his revelation so soon after these fanciful studies were published struck many observers as entirely too coincidental. Thus, Abelard Tomlinson's excavation of the sandstone tablet with its strange figures ignited the passions of both Smith's followers and his detractors.

ENTER THE SCHOLAR

Into this theological, and ultimately anthropological, maelstrom strode Henry Rowe Schoolcraft, a mineralogist whose keen interest in Native American history had led to his appointment as head of Indian affairs. While working in Sault Ste. Marie, Schoolcraft married a native woman and mastered the Ojibwa language. Schoolcraft traveled to Grave Creek to examine Tomlinson's tablet and concluded that the figures were indeed a language but deferred to more learned scholars to determine just which language they represented. The opinions were many and varied— from Celtic runes to early Greek; experts the world over weighed in with their opinions. Nevertheless, Schoolcraft was more concerned with physical evidence and close study of the mounds themselves, and he remained convinced that the mounds and the artifacts they carried were the products of ancestors of the Native Americans. Schoolcraft's theory flew in the face of both those who sought to defend and those who sought to debunk the Mormon belief, and it would be more than three decades until serious scholarship and the emergence of true archeological techniques began to shift opinion on the subject.

ANSWERS PROPOSED, BUT QUESTIONS STILL ABOUND

History has vindicated Schoolcraft's careful and thoughtful study of the mounds. Today, we know that the mound builders were not descendents of Israel, nor were they the offspring of Vikings. They were simply the ancient and more numerous predecessors of the Native Americans, who constructed the mounds for protection from floods and as burial sites, temples, and defense strongholds. As for the Grave Creek tablet: Scholars today generally agree that the figures are not a written language but simply a fanciful design whose meaning, if ever there was one, has been lost to the ages. Though the Smithsonian Institute has several etchings of the tablet in its collection, the whereabouts of the actual tablet have been lost to the ages.

The Native American earth mounds are among the most interesting and studied features of primitive America. Many have been lost to the plow and the elements since Europeans first settled in North America, but some of the more prominent have been preserved for study and observation, including:

- *Cahokia Mounds State Historic Site (Collinsville, Illinois) With an estimated population of 30,000, the city that once existed here was among the largest in the world in A.D. 1050. Then, suddenly, mysteriously, it ceased to exist. Today, visitors can walk among the 68 surviving mounds.*

- *Serpent Mound State Memorial (near Cincinnati, Ohio) Originally constructed in an area inhabited by the Adena people, the serpent-shape mound is more than 1,300 feet long and once inspired theories that it marked the original site of the biblical Garden of Eden. The notoriety generated by the mound led to the creation of Ohio's first state park to protect the grounds upon which it is situated.*

- *Hopewell Culture National Historical Park (Hopewell, Illinois) Known more commonly as "Mound City," this collection of gentle mounds was nearly annihilated by amateur archeologists lured to the site by the wealth of artifacts recovered there. The Hopewell culture flourished between 200 B.C. and A.D. 500, with an extensive trading network that allowed them to acquire copper, which they fashioned into ornate jewelry. The presence of copper in burial mounds convinced many early archaeologists that the mound builders could not have been Native Americans since none of the tribes retained the practice by the time Europeans arrived in the New World.*

GOLIATHS OF GERMANY

King Frederick William I of Prussia wanted only the best for his country: the best civil service, the best farms, and—most important of all—the best army. As Prussia came into its own, the king formed an exclusive club, the pride of his armed forces: a regiment of the tallest soldiers in Europe.

The eccentric Frederick William I, nicknamed "The Soldier King," was in some ways a model monarch. He lived frugally, encouraged farming and settlement, avoided wars, and reformed the country's civil service. He replaced mass conscription with a national sales tax (which he paid along with everyone else) and established primary schools. But he had one "huge" obsession.

A REGIMENT OF GIANTS

After becoming king in 1713, Frederick William set out to create a regiment of unusually tall soldiers. Sending agents to scour the countryside for farmers, soldiers, craftsmen, and peasants who were at least five feet, eleven inches tall—and preferably much taller—Frederick William assembled his collection of abnormally tall men into an elite unit of grenadiers. Thus was born the *Potsdamer Riesengarde,* or "Giant Guards of Potsdam."

Ranging from "small" men, who met the minimum height requirement, to at least two 8-foot goliaths, the Potsdam Giants were the king's favorites. Clad in blue jackets, scarlet trousers, and tall red hats that exaggerated their already ponderous height, the guards enjoyed the best pay and the special attentions of their sovereign. Frederick William paraded them before foreign dignitaries and kept them out of combat. Pleased to the point of obsession with his unique regiment, he painted the men's portraits, reviewed them daily, and had them march behind their mascot (a bear) for his pleasure whenever he suffered from sickness or depression. He once confessed to the French ambassador, "The most beautiful girl or woman in the world would be a matter of indifference to me, but tall soldiers—they are my weakness."

HUNTING TALL FELLOWS

The obvious problem was how to keep a three-battalion regiment up to strength. Every army unit loses men to disease, age, accident, and desertion, and Frederick William had to search far and wide for men tall enough to fill out his ranks. He transferred tall soldiers from other regiments, promoted captains of other companies who recruited tall soldiers, and let it be known in the courts of Europe that the Prussian king's goodwill could be encouraged by sending a few dozen impressively tall soldiers into his service.

When those sources failed to keep up with the king's demand for ever-taller specimens, he sent recruiting agents to other lands to recruit (or even kidnap) tall men—priests, innkeepers, even unwary diplomats—for his regiment. He bypassed his diplomats and sent agents to hire giants directly from foreign armies. He even forced tall Potsdam women to marry tall men to ensure an ongoing supply of giants for his beloved grenadier guards.

Upon Frederick William's death in 1740, his son, Frederick the Great, a five-foot, five-inch former major of the Potsdam Giants, disbanded the regiment, finding it to be a useless, ornamental expense. Men recruited or kidnapped from foreign lands were sent home, and lumbering giants, knapsacks over their shoulders, could be seen making their way along roads leading from Berlin.

- *The world's tallest woman? That would be "Rodina-Mat," or "Motherland," towering over Kiev, Ukraine, at 203 feet. She's still pretty short compared to the world's tallest man, Japan's Ushiku Amida Buddha, nearly 394 feet tall—three times the height of the Statue of Liberty.*

MARY AND HER MESSAGE

Did the Virgin Mary appear to little children in France and Portugal? Catholics seem to think so.

Pious Catholics hold a special place for Mary, the mother of Jesus, praying to her daily for favors and blessings. Some say that the Virgin has appeared to them right here on Earth. Many of these claims are not verified—dismissed as products of overactive imaginations or as outright hoaxes, but two apparitions—which defy scientific explanation—have stood the test of time and remain highly cherished by Catholics around the world.

OUR LADY OF LOURDES

In February 1858, Bernadette Soubirous, a poor, sickly 14-year-old peasant girl, was gathering firewood near a stream when she suddenly had a vision of a beautiful lady dressed in white. Overcome with fear, she rushed home to tell her mother, who told her to keep away from that place. However, Bernadette returned and would repeatedly see the Virgin—18 times in all. One message stood out: A chapel must be built on the site where Bernadette had first seen Mary.

Bernadette's parish priest was highly skeptical of the visions and dismissed the little girl and her childish fantasy. In spite of ridicule, Bernadette stuck to her story. It was only after people began reporting that their ailments had been cured after washing in the stream where the visions occurred, that the Church decided to endorse the apparition. A shrine was built on the site and, to this day, is visited annually by millions. These pilgrims flock to Lourdes, hoping to cure physical ailments by washing in its now famous waters. Hundreds of miraculous healings have been reported, all of them verified by church and medical experts.

OUR LADY OF FATIMA

In May of 1917, Lucia Santos and her cousins Jacinta and Fransisco were tending their sheep in the town of Vila Nova de

Ourém in the parish of Fatima, Portugal. Suddenly, they saw a tremendous flash of light. Thinking it was lightning, the children rushed for cover, only to see the same flash again. The children described seeing "a Lady more brilliant than the sun." This was the first in a series of Marian apparitions reported by the children. Mary impressed upon the children the importance of daily prayer (especially reciting the rosary) and penance. She also told the children that there would be a second war, much worse than the first. When World War II began almost two decades later, many saw this as the fulfillment of the prophecy. The Virgin also gave the children a brief glimpse of hell and further revealed a mysterious secret, which Church authorities kept under wraps until 2000. (The third secret was revealed to be a vision of the deaths of the pope and other individuals.)

Word of the apparitions soon spread, and by October 13, 1917, a crowd of 70,000—believers and skeptics alike—flocked to Fatima on the hot rumor that a miracle was about to occur. They were not disappointed. Newspaper reports of the day document how onlookers saw the sun burst through rain clouds and then begin dancing and spinning across the sky in a zigzag pattern, trailed by a brilliant array of colors. The so-called "Miracle of the Sun" solidified belief in the apparition, and a shrine was built on the site. Each year, scores of pilgrims visit the site, hoping to get the graces of Mary first experienced by the three children.

FAMOUS LAST WORDS

"All the ills of mankind, all the tragic misfortunes that fill the history books, all the political blunders, all the failures of the great leaders have arisen merely from a lack of skill at dancing."
—Molière

"The whole history of the world is summed up in the fact that, when nations are strong, they are not always just."
—Winston Churchill

KILLER QUEENS

When playwright William Congreve wrote,
"Hell hath no fury like a woman scorned," he may have had
these warrior queens in mind.

BOUDICCA (A.D. 61)—NEMESIS OF NERO

She stood six feet tall, sported a hip-length mane of fiery red hair, and had a vengeful streak a mile wide. She was Boudicca, queen of the Celtic Iceni people of eastern Britain. In A.D. 61, she led a furious uprising against the occupying Romans that nearly chased Nero's legions from the island.

Boudicca didn't always hate the Romans. The Iceni kingdom, led by her husband, Prasutagus, was once a Roman ally. But Prasutagus lived a life of conspicuous wealth on borrowed Roman money, and when it came time to pay the piper, he was forced to bequeath half his kingdom to the Romans; the other half was left for his daughters.

The Romans, however, got greedy; on Prasutagus's death, they moved to seize all Iceni lands as payment for the dead king's debt. When the widow Boudicca challenged the Romans, they publicly flogged her and raped her daughters. While most of the Roman army in Britain was busy annihilating the Druids in the west, the scorned Boudicca led the Iceni and other aggrieved Celtic peoples on a bloody rebellion that reverberated all the way back to Rome.

Boudicca's warriors annihilated the vaunted Roman Ninth Legion and laid waste to the Roman cities of Camulodunum (Colchester), Londinium (London), and Verulamium (St. Albans). Boudicca's vengeance knew no bounds and was exacted on both Romans and fellow Britons who supported them. Upwards of 80,000 people fell victim to her wrath.

The Romans were floored by the ferocity of Boudicca's attack, and Nero actually considered withdrawing his army from Britain. But the Romans regrouped, and later a seasoned force of 1,200 legionnaires trounced Boudicca's 100,000-strong rebel army in a decisive battle. The defeated Boudicca chose suicide by poison over capture.

Today, a statute of the great Boudicca can be found near Westminster Pier in London, testament to the veneration the British still hold for Boudicca as their first heroine.

EMPRESS JINGO (A.D. 169–269)— PERSUADER OF GODS AND MEN

She led the Japanese in the conquest of Korea in the early 3rd century. In 1881, she became the first woman to be featured on a Japanese banknote—no small feat given the chauvinism of imperial Japan. More than 1,700 years after her rule, Empress Jingo is still revered as a goddess in Japan.

Perhaps Jingo's success as a warrior queen can be attributed to the irresistible sway she held over both the ancient deities and mortal men. As regent ruler of imperial Japan following the death of her emperor husband, Chuai, Jingo was determined to make Korea her own. According to Japanese lore, she beguiled Ryujin, the Japanese dragon god of the sea, to lend her his magical Tide Jewels, which she used to create favorable tides that destroyed the Korean fleet and safely guided the Japanese fleet to the Korean peninsula. From there, she commanded and cajoled her armies to an illustrious campaign of conquest that secured her exalted status within Japanese cultural history.

Jingo purportedly had amazing powers of persuasion over the human reproductive cycle as well. Pregnant with Chuai's son at the time of the invasion, Jingo remained in Korea for the duration of the campaign, which by all accounts lasted well beyond the length of a normal pregnancy term. Legend has it, however, that she delayed giving birth until after the conquest so that her son and heir, Ojin, could be born in Japan.

Once home, Jingo cemented her power by using brute force to convince several rivals to the throne to concede to her rule, which would ultimately last for more than 60 years.

ZENOBIA (A.D. 274)—
MISTRESS OF THE MIDDLE EAST

Like Boudicca before her, the warrior queen Zenobia made her name by leading an army against the mighty Romans. Unlike the Celtic queen, however, Zenobia would experience a much different fate for her actions.

Zenobia and her husband, Odenathus, ruled the prosperous Syrian city of Palmyra. Though technically subordinate to Odenathus, she certainly didn't take a backseat to him. She established herself as a warrior queen by riding at her husband's side into battle against the Persians—often overshadowing her more reserved mate by shouting loud battle cries, walking for miles within the ranks of the foot soldiers, and drinking the boys under the table in victory celebrations.

Zenobia became the undisputed ruler of Palmyra in 267 following the assassination of Odenathus (which some attribute to Zenobia herself). As an ostensible ally of Rome, Zenobia launched a campaign of conquest in the Middle East, leading, walking, and drinking with her men as always. Within three years she expanded her realm to Syria, Egypt, and much of Asia Minor.

Flushed with success, Zenobia declared Palmyra's independence from Rome. But in 272, the Romans struck back. Zenobia was up for the fight, but her forces were overextended. The Romans easily recaptured Zenobia's outlying territories before laying siege to Palmyra itself.

After its fall, Palmyra was destroyed, and Zenobia was captured. She was taken to Rome and paraded in golden chains before Emperor Aurelian. But even in defeat, Zenobia triumphed. The striking beauty with the defiant stride struck a chord with Aurelian, who later pardoned her and allowed her to live a life of luxury on an estate outside Rome.

AETHELFLAED (A.D. 869–918)— "NOBLE BEAUTY" OF THE ANGLO-SAXONS

At the beginning of the 10th century, the Anglo kingdom of Wessex and Saxon kingdom of Mercia in southern England were under siege by the Danish Vikings. The cocksure Vikings were confident of victory, but they hadn't counted on the rise of the Mercian queen, Aethelflaed (her name means "noble beauty"), who would earn her warrior reputation by leading her armies in victory over the Vikings and emerging as one of Britain's most powerful rulers.

Aethelflaed's father, Alfred the Great, was king of Wessex. Aethelflaed, at age 15, married the Mercian nobleman, Ethelred, thus forming a strategic alliance of the two kingdoms against the Vikings. Her first fight against the Vikings occurred on her wedding day when the Norsemen tried to kill her to prevent the nuptial and political union. Aethelflaed took up the sword and fought alongside her guards while holed up in an old trench, eventually driving the Vikings away.

From then on, battling Vikings became old hat for Aethelflaed. When her husband died in 911, she assumed sole rule of Mercia and began taking the fight to the Vikings. Perhaps remembering her wedding-day experience in the trench, she built formidable fortifications to defend Mercia. She also used exceptional diplomatic skills to form alliances against the Vikings. By the time of her death in 918, she had led her armies in several victories over the Vikings, had them begging for peace, and had extended her power in Britain.

Aethelflaed made her name as a Viking killer, but her most important legacy was her success in sustaining the union of the Anglos and the Saxons, which would later germinate into the English nation.

ROME'S IMPERIAL APPETITE

The Romans loved their meals. Their food tended toward sweet, sour, and tangy flavors, and their main meal of the day was cena *(dinner), eaten in the early afternoon. Romans drank wine between courses and* posca *(vinegar and water) if they couldn't afford wine. Ancient wine was more concentrated than modern wine, and Romans diluted it (it was considered crass to drink it straight) with water and flavored it with various ingredients.*

SO, WHAT'S FOR DINNER?

In the country, Romans ate primarily what they could raise, harvest, and forage. In the cities, poor urbanites scraped by on a steady diet of subsidized grain, which they boiled into *puls* (porridge) or baked into *panis* (bread) if they had access to an oven. Many Romans of modest means took their meals at a *popina* (deli) or *taberna* (tavern), which provided food and drink as well as a place to enjoy a game of dice or conversation away from cramped quarters. But for those who could afford them, Rome's broad conquests gave access to foods from Britain to the Black Sea. Wealthier Romans dined at home, reclining on couches with family, friends, and clients in the *triclinium* (dining room). Meals were cooked and catered by slaves. At special banquets, the courses and items could reach fabulous proportions and featured entertainment, party favors, and convivial conversation. Descriptions of over-the-top banquets, such as Petronius's satirical *Dinner with Trimalchio,* have become infamous pictures of debauched overindulgence.

The menus on pages 140–141 come from a variety of sources but represent banquet settings for the urban poor (*Cena Proletaria*), small rural farmer (*Cena Rustica*), city dweller (*Cena Urbana*), and aristocrat (*Cena Nobilis*).

GUSTATIO ET PROMULSIS
(APPETIZERS AND STARTERS)

Proletaria	Rustica	Urbana	Nobilis
	Olive Medley Bunch Berry and Wine Preserve Fresh Endive and Radishes Slow-Cooked Eggs	Cappadocian Lettuce Fresh Leeks Pickled Tuna Garnished with Sliced Eggs and Rue Slow-Cooked Eggs "Velabrum Street" Cheese	Bottomless Treasure Chest of Sea Urchins, Oysters, and Mussels with Carrots Warbler "Trimalchio" (Whole warbler baked in a peppered egg-crème dumpling and decorated to look like peacock eggs) Thrush Baked with Asparagus Roasted Capons and Figpeckers Oyster and Mussel Pasties Black and White Barnacles with Carrots, Sea-Smelt, and Jellyfish

PRIMA MENSA (DINNER AND ITS COURSES)

Proletaria	Rustica	Urbana	Nobilis
Puls (boiled wheat cereal) or *Panis* (bread)	Boiled Farm Cabbage with Rafter-Smoked Bacon	Boiled Green Cabbage Sausage on a Bed of Couscous White Beans and Bacon	Wild Boar with Turnips, Lettuce, and Radish Set in a Tangy Caraway Wine Sauce Platter of Lamprey and Shrimp Glazed with Capanian Olive Oil, Spanish Mackerel Caviar, Wine, White Pepper, Lesbos Vinegar; Reduced in New Wine infused with Arugula, Yellow-head, and Fresh Sea Urchins Crane Encrusted in Meal and Sea-Salt; served with Fig-Fed Goose *Foie Gras* and Leg of Rabbit Parrot Rotisserie Fish and Boar Pasties

SECUNDA MENSA (DESSERTS) AND MATTEAE (SAVORIES)

Proletaria	Rustica	Urbana	Nobilis
Puls or Panis	Basket of Nuts, Figs, Dates, Plums, and Apples with Honeycomb Homemade Ricotta Cheesecake with Honey	Neapolitan Chestnuts Roasted with Raisins and Pears Picenum Olives Cooked Chickpeas and Lupines	Mixed Pastry and Fruit Tray Dusted in Saffron Dates "Apicius" (pitted dates stuffed with nuts and pine kernels and fried in honey) Spits of Blackbird and Squab Breasts Chicken with "Capped" Goose-Eggs

BIBENDA (DRINKS)

Proletaria	Rustica	Urbana	Nobilis
Posca or Cheap Wine	Posca or Homemade Wine Mixed with Water and Honey or Herbs	Table Wine Mixed with Water and Honey or Herbs	Vintage Domestic and Provincial Wines, Cooled with Snow and Flavored with Honey, Herbs, or Spices

FAMOUS LAST WORDS

"*Appetite, a universal wolf.*"

—WILLIAM SHAKESPEARE

"*Let the stoics say what they please, we do not eat for the good of living, but because the meat is savory and the appetite is keen.*"

—RALPH WALDO EMERSON

Fast Facts

- *"Some Assembly Required": It took an estimated 30 million hours for Stone-Age builders to complete the rock structure at Stonehenge, England.*

- *Of the Seven Wonders of the Ancient World, only one has survived the test of time: the two-million-block Great Pyramid of Giza.*

- *The Great Wall of China, at 3,977 miles, is the world's longest artificial structure. If you broke it up for materials, you could build 120 of Egypt's Great Pyramids.*

- *The Greeks had a working steam engine in the first century B.C.—about 1,700 years before an English engineer patented the steam engine. To the ancients, the steam engine was just an amusing toy, since they hadn't figured out how to hook it up to anything useful.*

- *In 1931, the immense Boulder Dam on America's Colorado River was renamed the "Hoover Dam" after the incumbent Republican president, Herbert Hoover. When Democrat Franklin Roosevelt defeated Hoover the next year, Congress changed the name back to "Boulder Dam." After Roosevelt died, Congress changed the name yet again—back to "Hoover Dam."*

- *Constructing a tunnel under the English Channel has been discussed since the time of Napoleon. A brief attempt was made in the 1870s, but the British government refused to allow a tunnel that could give French soldiers a route to invade England. The "chunnel" finally opened in 1994.*

- *The first calendar was invented by the Egyptians to let everybody know when the Nile River was scheduled to flood its banks.*

- *The first bomb dropped by the Allies on the city of Berlin during World War II claimed an unusual casualty—the only elephant in the Berlin Zoo.*

GREATEST SHORTCUTS

*The construction of great canals such as Suez and Panama
cost vast amounts of money and required incredible feats of
engineering to link seas and oceans with only a few miles
of artificial waterway. But it sure beat sailing
thousands of miles around entire continents.*

In September 1513, Vasco Núñez de Balboa left the Spanish
colony of Darién on the Caribbean coast of the narrow Panama-
nian isthmus to climb the highest mountain in the area—literally,
to see what he could see. Upon reaching the summit, he gazed
westward and became the first European to see the eastern shores
of the vast Pacific Ocean.

From there, he led a party of *conquistadores* toward his discovery.
They labored up and down rugged ridges and hacked their way
through relentless, impenetrable jungle, sweating bullets under
their metal breastplates the entire way. It took four days for Balboa and his men to complete the 40-mile trek to the beach.

Of course, Balboa's journey would have been much easier if someone had built the Panama Canal beforehand.

For 2,500 years, civilizations have carved canals through bodies
of land to make water transportation easier, faster, and cheaper.
History's first great navigational canal was built in Egypt by the
Persian emperor Darius I between 510 and 520 B.C., linking the
Nile and the Red Sea. A generation later, the Chinese began their
reign as the world's greatest canal builders, a distinction they
would hold for 1,000 years—until the Europeans began building
canals using technology developed centuries earlier during the
construction of the world's longest artificial waterway: the 1,100-
mile Grand Canal of China.

It's been a long time since a "great" canal was built anywhere in
the world. Here's a brief look at the most recent three.

THE ERIE CANAL—CLINTON'S BIG DITCH

At the turn of the 19th century, the United States was bursting at its seams, and Americans were eyeing new areas of settlement west of the Appalachians. But westward overland routes were slow and the cost of moving goods along them was exorbitant.

The idea of building a canal linking the Great Lakes with the eastern seaboard as a way of opening the west had been floated since the mid-1700s. It finally became more than wishful thinking in 1817, when construction of the Erie Canal began.

Citing its folly and $7-million price tag, detractors labeled the canal "Clinton's Big Ditch" in derisive reference to its biggest proponent, New York governor Dewitt Clinton. When completed in 1825, however, the Erie Canal was hailed as the "Eighth Wonder of the World," cutting 363 miles through thick forest and swamp to link Lake Erie at Buffalo with the Hudson River at Albany. Sadly though, more than 1,000 workers died during its construction, primarily from swamp-borne diseases.

The Erie Canal fulfilled its promise, becoming a favored pathway for the great migration westward, slashing transportation costs a whopping 95 percent, and bringing unprecedented prosperity to the towns along its route.

THE SUEZ CANAL—GRAND TRIUMPH

The centuries-old dream of a canal linking the Mediterranean and the Red Sea became reality in 1859 when French diplomat Ferdinand de Lesseps stuck the first shovel in the ground to commence building of the Suez Canal.

Over the next ten years, 2.4 million laborers would toil—and 125,000 would die—to move 97 million cubic yards of earth and build a 100-mile Sinai shortcut that made the 10,000-mile sea journey from Europe around Africa to India redundant.

De Lesseps convinced an old friend, Egypt's King Said, to grant him a concession to build and operate the canal for 99 years. French investors eagerly bankrolled three-quarters of the 200 million francs ($50 million) needed for the project. Said had to kick in the rest to keep the project afloat because others, particularly the British, rejected it as financial lunacy—seemingly justified when the canal's final cost rang in at double the original estimate.

The Suez dramatically expanded world trade by significantly reducing sailing time and cost between east and west. De Lesseps had been proven right and was proclaimed the world's greatest canal digger. The British, leery of France's new backdoor to their Indian empire, spent the next 20 years trying to wrest control of the Suez from their imperial rival.

THE PANAMA CANAL—SPECTACULAR FAILURE

When it came time to build the next great canal half a world away in Panama, everyone turned to de Lesseps to dig it.

But here de Lesseps was in over his head. Suez was a walk in the park compared to Panama. In the Suez, flat land at sea level had allowed de Lesseps to build a lockless channel. A canal in Panama, however, would have to slice through the multiple elevations of the Continental Divide.

Beginning in 1880, de Lesseps, ignoring all advice, began a nine-year effort to dig a sea-level canal through the mountains. This futile strategy, combined with financial mismanagement and the death of some 22,000 workers from disease and landslides, killed de Lessep's scheme. Panama had crushed the hero of Suez.

THE PANAMA CANAL—SUCCESS!

The idea of a Panama canal, however, persevered. In 1903, the United States, under the expansionist, big-stick leadership of Theodore Roosevelt, bought out the French and assumed control of the project. Using raised-lock engineering and disease-control methods that included spraying oil on mosquito breeding grounds to eliminate malaria and yellow fever, the Americans completed the canal in 1914.

The Panama Canal, the last of the world's great canals, made sailing from New York to San Francisco a breeze. A trip that once covered 14,000 miles while circumnavigating South America was now a mere 6,000-mile pleasure cruise.

DANCE OF
THE BLACK DEATH

The Black Death, the epidemic best known for devastating Europe between 1347 and 1350, was as deadly in the east as it was in the west. By the time the plague reached the outskirts of Europe, it had already killed an estimated 25 million people. Within three years, approximately 25 million more Europeans would follow in the first wave of a cycle of plagues that continued to hound Europe for three centuries.

The plague isn't pretty. Whether primarily in the lymph nodes (bubonic), blood (septicemic), or lungs (pneumonic), the plague is caused by the bacterium *yersinia pestis,* which lives in the digestive tract of fleas. It primarily transmits from animals to humans through flea bites, though humans in close contact can transmit pneumonic plague to each other. The bacteria was discovered by Japanese and European researchers in the late 19th century. Patients manifest symptoms such as swollen and tender lymph nodes (*buboes*) in the area of the bite, fever, bloody sputum and blotching, rapidly worsening pneumonia, and—as the bacteria overwhelms the nervous system—neurological and psychological disorders. Untreated, plague has a morbidity rate of 50–60 percent; the rate is even higher for pneumonic plague. Between 1,000 and 3,000 cases are reported each year worldwide.

ORIGINS OF A DISEASE

The Black Death originated in China in the 1340s. Making its way along the Silk Road, the epidemic ravaged India, Egypt, the Middle East, and Constantinople before spreading rapidly through trading ports to Europe. Even Greenland and Iceland were struck. From 1347 to 1350, a third of Europe's population died an agonizing, dramatic, mysterious—and sudden—death. In cities such as Florence, the death toll reached 75 percent, and many rural villages were wiped out completely. Nearly annual outbreaks of the plague continued, culminating in the great 1665 plague of London, in which perhaps 100,000 Londoners died. Overall, some estimates of the combined death toll reach 200 million people.

It would be hard to underestimate the pervasive effects of the plagues on Europe. All aspects of society and culture suffered intense disruption and experienced profound change as the plagues brought on economic stress, social dissolution, religious extremism, and skepticism. The trauma on the European psyche as a result of living in circumstances where, as the 14th-century Italian writer Boccaccio put it, people could "eat lunch with their friends and dinner with their ancestors in paradise," can be seen in the pervasive use of skeletons in art and drama. They act as grim and often ironic reminders of *memento mori* ("Remember, you die"), illustrations of *quod es fui, quod sum eris* ("what you are I was; what I am you will be"), and participants in the "Dance of Death" (*Danse Macabre, Totentanz*) throughout this period.

WAS THAT THE LAST DANCE?

Although the Black Death and its subsequent outbreaks ended in the 17th century, its rapid spread and descriptions, as well as the patterns of outbreaks do not—in some cases—correspond well to *y. pestis,* nor to the complex conditions required for the bacteria to find its way into fleas that can then infect humans. This has recently led some researchers in Britain and the United States to advance the theory that the plague was actually caused by a human-borne virus that lies dormant in the earth until it is introduced into the population. If so, another round of "Black Death"—especially in an age of continuous global travel and trade—remains a frightening possibility.

- *Nearly half of medieval Europeans were wiped out by the plague.*

- *Although many sources claim that the popular children's rhyme "Ring Around the Rosy" is about the plague, this does not appear to be true. Five centuries passed between the plague and the first mentions of the rhyme.*

History of the Weird
FOLLOWING FREUD

*As it turns out, the "Father of Psychoanalysis"
was a case study of neurotic behavior.*

A neurologist and pyschiatrist, Sigmund
Freud's research on human behavior left a
lasting impact on the field of pyschology.

Freud himself was not without issues. He
was a heavy smoker—smoking as many as
20 cigars a day for most of his life—and as a
result, endured more than 30 operations for
mouth cancer. In the 1880s, he conducted extensive research on
cocaine, advocating use of the drug as a cure for a number of ills,
including depression. Reports indicate that Freud was probably
addicted to cocaine for several years during this time period. And
a friend for whom he prescribed cocaine was later diagnosed with
"cocaine psychosis" and subsequently died in what is referred to
by biographers as the "cocaine incident."

Freud suffered psychosomatic disorders and phobias, including agoraphobia (a fear of crowded spaces) and a fear of dying.
Though his Theory of Sexuality was being widely denounced as a
threat to morality, he decided that sexual activity was incompati-
ble with accomplishing great work and stopped having sexual relations with his wife. Yet he is thought to have had a long affair with
his wife's sister, Minna Bernays, who lived with the couple. Freud
denied these persistent rumors, but in 2006, a German researcher
uncovered a century-old guest book at a Swiss hotel in which
Freud registered himself and Minna as "Dr. Freud and wife."

Freud fled his native Austria after the Nazi Anschluss in 1938 and
spent his last year of life in London. Dying from mouth cancer,
in September 1939, he convinced his doctor to help him commit
suicide with injections of morphine.

NIGHT FLIGHT

Muhammad was just another guy running a caravan business.
Then, in A.D. 610, the angel Gabriel came calling with news that
Muhammad had been chosen to spread the word of God.

(Editor's note: This story has many variations. This is one of them.)
The Qur'an tells the story of the miracle of Muhammad's trip
from Mecca to Jerusalem to heaven and back to Mecca—all in a
single night. Often referred to as "Muhammad's Night Flight," or
the "Night of Ascension," this tale starts with Muhammad receiving a visit from the angel Gabriel on the 27th night of Rajab (the
seventh lunar month of the Islamic calendar) in A.D. 621. To prepare for his trip, Gabriel cut open Muhammad's chest, washed his
heart to purify it, then emptied a powder into his chest to increase
his wisdom and strengthen his faith.

Gabriel also provided a special means of transportation for
Muhammad called *al-Buraq*, a magical white horse with a stride
as far as the eye could see. Mounting the creature, Muhammad
and Gabriel began their journey.

THE GOOD, THE BAD, AND THE UGLY

During the trip to Jerusalem, the prophet saw people who were
planting and harvesting in just two days. Gabriel explained that
they were being rewarded for fighting for Allah. When they rode
by people whose lips and tongues were pinched shut with scissors
of fire, Gabriel explained that they were being punished for lying.
Muhammad also saw angels using stones to repeatedly crush
people's heads; these people would regain their shape only to be
smashed again. According to Gabriel, these people were being
punished for not praying before sleeping.

With prayer stops at Mt. Sinai and Bethlehem, Muhammad and
Gabriel made it to Jerusalem. There, waiting for them at the
Temple Mount, were all of the previous prophets of God. Because
God held Muhammad in higher regard than the others, he was
chosen to lead the other prophets in *salat* (ritual prayer).

ALL PROPHETS GO TO HEAVEN

Then it was time for Muhammad to ascend to heaven on a staircase of alternating steps of gold and silver. Muhammad and Gabriel entered the first level of heaven and journeyed through all seven levels, meeting such prophets as John, Jesus, Joseph, Idris, Aaron, Moses, and Abraham. Each prophet gave Muhammad their blessing to become the last prophet of Allah.

From the seven levels, Muhammad went on to paradise, witnessing the favors that God had for the faithful including the *Hur ul-^In*, women created by Allah who were neither human or *jinn* (creatures created from a smokeless flame), and the *wildan ul-mukhalladun*, very beautiful servants of the inhabitants of paradise. It was promised that even the person who had the least status in paradise would have 10,000 *wildan ul-mukhalladun* to serve him, each carrying a tray of gold and a tray of silver.

Muhammad then ascended past paradise to meet Allah, who told Muhammad to command the faithful to pray 50 times a day. Moses, concerned that the faithful would not keep to God's commandment, convinced Muhammad to return to the presence of Allah repeatedly to reduce the number of daily requirements. Eventually, God reduced the requirement of daily prayer to five.

THERE AND BACK AGAIN

Heading back to Jerusalem via the gold and silver stairway, Muhammad rode his magical horse back to Mecca. Many people questioned his story the next day, but Muhammad described every aspect of the mosque in Jerusalem and also said that he noticed on his way back to Mecca where their sheep were grazing and described shepherds looking for a lost camel. Muhammad even described the camel in detail; his description was confirmed when the shepherds returned from the fields.

Although some assert that Muhammad's journey was spiritual, most of the faithful believe it was a physical journey. The Night of Ascension is usually celebrated with prayers, the lighting of cities with electric lights and candles, and readings of the legend, called *Laylat al-Mi'raj* ("Night of the Ascension").

JULIUS CAESAR: OPPRESSOR OR ENLIGHTENED LEADER?

Julius Caesar is one of the most recognized figures in all of human history. However, most people don't know as much about him as they think.

Caesar was not the first Roman emperor; indeed, he was never an emperor at all. He *was* a dictator, but in his time that word had a reasonable and legitimate political connotation. As history suggests, Caesar was able in many areas. He led men into battle with courage and skill and was also a brilliant administrator and politician who instituted reforms that benefited the common people of Rome.

RISING OUT OF CHAOS

Caesar's birth in 100 B.C. (sometimes listed as 102 B.C.) coincided with great civil strife in Rome. Although his parents' status as nobles gave him advantages, Caesar's childhood was spent in a politically volatile Rome marked by personal hatreds and conniving. As an adult, he learned to be wary in his dealings with other powerful people. By the time Caesar was 20, a patrician named Sulla had been the Roman dictator for about 20 years. Although Caesar and Sulla were friends, Sulla later became enraged when Caesar refused to divorce his wife, Cornelia, who was the daughter of a man Sulla loathed (and murdered), Cinna. In order to save his neck, Caesar promptly left Rome for Asia.

When Sulla died in 78 B.C., Caesar returned to Rome and took up the practice of law. Caesar had everything necessary for success: He had received the best possible education, developed impressive oratorical skills, and made himself an outstanding writer. He also spent huge sums of money, most of which he had to borrow. The money went to bribes and sumptuous parties for the influential and bought Caesar access to power. Leading politicians looked on him favorably and rewarded him with a series of increasingly important political positions in Spain and Rome. Caesar's time in Spain was especially useful, as he used his position there to become very wealthy.

COMING OUT ON TOP

In 59 B.C., Caesar, who was by now a general, made a successful bid for power in concert with Marcus Licinius Crassus, the richest man in Rome; and Pompey, another ambitious general who was known, to his immodest pleasure, as Pompey the Great. These three Type-A personalities ruled Rome as the First Triumvirate, with Caesar becoming first among equals as consul. Caesar had always been popular among the common people and with Rome's soldiers, and he aimed to cement that loyalty with reforms that would benefit them. Soon, Caesar was made governor of Gaul and spent the next 11 years conquering all of what is now France, with a couple of profitable trips to Britain for good measure. While on campaign, he wrote an account of his actions, called *Commentaries*, which is among the finest of all military literature.

OLD FRIENDS AND NEW

To leave Rome, even for military glory, was always risky for any of the empire's leaders. While Caesar was abroad, Crassus was killed in battle. This void encouraged Pompey, who made it clear that Caesar was no longer welcome in Rome. Caesar and his army responded by crossing the Rubicon River in 49 B.C. to seize control of the city. Within a year of the civil war that followed, Caesar defeated Pompey. He also began a torrid affair with Egypt's Queen Cleopatra. After a few other actions against Rome's enemies, Caesar was acclaimed by all of Rome as a great hero. In turn, he pardoned all who had opposed him.

HAIL, CAESAR

Mindful of the fleeting nature of popularity, Caesar continued to promote a series of important reforms:

- Some of the land that had been held by wealthy families was distributed to common people desperate to make a living. As one might expect, this didn't go over well with the wealthy.

- Tax reforms insisted upon by Caesar forced the rich to pay their fair share. This innovation didn't win Caesar many new friends among the powerful.

- Retired soldiers were settled on land provided by the government. Because this land was in Rome's outlying territories, it became populated with a happy, well-trained cadre of veterans meant to be Rome's first line of defense, if needed. Unemployed citizens were also given the opportunity to settle in these areas, where jobs were much more plentiful. This reduced the number of poor people in Rome and decreased the crime rate.

- As he had done earlier, Caesar made residents of the provinces, such as people living in Spain, citizens of Rome. This idea proved quite popular. Many years later, some of the Roman emperors actually came from Spain.

- Working people are happy people (so it's said). In a clever move, Caesar instituted a massive public works program that provided both jobs and a sense of pride among the citizens of Rome.

BEWARE THE IDES OF MARCH

All these reforms notwithstanding, Caesar's enemies feared he would leverage his great popularity to destroy the Roman Republic and institute in its place an empire ruled by one man. So, in one of those moments of violence that turns the wheel of history, Caesar was assassinated by people he trusted on March 15, 44 B.C.—the Ides of March, for those of you who remember your Shakespeare. The civil war that followed was ultimately won by Caesar's nephew, Octavian, who changed his name to Caesar Augustus ... and who replaced the republic and instituted in its place an empire ruled by one man! Augustus was the first of a long succession of emperors who ruled virtually independent of the Roman Senate. It was the rulers who followed Caesar, then, and not Caesar himself, who proved the undoing of the system so cherished by Caesar's enemies.

BETTER LATER THAN SOONER: OKLAHOMA'S GREAT LAND LOTTERY

They trekked in by the tens of thousands to Oklahoma, by horse and by foot, under the blazing July sun. Hungry for land, they formed great lines, with hundreds sleeping in place. During this great 1901 migration, thousands of people camped out in one valley alone.

This was not the pell-mell, anything-goes 1889 land rush that gave Oklahoma Territory land to the "Sooners." No, this was quite the reverse. So contentious and confused had been the five land races between 1889 and 1895 that, to divvy up Oklahoma's remaining land, the federal government had opted for a civilized approach: a lottery. Vast crowds came from across the nation to register for it.

Some groups were opposed to the giveaway. Ranchers wanted to continue grazing their stock on the lottery lands. Kiowa Chief Lone Wolf sued the Interior Department to keep the Indian lands settler-free.

OKLAHOMA BEFORE THE LOTTERY

From the end of the Civil War, the Indian Territory, later known as Oklahoma, had come under irresistible pressure for land. In 1866, the federal government coaxed the local Indian tribes into ceding two million acres. Soon, Anglo leaders such as William Couch were leading expeditions of "Boomers"—prospective settlers—into these "Unassigned Lands." In 1889, a group of Creek Indians, in defiance of the opposition of the "Five Civilized Tribes"—sold the government three million more acres. That same year, the Indian Appropriations Act opened 160-acre blocks of Oklahoma land to homesteaders on a first-come basis.

A multitude—50,000 on the first day—swarmed into Kickapoo country on horse, foot, and wagon. Many of the arrivals were former slaves. Thousands more—the Sooners—sneaked into the territories before the official start date. Gunfights broke out between Boomers and Sooners. Lawsuits between claimants dragged on for decades. Of every 14 Boomers, only one wound up with an irrefutable land claim. Four other land rushes through 1895 had similar woes. When the time came to redistribute the remainder of Oklahoma's turf, Washington resolved to find a better way.

A BETTER WAY?

On July 4, 1901, President McKinley proclaimed that land 4,639 square miles from the Comanche, Apache, Wichita, and Kiowa reservations would be parceled out on the basis of a vast lottery.

Registration for a chance to own a block of land took place at Fort Sill and in the town of El Reno, between July 10 and 26. Tens of thousands of would-be settlers swarmed in from Texas, Kansas, and, most of all, from settled parts of Oklahoma.

Under the arrangement, 480,000 acres of pasture were reserved for the Indian tribes, though most of this was leased to ranchers for pennies an acre. Thousands of Indians did receive homesteads; many Native Americans leased most of their acreage to farmers for a yearly per-acre fee of $1.50. Off-limits to the land rush were the War Department's Fort Sill and the Wichita Mountain Forest Reserve.

At the registration offices, each applicant filled out a card with his or her name, birthdate, height, and other identifying information. The cards were placed in large, wheellike containers for mixing and selection. Land parcels were divided into two huge swaths of territory around Lawton and El Reno.

As vast crowds waited to apply in heat over 100 degrees, trouble broke out. A Mexican was taken out and killed for trying to jump to the front of a registration line. People were required to notarize their applications: A mob almost lynched a fake notary, and lawmen arrested another notary who used an outdated seal. In the meantime, grifters and gamblers taking advantage of the bored multitudes waiting in line were banished from the streets. More welcome were painted Cheyenne Indians who offered spectators war dances for 25 cents.

Most registrants were farmers of limited income. No one owning more than 160 acres in another state was permitted to register. One registration card per person was the rule; hundreds trying to game the lottery with multiple applications were barred.

Single-day registration peaked at 16,700. In all, approximately 160,000 hopefuls signed up for a chance at 13,000 homesteads.

THE WINNERS ARE REVEALED

Drawings began on July 29 in El Reno in front of 50,000 witnesses, whose tents and booths packed the dusty streets. From a platform on the grounds of a school, officials pulled the lucky registrations out of twin containers, representing the El Reno and Lawton parcels.

At 1:30 P.M., to a great hurrah, Commissioner Colonel Dyer called out the first name from the El Reno bin—Stephen A. Holcomb of Pauls Valley in Indian Territory.

The first lottery winner for Lawton was James R. Wood, a hardware clerk. The second was Miss Mattie Beal, a telephone operator from Wichita. After Commissioner Dyer read out her description—5-foot-3, 23 years old—the crowd cried: "They must get married!"

On August 6, winners began filing claims for their new properties at a land district office. There they got to choose the shape of their new 160 acres: a narrow strip, a square, or even the shape of a Z. In an unlucky stroke, 1,362 winners who failed to show up for the filings forfeited their claims for good.

The land rush immediately led to the creation of new Oklahoma counties—Comanche, Caddo, and Kiowa. Lots in the county seats were sold to raise some $664,000 to build roads, bridges, and a courthouse.

In 1907, boosted by the growing number of settlers and the economic growth that followed, Oklahoma became the 46th state.

Fast Facts

- The oldest military medal? Probably the Gold of Valor. It was awarded by the Egyptian pharaohs around 1500 B.C.

- The Hundred Years War lasted 116 years.

- What's with General George Patton's ivory-handled revolvers? He started carrying revolvers in 1916 after he nearly blew his own leg off with the Army's newfangled automatic pistol.

- The last soldier of World War II, Japan's Lieutenant Hiroo Onoda, didn't surrender until 1974, having fought a guerilla war on the Philippine island of Lubang since early 1945. For 29 years, he refused to be fooled by ridiculous Allied stories about the war ending in 1945 and only gave up the fight after his old unit commander was flown to the Philippines and ordered him to lay down his arms.

- Sailing into space: Pieces of Germany's High Seas Fleet, scuttled off Scotland at the end of World War I, have been used to build deep-space probes.

- The longest-running mercenary contract belongs to the world's smallest standing army—the Vatican's Swiss Guards, a 100-man company first hired by Pope Julius II in 1506.

- Britain's early 20th-century super-weapon, the battleship H.M.S. Dreadnought, was fitted with ultramodern weapons, so her builders naturally omitted the ancient ram from her design. Her only kill was a submarine, which she sunk by ramming it.

- During his invasion of England in 1014, King Olaf's fleet of Viking ships managed to pull down London's wooden Thames River bridge. (Hence, the children's song "London Bridge Is Falling Down.")

- Among his numerous contributions to astronomy, Galileo was the first to observe that the Milky Way was composed of stars.

ELEVATING INVENTION TO NEW HEIGHTS

When Elisha Graves Otis and his sons began their elevator business in the 1850s, the solid brick buildings of America's cities had four-story height limits. By the 1920s, with the widespread adoption of safe, power-driven lifts, skyscrapers had replaced church steeples as the hallmarks of urban design.

Elevators to lift cargo have been around since the pyramidal ziggurats of ancient Iraq. In 236 B.C., the Greek scientist Archimedes used his knowledge of levers to deploy beast- and slave-drawn hoists. In 1743, technicians of French King Louis XV devised a "flying chair," with pulleys and weights running down the royal chimney, to carry his mistress, Madame de Pompadour, in and out of the palace's upper floor.

AN UPLIFTING BACKGROUND

A descendant of American Revolutionary James Otis, Elisha Otis won a hard-earned path to success. Born in Vermont in 1811, Otis was a stereotype of Yankee ingenuity. In the 1840s, as a senior mechanic in a bedstead factory in Albany, New York, he patented a railroad safety brake, critical to quickly and safely hauling freight in and out of the factories of the Industrial Revolution. By 1852, Otis was a master mechanic at another bedstead firm in Yonkers, New York. He began tinkering with a safety lift for its warehouse, but the company went belly-up. Otis was mulling a move to California's Gold Rush country when a furniture maker asked him to build two safety elevators. A pair of workers at the manufacturer had died when a cable to their lift broke. Fighting off chronically poor health, Otis established his own company and set to work.

ALL SAFE

In 1854, Otis—looking quite distinguished in a full beard and top hat—took to a platform at the Crystal Palace exposition in New York. A rope had pulled his newfangled "hoisting apparatus" high up a shaft, its side open to public view. With a flourish, he waved an ax toward the nervous onlookers crowding the hall. Then, with a quick motion, Otis cleaved the rope with the ax. The onlookers gasped as the elevator began its downward plunge—only to suddenly stop after a three-inch fall.

Elisha Otis tipped his hat and proclaimed: "All safe, gentlemen, all safe."

Otis's means of making his freight elevators safe was straightforward. He attached a wagon wheel's taut springs to the elevator ropes. "If the rope snapped," explained *Smithsonian* magazine, "the ends of the steel spring would flare out, forcing two large latches to lock into ratchets on either side of the platform."

Otis soon patented an elevator driven by a tiny steam engine, permitting small enterprises like retail stores to purchase their own lifts. Modern department stores with multiple floors, such as Macy's, began to appear.

Despite the technical wizardry, Elisha Otis's commercial success and business sense were limited. Two years after his successful demonstration—despite a follow-up exhibit at P. T. Barnum's Traveling World's Fair—sales of Otis elevators totaled less than $14,000 a year. Even if proceeds picked up, wrote Otis's son Charles, "Father will manage in such a way [as] to lose it all," going "crazy over some wild fancy for the future." Five years later, in 1861, Otis died at age 49 of "nervous depression and diphtheria." He left his two sons a business that was $3,200 in the red.

SUCCESS

Charles and Norton Otis proved better businessmen and rivaled their father as technicians, making important improvements to their useful device. By 1873, Otis Brothers & Company, revenues soaring, had installed 2,000 elevators into buildings. Replacing steam-powered lifts, their hydraulic elevators sat on steel tubes sunk into shafts deep below the buildings. An influx of water pushed the platforms up. Reducing the water pressure lowered the elevators.

Where hotel guests previously had preferred the accessible first floor, they now opted to "make the transit with ease," boasted an Otis catalog, to the top floors, which offered "an exemption from noise, dust and exhalations of every kind."

Though taken for granted today, elevators were the height of opulence then. The Otis elevator in Gramercy Park, New York, which dates from 1883 and is still running, was made of upholstered seating and walnut paneling. Another elevator from that era in Saratoga Springs, New York, was outfitted with chandeliers and paneled in ebony and tulipwood.

Riding the skyscraper boom, the Otis firm went from one noted project to another. In 1889, the firm completed lifts for the bottom section of the Eiffel Tower. Around 1900, it bought the patents to a related invention, the escalator. In 1913, the Otis firm installed 26 electric elevators for the world's then-tallest structure, New York's 60-story Woolworth Building. In 1931, Otis installed 73 elevators and more than 120 miles of cables in another record-breaker, the 1,250-foot Empire State Building.

SETTING THE CEILING

All the while, along with enhancements, such as push-button controls, came improvements in speed. Cities constantly changed their elevator "speed limits"—from a leisurely 40 feet a minute for Elisha Otis's original safety lifts, to a speedy 1,200 feet a minute in the 1930s, to today's contraptions, which, at 2,000 feet per minute can put a churning knot of G-force in the stomachs of passengers hurtling to their destination.

"That's probably as much vertical speed as most people can tolerate," says an Otis engineer.

Along the way, the elevator industry quashed early fears that speedy lifts were bad for people. In the 1890s, *Scientific American* wrote that the body parts of elevator passengers came to a halt at different rates, triggering mysterious ailments.

Like the earlier notion that fast trains would choke passengers by pushing oxygen away from their mouths, that theory has since been debunked.

Timeline

Continued from page 115.

1500–1250 B.C.

Dawn of the Iron Age. Monotheism raises eyebrows in Egypt. The Hittites establish an empire in Anatolia, but in 1274 Egypt's King Ramses II roundly defeats the Hittites at the Battle of Kadesh; ten years later the Egyptian and Hittite empires sign the world's first recorded peace treaty. Moses leads Israelites out of Egypt and into Canaan. Nigerian metalworkers begin working with iron. Phoenician seafarers settle on Cyprus. A massive volcanic eruption destroys royal palaces on Crete; Minoan dominance of the eastern Mediterranean comes to an abrupt end, and Greco-Phoenician sea trade flourishes.

1250–1000 B.C.

Greeks invade Troy and level it, inspiring Homer's epic, the *Iliad,* centuries later. In Palestine, King David rules an Israelite monarchy. Mexico's Olmecs produce stone monuments, obsidian tools, and picture writing. Phoenicians develop an alphabet and begin colonizing Carthage and Spain. Mycenaean armorers develop bronze helmets and plate armor.

1000–800 B.C.

Solomon builds his temple in Jerusalem as Hebrew elders begin compiling the Old Testament. Assyrian power expands, and by 850, the empire extends from the Tigris River to the Mediterranean Sea. Egyptians develop the sundial to keep time. Etruscans immigrate into the Italian peninsula. Homer composes the *Iliad.* Siberians raise reindeer in herds, and writing systems develop among the Olmecs in Mesoamerica. Chinese develop gunpowder, an organized postal service, and an early feudal system under the ruling Zhou Dynasty.

800–700 B.C.

Rise of the Greeks. Greek mythology is described in Hesiod's *Theogeny.* Across the Aegean, 50-oared *pentekonter* boats, soon succeeded by their larger cousins, double-banked *biremes,* form the backbone of naval power in the Greek world. Greeks inaugurate the Olympic Games, build wooden temples on the Acropolis, and colonize Byzantium and Sicily. Etruscans dominate central Italy; Rome is founded by Romulus; and a Latin alphabet develops. The Brahmi writing system develops in India, and the oldest of the Hindu Upanishads are written.

700–600 B.C.

A tough set of Athenian laws are codified by the tyrannical Draco (giving us the word "draconian"). Assyria's King Sargon II conquers much of Palestine and Syria and defeats the Hittites, Chaldeans, and Samarians; his successors conquer much of Egypt but cannot hold it for long. The Assyrian Empire promotes art and culture and even assembles a great library at Nineveh, but it falls to the Medes (Persians) and succumbs to a Chaldean revolt in Babylonia. Babylon, the center of the Chaldean Empire, is the world's largest city, with a population exceeding

Timeline

200,000; to beautify his imperial seat, King Nebuchadnezzar II builds Babylon's famed Hanging Gardens. In Japan, the Jimmu Dynasty begins, inaugurating the island's legendary period.

600–500 B.C.

Babylonians capture and destroy Jerusalem, but soon fall to Cyrus the Great and the Persian Empire 50 years later. Cyrus and his successors build the most powerful empire until the era of Alexander the Great. To the west, Carthage breaks away from Phoenicia and rules the western Mediterranean. In Greece, Anaximander draws the first map of the world, while primitive democracy, drama, poetry, and Pythagorean mathematics flourish. Greek colonists battle the Carthaginians at sea and compete for dominance along the lucrative sea trade routes. Romans overthrow their Etruscan rulers. Taoism and Confucianism take root in China, which uses blast furnaces to produce iron and makes great advances in herbal medicine. Buddhism is founded in India.

500–479 B.C.

Three Strikes, You're Out. Persia invades Greece three times, losing its transport fleet in a storm off the Greek coast in 492, then losing to the Athenians at Marathon in 490. On the third try, the Persians sweep through Greece and destroy Athens, but are soundly defeated at sea by the Greeks at Salamis. Persia's King Xerxes returns to Persia in defeat, and the remnants of his army are destroyed at Platea a year later, ushering in the Golden Age of Greece. Herodotus, the "Father of History," is born. Elsewhere, Chinese astronomers document the planetary grouping as China enters its period of the "Warring States." Sicilian Greeks repel a Carthaginian invasion.

476 B.C.

China's Zhou Dynasty collapses, and the empire's vast lands are carved up among petty kingdoms. The so-called "Period of the Warring States" will last until the rise of the Ch'in Dynasty in 221 B.C.

c. 469 B.C.

Earthquake! Some 20,000 Spartans die in one of the most devastating earthquakes ever recorded, disrupting—but not halting—the growing power of Sparta.

431–403 B.C.

The Peloponnesian War pits the Athenian empire against Sparta and her allies. Athens takes the lead with early victories at sea, but the Peloponnesian coalition eventually defeats the Athenian fleet and breaks Athenian power in eastern Greece.

335 B.C.

It's All Greek to Me. Alexander the Great goes on a rampage across the Balkans, the Middle East, Asia Minor, and India, establishing the ancient world's greatest empire and spreading Hellenic culture across southern Asia. He dies, allegedly of a fever, in 323 B.C., one month short of his thirty-third birthday.

Wondering what happened next?
Turn to page 236 to find out!

THE OTHER SECESSIONISTS

Until 1851, Mormons had their very own state called Deseret.
But the dream of Mormon autonomy was not ultimately achieved.

The Church of Jesus Christ of Latter Day Saints values purity and hard work paramount among the virtues of the faithful. Certainly, the Mormons who fled persecution in the early 19th century, moving westward across North America, were a resilient lot determined to maintain their faith in the face of increasingly hostile gentiles. When their leader Joseph Smith was killed by a mob in Illinois, the Mormons fled to a sparsely inhabited region in the Great Basin. Under Brigham Young's leadership, pioneer settlements of Mormons prospered as far north as the Oregon territory and as far west as the Pacific Ocean. When the United States annexed this land following its war with Mexico, the Latter Day Saints saw an opportunity to achieve statehood. To some, it seemed that the promised Zion in the New World was prepared— the place where the church elders could maintain the people's virtue until the prophesied fall of the U.S. government.

DESERET BECOMES UTAH

Meeting in Salt Lake City in early 1849, the Latter Day Saints established the state of Deseret—the name taken from the Book of Mormon in reference to the industrious, communal, and admirable honeybee. Brigham Young, the nominal head of the new state, sent representatives to the U.S. Congress with a proposed state constitution borrowed hastily from that of Illinois. The Saints proposed that their new state encompass all the territory from Mexico to Oregon and from the Green River to the Sierra Madre, including a portion of the California coast where Los Angeles now stands. The House of Representatives denied the Mormon's claim to statehood and opted instead to create the Utah Territory, with Brigham Young as provisional governor. For their part, the Mormon representatives considered the choice of an Indian name for their perceived Zion particularly offensive.

NOT GOOD ENOUGH

Territorial status was not what the Deseret General Assembly had envisioned when they sent their request for statehood to Congress. Only with statehood, on their own terms, could they set the agenda for their land. Moreover, while its representatives were being dismissed by the federal government, the Deseret General Assembly had truly been industrious. In a short time, it had appointed judges, formed a militia, enacted taxes, outlawed gambling, and incorporated the Church of Latter Day Saints.

Whatever the federal government chose to call it, the new territory was fiercely loyal to the Church of Latter Day Saints, and its inhabitants were determined to defend it from encroachment. Mormon zealots began to lash out at gentiles who traveled through their land. For its part, the federal government became increasingly frustrated by this group of religious separatists who seemed determined to remain autonomous. Several non-Mormon, territorial governors were sent to the area with the intention of replacing Young, who ceded his title but did not relinquish his power.

THE UTAH WAR

The situation reached a boiling point in 1857 after a band of church zealots massacred a group of pioneers traveling through the territory. President Buchanan dispatched Colonel A. S. Johnston with a federal army to assert authority over the territory and quell its inhabitants. Disdainful of the federal troops, yet incapable of mounting an effective defense, the Mormon settlers fled from their villages ahead of Johnston's army. Hundreds of men, women, and children laden with supplies trekked across the barren land toward Salt Lake City. With troops approaching, Brigham Young threatened to burn the city rather than allow a "foreign army" to enter it.

Contrary to Buchanan's expectations, the war was immensely unpopular with the American public, who considered the entire expedition unnecessary and expensive. Therefore, Buchanan was happy to end it peacefully in 1858 after the Mormons allowed federally appointed Governor Alfred Cumming to take office. Aside from destroyed property, the Utah War, or "Buchanan's Blunder" as it was called, ended without a single pitched battle.

GHOST GOVERNMENT

Officially, the State of Deseret was dissolved in 1851 when the U.S. government established the Utah Territory. Unofficially, however, it continued to exist, as the Utah General Assembly disregarded the protests of a succession of federal governors and continued to meet and pass resolutions for the State of Deseret. In 1862, Brigham Young officially reconvened the Deseret General Assembly, which drew up a new resolution for statehood. This and subsequent efforts, including one in 1872 that dropped the demand for the name "Deseret" from the text, failed to meet federal approval. When the Eastern and Western railroads joined with the ceremonial driving of the golden spike at Promontory Point, Utah, in 1869, the dream of Deseret ended with the promised flood of new arrivals that would soon dilute the Mormon population.

• *The Utah stone at the Washington Monument contains two references to "Deseret."*

• *The hard-working Deseret honeybee survives today in the beehive on the Utah flag.*

• *The Mormon attempt to create a state was not unprecedented in American history. Settlers in both Tennessee and Oregon had taken similar steps until suitable territories were established by Congress.*

• *Coins were minted for use in Utah by the Church of Latter Day Saints in 1849, 1850, and 1860.*

• *Approximately 30,000 people were evacuated from their homes during the Utah War.*

Fast Facts

- Of the classical Greek city-states, Sparta gets the women's rights prize (such as it might be). Sparta was the only city to mandate public education for girls, and only at Sparta did women strip for athletics, just as all Greek men did.

- What kind of a guy was Socrates? He wandered around barefoot and shirtless, dependent upon handouts from friends. He never had a real job to speak of.

- The ancient Olympics weren't always a fun time. The heat was miserable, the site was buggy, and the concessions served shabby, overpriced food. Sanitation was minimal. A slave-owner once threatened to send an errant charge to the Games as punishment.

- All those splendid Greek statues you see in off-white marble? Most used to be painted in realistic colors. We know because tiny bits of paint remain embedded in nooks and crannies.

- The pigtail common to Chinese peasant men until early in the 20th century dated back to a Manchu emperor in the 1600s. Enforcing this Manchu style on the Chinese served as a constant reminder of Manchu overlordship.

- Footbinding—the deformation of girls' feet into barely walkable little triangles—began in China around A.D. 1000. It took hundreds of years for this painful, crippling practice to die out.

- Those who attended Genghis Khan's burial (A.D. 1227)—all 2,900 of them—were executed. Evidently the Mongols were fairly sure someone would try to plunder the grave.

- Ancient Chinese used ants to kill citrus pests.

- Early medieval European monarchs had outstanding names. Who can resist Charles the Bald (reigned 823–877), Louis the Stammerer (877–879), Charles the Fat (881–887), Louis the Blind (901–905), or Charles the Simple (893–922)?

CRACKING THE CODE OF DA VINCI'S MASTERPIECE

After centuries of beguiling viewers—and maddening artists and scientists who tried to uncover its secrets—Leonardo da Vinci's Mona Lisa *may have finally revealed her secret code.*

The Renaissance genius began his portrait of Lisa del Giocondo, a Florentine gentlewoman, in 1503 and is believed to have finished the painting just before his death in 1519. Using a process of brushwork he called "sfumato" (from the Italian *fumo*, meaning smoke), da Vinci said his technique created a painting "without lines or borders, in the manner of smoke or beyond the focus plane." Although he left many notes on his other projects, Leonardo never explained how he created the subtle effects of light and shadow that give his masterwork an unworldly, three-dimensional quality.

Although the painting has been studied extensively over the centuries, even the most modern scientific instruments have been unable to uncover its secrets. Much of the brushwork on the portrait's face and hands is too small to be studied by X-ray or microscope. French artist and art historian Jacques Franck, however, believes he has discovered da Vinci's methods through his own trial and error. According to Franck, after completing a conventional sketch of his subject, da Vinci applied a base coat of pale yellow imprimatura—a diluted semiopaque wash—then began one of history's greatest creative marathons. Using minute crosshatching techniques, da Vinci spent more than 15 years brushing on 30 successive layers of paint. Apparently requiring a magnifying glass, the process took 30 to 40 small dots of oil paint smaller than the head of a pin to cover one square millimeter of canvas. Franck believes da Vinci applied additional layers of imprimatura between each layer of paint to further soften lines and blend colors, creating successively finer layers of shading and tones.

Although Franck's conclusions have been disputed by some art historians, he has convincingly reproduced the effects with his own copies of small sections of the painting. A recent exhibit at the Uffizi Gallery in Florence displayed six panels by Franck re-creating one of Mona Lisa's eyes, illustrating the step-by-step process of how Leonardo may have worked. Though his artistic sleuthing remains controversial, Franck points out that the use of minute dots of paint—similar to the pointillism developed by modern artists—had been used since Roman times and is clearly evident in some of da Vinci's earlier paintings. With the *Mona Lisa*, Leonardo apparently took the technique to an unmatched level of virtuosity.

FAMOUS LAST WORDS

"Art is never finished, only abandoned."

"A picture or representation of human figures, ought to be done in such a way as that the spectator may easily recognise, by means of their attitudes, the purpose in their minds."

"I have been impressed with the urgency of doing. Knowing is not enough; we must apply. Being willing is not enough; we must do."

"Life is pretty simple: You do some stuff. Most fails. Some works. You do more of what works. If it works big, others quickly copy it. Then you do something else. The trick is the doing something else."

—ALL QUOTES FROM LEONARDO DA VINCI

THE SECRET OF
THE STONES

Part of the enduring charm of Stonehenge—
that curious structure of rocks located in Wiltshire County,
southern England—is that it continues to defy explanation,
baffling experts throughout the centuries.

Though no one can definitively say who erected this massive monument, when and why they built it, and how they did so without the aid of modern machinery, there are no shortage of theories. So let's hear from the experts:

Archaeologists: Speculate that the site first took shape about 5,000 years ago, with the first stones being laid in 3000 B.C. The monument was finally completed in 1500 B.C., perhaps serving as a memorial to fallen warriors, as the burial mounds that surround the site might indicate.

Geologists: Claim that 80 of the 4-ton rocks at Stonehenge, known as bluestones, were quarried from the Prescelly Mountains in Wales—240 miles away—and then transported by sled and barge to their current location.

Astronomers: Observe that builders placed the rocks in concentric circles, thus creating a massive solar observatory through which early man could predict the arrival of eclipses and follow the passage of the seasons. On the longest day of the year, the rising sun appears directly behind one of the main stones, the so-called "Heel Stone."

Historians: Think that the stones form the walls of an ancient temple—a place for people to worship the heavens. In later times, it was used by Druids to celebrate their pagan festivals.

Conspiracy theorists: Believe Stonehenge was placed there by a UFO.

CULTURE AND HISTORY OF THE CHEROKEE

*When 16th-century European explorers first began exploring what
would later be called the United States, they found
a land already inhabited by a variety of groups. Among these
were a people living in the southeast corner of the continent
who referred to themselves as the* Aniyunwiya, *or "the principal
people." Their Creek Indian neighbors, however, called them the*
Tsalagi, *and the white tongue morphed that word
into Cherokee, the name generally used today.*

The origin of the Cherokee is uncertain at best. Tribal legend
speaks of an ancient time of migration, which some historians
have projected as far back as the time of a land bridge linking
North America to Asia. Linguists report that the Cherokee language is linked to the Iroquois, who lived far to the north; others
point out that traditional Cherokee crafts bear a resemblance
to those of the people of the Amazon basin in South America.
Regardless of their origin, the Cherokee held sway over a great
deal of land when Spaniard Hernando de Soto made contact with
the tribe in the 1540s.

De Soto did not find the gold he was looking for in Cherokee territory. What he did find was a people who had heard of his treatment of other tribes and did everything they could to hasten his
exit from their land. They quickly traded him some food and other
supplies—including two buffalo skins, the first European contact
with the animal, which at the time ranged as far east as the Atlantic coast—and suggested that he might be better off looking to
the west. With that, de Soto headed off. The total number de Soto
found living in their traditional lands is a matter of speculation;
the oldest reliable count dates from 130 years later, long after the
smallpox the Spaniard left behind had wreaked havoc on the tribe.
The disease left somewhere between 25,000 to 50,000 people
alive after killing an estimated 75 percent of the natives.

CULTURE SHOCK

The Cherokee were quick to realize that white intruders were there to stay, and they did what they could to adapt to the changing world. On the arrival of the British, they became active trading partners, seeking to improve their situation through the acquisition of European goods and guns. They also became military allies—by many accounts, a trade at which they excelled—fighting with the British against the French and later against the Colonists in the American Revolution. The British, however, always viewed their Cherokee allies with suspicion, the effects of which ranged from the occasional massacre to the imposition of treaties demanding that the British be allowed to construct forts in Cherokee territory. This ceding of property was only the beginning of one of the biggest land-grabs in history, culminating in the 1838 Trail of Tears, in which 17,000 Cherokee were forcibly sent west, resulting in thousands of deaths along the way.

Part of the difficulty with the early treaties was that the Europeans were in the habit of making them with anyone who claimed they represented the tribe; in reality, nobody could speak for all of the Cherokee. Their system was one of local autonomous government, with each village being responsible for its own affairs. The individual villages even had two chiefs: a White Chief in charge of domestic decisions and a Red Chief in charge of war and general relations with outsiders. The society itself was matrilineal and focused on a spiritual balance that the Cherokee believed existed between lower and higher worlds, with the earth caught in the middle. Europeans were ill-suited to understanding such a culture. In turn, the Cherokee realized that their society was ill-suited to dealing with Europeans.

THE TIMES, THEY ARE A-CHANGIN'

Cherokee society proved up to the challenge, however. Part of the advance was because of Sequoyah. Sequoyah was a silversmith who devised the first syllabary for the Cherokee language in 1821. Although he was illiterate, he had observed the white man's system of written communication. His Talking Leaves system, consisting of more than 80 symbols that each represented a syllable of Cherokee speech, was rapidly adopted and soon the Cherokee had a higher literacy rate than most of their white neighbors. One immediate result was the publication of a newspaper, *The Cherokee Phoenix*, in 1828; it was soon renamed the *Cherokee Phoenix and Indian Advocate* to indicate that its pages addressed issues faced by Native Americans of all tribes.

Along with the alphabet, the 1820s proved a time of change for Cherokee society as a whole. Realizing that they must deal with the white man on his terms, the Cherokee had unified their autonomous tribes by the close of the decade, adopting a constitution that provided for a formal judiciary and elected legislature, electing John Ross as principal chief, and declaring themselves to be an independent nation. They took the nearly unheard of step of sending Indian representatives to Washington, D.C., to persuade both the Congress and the Supreme Court that the United States ought to be held to both the spirit as well as the letter of various treaties that were signed over the years. However, despite favorably impressing many with the quality of their arguments, their efforts proved fruitless, and the Cherokee joined their Native American brothers—being treated as second-class citizens for decades to come.

The repercussions from the almost unimaginable changes imposed on the Cherokee as European settlers came to dominate the continent echo to the current day. However, Cherokee society has proved itself equal to the task, and today its people are the most numerous of any Native American population, and the leadership of various parts of the tribe continues to actively work to remedy past inequities.

FAMOUS LAST WORDS

"It is but a little spot of ground that you ask, and I am willing that your people should live upon it."

—CHEROKEE CHIEF ATTAKULLAKULLA,
WRITING TO JOHN STUART, BRITISH AGENT

THE MAID OF ORLÉANS

The Hundred Years War was a disaster for France.
They had not won a major battle in a generation. The population
was still reeling from the ravages of the Black Death. England
controlled most of northern France. To add insult to injury, their
ruler, Charles VI, suffered from spells of insanity that made him
unfit to rule. When he died, a civil war broke out among the royal
family over who would rule next. France needed a savior.
They found her in a 17-year-old peasant girl named Joan.

Joan was born on January 6, 1412, in the eastern
French village of Domremy. It seems that she
led a normal life until around 1424, when she
started having visions of St. Michael (commander of the armies of heaven) as well as
St. Catherine and St. Margaret (both early
Christian martyrs). God had taken pity on
the French people, they told Joan, and
she was chosen to drive the English out
of France and ensure the coronation of
Charles VII.

FROM SERF TO SAVIOR

In March 1429, Joan managed to get an audience with Charles,
the leader of the French army (the other side of the royal family
had taken sides with the English). She got his attention by repeat-
ing for him a private prayer he had made the previous November.
Charles sent her to be evaluated by a group of theologians, and
when they gave their approval, he placed her in titular (or ceremonial) command of the French army.

Charles's first mission for Joan was to break the siege on the city
of Orléans. When Joan joined the army, she restored discipline by
running off the prostitutes, outlawing swearing, and requiring all
soldiers to go to church. She led the army into battle at Orléans,

giving encouragement to the troops by sharing the same dangers they did. Within nine days, she had lifted the siege and had the English army on the run. Her discipline and her victory had raised the morale of the army and attracted many more volunteers, who wanted to fight for the "Maid of Orléans."

Fulfilling her vision, Joan led Charles and 12,000 men through English-controlled territory to Reims where, on July 17, 1429, he was crowned Charles VII.

FROM SAVIOR TO HERETIC

Joan continued to lead men into battle after Charles's coronation, but court politics and a wound she had suffered while trying to liberate Paris restricted her command to only minor companies.

Just as the saints told of her future, they also foretold her end. Around Easter 1430, Joan revealed that she would be captured "before St. John's day" (June 24). The saints were true to their word: On May 23, 1430, during a skirmish with the Burgundians (the rival faction of the French royal family), Joan was taken prisoner.

Some say that Charles offered a ransom for Joan and tried to rescue her. Others contend that he did nothing to try to save her. Whatever the case, after four months the French sold her to the English for 10,000 francs.

The English put her on trial from February 21 to March 17, 1431. Convicted of heresy, she was burned at the stake on May 30, 1431; her ashes were thrown into the Seine River.

FROM HERETIC TO SAINT

The Hundred Years War continued for another 22 years after Joan's death, but her efforts had turned the tide in France's favor. Immediately after the war, Pope Callixtus II reopened her case and—declaring her a martyr—found her innocent of heresy. Joan of Arc was beatified in 1902 and canonized as a saint in 1920.

THE SHORT-LIVED 1942 GERMAN INVASION OF AMERICA

Why did the least effective sabotage operation in history fail so miserably?

In June 1942, two Nazi submarines delivered eight saboteurs to America's coast—four to Long Island and four to Florida. Their mission: implement a series of industrial bombings and spread fear in the heart of the enemy. The men, trained agents of the Nazi intelligence unit known as the *Abwehr*, were chosen for their impeccable Nazi credentials, knowledge of American culture, and fluent English. The teams were trained to use explosives, given approximately $50,000 for expenses and bribes, and supplied with a list of contacts written in invisible ink on handkerchiefs.

Within two weeks of landing, however, all eight members of Operation Pastorius were in FBI custody and waiting to stand trial for their lives.

FLAWED FROM THE START

The captain of submarine U-202, Kptlt. Lindner, was decidedly unhappy with his mission. He was to deliver four saboteurs to the New York coast and then make his way south to prey on enemy shipping. Lindner suspected that the saboteurs lacked true Nazi fervor and dedication to their mission. He was nervous that, if captured, they would reveal essential details about the U-boats. If Lindner had known how much information the saboteurs' leader, George Dasch, would eventually relay to the Americans, he would certainly have shot him on sight.

As it was, Kptlt. Lindner successfully got the men ashore, after which U-202 became moored on a sandbar. With daylight only a few hours away, Lindner could not afford to await the tide. He ordered a series of furious, noisy maneuvers, which—after several attempts—succeeded in freeing the submarine.

On the beach, Dasch and the members of his team encountered a young Coast Guard seaman named John Cullen who soon became suspicious. Rather than kill the guardsman, Dasch offered a bribe, which Cullen, outnumbered, pretended to accept. When Cullen returned with other seamen, they were in time to see the conning tower of U-202 slip beneath the waves; soon thereafter they unearthed explosives and uniforms hastily buried by the Germans.

ON THE MONTAUK HIGHWAY

The Montauk Highway runs east toward Montauk and west to the Amagansett Railroad Station with trains to New York City. Shaken by their encounter with the guardsmen, the Germans began to walk east, away from their immediate goal. The rising sun soon corrected their direction, however, and as the secret agents miserably retraced their steps alongside the highway, numerous cars—including a truck full of Coast Guard seamen—passed them. Against the odds, however, the Germans reached the rail station and—from there—the anonymous safety of the city.

HOW TO PROVE YOU'RE A NAZI

The saboteurs separated into two pairs and ensconced themselves in downtown New York City hotels. With the authorities alerted to their presence, the men grew increasingly nervous while Dasch did nothing beyond purchasing new clothes for nearly a week. After speaking at length about his intentions with fellow saboteur, Ernest Peter Burger, Dasch called the FBI office in New York and stated that he would have information for J. Edgar Hoover in two days. He then traveled by rail to Washington, D.C., where he checked into a hotel and phoned the FBI. Using the pseudonym Franz Daniel Pastorius, Dasch demanded to speak with J. Edgar Hoover regarding important information about German agents.

Whatever hopes for a sensational, thankful, or decisive response Dasch might have held prior to phoning the FBI, however, rapidly dissipated as the G-man took a message and subsequently dismissed him as a crank caller. Dasch then went to the bureau in person and was sent from office to office with his fantastic story of submarines, explosives, and German agents extant in both New York and Florida. Finally, after he dropped $84,000 in cash on an agent's desk, the FBI took Dasch seriously and interrogated him for nearly 13 hours. During the course of the interrogation, Dasch outlined everything from the probable whereabouts of the other agents to the diving depth of the submarines that had carried them to America.

WHY DID DASCH TURN TRAITOR?

George Dasch was 39 years old at the time of Operation Pastorius; he felt that the world had passed him over for too long. First, as a poor German immigrant to the United States in the 1920s, he detested the dreary, unimportant work available to him. And the Nazis were unable to provide him with the recognition and glory that he considered his due.

During the course of his confession to the FBI, Dasch claimed that he had never intended to carry out his destructive mission; rather, he had meant to turn himself in from the beginning. Whether Dasch really expected a parade in his honor or was merely hedging his confession in hopes of lenient treatment is uncertain. What is known is that Dasch and Burger's death sentences were commuted to lengthy prison terms while the other six would-be saboteurs died in the electric chair.

After the war, Dasch was deported to Germany where he was viewed as a traitor and a coward. A subsequent book by Dasch about his experiences failed to bolster his reputation. George Dasch died in 1992.

- *Operation Pastorius was over before it even started: One of the members got drunk in a Paris bar and loudly announced that he was a secret agent.*

- *Franz Daniel Pastorious was the leader of a 17th-century group of German immigrants to the New World who founded what would become Germantown, Pennsylvania.*

THE TRUTH AND THE MYTH OF THE NINJA

Ninjas were the special forces of feudal Japan.
Trained in assassination, espionage, and guerilla warfare,
ninjas inspired fear in both rulers and commoners alike.

Over the years, the ninja has taken on a mythical status. But like most myths, the story is filled with both fact and fiction.

HUMBLE BEGINNINGS

Ninjas got their start as priests living in the mountains of Japan. Harassed by the central government and local samurai, they resorted to using *Nonuse* (the art of stealth)—what we would call guerilla warfare. Their use of secrecy and stealth didn't win them many friends, but it secured them a role in the civil wars to come.

From roughly 794 to 1192, local rulers fought to gain control of Japan. While the Samurai fought the wars, it was left to the mountain priests to do those things that the Samurai considered cowardly—namely spying, sneaking around to gather information, and trying to assassinate their rivals. This is when the ninja (*nin*, meaning "concealment" and *sha*, meaning "person") was born.

FROM PRIESTS TO NINJAS

The ninja made their reputation during the Japanese civil wars. They worked for anybody—often for both sides at the same time. In addition to being scouts, a favorite ninja job was to sneak into a castle under siege and cause as much chaos as possible. Dressed like the enemy, they made their way into enemy camps to set fires, start rebellions in the ranks, steal flags, and generally keep the pressure on their opponents so that when the army outside stormed the gates, the defenders would give up without a fight.

Ninjas used weapons uniquely suited to them. They wore claws on their gloves to help them fight and climb. Because the ownership of weapons was forbidden to all but the samurai, ninjas used a common farming tool called a sickle for much of their fighting. And, of course, they used the throwing stars that everybody sees in the movies, though the real ninjas weren't nearly as accurate as their Hollywood counterparts. They also used invisibility weapons, usually an eggshell filled with an eye irritant or a bit of gunpowder with a fuse in case they had to make a quick getaway.

Eventually the Japanese civil wars came to an end, and the ninjas found themselves out of a job. The ninjas were gone but certainly not forgotten. The exploits of the ninja made their way into popular literature and eventually into legend.

NINJA FACT AND FICTION

The ninja were feared for their ability to assassinate their rivals, but there was never a documented case of any ruler being killed by a ninja. They tried, of course, but they were never successful.

Although ninjas are typically thought to be male, there were female ninjas as well. Whether male or female, one thing is certain: Ninjas didn't run around in black pajamas as Hollywood would have you believe.

This misconception originated in Kabuki Theater. During shows, the prop movers wore all black to shift things around while the play was going on. Everybody was supposed to ignore the people in black, pretending they were invisible. So when it became time for ninjas to be played in the theater, they wore the same black dress as the prop movers to symbolize their gift of invisibility. The crowds bought it, and the black ninja suit was born.

The exploits of the ninja came to the West mainly after World War II. Like the Japanese theater, Hollywood's version of the ninja portrayed them either as an almost unbeatable mystical foe or as a clumsy fighter that the hero of the movie could take on singlehandedly.

Although there are martial arts schools that teach ninja techniques, the ninja have faded into history and legend.

HOPE FLOATS

It was a given: Boats made of metal would sink straight to the bottom of the ocean. And a heavier-than-air flying craft? An impossibility!

Metal ships were so obviously an impossibility that no one made a serious effort to float steel until the end of the 18th century. Although an enterprising shipbuilder crafted a canal barge in 1787, and in 1815 England's Robert Dickenson patented a design for an iron ship, it was generally accepted—with almost no discussion—that seagoing vessels made of metal would sink.

It was nine years after Dickenson's patent before anyone attempted to build an iron passenger vessel—the Scottish vessel *Vulcan*—and no large navy dared field an iron-hulled fighting ship until Mexico bought one for its wars against Texas and Yucatán in the early 1840s.

At the other end of the transportation spectrum, the idea of a heavier-than-air flying machine was roundly ridiculed by the scientific establishment in the early 1900s. In 1902, the year before Wilbur and Orville Wright took their famous flight, the U.S. Navy's chief engineer declared the very idea to be "absurd." The following year, an eminent professor of mathematics and astronomy at Johns Hopkins University proved to the world that a heavier-than-air craft was "scientifically impossible." Undeterred by this scientific pronouncement, a few weeks later the Wright brothers took their "flyer" to Kitty Hawk, North Carolina, and changed the world. Even after photographs circulated of the historic flight, the Wright brothers's hometown newspaper refused to print anything about their revolutionary contraption because, as the editor admitted, "We didn't believe it."

THE MYSTERY OF EASTER ISLAND

On Easter Sunday in 1722, a Dutch ship landed on a small island 2,300 miles from the coast of South America. Polynesian explorers had preceded them by a thousand years or more, and the Europeans found the descendants of those early visitors still living on the island. They also found a strange collection of almost 900 enormous stone heads, or moai, *standing with their backs to the sea, gazing across the island with eyes hewn out of coral. The image of those faces haunts visitors to this day.*

ANCESTORS AT THE END OF THE LAND

Easter Island legend tells of the great Chief Hotu Matu'a, the Great Parent, striking out from Polynesia in a canoe, taking his family on a voyage across the trackless ocean in search of a new home. He made landfall on Te-Pito-te-Henua, the End of the Land, sometime between A.D. 400 and 700. Finding the island well-suited to habitation, his descendants spread out to cover much of the island, living off the natural bounty of the land and sea. With their survival assured, they built *ahu*—ceremonial sites featuring a large stone mound—and on them erected *moai*, which were representations of notable chieftains who led the island over the centuries. The *moai* weren't literal depictions of their ancestors, but rather embodied their spirit, or *mana*, and conferred blessings and protection on the islanders.

The construction of these *moai* was quite a project. A hereditary class of sculptors oversaw the main quarry, located near one of the volcanic mountains on the island. Groups of people would request a *moai* for their local *ahu*, and the sculptors would go to work, their efforts supported by gifts of food and other goods. Over time, they created 887 of the stone *moai*, averaging just over 13 feet tall and weighing around 14 tons, but ranging from one extreme of just under four feet tall to a behemoth that towered

71 feet. The *moai* were then transported across the island by a mechanism that still remains in doubt, but that may have involved rolling them on the trunks of palm trees felled for that purpose—a technique that was to have terrible repercussions for the islanders.

When Europeans first made landfall on Easter Island, they found an island full of standing *moai*. Fifty-two years later, James Cook reported that many of the statues had been toppled, and by the 1830s none were left standing. What's more, the statues hadn't just been knocked over; many of them had boulders placed at strategic locations, with the intention of decapitating the *moai* when they were pulled down. What happened?

A CULTURE ON THE BRINK

It turns out the original Dutch explorers had encountered a culture on the rebound. At the time of their arrival, they found two or three thousand living on the island, but some estimates put the population as high as fifteen thousand a century before. The story of the islanders' decline is one in which many authors find a cautionary tale: The people simply consumed natural resources to the point where their land could no longer support them. For a millennium, the islanders simply took what they needed: They fished, collected bird eggs, and chopped down trees to pursue their obsession with building *moai*. By the 1600s, life had changed: The last forests on the island disappeared, and the islanders' traditional foodstuffs disappeared from the architectural record. Local tradition tells of a time of famine and even rumored cannibalism, and it is from this time that island history reveals the appearance of the spear. Tellingly, the Polynesian words for "wood" begin to take on a connotation of wealth, a meaning found nowhere else that shares the language. Perhaps worst of all, with their forests gone, the islanders had no material to make the canoes that would have allowed them to leave their island in search of resources. They were trapped, and they turned on one another.

The Europeans found a reduced society that had just emerged from this time of terror. The respite was short-lived, however. The arrival of the foreigners seems to have come at a critical moment in the history of Easter Island. Either coincidentally or spurred on by the strangers, a warrior class seized power across the island, and different groups vied for power. Villages were burned, their resources taken by the victors, and the defeated left to starve. The warfare also led to the toppling of an enemy's *moai*—whether to capture their *mana* or simply prevent it from being used against the opposing faction. In the end, none of the *moai* remained standing.

DOWNFALL AND REBOUND

The troubles of Easter Island weren't limited to self-inflicted chaos. The arrival of the white man also introduced smallpox and syphilis; the islanders, with little natural immunity to the exotic diseases, fared no better than native populations elsewhere. As if that weren't enough, other ships arrived, collecting slaves for work in South America. The internal fighting and external pressure combined to reduce the number of native islanders to little more than a hundred by 1877—the last survivors of a people who once enjoyed a tropical paradise.

Easter Island, or Rapa Nui, was annexed by Chile in 1888. Currently, there are around 2,200 Rapanui living on the island, all descended from the 111 remaining in 1877. There are projects underway to raise the fallen *moai*. As of today, approximately 50 have been returned to their former glory.

- *The largest moai weighs between 145 and 165 tons.*

- *At one time, the moai had eyes made of coral.*

- *Easter Island's nearest neighbor is Pitcairn Island, which is 1,400 miles away.*

- *The size of Easter Island is only 64 square miles.*

HISTORY'S GREAT ESCAPES

Whether caught in the grip of wars hot and cold, palace intrigues, wilderness adventures gone wrong, or the consequences of their own misdeeds, men and women through the ages have risked great escapes to save their own lives and win their freedom.

THE BALLAD OF MARY

Though the throne of England would elude her, Mary, Queen of Scots, struggled most of her life to assume the crown she believed to be her birthright. Imprisoned in remote Lochleven Castle in 1567 during a rebellion of Scottish nobles, her pleas for help were ignored by Queen Elizabeth of England and Queen Catherine de Medici of France. In March 1568, Mary attempted to escape by disguising herself as a laundress and fleeing the castle's small island by boat. Her plan was thwarted when the boatmen, who were not part of the plot, noticed her beautiful hands and face and realized she was royalty. Mary managed to return to her cell without alerting her guards, however, and tried again with the aid of an orphan she befriended in the castle. On May 2, 1568, Mary escaped from the castle by boat to the mainland and rode to her freedom on a stolen horse, an exploit immortalized by Scottish poets, balladeers, and romantic novelist Sir Walter Scott. Her ultimate fate, however, was not as bright. She spent the last 19 years of her life imprisoned by her cousin, Queen Elizabeth I, until she was beheaded by order of the Queen in 1587.

THE WORLD'S GREATEST LOVER

Sentenced by a Venetian court to five years in prison in 1755 for Freemasonry, practicing magic, and numerous offenses of adultery, Giacomo Casanova was soon plotting his freedom. Incarcerated in a Vienna prison called "the Leads" for the lead coating its walls and roof, escape seemed impossible. Casanova, however, started work on a tunnel in his cell, using an iron rod he found in the prison yard as a digging tool. Several months into the project, he was forced to move to another cell where he would be under close surveillance. Casanova managed to slip his tool to the prisoner in an adjacent cell, a Catholic monk named Balbi. Hiding messages in the spines of books they were allowed to trade, he convinced the monk to dig a tunnel joining their cells. After digging a second tunnel from the monk's cell to the prison's roof, on the night of November 1, 1756, they used bed sheets as ropes to climb to an adjacent palace and used the iron rod to pry open several doors and reach the ground. Casanova fled Venice in a stolen gondola—the only prisoner to that time to carry out a successful escape from the Leads.

RACE WITH THE BLACKFOOT

In 1808, a member of Lewis and Clark's expedition to the Northwest, John Colter, and a hunter named Potts left the Corps of Discovery in the heart of Blackfoot Indian country to trap beaver on the Missouri River. A year earlier while traveling through the region—present-day Montana—Lewis had killed a Blackfoot trying to steal horses from their expedition. After a few weeks of trapping, Colter and Potts were paddling on a small creek when they were surrounded by Blackfoot warriors. Potts killed a Blackfoot who tried to take his rifle and was in turn shot full of arrows. Stripped naked, Colter was led to a nearby prairie and given a head start of a few hundred yards to run for his life. With hundreds of Blackfoot warriors behind him, he ran six miles across a cactus-strewn plain toward the Jefferson River, far outpacing the Indians except for one warrior who stayed close behind. Covered in cactus pins, with blood streaming from his nose, he finally turned on his pursuer. The Indian collapsed from exhaustion, and Colter killed him with his own spear before diving into the river. The Blackfoot surrounded both banks looking for Colter, at one point climbing on a pile of floating driftwood under which he had ducked to hide. The Indians gave up after dark, and Colter swam downriver for miles before coming ashore, naked and alone. Eleven days later, Colter walked into a trading post on the Yellowstone River more than a hundred miles away, sunburned and nearly starving but still alive.

ON THE LAM WITH PUBLIC ENEMY NO. 1

Among the gun-toting gangsters whose bank robbery sprees riveted America at the height of the Great Depression, none was more notorious than John Dillinger. Imprisoned in the county jail in Lima, Ohio, on October 12, 1933, Dillinger was sprung by three members of his gang who had escaped from jail in Indiana a month earlier. Posing as lawmen, they shot the sheriff, set Dillinger free, and made their getaway. Months later, they had fled to Tucson, Arizona, when their cover was blown during a fire at their motel hideout. Back in jail in Crown Point, Indiana, Dillinger was awaiting trial for the murder of a police officer when he bluffed his way out of his cell, reportedly using a wooden gun he had whittled. A few months later, Dillinger and his gang shot their way out of a bungled attempt by G-men to catch them at a remote resort in northern Wisconsin. The FBI finally caught up with Dillinger in Chicago on July 22, 1934, when he was gunned down leaving a movie theater with his girlfriend. Some researchers, however, believe that a petty criminal who had also dated Dillinger's girlfriend was the man actually shot. In 1963, *The Indianapolis Star* received a letter with a return address in Hollywood, California, from a person calling himself "John Dillinger." An attached photo resembled an older Dillinger.

UP, UP, AND AWAY, OVER THE IRON CURTAIN

On September 16, 1979, Peter Strelzyk, Günter Wetzel, their wives, and four children dropped from the night sky onto a field in West Germany, flying a homemade hot-air balloon. Strelzyk, an electrician, and Wetzel, a bricklayer, built the balloon's platform and burners in one of their basements. Their wives sewed together curtains, bed sheets, shower liners, and whatever other fabric was on hand to make the 75-foot-high balloon. A bid to escape communist East Germany during the days of the Berlin Wall, their famous flight was two years in the making, spanned 15 miles, and took 28 minutes to complete. Unsure whether they had reached freedom, the two families spent the next morning hiding in a barn, until they saw an Audi driving down a nearby road and realized they were in the West.

Fast Facts

- In the Viking Age (c. 800–1100), Britain only had about a million people.

- If Alexander VI (Renaissance era) wasn't the worst pope, it may have been John XII (955–964). He attained the Papacy as a teenager (18) and acted like a combination of lech and mobster. His reign ended, according to rumor, when an enraged husband caught his wife and His Unholiness being decidedly carnal.

- "Black" Agnes Dunbar (1312–69) is a Scottish national heroine for her defense of Castle Dunbar against an English army. She got special pleasure from standing on the battlements and shouting insults at the besiegers, who eventually gave up.

- Early medieval English coins were only legal tender for a few years, after which the authorities melted them down and gave out slightly fewer new ones. Today we call this "tax."

- During the Black Death of the 1300s, fanatical groups called Flagellants wandered Germany and France whipping themselves bloody. They believed God would call off the plague if they kept it up long enough.

- One of history's great unknown female generals was the Kahinah Dahiyan (680), a seeress and leader of a Jewish tribe in the Atlas Mountains (now Algeria) during the Islamic explosion. She led the region's diverse tribes in battle for years until the Arab armies finally overwhelmed her.

- Sati, the Indian practice of widows immolating themselves on their husbands' funeral pyres, was not limited to India. It is also recorded among some Slavic peoples in the post-Roman era before A.D. 1000.

- Frankish soldiers learned to throw the francisque (battle-axe) at the enemy's shield to shatter it for an advantage in close combat. A millennium later in World War II, the sordid Vichy French régime superimposed the Franciscan Axe on its short-lived version of the famous Tricolor flag.

187

MURDERESS

It was the trial of the century—for what may well have been the most poorly executed murder of the time.

It was a terrible thing to wake up to on that March morning in 1927. Nine-year-old Lorraine Snyder found her mother Ruth, her hands and feet bound, begging for help in the hall outside her bedroom. The girl rushed to her neighbors in the New York City suburb, and they called the police.

What the police found was more terrible still. Ruth Snyder's husband Albert lay dead in the bedroom—his skull smashed, wire strung around his neck, and a chloroform-soaked cloth shoved up his nose. His 32-year-old widow told the police that a large Italian man had knocked her out, stolen her jewelry, and assaulted her husband.

But the police found her jewels under a mattress; they also discovered a bloody pillowcase and a bloody, five-pound sash weight in a closet. As if this evidence wasn't damning enough, police located a check Ruth had written to Henry Judd Gray in the amount of $200. Gray's name was found in her little black book—along with the names of 26 other men. Little Lorraine told the cops that "Uncle Judd" had been in the home the previous night. A tie clip with the initials HJG was found on the floor.

A MARRIAGE ON THE ROCKS

Ruth Brown met Albert Snyder—14 years her senior—in 1915. He was an editor of *Motor Boating* magazine, and Ruth was a secretary. She and Albert married and had Lorraine, but their union was flawed from the start. Albert was still enthralled with his former fiancée of ten years ago, who had died; he named his boat after her and displayed her photograph in his and Ruth's home.

In the meantime, Ruth haunted the jazz clubs of Roaring Twenties Manhattan, drinking and dancing 'til the wee hours of the morning without her retiring spouse, whom she had dubbed "the old crab."

In 1925, the unhappy wife went on a blind date and met Judd Gray, a low-key corset salesperson. Soon the duo was meeting for afternoon trysts at the Waldorf Astoria—leaving Lorraine to play in the hotel lobby. Eventually, Ruth arranged for her unsuspecting husband to sign a life insurance policy worth more than $70,000.

THE JIG IS UP

At the murder scene, the police questioned Ruth about Gray. "Has he confessed?," she blurted. It wasn't long before she had spilled her guts, though she claimed it was Gray who'd actually strangled Albert.

Meanwhile, 33-year-old Gray—not exactly the sharpest knife in the drawer—was found at a hotel in Syracuse, New York. It didn't take police long to locate him; after leaving Ruth's house, he had actually stopped to ask a police officer when he could catch the next bus to New York City. Gray quickly confessed but claimed it was Ruth who'd strangled Albert. Ruth had mesmerized him, he stated, through alcohol, sex, and threats.

A month after the arrest of the murderous duo, a brief trial ensued. For three weeks, the courtroom was jammed with 1,500 spectators. In attendance were such luminaries as songwriter Irving Berlin and the producers of the Broadway play *Chicago*. Also on hand was novelist James M. Cain, who drew on the case for his novel *Double Indemnity,* later turned into a *film noir* classic by director Billy Wilder and writer Raymond Chandler.

The media frenzy over the courtroom drama even exceeded coverage of the execution of anarchist-bombers Sacco and Vanzetti. Miming the fevered reporting of city tabloids such as *The Daily News,* the stodgy *New York Times* carried page-one stories on the crime for months.

GUILTY!

Ruth and Gray were pronounced guilty after a 100-minute deliberation by an all-male jury. When their appeal failed and their plea for clemency to Governor Al Smith was denied, the deadly pair was driven 30 miles "up the river" to Sing Sing Prison's death row. En route, excited onlookers hung from rooftops to catch a glimpse of the doomed couple.

Robert Elliott, the man slated to execute the pair, professed angst over putting a woman to death; Ruth would be the first female executed since 1899. "It will be something new for me to throw the switch on a woman," he told reporters, "and I don't like the job." The former electrical contractor received threats because of his role as hangman. He asked the warden for a raise to help salve the stress. Yet, Elliott would long continue his grim work, sending a total of 387 convicts to the next world.

THE END

On January 12, 1928, at 11 P.M., 20 witnesses—chosen from the 1,500 who'd applied—watched Ruth enter the execution chamber. The Blonde Butcher, as she had been dubbed, was strapped weeping into a wooden chair, a leather cap clamped on her head. "Jesus, have mercy on me," she moaned, "for I have sinned."

In a room close by, Elliott threw a switch, and 2,000 volts surged through Ruth's body. At that instant, a reporter for the *Daily News* triggered a camera hidden in his pants. A garish photo of the murderess's last moment would appear on the paper's front page the next day. The headline read, "DEAD."

Minutes later, it was Gray's turn. Although his feet caught fire during the execution, for most witnesses it was Ruth's final moments that were stamped indelibly in their minds.

- *Ruth Snyder is often remembered—incorrectly—as the first woman put to death in America. In fact, a woman named Martha Place was executed in 1899 for the murder of her step-daughter.*

PULLING THE WOOL OVER THE EYES OF NEW YORK CITY

Throughout the 1860s and 1870s, a man named William "Boss" Tweed controlled New York City politics—and, subsequently, New York City itself. Graft, payoffs, cheating, and a healthy dose of high-quality corruption were the order of the day.

IT ALL STARTED WITH TAMMANY HALL

As the United States struggled to stand on its own following the American Revolution, political organizations began to spring up across the East Coast. The biggest and most influential was the Tammany, named after Native American Chief Tamanend. Founded on May 12, 1789, it was first a social and political organization. Then, under the leadership of Aaron Burr, the group embraced the politics of Thomas Jefferson and began supporting candidates. It was no small coincidence that Burr was elected vice president in 1800.

The strength of Tammany continued to grow, aiding the presidential election of Andrew Jackson in 1828 and 1832. By then, the powerful Democratic faction literally ran all of the politics in New York City, based out of their huge headquarters called "Tammany Hall." The organization became known by the same name.

Tammany Hall soon became a tool of the Irish Catholic community, which had quickly formed in New York City after the potato famine in Ireland drove its inhabitants to the shores of Manhattan in the mid-1840s. By the mid-1850s, Tammany Hall controlled the outcome of mayoral races, as well as other elected offices. Skilled in the art of politics, the leaders of this political machine kept New York City running—and their pockets filled.

WHO'S THE BOSS?

In New York City, a young Scottish-Irish bookkeeper and volunteer firefighter named William Tweed used his municipal position to become elected as an alderman in New York City in 1851. He soon became a member of Congress and, in 1857, became the leader of Tammany Hall.

The next 14 years became a swirl of voting fraud, judge-buying, and contract kickbacks for "Boss" Tweed and his cronies. In one instance, a carpenter received more than $360,000 for work done in a building that had very little wood in it. A furniture dealer was paid nearly $180,000 for three conference tables and 40 chairs. A plasterer received more than $130,000 for a mere two days of work. Tweed orchestrated the construction of the New York County Courthouse—a task that took nearly 20 years (2 years past his death, in fact) and cost $13 million. It was estimated that the project's price tag should have been half that figure. When an investigation was conducted into the excessive amount, the resulting report cost nearly $8,000 to print. The owner of the printing company was William Tweed.

GETTING TWEED OFF

The "Tweed Ring," which included the mayor and city comptroller, profited to the tune of an estimated $100 million to $200 million by the time the illegal activities were exposed in 1871. New York newspapers and magazines, featuring unflattering political cartoons of Tweed by illustrator Thomas Nast, revealed the graft under the Tweed Ring, and the "Boss" was brought to trial in 1874. Found guilty of embezzlement, he was sentenced to 12 years in prison, but served only a year on appeal.

Arrested the next year on a separate charge, Tweed escaped to Cuba but was found and held by Cuban officials. Before U.S. marshals could claim Tweed, however, he bolted to Spain. The Spanish government immediately grabbed him as he landed.

William Tweed was returned to a New York City jail (a jail that he may very well have had built under his regime), where he died two years later in April 1878. He was only 55.

What's in a Name?
TERRIBLY TERRIFYING

The first all-powerful Russian ruler,
Tsar Ivan the Terrible, was terrible indeed.

The Terrible One had an unhealthy dose of paranoia. It must have been his upbringing. As a child prince in Moscow, Ivan was under the thumb of *boyars,* or Russia's nobles. Feuding noble families such as the Shuiskis would break into young Ivan's palace, robbing, murdering, and even skinning alive one of the boy's advisors. The orphan (his mother had been poisoned) took out his frustrations on animals, poking out their eyes or tossing them off the palace roof. In 1543, at age 13, Ivan took some personal revenge, and had Andrei Shuiski thrown to the dogs—literally. After other vile acts, he'd sometimes publicly repent—by banging his head violently on the ground.

When his beloved wife Anastasia died in 1560 (Ivan beat his head on her coffin), the boyars refused allegiance to his young son Dmitri. Then Ivan really became terrifying. He set up the *Oprichniki,* a group of hand-picked thugs. After his forces sacked the city of Novgorod in 1570, he had its "archbishop sewn up in a bearskin and then hunted to death by a pack of hounds." Women and children fared no better; they were tied to sleds and sent into the freezing Volkhov River.

Over time, Ivan had the lover of his fourth wife impaled and had his seventh wife drowned. Perhaps afflicted by encephalitis, and likely by syphilis, his behavior grew ever stranger. He beat up his son's wife, who then miscarried, and later beat his son Ivan to death with a royal scepter (then beat his head on the coffin).

Ivan the Terrible may well have been mad as a hatter, and by the same cause that drove 19th-century hatmakers insane—mercury poisoning. When his body was exhumed in the 1960s, his bones were found to have toxic levels of the metal.

Fast Facts

- *Aphra Behn (1640–1689) was England's first female playwright and novelist.*

- *Henry VIII of England is well-known. So is Anne Boleyn, one of his beheaded wives. More famous still is Elizabeth I (queen 1558–1603), without whom the Elizabethan Era would have been a bore. Less known: Henry and Anne were Elizabeth's parents.*

- *Queen Elizabeth I was a beer and ale drinker. She also liked mead, but she drank very little wine. For Her Majesty, it was all about the hops.*

- *A powerful woman you haven't heard of: Diane de Poitiers, Duchesse de Valentinois (1499–1566). Mistress of King Henri II of France, she more or less ran the realm while Henri did his own thing. Odd detail: Her personal emblem looked very much like the modern symbol for a biohazard.*

- *In terms of per capita death and destruction, King Philip's War (1675–1676) between the Wampanoags and English settlers was the worst in U.S. history. Of 90 Puritan towns, 52 were attacked; 12 were completely destroyed.*

- *Tsar Peter the Great of Russia (1682–1725) decided to learn about shipbuilding the old-fashioned way: by going to the Netherlands and spending some time working in the shipyards. On his watch, Russia became a naval force to be reckoned with.*

- *France's great author Voltaire (1694–1778) had the memory and temper of an abused elephant. Feuding for decades with literary critic Elie Fréron, Voltaire went so far as to have a painting made in which devils were lashing Fréron. He hung it in his dining room.*

- *Salem witch trivia: If there wasn't witchery, why did several young girls suddenly act so bewitched? The answer may lie in moldy rye grain, a constant problem in the Colonies. Rye mold contains a hallucinogen called* ergot.

THE FIRST
MONTESSORI SCHOOLS

You may have heard of Montessori schools,
but what of the woman behind them?

When Maria Montessori was a schoolgirl, a teacher asked if she'd like to become famous. "Oh, no," she answered, "I shall never be that. I care too much for the children of the future to add yet another biography to the list."

By any standard, Maria cared for the children. She was born on August 31, 1870, at Chiaravalle, near Ancona, Kingdom of Italy. An excellent pupil, she went to technical school in 1886. After her graduation in 1890, she chose to study medicine—a strictly male field. At first, her father objected, and the medical school vetoed her desires—rather bluntly. Maria persisted, though, until they let her in.

As Montessori later explained, her movement really began on the street. She had just walked away from a dissection task, fed up with med school. As she moped down the street, a female beggar accosted Maria for money. The beggar woman's two-year-old sat on the sidewalk, her entire attention locked into play with a piece of colored paper. Seeing this child, oblivious to her poverty— silent, serenely happy—sent Maria straight back to her grisly assignment with a new will. She soon earned a title then unique for an Italian woman: *La dottoressa* Montessori, of medicine.

In 1896, Drsa. Montessori went to work with special-needs children. The status quo appalled her. Contemporary thinking classed them as "idiots" or "lunatics" and placed them in schools that were more jail than education. They were denied dignity, free-dom, even anything to manipulate with their little hands. Drsa. Montessori felt she knew what they needed. She believed she could help them through education.

Her chance came in 1899. Italy's educational bigwigs established Drsa. Montessori in a small school composed of children rejected from mainstream schools. Most couldn't read. After two years, she sent her kids to take standardized tests. Not only did many pass, some did better than the mainstream students. It was nothing short of miraculous. Now Drsa. Montessori had people's attention.

She spent the next few years traveling, studying, thinking, experiencing, and doctoring. Then in 1906 Drsa. Montessori was invited to take over an out-of-control preschool/daycare for the rowdiest preschoolers Rome had seen since Alaric the Visigoth. She was elated at the possibility: Given what happened with slower kids, what might children with normal intelligence manage?

Answer: Wonders. She found that preschoolers had phenomenal powers of concentration. They loved repetition. They liked order better than disorder; left to their own devices, they would put things away. They responded very well to free choice of activity; work—not play—was their natural preference. They had a strong sense of personal dignity and flourished when that dignity was respected; they thrived on adult attention. And perhaps most shockingly: They taught themselves to write, a phenomenon called "explosion into writing." Reading soon followed. Unruliness gave way to great self-discipline and strong respect for others. They were now "great kids."

They always had been. Drsa. Montessori had just found a way to let them show it.

From there, the Montessori movement gathered momentum. As she refined her methods, Montessori influenced educators all over the world, and her celebrity grew. By her death in 1952, a fair percentage of young adults in the child-development field were products of her approach. Fifty years and change since her passing, that approach remains popular.

Drsa. Maria Montessori didn't trademark her philosophy. You can use it without worrying about royalties, intellectual property lawyers, or cease-and-desist letters. Her life's work was her gift to humanity.

BLACK SUNDAY
DARKENS THE NATION

Sunday April 14, 1935, began as a clear, pleasant day over much of the Midwest. But within hours, daytime would be tranformed to night as a weather front with 60-mile-per-hour winds threw up a monstrous dust cloud from the barren fields of the Dust Bowl, burying homes in millions of tons of dirt.

People in the small towns and farms of Kansas, Oklahoma, Texas, and Colorado were used to dust storms and were ready to seal windows, doors, and every possible crack in their houses with sheets, blankets, and newspapers. But this particular storm, which came to be known as Black Sunday, was different. In Dodge City, Kansas, a strange nighttime fell for 40 minutes in the middle of the day, followed by three hours of near darkness. Inside their homes, men, women, and children huddled with handkerchiefs or wet sponges over their noses, struggling to breathe. Many believed the world was coming to an end. A few hours later in Chicago, the cloud dumped three pounds of soil for each person in the city. The next day, it blanketed New York and Washington, D.C., before sweeping out into the Atlantic Ocean.

ORIGIN OF A DISASTER

The April 1935 storm was the worst of the Dust Bowl, an ecological disaster that lasted for years at the height of the Great Depression. Affecting 100 million acres of the Great Plains, it brought poverty and malnutrition to millions and spurred an exodus of poor farmers to the West Coast. For years, the Plains region had enjoyed high grain prices and phenomenal crops, but farmers had been overproducing for more than a generation. Overgrazing by cattle and sheep had further stripped the landscape. By 1930, 33 million acres of southern plains once held in place by native prairie grasses had been laid bare. The crisis began in 1931.

Farmers enjoyed another bumper crop of wheat, but the resulting surplus forced prices down. Many farmers went broke, and others abandoned their fields just at the start of a severe drought that would last much of the decade.

STORMY WEATHER

In 1932, 14 dust storms—whipped skyward by strong, dry winds—were reported in the United States. The following year, the storms numbered 38, and a region centering on northern Texas, Oklahoma, and Kansas was dubbed the Dust Bowl. The first great storm occurred in May 1934, when high winds swirled 300,000 tons of soil from Montana and Wyoming skyward. By evening, the "black blizzard" began depositing dust like snow on the streets of Chicago. By dawn the next day, the cloud had rolled eastward over New York, Washington, D.C., and Atlanta, dimming the sun before moving out to sea and dusting ships 300 miles off shore. In the Midwest, summer temperature records were broken as thousands of livestock starved and suffocated. Hundreds of people died from heat stroke, malnutrition, and dust pneumonia.

BLACK SUNDAY

In March 1935, another big storm again blew topsoil from the fields of Kansas, Colorado, Texas, and Oklahoma all the way to the East Coast, but it was only a prelude of what was to come.

On April 14, 1935, 20 huge dust storms tore through the region, converging in a single front headed for the east. Witnesses reported that at times they could not see five feet in front of them. A pilot who encountered a dust cloud at 20,000 feet assumed it was a thunderstorm. She tried to climb above it, but could not, and had to turn back. In Oklahoma and Texas, humble homesteads were literally buried beneath feet of dust.

When the dust settled, a drastic migration began that would culminate in 15 percent of Oklahomans leaving the state. Called "Okies" in California, the uprooted people searching for a new life actually came from all the states of the Midwest affected by the continuing disaster. Working for the Farm Security Administration, photographer Dorothea Lange documented their lives, while novelist John Steinbeck immortalized their plight with *The Grapes of Wrath*.

AFTERMATH

Black Sunday would be an impetus for change. With dirt from the storm still falling over Washington, D.C., Hugh Hammond Bennett—a soil surveyor from North Carolina who helped found the soil conservation movement—won the support of Congress, which declared soil erosion a national menace. Later that year, President Roosevelt signed into law the Soil Conservation Act of 1935, establishing Soil Conservation Service in the Department of Agriculture. Under Bennett's direction, an aggressive campaign to stabilize the region's soil began. Roosevelt also undertook banking reforms and other agricultural policies to help rescue the Plains farmers. One of his decisions led to the planting of more than 222,000 trees.

For the next year, however, the drought continued, as summer temperatures soared to 120 degrees. Sporadic rains and floods in 1937 and 1938 joined the continuing dust storms, and wintertime brought a new kind of storm called a "snuster"—a mixture of dirt and snow reaching blizzard proportions. The fall of 1939 finally brought the rains that ended the drought. With new farming methods and increased agricultural demand due to WWII, the Plains once again become golden with wheat.

"GOD WILLS IT!"

*Pope Urban II's call to arms in 1095 set off a war
for the Holy Land that would change the course of history
for the next thousand years.*

The First Crusade (1096–1099) was born of a pope's desire to safeguard the holy sites of Palestine for Christian pilgrims and to assert papal influence over the kingdoms of Western Europe. One sermon, given in late 1095, did more to change the course of the second millennium than any other speech in history.

BIRTH OF THE CRUSADES

The Crusades were born of a desire to roll back a loose Islamic empire that stretched from Afghanistan to northern Spain. In the 7th and 8th centuries, while many European nobles spent their time fighting one another, a wave of Arab-led, Islam-inspired armies thundered across North Africa, Central Asia, the southern Mediterranean, and the Iberian Peninsula, gobbling up huge chunks of territory—many of which were torn out of the predominantly Orthodox Christian Byzantine Empire.

It did not take a political genius to figure out that Western Europe could set aside brewing political and social differences by uniting against a dangerous enemy espousing a different religion. In 1074, Pope Gregory VII issued a call for Christian soldiers to rush to the aid of the Byzantine Empire; they may have been Orthodox Christians, but they were Christians nonetheless, and they were being threatened by the great imperial powers of the age, the Islamic Caliphates.

Gregory's call went nowhere, but the publicity surrounding the pope's pleas attracted the attention of Christian pilgrims, who began visiting the Holy Land in record numbers. When priests with names like Walter the Penniless and Peter the Hermit began spreading tales of Muslims robbing Christian pilgrims on their way to Jerusalem, Europe was ripe for a battle over Palestine.

URBAN'S CALL TO ARMS

Enter Pope Urban II. Elected in 1088, this savvy French priest carried out his diplomatic duties with finesse, and when Emperor Alexius I of Byzantine called for help against the Muslim hordes, Urban was happy to oblige. He summoned bishops from all over Europe to Clermont, France, and when some 300 bishops had assembled in an open-air forum, Urban gave them a barn-burner of a sermon. He exhorted the Christians of Europe to take up arms, to drive back the Seljuk Turks and the other Muslim armies occupying the Holy Land.

Knowing his real audience was the kings, princes, and nobles who would be asked to send soldiers into battle, the cagy Urban was quick to point out the material benefits of a conquest of eastern lands. He proclaimed:

"This land which you inhabit, shut in on all sides by the seas and surrounded by the mountain peaks, is too narrow for your large population; nor does it abound in wealth; and it furnishes scarcely food enough for its cultivators... Enter upon the road to the Holy Sepulcher; wrest that land from the wicked race, and subject it to yourselves."

The kicker, of course, was that the crusaders would have a spiritual *carte blanche* to kill and conquer, all with divine sanction. "God has conferred upon you above all nations great glory in arms. Accordingly undertake this journey for the remission of your sins, with the assurance of the imperishable glory of the kingdom of heaven," Pope Urban II said.

Urban's sermon wowed the bishops and nobles in attendance, who left the council chanting, *"Deus vult!"* ("God wills it!"). Peasants, knights, and nobles from France, Italy, and Germany answered Urban's call, and over the next year, a hodgepodge of crusaders (generally grouped into the unsuccessful "People's Crusade" and the more successful "Princes' Crusade") took up the Cross, looking for heavenly rewards, material treasure, and great victory.

CONQUEST OF THE HOLY LAND

The Crusades didn't get off to much of a start. The thousands of hungry, ill-supplied peasants who had joined the People's Crusade were neither trained nor organized, and they were quickly massacred once they set foot into Seljuk Turk territory. But the roughly 7,000 knights of the Princes' Crusade managed to capture Antioch, north of Jerusalem, in 1098. The following year, the crusading army—about 1,500 knights, supported by some 12,000 men-at-arms—reached Jerusalem, which it captured after a brief siege. The crusaders capped their victory by massacring men, women, and children of all faiths in all sections of the holy city. They set up the Kingdom of Jerusalem, which they ran as a Christian fiefdom until it fell to Saladin and his Arabian armies in 1187.

ECHOES THROUGH THE AGES

The First Crusade set in motion a seesaw battle between the Christian west and the Islamic east that lasted another two centuries. As chunks of the Holy Land fell to one army or another, Urban's successor popes used the Crusades as a way to unite Europe. But the Crusades, and the orgies of blood they incited, left a bitter legacy. The rancor that the Crusades caused among both Christians and Muslims has persisted to this day, and even now the word "crusader" evokes very different feelings among Westerners and Middle Easterners.

- *Other famous crusades were the Third, in 1189, in which Richard the Lionheart, Philip II of France, and Fredrick Barbarossa took part; and the Seventh, in 1249, which was led by King Louis IX (St. Louis) of France.*

JEZEBEL—
PAGAN PRIESTESS OR
MANIPULATIVE MINX

*There are more seductresses, fallen women, temptresses,
adulteresses, and manipulative minxes in the Old Testament than
in the steamiest television soap opera yet written. None, however,
suffered so cruel a fate nor are still so reviled as Jezebel.*

Jezebel makes her first appearance in the Bible in the First Book
of Kings, Chapter 16, Verse 31, when Ahab, king of Israel "also
took to wife Jezebel, daughter of Ethbaal, king of the Sidonians."
One of Jezebel's first acts as queen was to convince her husband
to "rear up an altar for Ba'al," the god of her people, and to join
her in worshipping him. In so doing, as the Bible says, "Ahab did
more to provoke the Lord God of Israel to anger than all the kings
of Israel that were before him."

That is no small accomplishment, considering the sins of Ahab's
predecessors and the short temper of the frequently wrathful God
they served. Jezebel, of course, gets the blame for her husband's
fall from grace, even though initially all she was guilty of was convincing the king to come along with her to the ancient equivalent
of Sunday services.

A Phoenician people from what is now southern Lebanon, the
inhabitants of Sidon had worshipped the god Ba'al for at least
a thousand years before the Israelites and their God wandered
into the land of Canaan. Assyrians, Babylonians, and Egyptians
had each in turn conquered Sidon (which still exists and lies just
25 miles south of Beirut). While other gods came and went with
the occupying armies, Ba'al remained in the hearts and devotions
of the Sidonians.

Jezebel brought that devotion with her, which in hindsight was not
a particularly wise or politically correct thing to do in the land of

the Chosen People. Damned and challenged by the holy men of Israel for what they saw as her idolatry, she responded by convincing her husband to cut off their heads. As "Jezebel slew the prophets of Israel," so the Bible reports, she also imported some 450 priests of Ba'al—along with another 400 "prophets of the groves," caretakers of outdoor arboreal shrines where pagans gathered to dance, sing, party, and participate in lewd rituals.

This attempt to suborn the faith of the nation of Israel, turn their king away from God, and undermine the power of the religious elite brought Jezebel into direct confrontation with Elijah, arguably the "most valuable player" to ever carry a staff in the league of prophets.

Elijah and Jezebel battled for the soul and purse of Israel for some 20 years, their fight marked by tornadoes, earthquakes, and fires that the Lord God of Hosts brought down upon pagan sites. Even so, at first, things went Jezebel's way, thanks to her ability to get the king to do as she wished. As is written in 1 Kings 25: "There was none like unto Ahab, which did sell himself to work wickedness in the sight of the Lord, whom Jezebel his wife stirred up."

Ahab, however, began to repent, and for a time "put sackcloth upon his flesh and fasted." Soon after that, he died in battle. Jezebel continued to fight on through Ahab's son and heir Ahaziah, who as king of Israel, the Bible says "walked in the way of his father, and in the way of his mother." Ahaziah "made Israel to sin," notes the Book of Kings, "served Ba'al, and worshipped him, and provoked to anger the Lord God of Israel."

That anger was made manifest in the hero, Jehu. As the country devolved into revolt and civil war, Jehu arose, and in an epic chariot-to-chariot duel was able to "smite" the idolatrous king. The victorious Jehu then rode into Jerusalem, came to the palace as Jezebel was painting her face, and ordered the queen's servants to "throw her down." They dutifully tossed her out the window, makeup and all. Her "blood was sprinkled on the wall and on the horses" as she fell, or so the Bible records. Trampled by Jehu's chariot horses for good measure, her body was then consumed by dogs—which left "no more of her than the skull and the feet, and the palms of her hands."

Ever since her bloody demise, the pagan queen who was devoured by dogs in the street has been held up as a cautionary figure to warn men and women alike of the danger and eventual fate of femme fatales who use their sexual power to seduce the righteous and lead them astray. The lesson and legend of Jezebel has been and continues to be reinforced and perpetuated by literature, religious tracts, film, and music. The very name Jezebel has become a powerful marketing tool and literary device used to conjure up the image of the coquette, the seductress, the insatiable demonic spirit made supple flesh to sow discord among men. An impressive, if unflattering, legacy for a Phoenician princess from south Lebanon.

FAMOUS LAST WORDS

"For most of history, Anonymous was a woman."
—Virginia Woolf

"The very ink with which history is written is merely fluid prejudice."
—Mark Twain

"Historians are gossips who tease the dead."
—Voltaire

THE LOUVRE: GIFT OF THE REVOLUTION

Built by French kings over six centuries, the famed Louvre Museum found its true calling with the bloody end of the dynasty that built it.

The art collection known throughout the world as the Musée de Louvre began as a moated, medieval arsenal erected to protect the city's inhabitants against the Anglo-Norman threat. Built by King Philippe Auguste in the late 12th century, the fortress lost much of its military value as the city expanded far beyond the castle walls over the next 150 years. In 1364, King Charles V had the Louvre redesigned as a royal residence.

During the next three centuries, French kings and queens remodeled and redesigned portions of the Louvre, connecting it with the nearby Tuileries palace. Apartments and galleries were added, and remnants of the medieval fortress were demolished.

During the reign of King Louis XIV, the famed "Sun King," the palace came into its own, as classical paintings and sculptures by the great artists of the day graced the palace's walls and ceilings. Work halted briefly in 1672, when Louis moved the French court to his fantastic palace at Versailles, but in 1692 Louis sent a set of antique sculptures back to the Louvre's *Salle de Caryatides*, inaugurating the first of the Louvre's many antique accessions. Academies of arts and sciences took up residence at the palace, and in 1699, the *Académie Royale de Peinture et de Sculpture* held its first exhibition in the Louvre's Grand Galerie.

The artistic treasures housed by the French monarchs were, of course, the property of the king and off limits to the masses. But in 1791, in the wake of the French Revolution, the French Assemblée Nationale declared all Bourbon property to be held by the state for the people of France. The government established a public art and science museum at the Louvre and Tuileries, and in 1793, the year King Louis XVI and his queen, Marie Antoinette, were sent to the guillotine, the Museum Central des Arts opened its doors to the public.

As Napoleon's armies marched through Italy, Austria, and Egypt in the late 1790s, the museum's collections grew with the spoils of war. Napoleon and Empress Josephine inaugurated an antiquities gallery at the Louvre in 1800, and three years later, the museum was briefly renamed the Musée Napoléon. With the emperor's fall in 1815, however, the Louvre's status diminished as many of its artifacts were returned to their rightful owners across Europe.

In the mid-19th century, the Louvre opened additional galleries to showcase Spanish, Algerian, Egyptian, Mexican, and other ethnographic artworks. As the Louvre soldiered on into the 20th century, its more exotic holdings—particularly Islamic and Middle Eastern art—expanded, and the museum was progressively remodeled to accommodate its growing collection.

At the outbreak of World War II, French officials fretted that the Louvre's magnificent holdings would become a prime target for Nazi pillage, so they removed most of the museum's treasures and dispersed them among chateaus in and around the Loire valley. The Nazis had the museum reopened in September 1940, though there was little left for the cowed Parisians to view until the country was liberated four years later.

In 1945, the restored French government reorganized its national art collections, and in 1983 the government announced a sweeping reorganization and remodeling plan under the direction of the famed Chinese-American architect I. M. Pei. Impressionist and other late 19th-century works were moved to the Musée d'Orsay, while Pei's famous glass pyramid, which towers over the Cour Napoleon, signaled a new stage in the Louvre's life. Further renovations from 1993 to the present have given the Louvre its distinctive look, as well as its status as one of the world's premier museums.

MISCALCULATED INSULT: THE BRITISH BURN THE WHITE HOUSE

On August 24, 1814, British forces brushed aside the Virginia militia and burned the White House. Why? To teach the upstart former colonists King George's lesson: "Don't mess with me." Unfortunately for the British, it only embarrassed and angered said colonists, who proceeded to mess with His Majesty anyway.

Coming a generation after the Revolutionary War, one might call the War of 1812 a grudge rematch—except this time King George had more than a colony to lose. From 1805–1815, crown forces were at full strain with Napoleon's France. Had the French fleet gotten loose at sea on a stormy day with a load of troops, England itself could have faced direct invasion.

THIS MEANS WAR!

One key British strategy was a blockade to deny France world trade, but the spunky Americans did business with Napoleon anyway. Britain seized such ships and cargos, which annoyed the Americans enough; worse still, the Royal Navy drafted the captured U.S. sailors into British service. Americans said: "This means war!" President James Madison asked Congress for a Declaration of War, and on June 18, 1812, Congress gave it to him.

The Canadian border and the Atlantic seaboard were the natural battlefronts in a low-intensity conflict. The border battles went back and forth without decisive results for either side. U.S. privateers and navy warships harassed the British at sea but lacked the big ships-of-the-line necessary to challenge the world's dominant navy. Even so, in 1813, U.S. forces managed to burn York (now Toronto), including the Canadian Parliament. Now it was Britain's turn to take things personally, but retaliation could wait until Napoleon was exiled to a lonely Mediterranean island.

ENGLAND SEEKS REVENGE

By 1814, Britain was ready to hit the yappy colonial terrier with a rolled-up newspaper. The man for the task was Admiral Sir George Cockburn, hater of all things American, who had taken great glee in raiding Chesapeake Bay the previous two years. On August 19, 1814, Cockburn landed General Robert Ross and a force of 4,700 British regulars at Benedict, Maryland—about 25 miles from the White House.

The D.C. militia was mustered in great haste. President Madison scrambled to organize the defense, such as it was; his wife Dolley rushed to pack up White House national treasures. The lightly armed minutemen prepared to make their stand at Bladensburg, Maryland, five miles from the White House, ready to teach King George how free men could fight. Just after noon, His Majesty knew the answer: "Very poorly." After a brief exchange of shots (now known as the Battle of Bladensburg), the militia panicked and fled, barely slowing Ross's redcoats in their march on D.C.

The capital's population focused on weighty matters: blaming everything on the president, looting, and running like hell. A small U.S. fleet scuttled itself in the Patuxent River to avoid capture.

The British waltzed into Washington, burning public buildings while sparing private structures. They set fire to the Washington Navy Yard, adding insult to the navy's self-inflicted injury. Redcoats heaped papers, desks, and chairs in the Capitol's House and Senate chambers, then set the structure gloriously ablaze with a newfangled Congreve artillery rocket. Then they headed up the road to the White House where a hastily abandoned meal awaited them. The officers devoured the meal, overindulged in the fine wine, then left a fiery tip by putting the White House to the torch. Only its gutted stone skeleton survived.

After a second day of organized arson, the British made for Baltimore. Here U.S. resistance held fast. The British attacked first by land, losing the battle and General Ross in the bargain. They tried next by sea, but the bombardment failed to reduce Fort McHenry. The next morning, a lyrical observer named Francis

Scott Key wrote a poem honoring the defiance of the flapping Stars & Stripes, visible at night thanks to exploding British shells and the reddish light of Congreve rockets. Most Americans know this poem. However, they probably don't know that its tune comes from an old British drinking song, "To Anacreon in Heaven."

The rest of the war was all United States. "Old Hickory" Andrew Jackson defeated the British-supported Creek Indians in Alabama in March 1814, then the British themselves at New Orleans in January 1815, before either force could learn that the war was over. The British agreed to leave U.S. shipping and seamen alone. No borders would change, but the young republic had asserted the right to avenge British slaps across its face. It had also gained a reality check. Reliance on a "people's army" of hastily raised militia sounded great but didn't work in practice. Many would not serve, and many—even when the stakes were the national capital—broke and ran as soon as they smelled gun smoke. The United States needed what the founding fathers had dreaded: a standing military.

- *You can tell just how short-handed the Royal Navy was from one of its preferred recruiting venues: gaols (jails). An officer would offer prisoners the option of navy service over a cell. Given the severity of navy discipline—where a man might be flogged nigh to death on an alcoholic captain's whim—many British considered gaol a better bargain.*

- *Admiral Cockburn might well have been called "Admiral Cocky." Bold, brash, and arrogant, his coastal raids made him a hated man in the United States. One American put a price on his head—and an equal price on his ears—should anyone bring him both.*

- *The most important national treasure Dolley Madison saved was a portrait of George Washington that she felt sure the British would desecrate.*

THE LEGENDARY MOHAWK IRONWORKERS

Employing the fearless Mohawk Indians as ironworkers, the Dominion Bridge Company set a constructive force into motion that six generations later has—in no small part— built up the entire New York City skyline.

In 1886, Dominion crews were building a cantilevered bridge for the Canadian Pacific railway to cross the St. Lawrence river, near Montreal. The path skirted an island reservation of the Mohawk nation Kahnawake, and, to ease any qualms that the bridge's new neighbors might raise, Dominion agreed to hire day-laborers from the reservation.

SPANNING NEW HEIGHTS

A Dominion official, consulting internal company documents and memoranda, told *The New Yorker* in 1949 that the Mohawks hired for the job were given menial tasks like unloading materials for the actual steelworkers to use. However, the official noted, "They were dissatisfied with this arrangement and would come out on the bridge itself every chance they got. It was quite impossible to keep them off. As the work progressed, it became apparent to all concerned that these Indians were very odd in that they did not have any fear of heights. If not watched, they would climb up into the spans and walk around up there as cool and collected as the toughest of our riveters, most of whom at that period were old sailing ship men especially picked for the experience in working aloft."

And so a legend was born. Sprouting cities across the American and Canadian northeast had no shortage of jobs for sky walkers who could wield a rivet gun. Kahnawake residents soon found work as actual riveters at the Soo Bridge, spanning Sault Ste. Marie, Ontario, and Michigan—a job that served as vocational college for these previously unskilled tradespeople. By 1907,

Kahnawake was home to some 70 bridgemen, who would hop as an ensemble from one project to the next.

DISASTER STRIKES

But 1907 was also when disaster transformed this would-be trade union. Hailed as one of the early 20th century's great engineering marvels, the Québec Bridge spanned the St. Lawrence from Québec City to Levis, Québec. On August 29, minutes after a foreman ended the workday with the sound of his whistle, the Québec Bridge collapsed, sending 76 men to a watery grave. In Kahnawake, which lost 33 bridgemen, this tragedy is known to this day simply as "The Disaster."

NEW YORK, NEW YORK

After The Disaster, the village women gathered in this matriarchal society and decided that to avoid another widespread tragedy, their ironworking husbands, fathers, and brothers would never again work *en masse* as a Nation. The practical upshot of this policy decision was to scatter Mohawk ironworkers to the winds, which led many of them to New York at a moment in history when buildings were pushing up like rows of sunflowers. From the 1920s onward, Mohawks from Kahnawake (and Akwesasne, near Québec City) riveted their way across patches of sky that became the Empire State Building, the Chrysler Building, Rockefeller Center, The Triborough Bridge, and of course, the World Trade Center.

On the morning of September 11, 2001, skywalkers from Kahnawake raced down to New York to be some of the first construction crews to dismantle what uncles, fathers, and cousins had assembled three decades ago.

Today, Mohawks from Kahnawake and Akwesasne are members of ironworkers' union locals in Montreal and New York, as well as New Jersey, Boston, Detroit, and Kentucky. Some are also laying the foundation—and will soon be scraping the sky—for the Freedom Tower.

GHOST TOWNS OF
THE ANCIENTS

*It's hard to think of great cities like New York or London ever
becoming the ghost towns of future centuries.
But many New Yorks and Londons of the ancient world did just
that—then kept archeologists and scientists busy
for hundreds of years looking for them.*

A WALL, A HORSE, AND A MYSTERY

Most people have heard of the siege of Troy, that epic battle over
a stolen princess that the blind poet Homer immortalized in the
Iliad. The image of a "Trojan Horse" has made its way into film,
literature, and even computer lingo. But the city that gave us the
famed wooden horse faded into legend around 700 B.C. For the
next 25 centuries, the city of Troy was dismissed as a fable—an
elusive ghost for archeologists and historians.

Details of the real Troy are fragmentary, handed down mostly
through Greek myths and Homer's poetry. The city, on the
Aegean coast of modern-day Turkey, lay along major trade routes
from the Mediterranean to the Black Sea, and it steadily prospered since its Bronze Age founding around 3000 B.C.

As Troy grew wealthy and powerful, its inhabitants protected
themselves with massive stone walls. Homer's Troy boasted towers
nearly 30 feet high and probably contained around 10,000 inhabitants at the time of the Trojan War. The city rose and fell several
times (the last around the end of the 8th century B.C.), and it
was rebuilt as a Roman outpost around the time of Christ. The
"Roman Troy" remained an important trading center until Constantinople became the capital of the Eastern Roman Empire and
traders began to bypass the ancient town.

Troy then began its final journey into decline and ruin. By the
time Europe emerged from the Dark Ages, the city had been lost
to the ages.

But in the 1870s, an eccentric German businessman named Heinrich Schliemann, who had been schooled on the *Iliad* as a boy, built a small fortune and began searching for the lost city. Over a 19-year period, Schliemann completed several amateur digs around a city that, in due course, yielded nine sites to bear the name "Troy." The seventh "Troy," a city (or succession of cities) from around 1200–1000 B.C., appears to have been destroyed by fire and is the most likely candidate for the Troy of Homer's epic.

GO TELL THE WHOM?

Today we think of the ancient Greek city of Sparta as the "Spartan" (austere, militant, and culturally empty) counterpart to the more enlightened, democratic Athenian society. But in ancient times, Sparta lay at the "cutting edge" of political and military arts.

Sparta, the capital of the Lacedaemon kingdom on Greece's Ionic coast, inaugurated many idealistic traditions for which the Greek world became famous. It established a democratic assembly years before the Athenians adopted the practice; it allowed women broad rights to own property and attend schools; and it took its religion and art seriously.

After the Greek city-states combined to defeat the Persian invasion of 480 B.C., a rivalry between Sparta and Athens led to the bitter Peloponnesian War (431–403 B.C.). The war ended in Spartan victory, but Sparta's defeat by Thebes 30 years later sent the city into a period of decline. It fell under Roman rule and succumbed to barbarian invasions, ultimately vanishing into ruin before A.D. 400.

In a passage from Thucydides's ancient work *The History of the Peloponnesian War,* the old chronicler muses: "Suppose the city of Sparta to be deserted, and nothing left but the temples and the ground-plan, distant ages would be very unwilling to believe that the power of the Lacodaemonians was at all equal to their fame."

Sure enough, the city left little of its original grandeur for later generations. It was not until some 1,500 years later that serious efforts were made to recover the home of the Spartans. In 1906, the British School at Athens did serious archeological work, discovering a theater, temples, and beautiful examples of early Spartan art, and opening the world's eyes to the cultural world that was Sparta.

ROME: TOTAL WAR

One of the ancient world's greatest cities had the misfortune of bumping up against the most powerful military force of its time. Set on the North African coast near modern Tunisia's capital city, Tunis, the great city of Carthage was the hub of a Mediterranean trading empire that rivaled that of the later Italian upstarts. This rivalry with Rome produced three great wars of antiquity, called the Punic Wars.

By virtue of its location—south of Sicily on Africa's Mediterranean coast—Carthage, a trading empire founded by the seagoing Phoenician people around 814 B.C., held a dominant position in Mediterranean trade from the 3rd and 2nd centuries B.C. In 264 B.C., Rome and Carthage got dragged by their allies into a war over Sicily. Round One went to the Romans. Two decades later, the Carthaginian general Hannibal led his elephants over the Alps into Italy on a legendary campaign of destruction, but the Romans eventually won that one, too.

A half century later, Rome goaded the Carthaginians into a third war. This time, the Roman general Scipio Africanus led a three-year siege of Carthage. After storming the walls and capturing the city, he burned the metropolis to the ground, destroyed Carthaginian ships in the harbor, and sold the populace into slavery. By 146 B.C., the destruction of Carthage was complete.

In the 1st century A.D., the Romans rebuilt the city as a shipping hub, and the "new" Carthage became a major food supplier for the Roman Empire. It remained a center of Roman Christianity until the end of the 7th century, when Arab invaders toppled the city and replicated Scipio's "complete destruction" formula. The city was supplanted by nearby Tunis, and today the ancient capital is a series of ruins in Tunis's suburbs, where archeologists are digging up statues, tombs, and other relics of one of the ancient world's lost empires.

EPITAPHS OF THE FAMOUS

CRYPT OF CHRISTOPHER WREN,
WHO DESIGNED ST. PAUL'S CATHEDRAL IN LONDON,
IN WHICH HE IS BURIED:
"Reader, if you seek his memorial, look around you."

DOC HOLLIDAY:
"He Died in Bed."

JOHN KEATS:
"Here lies one whose name is writ in water."

WILLIAM SHAKESPEARE:
"Good friend for Jesus' sake forbear,
To dig the dust enclosed here!
Blessed be the man that spares these stones,
And cursed be he that moves my bones."

CLARA BARTON:
"An Angel of the Battlefield"

EDGAR ALLAN POE:
"Quoth the Raven, nevermore."

WYATT EARP:
"Nothing's So Sacred As Honour And Nothing's
So Loyal As Love."

CARL JUNG:
"Bidden or unbidden, God is present."

MARTIN LUTHER KING, JR.:
"Free at last. Free at last. Thank God Almighty I'm Free At Last."

Fast Facts

- Louis XIV, the splendorous French Sun King (1643–1715), should have been called the Spend King. Between the lavish palace of Versailles, his expensive lifestyle, and a series of costly wars, he ran the French treasury into the toilet.

- King George III's coronation (1761) was nearly as big a fiasco as losing the Colonies. Someone forgot the royal chairs and Sword of State. The king's steward had trained his horse to walk backward, so it could exit with proper ceremony. Instead, it backed right into the room to begin with, presenting its hind-quarters to His Majesty.

- Worst pope in history? Probably Alexander VI (pope 1492–1503), the Borgia pope of the Renaissance. Chastity? He had numerous mistresses. Humility? He bought his way to the papacy. Poverty? He piled up every ducat he could.

- Anti-Freemason sentiment ran high enough in the United States in the 1820s and 1830s for Anti-Masonic Party politicians to be elected governors of Vermont and Pennsylvania.

- As sheriff of Erie County, New York, Grover Cleveland (president 1885–1889 and 1893–1897) carried out several hangings. He preferred not to ask his deputies to do the law's dirty work.

- The United States once invaded Russia. Siberia, actually. During the Russian Revolution, just after WWI, about ten foreign nations intervened in favor of the Whites (anti-Communists). The U.S. contingent wasn't even the largest—that honor goes to the Czechoslovakians.

- Blind, deaf, and mute, yes; shrinking violet, no. Helen Keller (1880–1968) was a radical socialist who lauded the new USSR. During the McCarthy years, the FBI kept a file on her.

- The Pilgrims didn't invent Thanksgiving; the Native Americans of the region had held fall harvest festivities going back centuries. Thanksgiving only became a U.S. national holiday in 1863, at the height of the Civil War.

217

MAO: A MIXED LEGACY

The "Great Helmsman" was responsible for modernizing China. But at what cost?

From his humble beginnings as a rural peasant to his eventual leadership of the world's most populated country, Mao Zedong left an indelible mark on modern China. In 1925, he became head of the Communist Party and led a 20-year civil war against the ruling Nationalists. In 1949, with the nationalists exiled to Taiwan, Mao proclaimed himself leader of the new People's Republic of China.

Hailed as a hero, Chairman Mao made a number of questionable moves that forever tarnished his reputation. In 1958, he launched the "Great Leap Forward"—an effort to modernize and collectivize China's farming and industry. The result was a total failure; millions died in the ensuing famine.

Throughout his tenure, Mao held on to power by suppressing opposition. He also invented a "cult of personality," a scheme whereby people were forced to idolize their leader—on pain of death. Statues and pictures of Mao went up everywhere, and people began to worship him as a god.

It was during this time that he released his infamous *Little Red Book*, a series of quotations from Mao. Every worker carried a copy of the book and learned to repeat its sometimes indecipherable sayings. The book was intended to restore Communist fervor but quickly became a tool to measure allegiance to the so-called "Great Helmsman." Schools were closed, and students formed the Red Guard, using the book to persecute enemies of the state—party members and "bourgeoisie" academics. Known as the Cultural Revolution, this movement saw more than one million killed.

As the cities began to slip into chaos, Mao called in the army to restore order. After that, his grip on power gradually began to slip. His last notable act occurred in 1972, when he invited U.S. President Richard Nixon to China. Mao died in 1976.

ORDER IN THE COURT?
ANIMALS ON TRIAL

During the Middle Ages, people believed that animals were
legally responsible for their crimes and misdeeds.
But punishment was not administered without fair trial.

The year was 1386. In the French city of Falaise, a child was killed and partially devoured by a sow and her six piglets. Locals refused to let such a heinous crime go unpunished. However, rather than killing the sow, they brought her to trial. The pig was dressed in men's clothing, tried for murder, convicted, and hanged from the gallows in the public square.

Porkers weren't the only animals to face trial during medieval times. Bees, snakes, horses, and bulls were also charged with murder. Foxes were charged with theft. Rats were charged with damaging barley. In the early 1700s, Franciscan friars in Brazil brought "white ants" (probably termites) to trial because "the said ants did feloniously burrow beneath the foundation of the monastery and undermine the cellars...threatening its total ruin."

HISTORY

The first record of animal trials exists in Athens. More than 2,000 years ago, the Athenians instituted a special court to try murderous objects (such as stones and beams) as well as animals that caused human deaths. They believed that in order to protect moral equilibrium and to prevent the wrath of the Furies, these murders had to be avenged.

Animal trials peaked in the Middle Ages, ranging from the 9th century to as late as the 18th century. During this time, people believed that animals committed crimes against humans and that, like humans, animals were morally and legally responsible for their actions. As a result, animals received the same punishment as humans, ranging from a knock on the head to excommunication or death.

LEGAL RIGHTS

Animals accused of crimes in Europe's Middle Ages received the same rights under the law as humans, which included a fair trial. Domestic animals were often tried in civil courts and punished individually. Animals that existed in groups (such as weevils, eels, horseflies, locusts, caterpillars, and worms) were usually tried in ecclesiastical courts. They weren't stretched on the rack to extract confessions, nor were they hanged with individual nooses. Instead, they received a group malediction or anathema.

The accused animals were also entitled to legal representation. When the weevils in the French village of St. Julien were accused of threatening the vineyards in 1587, Pierre Rembaud argued in their defense. The innocent weevils should not be blamed, said Rembaud. Rather, the villagers should recognize God's wrath and don sackcloth. The court ruled in favor of the weevils and gave them their own parcel of land.

As for the six little piglets in Falaise? They also must have had good counsel—they were acquitted on the grounds of their youth and their mother's poor example.

CAPITAL PUNISHMENT

Murder wasn't the only crime to carry a death sentence. Often, animals accused of witchcraft or other heinous crimes received similar punishment. In 1474, a cock was burned at the stake in Basel, Switzerland, for the crime of laying an egg. As was widely understood, this could result in the birth of a basilisk, a monster that could wreak havoc in a person's home.

Pigs were often brought to the gallows for infanticide (a perennial problem since 900-pound sows often ran free). A mother pig smothering her infants was most likely an accident, but in those times people saw it as a sign of evil thanks to the Biblical account of the demon-possessed herd at Gadarenes.

Animals had slim hopes for survival when accused of severe crimes. However, there is the amazing account of a jenny that was saved when the parish priest and the citizens signed a certificate that proclaimed her innocence. It stated that they had known the "she-ass" for four years and that "she had always shown herself to be virtuous and well-behaved both at home and abroad and had never given occasion of scandal to anyone."

CONTEMPORARY COURTROOMS

Although animals are not tried as humans in the United States, they are not immune to the gavel. In April 2007, a 300-pound donkey named Buddy entered the courtroom at the North Dallas Government Center in Texas.

While technically it was Buddy's owner who was on trial, the donkey was accused of the "crime." His owner's neighbor had been complaining about Buddy's braying and foul odor.

When the defense attorney asked Buddy if he was the said donkey, Buddy twitched his ears and remained silent. For the next few minutes, he was calm and polite—hardly the obnoxious beast that had been described in the accusations.

While the jury pondered, the neighbors reached an agreement. The day ended peacefully. Buddy—like his ancestors—had his day in court.

- *The Case for Animal Rights. In* The Criminal Prosecution and Capital Punishment of Animals *(1906), author E. P. Evans refers to the words of his contemporary, Henry Salt: "If animals may be rendered liable to judicial punishment for injuries done to man, one would naturally infer that they should also enjoy legal protection against human cruelty."*

- *The Ants' Defense: The monks wanted to excommunicate the termites for devouring their food, furniture, and foundation. But the termites' appointed lawyer defended them on several grounds, including their work ethic—the "white ants" were more industrious than the "gray friars."*

ST. PETER'S: CHURCH OF CHURCHES

Sprawling across nearly six acres in the Vatican, the Basilica of Saint Peter was the world's largest Christian church for almost four centuries.

St. Peter's is not the "official" church of the pope: That honor goes to another basilica, St. John's Lateran. But St. Peter's is the edifice most closely identified with the papacy because its enormous size—both inside and outside, in the form of St. Peter's Square—can accommodate tens of thousands of worshippers and pilgrims. (The term *basilica* comes from a Latinized Greek word describing a church built to a pattern dating back to the late Roman Empire, or a church accorded special ceremonial privileges by the pope.) The structure is built on the site on which, according to tradition, the first bishop of Rome—St. Peter, the apostle whom Jesus called upon to lead the Church after his death—was crucified in the 1st century A.D.

STOREHOUSE OF MASTERPIECES

Pope Julius II laid the cornerstone for the basilica in 1506, but the structure wasn't completed until 1615, during the reign of Pope Paul V. Donato Bramante provided the original design, but after his death in 1514, a succession of artists/architects worked on the project, including such great figures as Raphael and Michelangelo. (The latter is often credited with designing the magnificent dome that rises almost 400 feet from the basilica's floor, but the dome was in fact modified from Michelangelo's original plans.) St. Peter's interior and exterior would eventually include Michelangelo's great sculpture, the *Pietà,* and other important Baroque artworks, including the baldacchino (altar canopy) by Lorenzo Bernini. Within St. Peter's is the Vatican Grotto, the burial place of 91 popes (most recently Pope John Paul II in 2005) and other Catholic notables.

CHARLEMAGNE: ILLITERATE READER

Charlemagne created a major Frankish Empire that unified most of what we now call western and central Europe, helped establish the dominance of the Roman Catholic Church in that area, began the Middle Ages, and brought about a revival of arts and literature that helped preserve the works of ancient Greek and Roman writers. Not bad for a fellow whose name isn't even known for certain!

The first mention of his name is the Latin *Carolus Magnus*, which translates as Charles the Great. The French, who claim him as one of their kings, call him Charlemagne (which translates more or less the same), while the Germans (who also claim him as *their* own) call him Karl der Grosse. The English-speaking world generally knows him by his French name, Charlemagne. We're not even entirely sure when he was born, though 742 is the commonly accepted date.

OF POPES AND KINGS

Charlemagne came from two lines of Frankish kings. His grandfather was the great Charles "The Hammer" Martel. Charles's tribe was known as the Merovingians, and Charles had largely unified modern-day France and had defeated the Arabian invaders at the Battle of Tours in 732. His son, Pepin the Short, was eventually made king and established a new line known as the Carolingians. The pope stated his approval for this, starting a tradition of kings seeking the pope's approval, a situation that often led to religious wars and other difficulties. When Pepin died, his two sons, Charles and Carloman, ruled together until Carloman died in 771, leaving Charles to rule the kingdom. Charles went on to gain historic renown.

Like so many great people in history, Charlemagne earned much of his reputation through military conquest. Over the years, he fought in Italy, Saxony, Spain, Bavaria, and pretty much anywhere else he was threatened. His campaign in Spain was immortalized by the epic poem, *Song of Roland*. A devout Christian, Charlemagne went to the aid of the pope several times; as it happens, the pope was often being threatened by assorted forces. On Christmas Day of 800, Pope Leo III crowned Charlemagne as holy roman emperor. There is some dispute as to whether or not Charlemagne was really aware that this was going to happen, but he is said to have remarked later that allowing it to happen had been a mistake. Kings and emperors wanted to rule as the top dog, and having a pope approve or, worse yet, actually crown you as king meant that even in temporal matters the pope was above the emperor. It wasn't until Napoleon crowned himself in 1804 that this conflict was finally resolved in favor of the secular power of the state.

SAVIOR OF WESTERN CIVILIZATION

One might think, given all this fighting, that Charlemagne didn't have much time for anything else. To the contrary, Charlemagne's biggest contributions to history may well be what he did *off* the battlefield. Here are just a few of the major cultural contributions made by Charlemagne:

• After the fall of the Roman Empire, education in Europe had gone into a steep decline. Charlemagne reversed that trend by increasing the number of schools. His palace school in the capital of Aachen featured Alcuin of York, perhaps the top scholar of his day. The school, and the nearby court, were crowded with other leading minds of that age, and Charlemagne and his sons attended classes from time to time. Not bad for a fellow who couldn't write. On the other hand, he could read, and most kings in those days were completely illiterate. Oh yes, one thing more: Education was normally reserved for the nobility, but Charlemagne made sure that really deserving commoners also had a chance to be educated. He understood that the more educated people there were, the more people there would be to help run things. Charlemagne also encouraged the education of women and established empire-wide curriculum standards.

- Speaking of writing, the script of the period was difficult to read. Scholars and scribes under Charlemagne eventually came up with a new system that used both upper- and lowercase letters. This script is called Carolingian Minuscule and is one of the foundations of modern Western script.

- Speaking of writing (again), the works of the ancients were in danger of being lost. Many ancient documents had been destroyed by Christian clergy who were determined that people should only have Christian materials to read. Since they were all handwritten, there were obviously not many copies available. So, when one was lost, that was likely all she wrote (so to speak). Charlemagne established writing centers where scribes spent all day making copies of these works. He sent other people all over the countryside, peeking into musty old monastic libraries, trying to find copies of ancient texts that could then be copied. Many, if not most, of the ancient works that we still have were saved due to this effort.

- Given all of this, it may not surprise you to hear that Charlemagne was a great fan of books. He would give and receive books, often bound in sumptuous ivory and jeweled bindings. A few of these survive today and are wonders to behold.

These educational and literary accomplishments, along with some other reforms, have led historians to give Charlemagne credit for starting the Carolingian Renaissance, or a rebirth of learning and of interest in the ancient texts. Some historians even feel that he was largely responsible for saving Western civilization. When he died in 814, his empire began a decline, and within a generation had broken into a feudal system that would last through much of the Middle Ages. Emphasis on learning and literature would decline as well, but thanks to Charlemagne it never completely died out. When the Italian Renaissance began several centuries later, scholars had a base upon which to begin their march to the modern era; a base that was created by one of history's greatest figures—Charlemagne.

A CONCRETE THREAT

Over a period of approximately 20 years, the invisible Iron Curtain was transformed into a very real concrete wall. A symbol of the confining Communist world, the Berlin Wall stood for more than 25 years.

LOWER THE IRON CURTAIN...

English statesman Winston Churchill coined the iconic phrase in a speech he delivered to Westminster College in Missouri on March 5, 1946, saying, "An 'iron curtain' has descended across the Continent [Europe]... behind... what I must call the Soviet sphere." Though his words were received with skepticism at first, the evidence mounted through the 1950s, confirming the Soviet stranglehold on Eastern Europe.

At the conclusion of World War II, conflict ensued over the division of the defeated country of Germany, namely who would occupy which section. The four Allied countries of France, Great Britain, the United States, and the Soviet Union originally agreed to share the caretaking of Germany equally. Plans were also made to split the capital of Berlin into eastern and western halves.

EAST VERSUS WEST

The division quickly led to cities with clearly different economic and political structures. While West Berlin became a free and democratic economy of "haves," East Berlin adopted a planned financial system based on a Soviet-style government that left them as "have nots." Many East Berliners envied the wealth and success that spread across West Berlin.

By 1961, thousands of East Germans had poured across the border into West Berlin to work, to visit, and to live. What's more, the open boundary provided access to a free Europe and beyond. Walter Ulbricht, the East German leader (along with Soviet premier Nikita Khrushchev) was not happy with this coming and going; a wall of barbed wire was proposed to restrict the free and easy travel. To the satisfaction of the East and the concern of the West, nearly 28 miles of wire fence were erected in August 1961. Eventually, chain-link fencing, booby traps, and armed guards split the entire border between East and West Germany.

Within a year, a second fence of barbed wire was built nearly 300 feet from the first, creating a "no-man's land" to discourage any attempts at defecting. Once the original fence went up, the first successful escape was pulled off within two days—ironically, by an East German border guard.

More than 5,000 East Germans successfully escaped into West Berlin during the Wall's existance. However, approximately 200 were not successful.

CEMENTING THE HOSTILITIES

By 1965, the East Germans had replaced the barbed-wire fence with an enormous concrete barrier. By 1975, it stood 12 feet high and 4 feet thick and was topped with barbed wire and a rounded pipe to discourage any escapes. More than 300 watchtowers were spaced along the wall, offering armed East German guards a clear and unobstructed view of the "death strip" between the barriers.

WELCOME TO CHECKPOINT CHARLIE

The Berlin Wall kept East and West German citizens in their respective "backyards." Allied and Soviet personnel, however, could cross the border at certain passage areas called "check-points." The most famous Allied station was known as "Check-point Charlie," located halfway along the border, where Allied personnel and foreign travelers crossed between West and East Berlin. Today, it is part of the Allied Museum in western Berlin.

"TEAR DOWN THIS WALL!"

In June 1987, President Ronald Reagan called for Soviet leader Mikhail Gorbachev to remove the long-standing icon of isolation. It took two and a half years for East German officials to announce that their citizens could openly cross the border. Drunk with freedom, many Germans attacked the wall with sledgehammers, breaking off pieces for posterity.

PHILOSOPHY 101

Most of our knowledge and thinking have been shaped by the work of philosophers. They spend their lives searching for truth, explaining our existence, and wondering why things happen. For all those who slept through philosophy class, here's a very brief overview of the great Western philosophers.

SOCRATES: 470–399 B.C.

Major works: Socrates's thinking was not written down until after his death.

In a nutshell: Devised the Socratic method of argument. Believed we all have souls that lead us to virtue, synonymous with truth. Once we find truth, we must order our lives by it.

Quote:
"In every one of us there are two ruling and directing principles, whose guidance we follow wherever they may lead; the one being an innate desire of pleasure; the other, an acquired judgment which aspires after excellence."

Fact: Socrates was tried for corrupting youth and was executed with a drink poisoned by hemlock.

PLATO: 427–347 B.C.

Major works: *Republic, Phaedo, Symposium*

In a nutshell: Devised an idea of Forms, which are the perfect representation of everything, assuring a constant thread of truth in an ever-changing universe. Plato also discussed ideal forms of government and determined that philosophers make the best leaders.

Quotes:
"Ignorance is the root and stem of every evil."

"The rulers of the state are the only persons who ought to have the privilege of lying, either at home or abroad; they may be allowed to lie for the good of the state."

"The people always have some champion whom they set over them and nurse into greatness…This and no other is the root

from which a tyrant springs; when he first appears he is a protector."
Fact: As a student of Socrates, Plato recorded his famous teacher's wisdom and expounded on it further.

RENÉ DESCARTES: 1596–1650

Major works: *Discourse on Method, Rules for the Direction of the Mind, Meditations on First Philosophy*
In a nutshell: Descartes believed that the only thing we know for certain is that we are thinking beings: "I think, therefore I am." All else is just hypothesis. By bringing everything else into doubt, Descartes attempted to arrive at fundamental truths—such as the existence of God.

Quotes:
"If you would be a real seeker after truth, it is necessary that at least once in your life you doubt, as far as possible, all things."
"All that is very clearly and distinctly conceived is true."
Fact: Descartes was also a trailblazing mathematician; he invented the Cartesian coordinate system, which provided great advances in algebra and geometry.

BLAISE PASCAL: 1623–1662

Major Work: *Thoughts: An Apology for Christianity*
In a nutshell: Pascal felt that reason and thought weren't enough to solve our problems; rather, we need to believe in God. He came up with a formula to measure the odds on the existence of God.
Quote:
"If I wager for and God is—infinite gain;
If I wager for and God is not—no loss.
If I wager against and God is—infinite loss;
If I wager against and God is not—neither loss nor gain."
Fact: At age 19, Pascal invented a calculating machine.

JOHN LOCKE: 1632–1704

Major works: *Essay Concerning Human Understanding, Two Treatises on Civil Government*
In a nutshell: Locke examined the mind and delved into the process through which it understands the world. He founded the

school of Empiricism, which maintains that everything we know is derived through experience. His political philosophy dwelt on a citizen's right to property and the right to revolution.

Quotes:
"New opinions are always suspected, and usually opposed, without any other reason but because they are not already common."
"Consciousness is the perception of what passes in a man's own mind. Can another man perceive that I am conscious of any thing, when I perceive it not myself? No man's knowledge here can go beyond his experience."

Fact: Locke's political writings were so controversial at the time that he was forced to publish them anonymously. He had a tremendous influence on the writers of the U.S. Constitution.

IMMANUEL KANT: 1724–1804

Major works: *Critique of Pure Reason, Foundations of the Metaphysics of Morals*
In a nutshell: Kant believed that morality and justice were governed by universal laws, just as nature is governed by laws. Kant's Categorical Imperative meant that even though we can't prove God's existence, everyone has a duty to act as if there is a God.

Quotes:
"Act only according to that maxim by which you can at the same time will that it should become a universal law."
"But although all our knowledge begins with experience, it does not follow that it arises from experience."

Fact: Generally regarded to be the greatest modern philosopher, Kant had significant influence on those who followed.

FRIEDRICH NIETZSCHE: 1844–1900

Major works: *The Birth of Tragedy, Twilight of the Idols, Thus Spake Zarathustra*
In a nutshell: Nietzsche is famous for his criticism of the entire culture: science, history, philosophy, art, and religion. He argued that you couldn't rely on the abstract—religion or philosophy—to find truth. Only superior individuals can rise above traditional concepts of good and evil to achieve a truly worthy human life.

Quotes:
"God is dead...and we have killed him."
"In the mountains of truth, you never climb in vain. Either you already reach a higher point today, or you exercise your strength in order to be able to climb higher tomorrow."
Fact: In 1899, one year before his death, Nietzsche saw a horse being whipped by a coachman. He threw his arms around the horse, and it is said he never regained his sanity.

MARTIN HEIDEGGER: 1889–1976

Major works: *Being and Time, The Basic Problems of Phenomenology*
In a nutshell: Heidegger investigated the nature of human existence, which he defined as active participation in the world, or "Being There." He also looked at our existence in relation to the pressures of modern society and our acknowledgment of our own mortality.
Quote:
"Man acts as though he were the shaper and master of language, while in fact language remains the master of man."
Fact: Although he rejected the title, Heidegger is often credited with being the founder of Existentialism.

FAMOUS LAST WORDS

"Even philosophers will praise war as ennobling mankind, forgetting the Greek who said: 'War is bad in that it begets more evil than it kills.'"

—IMMANUEL KANT

"I attribute the little I know to my not having been ashamed to ask for information, and to my rule of conversing with all descriptions of men on those topics that form their own peculiar professions and pursuits."

—JOHN LOCKE

A VIOLENT RUN FOR THE ROSES

Power—not flowers—was at stake in the Wars of the Roses, a series of battles and skirmishes between two branches of England's royal family. The Lancaster clan had the throne, and the York clan wanted it. Then the tables turned and turned again.

A FAMILY FEUD

One drawback of monarchies is that they often lead to quarrels over whose turn it is to sit on the throne. Brother turns against brother, son against father, and so on. More than 500 years ago, such a disagreement between noble cousins grew into a squabble that split England's ruling class into armed camps and repeatedly tore up the countryside.

The House of Lancaster and the House of York were branches of the royal Plantagenet family, descendents of King Edward III, who ruled from 1327 to 1377. The Wars of the Roses began in 1399, when Henry of Bolingbroke, a grandson of Edward III, ended the disastrous reign of his cousin, Richard II, and took the throne himself. Also known as the Duke of Lancaster, the new king, now Henry IV, founded the Lancastrian Dynasty. He passed his scepter down to son Henry V, who in turn passed it to his then nine-month-old son, Henry VI in 1422.

THE YORKIST CLAIM

Lancasterian heirs might have continued this streak indefinitely, but pious Henry VI preferred the spiritual realm of prayer to his worldly kingdom, which sorely needed leadership. Worse, the king developed a mental disorder resulting in periodic breakdowns.

After Henry VI lapsed into temporary insanity in 1453, the powerful Earl of Warwick appointed the Duke of York to fill in as protector of the realm. York, an able leader, was also a descendent of Edward III and boasted a family tree that arguably made him a better claimant to the crown than the sitting king.

York earned the fierce enmity of the queen, Margaret of Anjou, who wielded more actual power than her husband did and who feared York would steal the throne. Battles ensued, beginning in 1455, with York defeating the royal forces more than once. In 1460, Lancastrian forces killed York in a sneak attack. The Yorkist cause passed to his 18-year-old son, Edward, who won a decisive battle, ran King Henry and Queen Margaret out of the country, and had himself crowned Edward IV in 1461.

The wars went on, however, as the new king clashed with his father's old supporter, the Earl of Warwick. For a time, Warwick got the upper hand and put addled King Henry back on the throne. Edward prevailed in 1471, however, and maintained order until his death in 1483.

THE FIGHT RESUMES AND ENDS

Edward IV's young son briefly succeeded him as Edward V, but the boy's uncle, brother of the late king, appears to have pulled a fast one. The uncle pushed little Eddie aside and became Richard III, one of England's most notorious monarchs. His notoriety is based on the widespread belief that Richard III murdered his two defenseless young nephews—Edward V and a younger brother.

For that reason and others, Richard lost the backing of many nobles, who flocked to support another royal claimant, Henry Tudor, the Earl of Richmond. A Welshman, this new contender also descended from Edward III on the Lancaster side.

Tudor famously killed Richard III in battle and became Henry VII, founder of England's Tudor Dynasty. He married the Yorkist heiress, the late Edward IV's daughter Elizabeth, in 1485, consolidating the family claim and ending, finally, the Wars of the Roses.

HOLLYWOOD VERSUS HISTORY

You may not be surprised to learn that Hollywood doesn't always get history right.

How about "bed-wetter"?

Alexander (2004)—Macedonian soldiers accuse Alexander of being a tyrant, which was no insult in Alexander's day.

Computer age-progression was so cool in the 18th century

The Man in the Iron Mask (1998)—An old-age portrait of King Louis XVI pops up, but the Louis of the film is a young man.

Everything sank but the schnitzel

Titanic (1943)—In this opulent Nazi version of the famed ship disaster, only one person aboard isn't a schemer and a braggart—a German national who serves on the ship's crew.

And the mayor is Latino

Chicago (2003)—A black prison matron oversees the Chicago women's jail—something highly unlikely in the ferociously segregated Chicago of the 1920s.

No, just horse flatulence

High Noon (1952)—When Gary Cooper stands in the middle of the street and the camera executes a graceful crane shot well above the ground, smog from Los Angeles can be seen in the distance.

But history is apparently willing to bend the rules

Guns Don't Argue (1957)—Everybody in this account of 1930s gangsters John Dillinger, "Ma" Barker, and others drives 1950s cars and sports 1950s wardrobes.

Oh, it could fly, it just couldn't land

GoodFellas (1990)—During the 1963 airport robbery, a 747 flies overhead. The 747 didn't fly until 1966.

Just another piece in the sinister tapestry of conspiracy

JFK (1991)—The Minox C spy camera that figures in the story wasn't invented until 1969, six years after President Kennedy's assassination.

Everything went to hell when Himmler started wearing cowboy boots

The Eagle Has Landed (1977)—Uniforms of SS troopers in a scene set in Warsaw have appropriate SS markings on their coats, and incorrect *Wehrmacht* (regular army) insignia on their collars.

"Mischievous rascals" would work

Anna and the King (1999)—In this romantic adventure set in the 1860s, antimonarch killers are referred to as "death squads"—a term that would not come into use until well into the following century.

When the speculators get into it the whole hobby is ruined

The Dangerous Lives of Altar Boys (2000)—Kids in this drama set in the late 1970s collect comic books from the 1980s.

They're just showing off again

Where Eagles Dare (1968)—Antiaircraft guns at the castle redoubt are aimed straight up, but to be effective the barrels should be angled so that enemy planes are hit before they're on top of the emplacements.

She meant to say "Scarlett O'Birnbaum"

Mame (1974)—Mame tells Beauregard Burnside she "feels like Scarlett O'Hara," but the novel hadn't yet been written at the time Mame's story takes place.

Yeah, but who wants a blood blister on the ankle?

The Rookie (1990)—Charlie Sheen fires up Clint Eastwood's vintage Harley by pressing the electric start button—but a bike this old had to be vigorously kick-started.

It gets good gas mileage

Gladiator (2000)—During the "Battle of Carthage" Colosseum sequence, a gas cylinder can be seen on the underside of an overturned chariot.

Continued from page 162.

347 B.C.
An emerging Rome fights its Samnite neighbors for control of central Italy. With the defeat of coastal rival Tarentum in 272 B.C., Rome dominates nearly all of the Italian boot.

264 B.C.
Rome and Carthage (in modern-day Tunisia) begin the First Punic War. The Romans win a sea battle that isolates the Carthaginian army, and Carthage surrenders in 241.

216 B.C.
In the Second Punic War, Carthage's top general, Hannibal Barca, defeats Rome's finest at Cannae with a battlefield maneuver that will be studied and attempted by generals for the next 22 centuries. But the Romans are a resilient bunch, and they come back to win Round Two.

146 B.C.
Mare Nostrum. After a three-year siege, Roman General Scipio Africanus takes the city of Carthage to win the Third Punic War. This time Rome destroys the rival capital for good. Rome dominates trade throughout the Mediterranean, a position it will enjoy for more than a quarter millennium.

61–52 B.C.
Hail Caesar (Part I). Julius Caesar's legions conquer Switzerland, France, Belgium, and Germany. Caesar makes a brief appearance on the shores of Great Britain before declaring victory and heading back to Rome.

51 B.C.
Egypt's princess Cleopatra becomes Queen Cleopatra VII of Egypt, ruling her lands jointly with her ten-year-old brother, King Ptolemy XIII. Around this time, Heron of Greece invents the steam engine, but no one seems to know what to do with it.

48 B.C.
Hail Caesar (Part II). Caesar defeats Pompey the Great and the Roman Senate at the Battle of Pharsalus, making Caesar the undisputed leader of Rome.

44 B.C.
Caesar is assassinated. Resulting unrest quickly breaks into civil war.

31 B.C.
Hail Caesar (Part III). Julius Caesar's nephew, Octavian, defeats Marc Antony and Egypt's Queen Cleopatra at the Battle of Actium, ushering in the era of the Roman Empire.

C. 4 B.C.
Jesus Christ is born in Bethlehem, Palestine.

C. A.D. 1
Shintoism becomes the dominant religion in Japan.

C. A.D. 29
Christ crucified outside Jerusalem. Christianity quietly begins to spread throughout the Roman world.

A.D. 63
Joseph of Arimethea introduces Christianity to the British Isles.

Timeline

A.D. 79
Mount Vesuvius erupts, wiping cosmopolitan Pompeii, Italy, off the map.

A.D. 135
The Diaspora. Jewish revolt leads to a brutal Roman crackdown followed by the dispersal of the Jewish peoples from Jerusalem and surrounding territories for nearly 1,900 years.

A.D. 220
After a nearly 400-year run, China's Han Dynasty comes to an end. China will split into fragmented kingdoms for the next 81 years.

A.D. 306
Roman general Constantinus becomes emperor; Christians are officially tolerated, and by Constantine's death Christianity has become a dominant religion in Rome.

A.D. 320
Gupta Kingdom replaces the Kushana Empire in northern and central India, opening the door to a golden age of Indian civilization. Poetry, medicine, and other cultural achievements mark Gupta rule for nearly a century.

A.D. 324–330
Constantine I moves the capital of the Roman Empire to Byzantium, at the border of Europe and Asia.

C. A.D. 350
A small collection of tribes in Central America begins to form the Mayan civilization.

A.D. 395
With the death of Emperor Theodosius I, the Roman Empire is divided into eastern and western empires under the rule of his two sons. Barbarians continue to press the weakening empire from the north.

A.D. 407
Rome withdraws the last of its legions from Britannia, and Picts, Scots, and Saxons rush into the power vacuum. According to legend, King Arthur battles the Saxons toward the end of the 5th century.

A.D. 433–453
Attila, king of the Huns, runs wild from the Black Sea into France, threatening the dominions of the tottering Roman Empire. Rome and the Visigoths team up to defeat Attila in 451 at the Battle of Chalons in France, saving western Europe from "the scourge of God," but Attila threatens Italy the next year. Attila's unexpected death after a banquet in 453 ends one threat to the decrepit Roman Empire, but before long Attila's place is taken by other barbarian warlords.

A.D. 476
Look Out Below! Germanic leader Odocer topples the last Roman emperor in the west, and the fall of the Roman Empire is complete. Europe enters a period known as the Dark Ages. Franks, Vandals, Ostrogoths, and Huns, among other barbarian tribes, dismember the western empire's dominions.

Wondering what happened next?
Turn to page 265 to find out!

Misconceptions of History
GOING FOR THE JUGULAR

The human body has always been fertile ground for misconceptions.

The celebrated Greek doctor Hippocrates postulated that all human emotions flowed from four bodily fluids, or humors: blood (which makes you cheerful and passionate), yellow bile (which makes you hot-tempered), black bile (which makes you depressed), and phlegm (which makes you sluggish or stoic). Though the good doctor's humors have given behavioral scientists a nice structure for examining personality types (sanguine, choleric, melancholic, and phlegmatic), the idea that our bodily fluids make us angry, depressed, or elated died out in the 1800s.

The withering of the Hippocratic belief in humors proved to be good news for patients who were not thrilled with the practice of bloodletting, a process of opening a patient's veins to lower blood levels in an attempt to bring the humors into balance and cure all manner of mental and physical ills. Bloodletting, with a knife or with leeches, was an accepted medical practice from the time of the Greeks, Mayans, and Mesopotamians, and it was going strong at the end of the 18th century, when George Washington had almost two liters of blood let out to cure a throat infection. (He died shortly afterward.)

✧✧✧

- *Good Humor docs believed "toxic vapors" caused disease. Certainly, if you walked through London in 1500, stepping through all manner of noisome filth and breathing fermenting human and animal wastes, you could get sick. The waste attracted rats, which* did *carry disease. Cause: wrong. Association: dead on.*

Fast Facts

- Urine wasn't one of the humors, but Tudor doctors did take urine samples—just like your family physician. However, it's a fair bet your family M.D. doesn't taste them, like Tudor docs did.

- If you had the gout in Tudor England, the preferred remedy was goat grease mixed with saffron. It might have worked, too, if charlatans hadn't substituted cheap imitations for the expensive saffron. Anything to make a quick pound.

- Everyone in Tudor England—men, women, and children—drank beer. The water was entirely too filthy to drink.

- During plague times, doctors wore long facemasks, called "beaks," and filled them with herbs to ward off the epidemic (or at least its olfactory cues).

- One odd Tudor concept was "weapon salve." Let's suppose some antisocial Tudor Englishwoman slashed your arm with a sickle. If you could find her sickle and anoint the weapon with a healing potion, your arm would supposedly heal.

- Got a headache? In Tudor England, you'd use willowbark tea (naturally containing aspirin). If your head hurt too much to scrounge around for willowbark, you could resort to hair and urine. You'd take a lock of your hair, and boil it in your urine. Then you'd toss the hair into the fire. Headache cured!

- To remedy lung problems, Tudor English took licorice and comfrey root.

- The Greek physician Herodicus of Selymbria advocated maintaining health through nutrition and exercise rather than drugs as early as the 5th century B.C. His diet fell out of favor when he was criticized in Plato's Republic for living unnaturally "to a miserable old age."

BARBED-WIRE REVOLUTION

*In 1915, Robert Frost gave the world the line
"Good fences make good neighbors." But fences have often meant
much more than that; to the brave men and women defending
their property against the wilderness, they meant nothing less
than safety and survival. But what makes a "good" fence?
In the American West, the answer was barbed wire—
an invention that left its mark on an entire continent.*

As America's settlers spread out into its vast heartland, they tried
to take their fences with them. However, in comparison with the
rock-strewn fields of New England or the lush pine forests of
the South from whence they came, the pioneers found their new
environs to be lacking in suitable material with which to build
the barriers that would protect their land. At the time, it was the
responsibility of landowners to keep roving animals out of their
fields (rather than it being incumbent upon the owner of the
animals to keep them controlled). As a result, farmers were left to
deal with the problem of how to protect their crops in conjunction
with the impossibility of building their traditional fences. A new
solution simply had to be found. The answer came from the state
of Illinois, which was on the border between the civilized East
and the wild West.

AN IDEA WHOSE TIME HAD COME

In 1873, a farmer named Henry Rose was desperate to control
a "breachy" cow. His original idea was to attach a board covered
with metallic points directly to the head of his cow; when the
cow ran into a fence, the points would prick the cow and cause it
to retreat. It came as a surprise to Rose (though probably not to
anyone else) that requiring his cow to wear a plank all the time
proved impractical; he then decided to attach the boards to his
fence rather than to the cow. The solution seemed promising,

and Rose proudly showed off his invention at a county fair where it caught the attention of a number of other inventors, including Joseph Glidden.

Joseph Glidden, working with a hand-cranked coffee mill in his kitchen, soon found that by twisting two lengths of wire together with a shorter piece in between to form a prickly barb, he could make a fence as effective as Rose's. He put up a test fence demonstrating his new invention, and word quickly spread. Isaac Ellwood, who had also seen Rose's display at the county fair and had been working on his own version, drove out to see Glidden's fence only to ride off in a rage when his wife commented that Glidden's barrier was superior to his. Ellwood was a shrewd businessman, however, and after he cooled down, he purchased an interest in Glidden's invention, and the two went into business together making barbed-wire fencing. Joseph Haish, also inspired by the Rose invention, introduced a rival barbed-wire fence around the same time.

All that was left was to convince a doubtful public that a few strands of thin wire could hold back determined cattle. The innumerable herds of Texas would be the proving ground, as barbed-wire salesmen threw up enclosures and invited ranchers to bring their most ornery cattle. To the amazement of the onlookers, barbed wire proved equal to the task again and again, and sales skyrocketed.

DON'T FENCE ME IN

Ironically, even though barbed wire's most obvious use was to protect farmers' fields, it wasn't until the cattle ranchers seized on barbed wire that it began to transform the West. Large ranches quickly realized that by fencing off grazing land they could effectively control the cattle industry, and miles of fencing sprang up across Texas and other territories. The fences weren't always well received; they injured cows and were sometimes put up without regard to traditional pasture or water rights. The winters of 1885 to 1887 were particularly brutal; free-range cattle in northern ranges, accustomed to moving south in the face of impending blizzards, found their way blocked by the strange new fences.

The cows froze to death by the thousands—carcasses stacked 400 yards deep against the fences in some places—in an event forever remembered as the Big Die-Up. Tempers naturally ran high, and there were open hostilities across the West, as armed factions cut down rival fences and put up new ones.

Despite the controversy, however, it proved impossible to reverse the trend to fence in land. Within about 25 years of the introduction of barbed wire, nearly all of what had previously been free-range land was fenced and under private ownership. The open land of the West, at one time considered an inexhaustible resource for all to use, was divided up and made off limits to the general public. The new invention channeled people into fixed paths of transit centered around railroads and towns. These patterns evolved into the interstate highways and cities we know today. It's no exaggeration to say that barbed wire is responsible for the shape of the modern West as we see it today—and it can all be traced back to Henry Rose's breachy cow.

FAMOUS LAST WORDS

"Where a new invention promises to be useful, it ought to be tried."
—Thomas Jefferson

"An amazing invention—but who would ever want to use one?"
—Rutherford B. Hayes upon making a call from Washington to Pennsylvania with Alexander Graham Bell's telephone, patented on March 7, 1876

"Our inventions are wont to be pretty toys, which distract our attention from serious things. They are but improved means to an unimproved end."
—Henry David Thoreau

MANSA MUSA'S REVERSE GOLD RUSH

History's epic gold rushes were generally characterized by masses of people trekking to the gold. But in 1324, the legendary Mansa Musa bucked the trend by trekking masses of gold to the people—and severely depressed the Egyptian gold market as a result.

If you could talk to a gold trader from 14th-century Cairo, he might say that the worst time of his life occurred the day Mansa Musa came to town.

Musa, king of the powerful Mali Empire, stopped over in Cairo during his pilgrimage to Mecca. Arriving in the Egyptian metropolis in 1324, Musa and his entourage of 60,000 hangers-on were anything but inconspicuous. Even more conspicuous was the 4,000-pound horde of gold that Musa hauled with him.

While in Cairo, Musa embarked on a spending and gift-giving spree unseen since the pharaohs. By the time he was finished, Musa had distributed so much gold around Cairo that its value plummeted in Egypt. It would be more than a decade before the price of gold recovered from the Mali king's extravagance.

A FOOL AND HIS MONEY?—NOT MUSA

Musa's story conjures the old adage about fools and their money soon parting—especially when you consider he had to borrow money for the trip home. But Musa was no fool.

Musa ruled Mali from 1312 until 1337, and ushered in the empire's golden age. He extended Mali's power across sub-Saharan Africa from the Atlantic coast to western Sudan. Mali gained tremendous wealth by controlling the trans-Sahara trade routes, which passed through Timbuktu and made the ancient city the nexus of northwest African commerce. During Musa's reign, Mali exploited the Taghaza salt deposits to the north and the rich Wangara gold mines to the south, producing half the world's gold.

Musa's crowning achievement was the transformation of Timbuktu into one of Islam's great centers of culture and education. A patron of the arts and learning, Musa brought Arab scholars from Mecca to help build libraries, mosques, and universities throughout Mali. Timbuktu became a gathering place for Muslim writers, artists, and scholars from Africa and the Middle East. The great Sankore mosque and university built by Musa remain the city's focal point today.

MUSA'S *HAJJ* PUTS MALI ON THE MAP

Musa's story is seldom told without mention of his legendary pilgrimage, or *hajj*, to Mecca.

The *hajj* is an obligation every Muslim is required to undertake at least once in their life. For the devout Musa, his *hajj* would be more than just a fulfillment of that obligation. It would also be a great coming-out party for the Mali king.

Accompanying Musa was a flamboyant caravan of courtiers and subjects dressed in fine Persian silk, including 12,000 personal servants. And then there was all that gold. A train of 80 camels carried 300 pounds of gold each. Five hundred servants carried four-pound solid-gold staffs.

Along the way, Musa handed out golden alms to the needy in deference to one of the pillars of Islam. Wherever the caravan halted on a Friday, Musa left gold to pay for the construction of a mosque. And don't forget his Cairo stopover. By the time he left Mecca, the gold was all gone.

But one doesn't dish out two tons of gold without being noticed. Word of Musa's wealth and generosity spread like wildfire. He became a revered figure in the Muslim world and inspired Europeans to seek golden kingdoms on the Dark Continent.

Musa's journey put the Mali Empire on the map—literally. European cartographers began placing it on maps in 1339. A 1375 map pinpointed Mali with a depiction of a black African king wearing a gold crown and holding a golden scepter in his left hand and a large gold nugget aloft in his right.

THE SWASTIKA:
SACRED GOOD, NAZI EVIL

*For thousands of years, it stood as a sacred symbol of fortune
and vitality—until Adolph Hitler adopted its eye-catching
geometry to lead his rise to power, turning the swastika into
the 20th century's ultimate emblem of evil.*

Originating in India and Central Asia, its name comes from the
Sanskrit word *svastika*, meaning well-being and good fortune.
The earliest known examples of the swastika date to the Neolithic
period of 3000 B.C. A sacred symbol in Hinduism, Buddhism, and
Jainism, the symbol was most widely used in India, China, Japan,
and elsewhere in Asia, though archaeological examples have also
been found in Greco-Roman art and architecture, in Anglo-Saxon
graves of the pagan period, in Hopi and Navajo art from the
American Southwest, and in Gothic architecture in Europe. Syna-
gogues in North Africa and Palestine feature swastika mosaics, as
does the medieval cathedral of Amiens, France.

For thousands of years, the swastika was a symbol of life, the
sun, power, and good luck, though in some cultures a counter-
clockwise mirror image of the swastika, called a *sauvastika*, meant
bad luck or misfortune. Pointing to evidence in an ancient Chinese manuscript, astronomer Carl Sagan theorized that a celestial
phenomenon occurring thousands of years ago may have given
rise to the swastika's use around the world, when gas jets shooting
from the body of a passing comet were bent into hooked forms
by the comet's rotational forces, creating a similar shape. Other
scholars believe that it was so widely known because its geometry
was inherent in the art of basket weaving.

The modern revival of the swastika in the Western world began
with the excavation of Homer's Troy on the shores of the Darda-
nelles in the 1870s. German archaeologist Heinrich Schliemann
discovered pottery and other artifacts at the site decorated with

swastikas. Schliemann and other scholars associated his finds with examples of the symbol uncovered on ancient artifacts in Germany. They theorized that the swastika was a religious symbol linking their German-Aryan ancestors to the ancient Teutons, Homeric Greeks, and Vedic India. German nationalists, including anti-Semitic and militarist groups, began using the symbol at the end of the 19th century. But with its connotations of good fortune, the swastika also caught on in Western popular culture. Swastikas were used to decorate cigarette cases, postcards, coins, and buildings throughout Europe. In the United States, they were used by Coca-Cola, the Boy Scouts, and a railroad company. The U.S. Army's 45th Division used the symbol during WWI; and Charles Lindberg painted one inside the nose cone of the *Spirit of St. Louis* for good luck.

In 1920, Adolf Hitler adopted the symbol for the Nazi Party's insignia and flag—a black swastika inside a white circle on a field of red—claiming he saw in it "the struggle for the victory of the Aryan man." With Hitler's appointment as chancellor, the Nazi flag was raised alongside Germany's national flag on March 14, 1933, and became the nation's sole flag a year later. The symbol was used ubiquitously in Nazi Germany—on badges and arm bands, on propaganda material, and on military hardware. By the end of the war, much of the world identified the symbol only with Hitler and the Nazis. Its public use was constitutionally banned in postwar Germany. Though attempts have been made to rehabilitate its use elsewhere, the swastika is still taboo throughout the Western world.

In Asia, however, the swastika remains a part of several religious cultures and is considered extremely holy and auspicious. In India, it is a symbol of wealth and good fortune, appearing not only in temples and at weddings but on buses, on rickshaws, even on a brand of soap. Hindus in Malaysia, Indonesia, and elsewhere in Southeast Asia also continue its use. In China, the left-facing Buddhist swastika is the emblem of Falun Gong. In 2005, the government of Tajikistan called for adoption of the swastika as a national symbol.

THE DIRTY, DIRTY BOER WAR

The last great conflict of the 19th century and the first of the 20th century was a far cry from a "Gentleman's War."

THE BEGINNING

In the fall of 1899, hostilities broke out in the South African regions known as the Transvaal and the Orange Free State between the Dutch settlers, called Boers, who controlled the territory, and the British Army. The reasons for the conflict lay not only in the discovery of gold and diamonds in the region but in Britain's desire to consolidate its imperial holdings. Certain of British aggression, the Boers struck first and dealt the overly confident and ill-prepared British soldiers a series of swift defeats. The British quickly regained their footing, however, and within a year had captured all of the major cities in the region. Unfortunately for all involved, this was just the beginning.

A WHITE MAN'S WAR

With the capture of the Boer capital cities in the spring of 1900, the British Army considered its job complete. It was the first time since the Crimean War (1853–1856) that British soldiers had fought against white opponents, and many were proud that the indomitable spirit of the glorious British Empire had once again held sway against a worthy opponent. No doubt, more than one English soldier was already imagining the stories he would tell his grandchildren many years hence.

The only spot of difficulty was that the Boers, a proud farming people who considered the land theirs by right of seizure and dominance over the native black population, refused to surrender. With their leader Paul Kruger safely ensconced in Holland, the Boers began a guerrilla war that, with their keen knowledge of the terrain and superior Mauser smokeless rifles, soon began to extract a heavy toll. The Boers struck swiftly from horseback or ambushed select targets from well-concealed positions in the African veldt. They were excellent marksmen who could disappear at will into the countryside, live off the sympathetic farms, and reappear to attack elsewhere.

British commander Lord Kitchener soon realized that the only way to eliminate the Boers was to deprive them of their support. To this end, Kitchener established a policy of total war in which British troops were ordered to burn farms (more than 30,000 buildings were destroyed), kill livestock, take no prisoners, and round up the Boer wives and children. In addition, the British established a dense network of block-houses that could alert garrisons to the presence of belligerent Boers in a particular area. These tactics proved murderously successful, and after two years of bloody conflict, the Boers were forced to concede defeat.

THE WOMEN AND CHILDREN'S WAR

Before the start of the Second World War, British Prime Minister Neville Chamberlain complained to German Field Marshall Hermann Goering about the Nazis' use of concentration camps to contain political prisoners. Goering, obviously prepared for the assault, brandished an encyclopedia in which the invention of concentration camps was credited to the British. Chamberlain, apparently, had no rebuttal because it was true.

In 1900, Lord Kitchener began a policy of collecting all non-combatant Boers, mostly women and children, into "refugee" camps. This was done partly to protect them, since the British had burned their farms and killed their livestock, and partly to separate the women and children from the men fighting in the veldt. But 27,927 women and children died in the camps due to unsanitary conditions and inadequate nutrition. Moreover, the camps placed "Hands Uppers," those families that wanted to surrender, side-by-side with "Bitter Enders," those who vowed to resist the British at all costs. This often resulted in violence.

THE AFRICANS' WAR

Boer women and children were not the only ones to suffer in concentration camps; thousands of native Africans were similarly imprisoned. Unlike the Boers, however, the Africans were not issued a food ration but were expected to grow or earn their daily morsel. In the end, approximately 14,000 natives died in the camps, though the exact number will probably never be known.

The Boer War was significant not only as the first use of concentration camps, but because it also marked the first time that whites armed blacks against whites. Somewhere between 10,000 and 30,000 Africans were given arms by the British to suppress the Boers. What the tribal natives lacked in discipline they made up for in zeal, often using the opportunity to avenge past wrongs against the actively racist Boer settlers who had seized their land. The natives' belief that the British would prove better rulers than the Boers, however, was misguided. The Treaty of Vereeniging, which ended the Boer War, denied rights promised to the African population by the British.

The Boers, who became known as Afrikaners, eventually formed the white supremacist Union of South Africa in 1910 with European and British support.

- *Mahatma Ghandi, Winston Churchill, Rudyard Kipling, and Sir Arthur Conan Doyle all spent their formative years in the Boer War. Ghandi was a stretcher-bearer for the British medical corps. Churchill earned fame as a journalist for his daring exploits and eventually parlayed that distinction into a seat in Parliament. Kipling worked for an army newspaper and was inspired to write the popular* Just So Stories *based on his African experience. The consummate anglophile, Doyle served as a doctor in the war and was knighted for writing favorably of the British role; he later created the quintessential British literary character—Sherlock Holmes.*

- *The Boer War was the last occasion that the British soldiers wore their red coats into battle. After the Boer War, khaki was the norm.*

Fast Facts

- *Adding injury to insult:* Shortly after the American colonies became the fledgling United States (1776), citizens knocked down a lead statue of King George III. They then melted it down for bullets to use in the Revolution.

- *Miranda Stuart, aka Dr. James Barry (1795–1865), not only lived her whole life as a man—she also rose to become inspector-general of British military hospitals. After her death, a charwoman who had been asked to lay out "his" body broke the news. So much for the customary military funeral.*

- *Martha "Calamity" Jane Cannary (c.1852–1903), the loutish but colorful frontierswoman, essentially drank herself to an early grave. In her final years, she looked much older than her chronological middle age.*

- *Frenchwoman Charlotte Corday (1768–1793) was a history-changer of the highest magnitude. Sickened and disillusioned by the Revolution's carnage, Corday took matters into her own hands: She knifed radical Jacobin politician Jean-Paul Marat in his bathtub. Need we add that she met the guillotine herself soon after?*

- *The Soviet Union was famous for its big projects; some were successful, others less so. In the Urals, Russia possessed Magnitka—a mountain made of iron ore. Stalin ordered a city built there, Magnitogorsk (1930s). It was a great idea, except that the ore only lasted five years.*

- *The Godmother: Fredericka "Marm" Mandelbaum ran a major criminal empire in New York in the 1800s. In keeping with women's traditionally strong role in education, she operated a school for promising young shoplifters, pickpockets, and burglars.*

- *Was it a comet? An asteroid? Here's what's odd about the Tunguska blast that flattened a 57-mile-wide area of Siberia on June 30, 1908: It left no crater.*

PONZI: THE MAN AND THE SCAM

Do you want to get rich quick? Are you charming and persuasive?
Do you lack scruples? Do you have a relaxed attitude toward the
law? If so, the Ponzi Scheme may be for you!

Yes, there was a real Mr. Ponzi, and here's
how his scam works. First, come up with a
phony investment—it could be a parcel of
(worthless) land that you're *sure* is going to
rise in value in a few months or stock in a
(nonexistent) company that you're *certain*
is going to go through the roof soon. Then
recruit a small group of investors, promising
to, say, double their money in 90 days. Ninety
days later, send these initial investors (or at
least some of them) a check for double their investment. They'll
be so pleased, they'll tell their friends, relatives, neighbors, and
coworkers about this sure-fire way to make a fast buck.

You use the influx of cash from these new investors to pay your
initial investors—those who ask for a payout, that is. The beauty
part is that most of your initial investors will be so enchanted with
those first checks that they'll beg to reinvest their money with you.
Eventually, of course, your new investors will start to wonder why
they aren't getting any checks, and/or some government agency
or nosy reporter might come snooping around... but by then (if
you've timed it right) you'll have transferred yourself and your
ill-gotten gains out of the country and out of reach of the authorities. Like related scams that include the Pyramid Scheme and the
Stock Bubble, financial frauds like this one have been around for
centuries, but only the Ponzi Scheme bears the name of a particular individual—Charles Ponzi.

MR. AMBITION LEARNS HIS TRADE

As you might imagine—given that he was a legendary con man—
Ponzi gave differing accounts of his background, so it's hard to
establish facts about his early life. He was likely born Carlos
Ponzi in Italy in 1882. He came to America in 1903 and lived the
hardscrabble existence of a newly arrived immigrant. While working as a waiter, he slept on the floor of the restaurant because he
couldn't afford a place of his own. But the handsome, suave Ponzi
was determined to rise in the world—by fair means or foul. The
foul means included bank fraud and immigrant smuggling, and
Ponzi wound up doing time in jails in both the United States and
Canada.

THE CHECK IS (NOT) IN THE MAIL

While living in Boston in 1919, the newly freed Ponzi more or
less stumbled across the scheme that would earn him notoriety.
It involved an easily obtained item called an International Postal
Reply Coupon. In simple terms, the scam involved using foreign
currencies to purchase quantities of a kind of international postal
stamp, then redeeming the stamps for U.S. dollars. This brought a
big profit because of the favorable exchange rate of the time, and
it actually wasn't illegal. The illegal part was Ponzi's determination
to bring ever-growing numbers of investors into the scheme . . .
and just keep their money. Until the roof fell in, Ponzi became a
celebrity. Before long, people across New England and beyond
were withdrawing their life savings and mortgaging their homes to
get in on the action.

The end came in the summer of 1920, when a series of investigative reports in a Boston newspaper revealed that the House
of Ponzi had no foundations. By that time, he'd taken some
40,000 people for a total of about $15 million. In 21st-century
terms, that's roughly $150 million. Ponzi spent a dozen years in
prison on mail fraud charges. Upon release, he was deported and
continued his scamming ways abroad before dying—penniless—
in Brazil in 1948.

AESOP:
WAS THE FANTASTIC
FABLER A FABLE HIMSELF?

Aesop's tales of talking animals—the industrious ant and the irresponsible grasshopper, or the fast but arrogant rabbit and the plodding but persistent tortoise—have been a staple of traditional folklore for centuries. But as it turns out, Aesop himself may have been as much a fable as his famous tales.

It's fun to tell Aesop's tales—especially since many of them take the air out of someone else's inflated ego or show the comic consequences of someone else's bad behavior. And with talking animals to boot! What's not to love?

WHO WAS AESOP?

By various traditions, Aesop (620–560 B.C.?) was a slave from Phrygia (central Turkey), Thrace (northern Greece), Sardis (western Turkey), or Ethiopia (horn of Africa), who was brought to the Greek island of Samos in the early 6th century B.C. and was eventually set free because of his wit and wisdom.

What we actually know of his life may be as fictional as his stories. Aesop's first official biography wasn't composed until the 14th century, and it was composed for the purposes of entertainment—not history. In it, Aesop appears as an unsightly, ungainly, and clever rogue who is always undermining and outwitting his master with his clever use of language. In one instance, when his master Xanthus has given precise directions for fixing "a lentil soup" for a special dinner party, Aesop fixes one boiled lentil and then avoids punishment by forcing the embarrassed Xanthus to admit that Aesop was only following his directions. In this version, Aesop the fabler is a subversive figure who turns the tables on the powerful—a trickster as common to folklore around the world as animal stories. Later biographies frame Aesop as a serious moral teacher and take most of the fun out of him. He becomes, after meritoriously winning freedom, a famous personality of the court of the Lydian King Croesus in Sardis (modern Sart, Turkey). Besides amazing the king and all the wisest men of the day, Aesop traveled about Greece instructing the powerful with his fables.

Even Aesop's death became a fable with as pointed a moral as any of his tales. He was framed and executed by dishonest men at Delphi (a famous Greek shrine) when he refused to distribute some of Croesus's gold (which the king had sent to the shrine as a gift) because of the men's greed. However, ensuing disasters forced the guilty to fess up, and so the "the blood of Aesop" became a proverb for dishonest deeds that eventually come to light and come home to roost.

SO, WAS THERE AN AESOP?

Well, perhaps. The Greeks and Romans certainly thought there was. But, as with Homer, the famous bard who traditionally composed the *Iliad* and *Odyssey*, whether the author created the works or the works created the author is open for debate. Just as Demodocus, the blind bard who appears in Book Eight of the *Odyssey*, may have suggested the tradition that Homer was blind, so too the sly and satirical characters of the fables may have helped to create the character that became Aesop. In any case, both Aesop's fables and Aesop's life make for "fabulous" reading.

FAMOUS LAST WORDS

"Every truth has two sides; it is as well to look at both, before we commit ourselves to either."

—AESOP

SEALED WITH A KISS

*In the times when nations were led by families,
a great way to improve diplomatic relations with a neighboring
state was to marry into its ruling house.*

"I NOW PRONOUNCE YOU ALLY AND VASSAL"

The idea of using marriage to seal a deal or shore up shaky diplomatic relations dates back well before the time of Israel's King Solomon, who picked up 700 wives in his pursuit of alliances with neighboring kingdoms. Rome's Pompey the Great married the daughter of archrival Julius Caesar to seal their power-sharing agreement in 59 B.C., and Eastern kingdoms such as China regularly doled out daughters to vassal states as a matter of diplomatic protocol. But it was during the Middle Ages that political marriages became as much a finely honed tool of foreign policy as poison, coded messages, and trade agreements.

The marital record of the Duchess of Aquitaine, a beautiful, intelligent lass named Eleanor, is a case in point. Heir to France's largest and wealthiest province, Eleanor was first married to Prince Louis, the son of King Louis VI of France, in 1137. After Eleanor failed to produce a male heir, the couple had the marriage annulled, and she quickly married Henry, the count of Anjou, duke of Normandy, and—within two years—king of England. The couple had a stormy relationship—Henry had Eleanor locked up in a castle for 15 years—but they managed to sire five sons, and most of their royal offspring were wedded to cement alliances with other noble families. (The marriage was so dysfunctional that it inspired an award-winning play and movie, both titled *The Lion in Winter*.) In 1199, one of Eleanor's last duties was to select a Castilian niece of her son, King John, to marry off to Prince Louis, the heir to the French throne.

Though most political marriages provided a veneer of protection for participating states, they usually flopped in the romance department. In 1328, King Afonso VI of Portugal married off daughter Maria to King Alfonso XI of Castile. Although their marriage was not a happy one (the Castilian king was enamored with his mistress, who bore him ten children), Alfonso offered his niece Constanza to Afonso's son, Prince Pedro. That relationship soured when Pedro fell madly in love with Constanza's lady-in-waiting, and the prince and servant conducted a not-so-secret affair until Constanza's death in 1345. (Even that romantic link was ill-fated, as King Afonso—worried that his son would be too heavily influenced by the Castilian throne—had assassins murder Pedro's lover in 1355, inciting a revolt and a family rift that took a year to patch up.)

NOT-SO-JOLLY OLD ENGLAND

England has long been a fertile land for disastrous political marriages. Take the Tudors, whose love lives were as tangled as the ivy that graced their castles. In 1509, England's King Henry VII arranged the marriage of his son Henry (later King Henry VIII) to Catherine of Aragon, the daughter of King Ferdinand and Queen Isabella of Spain. Catherine was the widow of Henry's older brother, Arthur, who had died unexpectedly, and young Henry was offered up to take his brother's place. The idea was to shore up relations with the most powerful Continental power, but the marriage was allegedly never legal, and Henry VIII divorced Catherine to take up with the second of his six wives.

Henry VIII's eldest daughter, Queen "Bloody Mary" Tudor, married Spain's Prince Phillip strictly to produce a Catholic heir, which the queen hoped would keep her Protestant half-sister Elizabeth off the English throne. But that effort failed, too. Mary's love for Prince (later King) Phillip went sadly unrequited—they had not met until two days before their wedding—and she died childless in 1558, whereupon the unconcerned Phillip proposed marriage to the incoming queen, Elizabeth I. For diplomatic reasons, Queen Elizabeth entertained marriage proposals from nobles of Spain, France, Austria, Sweden, Saxony, and Denmark, to name but a few. None of the would-be royal consorts ever made the cut.

WEAVING TANGLED WEBS

The practice of sealing relationships through marriage continued through the early 19th century, when Napoleon I of France negotiated with Tsar Alexander I of Russia for a marriage to Alexander's daughter, to strengthen the 1807 Treaty of Tilsit between the two countries. Negotiations broke down (Napoleon's influential foreign minister, Charles Tallyrand, opposed the prospective nuptials), and the French emperor instead married the daughter of Emperor Francis I of Austria. Like most other political marriages, this one didn't last; when Napoleon was sent into exile on a South Atlantic island in 1815, his Austrian wife returned to Vienna and took up with an Austrian count two years later.

The entwined family trees that took root in Europe's early centuries left the royal houses in such an incestuous mess that by the time World War I broke out, three of the five chief belligerents—Kaiser Wilhelm II of Germany, Tsar Nicholas II of Russia, and King George V of England—were first cousins. (Nicholas and George were grandsons of the King of Denmark, and George and Wilhelm were grandsons of Queen Victoria.) Virtually all established royal houses, from the Thames to the Danube, could boast some family ties to every other ruling house.

- *Spousal abuse was likely common in ancient Egypt. A disturbing percentage of healed arm fractures on mummified women seem to be defensive injuries consistent with shielding one's head from a heavy blow.*

- *Madame de Pompadour (1721–1764) was every bit as influential and clever as history paints her. What most don't know is that this famous mistress of King Louis XV was born Jeanne Antoinette Poisson ("Fish"), a disgraced financier's daughter. Quite the step up!*

LAIKA—FIRST CASUALTY OF THE SPACE RACE

The first living being to be launched into orbit was a three-year-old mongrel named Laika, an unassuming stray who became an unwilling pawn in the space race. Unfortunately, contingency plans to bring the dog back to Earth were never developed, and Laika also became the first animal to die in space.

The space race was launched on October 4, 1957, when the Soviet Union successfully sent *Sputnik 1* into orbit. And with that, the mad dash to be the first country to get a man into space began.

Russian Premier Nikita Khrushchev ordered members of his space program to launch a second spacecraft into orbit on the 40th anniversary of the Russian Revolution. The primary mission of *Sputnik 2* was to deliver a living passenger into orbit. The spacecraft—which was designed and built in just four short weeks—blasted into space on November 3, 1957.

Initially, three dogs were trained for the *Sputnik 2* test flight. Laika, a 13-pound mixed-breed rescued from a Moscow shelter, was ultimately chosen for the historic mission. Though the Soviets affectionately nicknamed the dog Little Curly, the Western press referred to her by a more derogatory nickname—Mutt-nik.

3, 2, 1...BLAST OFF!

Sputnik 2's capsule was equipped with a complete life-support system, padded walls, and a harness. During liftoff, Laika's respiration rocketed to four times its prelaunch rate, and her heartbeat tripled. Sensors indicated the cabin's temperature soared to 104 degrees.

The Soviets waited until *after* the spacecraft was launched to reveal that Laika would never return to Earth. The mission had been so rushed there hadn't been time to plan for the dog's return. She had only enough food and oxygen to last her ten days.

The Soviets issued conflicting information regarding Laika's death. Initial reports indicated that Laika survived four days in orbit—evidence that a living being could tolerate space. Her eventual death was attributed to either oxygen deprivation or euthanization via poisoned dog food—depending on the source.

Laika's remains were destroyed when *Sputnik 2* fell out of orbit and burned up reentering the earth's atmosphere.

Russians named postage stamps, cigarettes, and chocolate in Laika's honor, treating the dog as a national hero. In the meantime, there was outrage in the West over what many perceived to be the cruel and inhumane treatment of the animal.

THE AFTERMATH

In October 2002, a Moscow scientist revealed that Laika had actually died *hours* into the mission due to overheating and stress.

In March 2005, a patch of soil on Mars was unofficially named in Laika's honor. Dozens of other animals—including monkeys, frogs, mice, worms, spiders, fish, and rats—have since successfully made the journey into space.

- *Between 1957 and 1966, the Soviets successfully sent 13 more dogs into space—and recovered most of them unharmed.*

- *Dogs were initially favored for space flight over other animals because scientists believed they could best handle confinement in small spaces.*

- *To train for her space flight, Laika was confined to smaller and smaller boxes for 15 to 20 days at a time.*

- *In 1959, the United States successfully launched two monkeys into space. Named Able and Baker, the monkeys were the first of their species to survive spaceflight.*

FRESH INGREDIENTS FOR THE MELTING POT

This is the story of how foreigners built the United States.

Founded as a nation of immigrants, the United States has seen four major waves of immigration that have shaped its history. Like ocean waves devouring a shoreline—chewing up the existing landscape, only to leave behind new sand and soil in its place—the tides of demographics left their mark on America.

FIRST WAVE: WESTERN EUROPE AND AFRICA

The first major influx to North America began long before the nation's founding. From the early 1600s until about 1820, immigration came predominantly from colonial powers. England was the major contributor to what would become the United States of America, though the other mercantile and colonial powers—France and Holland, in particular—would enrich the new nation's settlements as well.

What drove these Europeans to the New World's coasts? Dreams of land ownership, freedom from religious and political persecution, and a chance to break loose from the caste system that characterized Europe in one form or another since the end of the Dark Ages. In the late 1700s, as democracy shook Europe's established kingdoms, newcomers also included French families, many of whom found their way to New Orleans, forming a colorful part of the Deep South's culture.

By the early 1800s, New York City began overtaking Philadelphia as the nation's premier city and became a major entry point for immigrants—though major eastern seaports from Newport to Savannah also brought in would-be citizens by the thousands. North and south of the forbidding Appalachian Mountains, the hardiest of these immigrants pushed westward in search of land on which to build new lives.

The major exception to this trend was, of course, the African slave trade. Africans kidnapped and brought to the United States formed a substantial minority whose numbers (together with their U.S.-born children) grew from nearly 750,000 in 1790 (the first year of the U.S. census) to a little more than 1.1 million by 1808, the  year the slave trade was officially abolished. As Thomas Jefferson and other founding fathers foresaw, the problem of slavery would grow exponentially every decade, as the slave population multiplied throughout the east and south.

SECOND WAVE: CENTRAL EUROPE AND CHINA

The next wave spanned the period from 1830 to about 1870, when the nation's growth beckoned to men and women of northern and central Europe. In a 20-year period, some 2.5 million people came to the United States; about a third were Irish nationals who came to escape a terrible potato famine that condemned many of their countrymen to starvation. Because the Irish immigrants generally had little money when they arrived, they tended to remain in eastern cities such as New York and Boston. More affluent immigrants, such as Germans and Scandinavians, tended to move west in a band running from central Pennsylvania to the Dakotas and Great Plains.

By the time Manifest Destiny brought the United States to the Pacific shores at the end of the Mexican–American War, immigrants began coming in from the other direction—the Far East. Exaggerated tales of California gold prompted many young Chinese men to embark for America. Though the majority of them took their earnings back to China, some established small businesses along the western seaboard or worked in the mining and rail industries. Their numbers grew until 1882, when Congress passed the Chinese Exclusion Act, which all but prohibited Chinese immigration for the next 80 years.

THIRD WAVE: EASTERN AND SOUTHERN EUROPE

From the 1870s through the early 1920s, America found a new source of fresh blood. Wars of liberation and nationalization forced legions of immigrants across the ocean on a growing network of transatlantic steamship lines. Between 1870 and 1900, approximately 12 million immigrants entered the United States, creating chaos among states that were charged with regulating immigration. To oversee this influx, the United States established a federal immigration facility on New York's Ellis Island. This new gateway to America opened for business on January 1, 1892.

One of the largest groups of "new" immigrants hailed from Italy, a nation reeling from poor harvests, disease, and the economic and political aftershocks of the wars of unification. From 1880 to 1900, America's Italian population increased tenfold, from around 44,000 in 1880 to more than 484,000 in 1900. Hailing from rural areas of Italy, they quickly adjusted to urban life, forming rich, distinctive "Little Italy" communities in many American cities.

In addition to national groups, Jews fleeing persecution in Russia, Germany, and other eastern European nations brought new talents to the nation's shores. Between 1880 and the early 1920s, about two million Jews left their homelands to come to America.

When the United States slumped into the Great Depression and World War II recalled millions of citizens to the colors of their motherlands, immigration trailed off.

FOURTH WAVE: FAR EAST AND LATIN AMERICA

The mid-1960s saw the start of a new immigration wave that continues today. Communist revolutions in Eastern Europe and Southeast Asia and an economic boom in the United States coincided with a removal of legal immigration quotas to produce the largest wave of immigration ever seen. This latest round of mass immigration was driven by conditions in Asia, Africa, and Latin America, three regions whose numbers of emigrants to the United States grew almost tenfold between 1960 and 1990.

POPE JOAN:
WAS SHE OR WASN'T HE?

Posing as a man, a scholarly German woman of English descent entered the Catholic Church hierarchy, rising to become pope in A.D. 855. Her secret emerged, literally, when she gave birth to a son while riding in a papal procession through the streets of Rome. The populace, which just couldn't take a joke, tied her to a horse's tail and dragged her to death while stoning her.

So here's the question: Is this story fact or fiction?

What Does the Holy See Say?

Not a chance. They list Pope Benedict III, A.D. 855–858, with no suggestion that the Holy Father might have been a Holy Mother. The Church has long blamed anti-Catholic writers and saboteurs said to have doctored the evidence.

Surely that's plausible, given the avalanches of anti-Catholic hatred since the Reformation.

Up to a point, yes. Catholic-bashers pummelled the papacy with Pope Joan taunts. However, that cannot explain the pre-Reformation references, not all of which meant woe unto St. Peter's Basilica.

An example, please.

Jan Hus, the Czech heretic burned at the stake in 1415 (a century before Luther picked up steam). In the trial record, Hus rebukes the papacy for letting a woman become pope. Why didn't they strappado him on the spot for rank blasphemy?

That indicates only that the Inquisitors believed the legend at the time, not that it's true.

Good point. But then there's Martin of Poland, a Dominican who wrote his history of the papacy in 1265. He's the primary source for Pope Joan, the hardest to dismiss. He didn't hate the church; he held high rank as papal chaplain. Did someone doctor our oldest copy of his account (circa 1300s)? Hard to say.

Could a woman have pulled it off?

Possibly. Medical checkups were even rarer than baths. The clergy shaved, solving the dilemma of facial hair. Papal garments were heavy and hanging. Every reference to Joan attests to her great intellect, a necessary aspect since no idiot could have been elected pope in drag. It wouldn't be easy, but it's possible.

Okay: If Joan was so smart, she knew she was pregnant. How did she plan to dispose of the child?

That's a big weakness in the pro-Joan theory. You can cover up your body and tonsure your head, but ask anyone who's ever flown commercially: You can't keep a baby quiet. How would she care for the infant if she managed to give birth in secret? If it's possible to insult a mythical figure's legacy, suggesting that she might abandon the infant would be that insult. She'd have had to know this pregnancy wouldn't end well.

So, historian, what of this? Legend or covered-up truth?

Stoning a pope to death in the streets would have been a big event, which should have spawned at least a few contemporary accounts. Where are they? There isn't enough strong evidence to say, "Pope Joan existed." There is just enough to make us wonder if the legend has some basis in reality.

How could that be?

Stories morph and change. About 700 years span the time between Joan and the Protestant Reformation—nearly the lifespan of the Roman Republic and Empire combined. The story could have wandered far enough into time's misty fog to place the papal mitre upon this mysterious woman's head.

But we do not know.

Without compelling new evidence, we never will.

Timeline

Continued from page 237.

A.D. 538
Korean missionaries introduce Buddhism to Japan; before long, "Shinto" is used to differentiate Japan's native religion from Buddhist and Confucianist imports. By 605, Buddhism and Confucianism become the state religions of Japan.

C. A.D. 613
The prophet Muhammad begins preaching; seven years later, he speaks of a spiritual journey with the archangel Gabriel, and in 622 he moves to Medina, marking a new phase of the Muslim calendar. Over the next hundred years, the Muslim faith drives an explosive campaign of conquest stretching from India to southern France.

A.D. 732
Charles Martel ("the Hammer"), ducal leader of the Frankish kingdom, halts the Muslim tide at Poitiers; Muslim gains in the west are held to the Iberian Peninsula.

A.D. 751
In return for military protection and service, Pope Zachary confirms Pepin the Short, son of Charles Martel, as the first Carolingian king of the Franks, creating a dynasty that will rule France until the early 10th century. Arab forces defeat Chinese armies at the Battle of Talas, extending Islamic influence into central Asia's trade routes.

C. A.D. 862
According to tradition, Byzantine missionary Saint Cyril invents the Cyrillic alphabet to spread the gospel among Slavonic peoples.

C. A.D. 867
A doctrinal argument between Pope Nicholas I and Byzantium's Patriarch Photius inflames estrangement between the two churches; a full-blown schism between the Orthodox and Roman Christian faiths erupts in A.D. 1054.

A.D. 871
Viking settlers establish villages in Iceland.

C. A.D. 900
Mass migration into Mexico's Yucatán peninsula leads to the emergence of a new Mayan kingdom.

A.D. 919
Frankish noble Henry of Saxony becomes King of Germany, which at the time is little more than a hodgepodge collection of duchies sharing a common language.

A.D. 929
Abd-ar-Rahman III declares himself Caliph of Spain, formalizing a Moorish kingdom in which literature, architecture, and medicine flowers.

A.D. 961
Otto of Saxony (son of King Henry I) marches to the rescue of the pope and is crowned the first Holy Roman Emperor. Before long, the Holy Roman Empire becomes one of the most powerful political forces in Europe.

Timeline

A.D. 987
Frankish noble Hugh Capet is crowned King of France and establishes the Capetian Dynasty; branches of the Capetian Dynasty, such as the Bourbons, will rule France until revolution hits in 1789.

A.D. 988
Vladimir I, Grand Prince of Kiev and Novgorod, orders his subjects to convert to Orthodox Christianity, establishing what will become Russia's dominant religion.

c. A.D. 1000
Viking captain Leif Erikson travels across the Northern Atlantic to Greenland and down the Canadian coast into Newfoundland nearly a half-century before Christopher Columbus reaches the "New" World.

1066
The last successful invasion of England reaches its climax at the Battle of Hastings, where William the Conqueror trounces King Harold Godwinson to claim the English throne.

1095
It Is God's Will! Pope Urban II calls for a crusade to retake Jerusalem from its Arab conquerors. The campaign becomes the first of eight major crusades, and a smattering of smaller crusades, to the Holy Land.

c. 1125
In Cambodia, Kambuja's King Suryavarman II embarks on a building project that includes Angkor Wat, the world's largest temple.

c. 1150
Peru's Inca tribes begin their expansion into one of the three great Western empires, creating a state that will last until 1533. Meanwhile, the Aztecs of central Mexico begin replacing the Toltec civilization and build their capital at Tenochtitlán.

c. 1200
Mayan leader Hunac Ceel and his allies fight a "Mayan Trojan War" against the empire's government at Chichen Itza.

1204
Crusaders Behaving Badly. Unruly Crusaders sack the Orthodox capital of Constantinople, unleashing an orgy of violence and looting that feeds animosity between western and eastern Christians for the next 800 years.

1206
An even more unruly Mongol named Temujin takes the title Ghengis Khan and launches an empire that will reach from the Pacific Ocean to Eastern Europe.

1215
An Offer He Can't Refuse. Menacing English barons force King John to sign the Magna Carta, a document acknowledging the king's fealty to the rule of law.

1242
Novgorod's Prince Alesandr Nevskii defeats the Teutonic Knights on a frozen Lake Peipus, turning back Germanic threats to western Russia. He pays tribute to the Mongol khans to the east to preserve Russian society throughout his domains.

Wondering what happened next? Turn to page 310 to find out!

Fast Facts

- Egyptian pharaoh Thutmose III (probably reigned 1479–1425 B.C.) resented his powerful stepmom, Hatshepsut. After she died, Thutmose vandalized her statues and dumped them in a quarry. Then he set out to chisel every instance of her name off all stone inscriptions. Despite his best efforts, we still know she existed.

- Herodotus reports that the Scythians, a fierce nomadic people from the Caspian Sea region of Central Asia, made drinking cups by gilding the interiors of human skulls. This died out when the Vikings took over.

- Paul Gauguin, the famous French painter, worked as a laborer on the Panama Canal.

- The White House hasn't always been known as such. This presidential domicile has also been called the "President's Palace," the "President's House," and the "Executive Mansion." In 1901, President Theodore Roosevelt officially gave the White House its current name.

- Presidents today are photographed as a matter of course, but that wasn't always the case. James Polk (1845–1849) was the first president ever to have his photograph taken. Not long after, President Theodore Roosevelt (1901–1909) celebrated another presidential milestone when he became the first of his office to ride in a car. A few decades later, President Franklin Roosevelt (1933–1945) became the first to ride in an airplane.

- Catherine of Aragon was both a widow and a virgin (allegedly) when she married Henry VIII.

- The colonists inadvertently chose a low tide to execute the Boston Tea Party. Due to this fact, nearly 350 crates of tea piled up in the shallow water. The colonists had to jump overboard and actually smash open the tea crates in order to make sure it was ruined.

WHY WE BUY

Advertising executives know how to push our buttons. They know what we want to buy, when we want to buy it, how much we're willing to pay for it, and how much of it we want. And they know how to inspire us to run right out and buy it—today!

IN THE KITCHEN

Ad agency McCann-Erickson Worldwide took a simple, two-sided slogan and turned Miller Lite beer into a top-selling brew in 1974. Actors, actresses, mystery authors, bronco riders, former and current athletes—all took a crack at debating whether Lite beer "Tastes great" or is "Less filling." The argument was never settled.

Candy-coated chocolate bits known as M&Ms were a blessing for moms who feared the dreaded "chocolate mess" on their children's hands. In 1954, the Ted Bates & Co agency informed America that M&Ms "Melts in your mouth, not in your hands." The candy was named after two executives at Hershey's—Forrest Mars and William Murrie.

Kellogg's Rice Krispies, a noisy breakfast favorite introduced in 1928, offered three cute elves named "Snap!, Crackle!, and Pop!" courtesy of the Leo Burnett ad agency. Worldwide favorites, they're known as "Piff!, Paff!, and Puff!" in Sweden, "Pim!, Pum!, and Pam!" in Mexico, and "Knisper!, Knasper!, and Knusper!" in Germany.

IN THE BATHROOM

In 1957, Clairol, a leader in hair-coloring and hair-care products, focused on the vanity of women when they asked, "Does she . . . or doesn't she?" Foote, Cone & Belding was the agency that boldly questioned the real hair color of the women of postwar America.

Benton & Bowles was an agency that developed clever slogans that brought booming sales for Crest toothpaste in 1958. A beaming boy flashed his smile following a successful visit to the dentist and cried, "Look, Ma! No cavities!" The agency also brought us the grouchy grocer Mr. Whipple, famous for the line "Please don't squeeze the Charmin!" in 1964.

Portly actor Jack Somack sat stone-faced, having wolfed down way too much dinner. Thanks to ad agencies like Jack Tinker & Partners; Doyle Dane Bernbach; and Wells Rich Greene, the overstuffed eater had Alka-Seltzer in the '60s and '70s. Somack claimed, "I can't believe I ate the whole thing," and the effervescent antacid tablets replied with, "Plop, Plop, Fizz, Fizz, Oh, what a relief it is."

FAST FOOD

A three-way tussle for the food dollar outside the home rumbled through the '70s and '80s. McDonald's told America, "You deserve a break today," while Burger King insisted that customers could, "Have it your way." Late arrival Wendy's Hamburgers countered with a feisty old lady named Clara Peller who demanded that an invisible cashier answer this famous question: "Where's the beef?"

SODA POP

In a soft drink battle that waged for decades, Pepsi-Cola, with the help of agency BBD&O, assured America that it belonged to "The Pepsi Generation" in 1964. Atlanta's Coca-Cola, with a typically top-notch jingle, responded that Coke was "The real thing." Also-ran 7-UP, however, was not caught lying down, as it cleverly positioned itself as "The Uncola" in the 1970s.

TRANSPORTATION

Avis Rent-A-Car, trailing the industry leader Hertz, admitted their work was cut out for them as they proudly stated, "We try harder," courtesy of agency Doyle Dane Bernbach in 1963. As America built its interstate highway system in the mid-1950s, Chevrolet invited everyone to "See the USA in your Chevrolet." Meanwhile, the Greyhound Bus Company responded by suggesting that travelers "Leave the driving to us."

A POX ON YOUR HOUSE...
OF COMMONS

It was a sordid little 1963 drama so outrageous it would have played well on the big screen. The players included a top official in English government, a beautiful showgirl/call girl, a prominent medical man, and a military member of the Communist Party. When it was all over, the outrage accelerated the paranoia of the Cold War and threatened the national security of Britain— not to mention the rest of the world.

THE CAST MEMBERS

John Profumo was the secretary of state for war under Harold Macmillan, England's prime minister for the Conservative Party in the early 1960s. Profumo was married to a beautiful movie actress named Valerie Hobson, whose biggest role was starring in *The Bride of Frankenstein.*

Christine Keeler was a young, vivacious model and topless showgirl in the Soho area of London, where she often posed for noted osteopath Stephen Ward, who fancied himself a sketch artist as well as a socialite. Ward had introduced Keeler, along with fellow showgirl Mandy Rice-Davies, to the world of the rich and famous.

Yevgeny Ivanov was a Soviet naval officer based at the Russian Embassy in London. He was acquainted with Dr. Ward. The British security service MI5 had tagged Ivanov as a KGB agent and had asked Ward to work on getting Ivanov to shift his allegiance to the West. With just a little prodding, they reasoned, Ivanov could be persuaded to join their side.

THE STORY UNFOLDS

All of these characters found themselves under one enormous roof in July 1961. Ward was throwing a party at Cliveden, the Buckinghamshire mansion of England's Lord Astor. Profumo was immediately attracted to Keeler and began seeing her after the party. But, on the quiet advice of a government official, Profumo called off the affair just a few months later.

What Profumo didn't know, however, was that Keeler had also been sleeping with Ivanov. Indeed, Christine Keeler was playing both sides of the Iron Curtain.

THE PLOT THICKENS

This might have been the end of the story. But Keeler had also been involved with two other men, Aloysius "Lucky" Gordon and Johnny Edgecombe, who got into a bloody brawl over Keeler at a club in Soho. In December 1962, Keeler was at Ward's house visiting Mandy Rice-Davies when Edgecombe showed up. Keeler refused to let him in, so Edgecombe shot at the door, attracting the attention of police and blowing the whole story wide open.

In the end, Keeler served nine months for committing perjury in a trial involving "Lucky" Gordon. Ward was charged with living off the "earnings of prostitutes"—namely Keeler and Rice-Davies. On the final day of the trial, Dr. Ward cheated the Royal Courts of their justice by committing suicide. The ensuing publicity brought Profumo's name to light, suggesting an affair with Keeler.

THE (AHEM) CLIMAX

Profumo intensified his troubles and broke the scandal wide open in March 1963 by lying to the House of Commons. He claimed that his relationship with Keeler involved "no impropriety whatever." But his story didn't hold water, and he admitted his indiscretions only two months later. The facts of Keeler's two-timing affair with Profumo and Ivanov became public, along with Keeler's assertions that both Ward and Ivanov had asked her to pump Profumo for information regarding the transport of American nuclear missiles to what was then West Germany.

The implications of this—in a time of heightened Cold War paranoia—led to Profumo's resignation in early June.

The scandal also led to the resignation of Prime Minister Harold Macmillan several months later. Although he claimed ill health, the real reason was clear—the breach of security had occurred during his watch, even though no exchange of sensitive data had actually occurred.

THE EPILOGUE

The aftermath of the Profumo Affair was a curious one. In disgrace, the former Parliament secretary wound up as a janitor for a London settlement house. On the upside, his wife forgave his transgressions. And in the end, his ability as a charity fundraiser led Queen Elizabeth II to award him Commander of the British Empire (CBE) in 1975.

Christine Keeler sold her story to a London tabloid for tens of thousands of dollars. She starred as herself in a British/Danish film called, appropriately, *The Keeler Affair*. In a photo shoot for the film, Keeler posed naked in a strategically positioned chair in what would become a famous and often copied image.

In 2001, Keeler published a "tell-it-all" autobiography entitled *The Truth at Last: My Story*, which made some wild and unsubstantiated claims about Profumo, Ward, and the British government.

- *In 1987, Keeler appeared in a music video for Bryan Ferry's single* Kiss and Tell.

- Scandal, *a 1989 film about the Profumo Affair, featured actress Joanne Whalley as Christine Keeler.*

- *In 1998, the Spice Girls copied Keeler's famous chair pose for their song* Naked.

GREAT OBSCURE QUOTES

"Capital punishment is as fundamentally wrong as a cure for crime as charity is wrong as a cure for poverty."
—HENRY FORD

"I am oppressed with a dread of living forever. That is the only disadvantage of vegetarianism."
—GEORGE BERNARD SHAW

"The art of procreation and the members employed therein are so repulsive, that if it were not for the beauty of the faces and the adornments of the actors and the pent-up impulse, nature would lose the human species."
—LEONARDO DA VINCI

"Happiness in intelligent people is the rarest thing I know."
—ERNEST HEMINGWAY

"The final reward of the dead—to die no more."
—FRIEDRICH NIETZSCHE

THE UNDERGROUND RAILROAD

The very mention of the Underground Railroad reaches deep into the American psyche, invoking images of daring midnight escapes, secret tunnels, and concealed doors, as well as the exploits of thousands of daring men and women.

"...THAT ALL MEN ARE CREATED EQUAL"

The story of American slaves seeking escape from their masters long predates the invention of the railroad and its associated terms. The reasons for escape are easily understood and existed equally across slaves of all levels of privilege, from field hands to highly skilled laborers. Even before the Underground Railroad, escapees were often aided by individuals or organizations opposed to the institution of slavery. In fact, one prominent slaveholder—George Washington—complained in a letter that some of his fellow citizens were more concerned with helping one of his runaway slaves than in protecting his property rights as a slaveholder.

As the United States careened toward civil war, the arguments between supporters of slavery and those opposed to it became increasingly heated. Northern states began abolishing slavery on an individual basis—and became instant magnets for those fleeing servitude. In response, Congress passed Fugitive Slave Acts in 1793 and 1850, rendering escaped slaves fugitives for life, eligible for return to bondage on nothing more than the word of a white man. Any constable who refused to apprehend runaway slaves was fined. With the Northern states thus a less attractive final destination, runaways headed to Canada, where slavery had been outlawed in 1834. Meanwhile, abolitionist societies began to spring up, though a surprising number of them supported the return of escaped slaves to their masters, believing they could end the practice through moral persuasion rather than by violating the law.

ALL ABOARD

Despite hesitation on the part of some abolitionist societies, however, there were always
individuals and groups who were sympathetic to the cause of the runaway slave and
willing to place themselves at risk to help
slaves find freedom. These benefactors
ranged from white citizens to free blacks to
other slaves willing to risk being beaten or sold
for giving aid to runaways. Often, these protectors
acted alone with little more than a vague idea of where to send a
fugitive slave other than in the general direction of north. When
a sympathetic individual discovered a runaway, he or she would
often simply do what seemed best at the moment, whether that
meant providing food and clothing, throwing pursuers off the
track, or giving the slave a wagon ride to the next town.

By the 1840s, the expansion of the railroad was having a major
impact on American society, and abolitionist activists quickly
adopted its terminology. *Conductors* were those people who
helped their *passengers*—runaway slaves—onto the next *station*,
or town, where they made contact with a *stationmaster*—the
person in charge of the local organization—and guided them
down the rails. The most famous conductor, Harriet Tubman, was
herself an escaped slave who risked no less than 19 trips back into
slave country to guide out family members and others. Despite
her evident kindheartedness, she could be as ruthless as the life
or death stakes of the game demanded; she dosed infants with
sedatives to keep them quiet during the trip and once threatened
to shoot one of her passengers for having a change of heart rather
than let him leave and threaten the freedom of the entire party.

In some areas, small cells sprang up in which each person knew
only about a contact on the next farm or in the next town, perhaps
with the nebulous goal of somehow sending escapees into the
care of well-known abolitionist societies in far-off Philadelphia or
Boston. The image of one overriding national organization guiding the effort is largely a misleading one, but it was one encour-

aged by both abolitionists and slaveholders. The abolitionists were not hesitant to play up the romantic railroad imagery in an effort to bolster their fund-raising efforts. Their descriptions were so vivid that Frederick Douglass himself suggested they cease talking about it, lest they reveal their methods to their enemies. Likewise, Southern plantation owners were quick to play up the reports as proof that there was a vast abolitionist conspiracy bent on robbing them of their legal investment in slaves. As a result, some slave owners in border states converted their slaves to cash—selling them to the deep south rather than risking their escape, a fate many slaves considered nothing less than a death sentence.

Efforts at undermining the institution of slavery did exist but were scarcely clandestine. Many abolitionists were quite open about their intentions.

"DEVILS AND GOOD PEOPLE, WALKING IN THE ROAD AT THE SAME TIME"

Despite the presence—even the widespread prevalence, in some locations—of Underground Railroad workers, the experience of a runaway slave was never anything other than harsh. On striking out for freedom, even successful escapees faced an ordeal that could last months. During their journey, they rarely had food, shelter, or appropriate clothing. Every white face was a potential enemy, as were some of their fellow black people, who were sometimes employed as decoys to help catch runaways. A false Underground Railroad even existed. Participants would take a runaway in and promise him safe passage only to deliver him to the local slave market. Often the escapees had no idea where they were going or the distance to be covered.

Although estimates vary wildly, one widely reported figure is that approximately 100,000 slaves found freedom either through their own initiative or with the aid of the Underground Railroad before the rest of those in bondage were freed during and after the Civil War. The history of the Railroad was largely written decades after the fact, and it is occasionally hard to separate reliable facts from the aged recollections of those justifiably proud of their efforts at securing liberty for their fellow man.

THE "TENTH MUSE"

In a literary cannon that is almost exclusively male, Sappho, the captivating poet from the Greek island of Lesbos (modern Lesvos) stands out as a female author whose works achieved popular acclaim in antiquity.

Born around 630 B.C., Sappho belonged to an aristocratic Lesbian family at a time when colonization, the creation of pan-Hellenic festivals (such as the Olympic Games), and the works of Homer (the *Iliad* and *Odyssey*) fueled the growth of a common aristocratic Greek culture. Within this culture, Greek aristocrats used lyric poetry to reflect on politics, values, and personal experience. Sappho's poetry addresses all these issues, but it is most famous for capturing the powerful, poignanant—yet playful—sincerity of desire, longing, and affection.

An intriguing and sometimes controversial element of Sappho's poetry is that many poems are directed toward other women. It is, in fact, from these poems that the term "lesbian" was coined in the 19th century to mean "homosexual." However, though Sappho's world fostered intense and even erotic relationships among social peers, the relationships she wrote about would not have neatly corresponded to modern terms.

Despite these ambiguities, the continued popularity of her poetry remains a testament to its universality and to her talent and insight. Sappho's language and unique meter (which came to be known as "Sapphic stanza") have influenced many other poets and authors since her time. Plato, writing nearly 200 years after her death, called Sappho the "tenth Muse," and writers from the Roman poets Catullus and Horace, to contemporary authors such as Erica Jong and Guy Davenport, have been inspired to evoke her character or poetry in their own work.

Today, only one complete Sappho poem survives.

PHILO T. FARNSWORTH— THE TEENAGER WHO INVENTED TELEVISION

Responsible for what may have been the most influential invention of the 20th century, this farm boy never received the recognition he was due.

Philo T. Farnsworth's brilliance was obvious from an early age. In 1919, when he was only 12, he amazed his parents and older siblings by fixing a balky electrical generator on their Idaho farm. By age 14, he had built an electrical laboratory in the family attic and was setting his alarm for 4 A.M. so he could get up and read science journals for an hour before doing chores.

Farnsworth hated the drudgery of farming. He often daydreamed solutions to scientific problems as he worked. During the summer of 1921, he was particularly preoccupied with the possibility of transmitting moving pictures through the air.

Around the same time, big corporations like RCA were spending millions of research dollars trying to find a practical way to do just that. As it turned out, most of their work was focused on a theoretical dead-end. Back in 1884, German scientist Paul Nipkow had patented a device called the Nipkow disc. By rotating the disc rapidly while passing light through tiny holes, an illusion of movement could be created. In essence, the Nipkow disc was a primitive way to scan images. Farnsworth doubted that this mechanical method of scanning could ever work fast enough to send images worth watching. He was determined to find a better way.

His "Eureka!" moment came as he cultivated a field with a team of horses. Swinging the horses around to do another row, Farnsworth glanced back at the furrows behind him. Suddenly, he realized that scanning could be done electronically, line-by-line. Light could be converted into streams of electrons and then back again with such rapidity that the eye would be fooled. He immediately set about designing what would one day be called the cathode ray tube. Seven years would pass, however, before he was able to display a working model of his mental breakthrough.

Upon graduating from high school, Farnsworth enrolled at the University of Utah but dropped out after a year because he could no longer afford the tuition. Almost immediately, though, he found financial backers and moved to San Francisco to continue his research. The cathode ray tube he developed there became the basis for all television. In 1930, a researcher from RCA named Vladimir Zworykin visited Farnsworth's California laboratory and copied his invention. When Farnsworth refused to sell his patent to RCA for $100,000, the company sued him. The legal wrangling continued for many years and, though Farnsworth eventually earned royalties from his invention, he never did get wealthy from it.

By the time Farnsworth died in 1971, there were more homes on Earth with televisions than with indoor plumbing. Ironically, the man most responsible for television appeared on the small screen only once. It was a 1957 appearance on the game show *I've Got a Secret*. Farnsworth's secret was that "I invented electric television at the age of 15." When none of the panelists guessed Farnsworth's secret, he left the studio with his winnings—$80 and a carton of Winston cigarettes.

- *The first public demonstration of television took place in Soho, London, in 1926.*

- *Estimates suggest that more than one billion television sets have been sold worldwide.*

- *In 1946, only .5 percent of American households had a television. By 1962, this number had increased to 90 percent.*

Fast Facts

- The average 17th-century American woman gave birth to 13 children.

- The great Pharos Lighthouse of Alexandria was one of the Seven Wonders of the Ancient World.

- In ancient Rome, urine was as much a commodity as a waste product. The ammonia in pee was useful for bleaching togas and tunics.

- The ancient Incas had llamas large enough to pull wheeled carts, but no wheeled carts to pull. The ancient Aztecs had tiny wheeled carts as toys, but no animals big enough to pull a full-size cart. The two groups were about 2,600 miles apart, and neither had a working cart.

- Julius Caesar built a bridge over the imposing Rhine River to impress the Germanic inhabitants with Rome's engineering skills. To drive home his point, he had the bridge torn down two weeks later.

- Vikings didn't just raid England, France, and Ireland. Besides sailing to America and colonizing Greenland and Iceland, they assailed Portugal, Spain, the French Riviera, Italy, and Arctic Russia. Swedish Vikings traded all the way down to Byzantium.

- Arab ambassador Ibn Fadlan on the Swedish Rus (Vikings, c. 923): "They are the filthiest of God's creatures. They do not wash after discharging their natural functions, neither do they wash their hands after meals. They are as stray donkeys."

- Big Ben is neither the name of the clock, nor the name of the actual tower. What it refers to is the thirteen-and-a-half ton bell that is inside the clock tower. It was cast in 1858 and named for Benjamin Hall, the commissioner of works during the period when the bell was being installed.

SORRY, MATES, BUT AUSSIES DIDN'T INVENT THE BOOMERANG

Contrary to popular myth, lore, and Australian drinking songs, boomerangs, or "The Throwing Wood," as proponents prefer to call them, did not originate down under.

The colonists, adventurers, prisoners, and explorers who ventured into the heart of the Australian wilderness may be excused for believing that the local aborigines created these little aerodynamic marvels, considering the proficiency with which they used the wooden devices to bring down wild game and wilder colonials. The gyroscopic precision with which boomerangs were (and still are) crafted by primitive peoples continues to intrigue and astonish those who come in contact with the lightweight, spinning missiles, which—if thrown correctly—actually will return to their throwers.

MANY RETURNS

As a weapon of war and especially as a tool for hunting small game, the boomerang has been around for nearly 10,000 years. In fact, evidence of boomerangs has been discovered in almost every nook and cranny in the world. Pictures of boomerangs can be found in Neolithic-era cave drawings in France, Spain, and Poland. The "lagobolon," or "hare club," as it was called, was commonly used by nobles in Crete around 2000 B.C. And King Tut, ruler of Egypt around 1350 B.C., had a large collection of boomerangs—several of which were found when his tomb was discovered in the 1920s.

The Greek mythological hero Hercules is depicted tossing about a curved "clava" or "throwing stick" on pottery made during the

Homeric era. Carthaginian invaders in the 2nd century B.C. were bombarded by Gallic warriors who rained "catela" or "throwing clubs." The Roman historian Horace describes a flexible wooden "caia" used by German tribes, saying "if thrown by a master, it returns to the one who threw it." Roman Emperor Caesar Augustus's favorite contemporary author, Virgil, also describes a similar curved missile weapon in use by natives of the province of Hispania.

However, Europeans can no more claim the invention of the boomerang than their Australian cousins can. Archaeologists have unearthed evidence of boomerang use throughout Neolithic-era Africa, from Sudan to Niger, and from Cameroon to Morocco. Tribes in southern India, the American southwest, Mexico, and Java all used the boomerang, or something very similar, and for the same purposes.

Australians, however, can be credited with bringing the boomerang to the attention of the modern world. They helped popularize it both as a child's toy and as an item for sport. A World Cup is held every other year, and enthusiasts and scientists still compete to design, construct, and throw the perfect boomerang.

Though the tool, weapon, or toy known today as a boomerang did not originate in Australia—or at least did not originate exclusively in Australia—the word itself *is* Australian. *Boomerang* is a blending of the words, *woomerang* and *bumarin*, terms used by different groups of Australian aborigines to describe their little wooden wonders.

- *From boomerang to helicopter? David Unaipon, a 1914 inventor, drew preliminary mechnical illustrations of a helicopter based on the principles of boomerang flight. Today, Unaipon appears on the Australian $50 note.*

BY REASON OF INSANITY

However contentious the issues they decide, the members of the U.S. Supreme Court are usually known for sober, even-minded temperament. But that has not always been the case. At least two justices in the history of that hallowed court, including one acting chief justice, were insane for portions of their tenure.

A DERANGED JUSTICE

Henry Baldwin, who served on the Court from 1830 to 1844, had an abrasive personality that angered his fellow justices and eventually morphed into lunacy. A brilliant student at Yale and a law clerk for Alexander Dallas, Baldwin established the Constitution's privileges and immunities clause, whereby a right granted by one state must be upheld by all other states. Born in 1780, the independent-minded Baldwin set a giant precedent by writing the Court's first dissenting opinions; previously the Court had issued only unanimous rulings. In the famous *Amistad* case, where the Court ruled on the side of slaves who had seized their slave ship, Baldwin—though personally opposed to slavery—argued for sending the slaves back into captivity. He also irked the other justices by criticizing the fact that they shared the same Capitol Hill boarding house, which he felt fostered groupthink.

Baldwin was burdened by terrible financial woes: He lost a small fortune in the Depression of 1820, had to rescue grown children of his who fell into debt, and saw several of his businesses go belly up. On the circuit courts of New Jersey and Pennsylvania, he tried to make money by selling copies of his judicial opinions. Like Thomas Jefferson, he sold his personal book collection to the Library of Congress to raise cash.

In 1832, Baldwin suffered a seizure, was hospitalized for "incurable lunacy," and missed the 1833 term. Senator Daniel Webster noted the "breaking out of Judge Baldwin's insanity." On the Court, Baldwin grew violent-tempered. In 1838, a Court officer, after talking with Baldwin's fellow judges, noted his "mind is out of order...five persons say he is crazy." In his later years, Baldwin fell victim to paralysis. At age 64, "Crazy Henry" died, impoverished but still on the Court. His family and friends paid for his funeral.

A SUICIDAL JUDGE

Few could have guessed, knowing his resume, that Judge John Rutledge would lose his mind.

Born in 1739, Rutledge was coauthor of South Carolina's constitution and a former governor. His brother was a signer of the Declaration of Independence. During the Revolution, Rutledge helped rebuild American forces in the South after the crushing British victory at Camden, South Carolina. His efforts paid off, and a new army—under General Nathanael Greene—chased the Redcoats out of most of the state.

In his private life, Rutledge was prudent with his money. "By doing good with his money, a man, as it were, stamps the image of God upon it, and makes it pass, current for the merchandise of heaven." In the public realm, Rutledge was by inclination a moderate. Early on, he opposed separation of the colonies from Great Britain. In the years leading to the American Revolution, he opposed separating from the motherland, instead pressing for voting rights while forbidding trade with British merchants. As a political pragmatist, however, he made an exception for the export of rice, a South Carolina staple. Once war began, he was temperate toward the enemy: As governor, he pardoned pro-British loyalists willing to join the state's militia even though the British confiscated his considerable property—which he never got back.

A distinguished-looking man with gray hair and prominent eyebrows, Rutledge was a pivotal figure at the Constitutional Convention. He got everyone to take an oath of secrecy, placing a clamp on media-fed rumors that might have sunk an agreement. As chairman of the committee on detail, which controlled the agenda, he got almost all he wanted. The new government assumed the states' debts, permitted slavery, and set up a system where Congress elected the president. At the same time, Rutledge was willing to compromise, stating eloquently: "Is it not better that I should sacrifice one prized opinion than that all of us should sacrifice everything we might otherwise gain?"

Things began turning for him after President Washington named him to the Supreme Court in 1789. He was very dis-appointed that John Jay was named chief justice instead of him-self. For two years, to discharge his duties, he rode throughout the South to preside over the region's circuit courts. During this period, remarkably, the newly formed Supreme Court heard no cases. Bored, Rutledge resigned in 1791 to become chief justice of his home state's court of common pleas.

Things got much worse in 1792, when his wife Elizabeth, who had borne ten children, died. Driven by despair, Rutledge became mentally unstable. According to Senator Ralph Izard of South Carolina, he was "frequently so much deranged . . . in a great mea-sure deprived of his senses."

Rutledge made a critical political error in July 1795, after Presi-dent Washington nominated him for chief justice to replace John Jay, the nation's first supreme Supreme. Jay had negotiated a con-troversial treaty with Britain to settle commercial and military dis-putes between the two countries. Washington's political foes, led by Thomas Jefferson, bitterly attacked the accord. Irate crowds burned Jay in effigy, crying out: "Damn every one that won't put lights in his windows and sit up all night damning John Jay!"

As an appointee of Washington and as acting chief justice, Rut-ledge was naturally expected to back Jay's treaty, a priority of the Washington Administration. Instead, just two weeks after his selection, he denounced it at a public meeting in Charleston. Calling the treaty "prostitution of the dearest right of free man," Rutledge said he'd "rather the President should die than sign that puerile instrument." Rutledge added he "preferred war" with England to its adoption. Meanwhile a reporter at the forum eagerly took down his words, which soon appeared in newspapers around the nation.

The president's Cabinet was aghast. Treasury Secretary Alexander Hamilton, under the pen name Camillus, wrote that Rutledge was an "unfit character" who had again veered into insanity. Vice President John Adams informed wife Abigail that "C. Justices must not propagate Disunion, Division, Contention and delusion among the people." Rumors spread that the South Carolinian had taken to eating his gavel. Journals alleged he'd reneged on personal debts.

On December 15, the Senate, controlled by Washington's Federalist party and jawboned by Hamilton, rejected Rutledge's nomination by a vote of 10 to 14.

Humiliated by the torrent of criticism, Rutledge resigned from the court. He attempted to drown himself by jumping into Charleston Bay but was saved by two slaves who happened along at the right moment.

He never held another office and died in 1800.

FAMOUS LAST WORDS

"The foundation of justice is good faith."
—Marcus Tullius Cicero

"He reminds me of the man who murdered both his parents, and then when sentence was about to be pronounced pleaded for mercy on the grounds that he was an orphan."
— Abraham Lincoln

HOLLYWOOD VERSUS HISTORY

You may not be surprised to learn that Hollywood doesn't always get history right.

Sometimes being ahead of your time just doesn't pay off

Almost Famous (2001)—An Eastern Airlines plane has a wing configuration that wasn't introduced to commercial jetliners until after Eastern ceased to exist.

And who's the character with the checkered flag?

Ben-Hur (1959)—During the chariot race, tire tracks from the camera cars are plainly visible in the dust.

Au revoir!

Messenger: The Story of Joan of Arc (1999)—A cannonball is sent flying with "Hello" scrawled on it, but the word wasn't coined until around 1889.

History lite: half the calories and all the distortion

Mississippi Burning (1988)—Although based on real-life white persecution of blacks in the 1960s, the movie focuses almost exclusively on a pair of white FBI agents; black characters are peripheral.

Seventy-five pirates came on board and stole all the deck chairs

The Crimson Pirate (1952)—An establishing shot of Burt Lancaster's sailing ship near the end of the film inadvertently reveals a 20th-century ocean liner on the horizon.

But you can't undertake a journey to infinite truth without one

Dead Man (1995)—Teddy bears, one of which shows up in this mystical 19th-century Western, weren't created until the early 20th century.

A Day in the Life
HIP, HAPPENING FLORENCE

The wealthy merchants of Renaissance Florence actively cultivated the monumental cultural and intellectual movement that originated in their city. The following fictionalized account offers a glimpse into a day in Renaissance life.

Nicolo peers from the fifth-story bedroom window of his townhouse overlooking the streets of mid-15th century Florence. It's early morning, and Europe's most vibrant city is jumping.

Florence is the epicenter of the Renaissance, the great cultural and intellectual reawakening sweeping Europe. The city-state of 60,000 people is thriving as it sets the tone for Europe commercially, politically, and artistically.

And Nicolo, a wealthy Florentine merchant, embarks on another day as the quintessential man of his times.

AT WORK AT HOME

Nicolo's home also accommodates his prosperous cloth manufacturing business. Nicolo is a leading member of Florence's influential textile guild, and the exquisite goods he produces are among the finest in a city that dominates Europe's cloth industry.

Nicolo spends the morning in the ground-floor store, arranging displays and tending to customers.

At mid-morning, he retreats to the fourth floor for the first of the two daily meals Florentines typically eat. He, along with his wife, Leonarda, and their two children eat fruit, salad, cheese, and pasta—a new culinary delight that's all the rage in Florence.

HANGING WITH THE MOVERS AND SHAKERS

After, Nicolo changes into an outfit befitting a man of his stature. Overtop his green long-sleeve collarless shirt, he wears a burgundy velvet doublet, a long vest belted at the waist to create a skirt effect. White hose leggings and brown leather boots round out the ensemble. He also dons his *cioppa,* a red, full-length, fur-lined velvet gown worn by influential Florentine men.

Nicolo hires a horse-drawn carriage to take him to the Palazzo Vecchio, where 12 powerful merchant guilds conduct the business of Florence. Here, Nicolo makes his real money as he haggles with other textile merchants, arranging for the purchase of 300 wool bales from England and Spain and sales of finished cloth for export all over Europe.

Later, Nicolo and members of other guilds transform into political powerbrokers. In Florence, those who create the city's wealth also run it, and the 5,000 guild members, led by the powerful de Medici banking clan, provide Florence with an enlightened form of government unseen in Europe since the ancient Greeks—one that emphasizes republicanism, democracy, and the welfare of the city over despotic rule.

NICOLO GETS CULTURED

With the day's business done, Nicolo returns home for dinner. As on most days, Nicolo and Leonarda are entertaining. They serve up the usual guest-impressing cuisine: fruit and cake appetizers, a main course featuring roast lamb (only the well-to-do serve meat), a cheese plate, and dessert pastries.

After, Nicolo proudly shows off a recently purchased painting by a young emerging local artist named Botticelli. He, like many wealthy Florentines with the money and time to explore the arts, is a devoted patron of the city's flourishing arts scene.

Later, Nicolo reads aloud from Plato's *Republic,* reflecting on Europe's rediscovery of classic Greek and Latin writings triggered by the humanist movement, the intellectual driving force of the Renaissance. He is enthralled by the humanist philosophy that stresses man's interaction with his world and the idea of determining one's own destiny.

Nicolo, a man of his times in Renaissance Florence, not only believes the hype—he lives it too.

THE HOUSE OF DAVID

Members of the House of David religious community didn't know
when Jesus Christ would return to Earth, but they were
certain of the where—Benton Harbor, Michigan.
While they waited for Christ's return, they built a settlement,
erected a roller coaster, and followed the biblical vow of
the Nazirites to never cut their hair.

THE BEGINNINGS

The House of David's beliefs were rooted in the teachings of
Joanna Southcutt (1750–1814). She believed that she was the first
of seven angelic messengers who would usher in the millennium
(Revelation 10:7).

Like other millennialists, she professed that Christ would reign
on Earth during a thousand-year period of peace. Gathered with
him would be the elect—the 144,000 descendants of the scattered
tribes of Israel.

In 1903, Kentucky-born Benjamin Purnell (1861–1927) started
the House of David commune. Trusting in a divine inspiration, his
wife, Mary, believed the 144,000 Christian-Israelites would
gather in Benton Harbor, Michigan, to await Christ's arrival. With
pamphlets and a 780-page book (*The Star of Bethlehem, The
Living Roll of Life*), the Purnells attracted followers from the
United States, England, and Australia.

The open invitation to join the House of David was hard for
some to resist. Although the followers were required to sell their
belongings and give the proceeds to the House of David, this
was considered a small, temporary sacrifice relative to what they
expected to receive in return. After all, they would be among the
144,000 who would rule with Christ on Earth and would accompany Christ to heaven, where they would rank higher than the
angels.

By the end of 1903, more than 300 people had joined the House of David, fully trusting in the authority of the Purnells. The group purchased property, shared living quarters, generated electricity, grew their own food, and became vegetarians (a diet they deemed appropriate for the Garden of Eden). Members also took a vow of celibacy.

ENTERTAINMENT

While members of the House of David were patiently waiting for the millennium, they turned to business to keep them busy. In 1908, the Purnells opened Eden Springs, an amusement park with a giant roller coaster, miniature trains, and a zoo with lions, bears, and wandering peacocks. Eden Springs also featured a baseball field, a bowling alley, silent movies, and a variety of musical entertainment, including a band that once performed under John Philip Sousa. In the 1920s, as many as 200,000 nonmembers visited the park each summer.

Baseball also became important. Around 1915, ballplayers from the House of David formed a traveling team that barnstormed across the country. Playing with long hair and beards (they were forbidden to cut their hair), they generated income and gathered converts.

TROUBLE IN EDEN

The Benton Harbor settlement may have looked like Eden on its surface, but scandal lurked. While some lived in luxury, others were allegedly given no more than turnips and carrots to eat. Meanwhile, leaders ignored their vows of celibacy.

Beginning as early as 1907, Purnell was accused of business fraud, sexual indiscretion, and rape, but it took years for the accusations and evidence to support a conviction. In 1927, the state of Michigan brought Purnell to court. Armed with 225 witnesses, 75 depositions, and 15,000 pages of recorded testimony, attorneys were certain Purnell would face time behind bars. However, he died in 1929 before he could be sentenced. The House of David divided.

In 1930, 218 members followed H.T. Dewhirst, the board director. The settlement flourished—though he turned the preaching auditorium into a beer garden. Meanwhile, Mary Purnell led 217 followers to a new location—just two blocks from the original House of David. She reorganized the group, calling it "Mary's City of David."

BASEBALL PREVAILS

Though neither of the new settlements garnered the popularity of the original community, both groups fielded baseball teams for the next two decades. (They both used the name "House of David.") They recruited some nonmembers to play, but they were still required to wear long hair and whiskers.

Games often boasted trumpets, donkeys, and the immensely popular "pepper game." During the fifth inning, three players stood on the mound, performing sideways tosses, fake throws, and behind-the-back moves before they actually threw the ball to the catcher.

Despite their carnival antics, the House of David teams were highly skilled, defeating 75 percent of their opponents. In 1933, a House of David team faced the Cardinals at Sportman's Park in St. Louis. Led by female southpaw Jackie Mitchell, the House of David won, 8–6. (Mitchell was not required to wear a fake beard.)

THE COLOR BARRIER

The House of David teams also played against Negro League teams, including the Kansas City Monarchs, and used their immense popularity to help erode the color barrier. According to some reports, the House of David team wouldn't play the local team unless the locals played a Negro League team first.

BEYOND BASEBALL

What's left of the House of David? The baseball teams are memories; few believers remain. Yet the grounds in Benton Harbor still exist—evidence of the colony's zealous faith and enterprise.

AARON BURR:
HERO OR VILLAIN?

*Mention the name Aaron Burr and the thing most people
remember is his famous duel with Alexander Hamilton.
That may have been the high point of his life,
because by the time Burr passed away in 1836, he was
considered one of the most mistrusted public figures of his era.*

HOW TO MAKE FRIENDS...

Burr seemed to have a knack for making enemies out of important
people. George Washington disliked him so much from their time
together during the Revolutionary War that as president, he had
Burr banned from the National Archives, didn't appoint him as
minister to France, and refused to make him a brigadier general.

After the war, Burr became a lawyer in New York, frequently
opposing his future dueling partner Alexander Hamilton. But it
wasn't until Burr beat Hamilton's father-in-law in the race for a
Senate seat that the problems between them really started.

In 1800, Burr ran for president against Thomas Jefferson. Back
then, the candidate with the most votes got to be president; who-
ever came in second became vice president—even if they were
from different parties. When the election ended in a tie in the
Electoral College, it was thrown to the House of Representatives to decide. After 35 straight tie votes, Jefferson was reelected
president, and Burr became vice president.

Like Washington, Jefferson didn't hold Burr in high regard. So
in 1804, Burr decided to run for governor of New York. When
he lost, he blamed the slandering of the press in general and the
almost constant criticism from Hamilton in particular.

Hamilton later shot off at the mouth at a dinner party, and Burr
decided he'd had enough. After giving Hamilton a chance to take

his comments back (Hamilton refused), Burr challenged him to the famous duel.

I CHALLENGE YOU TO A DUEL

On July 11, 1804, Burr and Hamilton met at Weehawken, New Jersey. Some say that Hamilton fired first, discharging his pistol into the air; others say that he just missed. Burr, on the other hand, didn't miss, shooting Hamilton. He died the next day.

After the duel, Burr fled to his daughter's home in South Carolina until things cooled down. He was indicted for murder in both New York and New Jersey, but nothing ever came of it, and he eventually returned to Washington to finish his term as vice president. But his political career was over.

KING BURR?

After his term as vice president, Burr decided to head west, to what was then considered Ohio and the new lands of the Louisiana Purchase. It seemed that Burr had things on his mind other than the scenery, however. According to some (mostly his rivals), Burr intended to create a new empire with himself as king. As the story goes, he planned to conquer a portion of Texas still held by Mexico, then convince some of the existing western states to join his new confederacy. Called the Burr Conspiracy, it got the attention of President Jefferson, who issued arrest orders for treason. Eventually, Burr was captured and in 1807 was brought to trial.

But Burr caught a break. The judge was Chief Justice John Marshall. Marshall and Jefferson didn't get along, and rather than give his enemy an easy victory, Marshall demanded that the prosecution produce two witnesses that specifically heard Burr commit treason. The prosecution failed to come up with anybody, and Burr was set free.

Burr then left the United States to live in Europe. Returning to New York in 1812, he quietly practiced law until his death in 1836.

Fast Facts

- Here's an example of how far modern English has wandered in a thousand years: "Do you have a horse for sale?" was once "Haefst thu hors to sellenne?"

- Moss has its uses. In medieval England, it served as toilet paper.

- In the 1600s and 1700s, French women were known to duel with swords or pistols, just as the men did.

- Pocahontas, credited with saving John Smith from execution in 1607, ended up dying in England. Baptized Rebecca, she married a tobacco planter named John Rolfe. Something of a toast of English society, she died in 1617 as she and John were preparing to return to the Colonies.

- The Chinese of the Tang Dynasty (A.D. 618–907) played their own version of golf, called Buda.

- Freemasonry dates back to the 17th century. Famous Masons include Wolfgang Amadeus Mozart, George Washington, Voltaire, Benjamin Franklin, Douglas MacArthur, Franklin D. Roosevelt, Harry S. Truman, John Jacob Astor, Kit Carson, Mark Twain, King George VI, Patrick Henry, and Paul Revere.

- Chinese Checkers did not originate in China, nor does it involve checkers. It was invented in Europe and is played with marbles on a star-shape board. It was popular in Japan and the United States before it even reached China.

- Women in American law practice ought to venerate Belva Ann Lockwood, the first woman allowed to plead before the U.S. Supreme Court (1879).

- On the night that John Wilkes Booth killed Lincoln, he also intended to kill General Grant. However, the Grants turned down the invitation to go to the theater in order to visit their children in New Jersey.

THE OLD SALT MINE

In ancient times, salt was extremely hard to come by.
Vital to the preservation of food, the tanning of hides,
and even the production of gunpowder, salt was fought
over and even traded for slaves.

Salt can be obtained through several different production methods, including primitive solar evaporation, mining, and complex refining techniques.

However, the most common method of obtaining salt is by mining. Many countries have salt mines, and one of the oldest such mines can be found near Krakow, Poland. Salt was first mined in the area around 1044. During the Middle Ages, salt was one of Poland's most important exports.

Eight miles southeast of Krakow is the tiny town of Wieliczka. Founded in 1290, the town is built atop one of the world's oldest salt mine operations. Legend has it that the mine was a wedding gift presented to the Polish Prince Wstydliwy from his bride-to-be, the Hungarian Princess Kinga.

Tons of salt have been taken from the ground under the town over the course of 700 years. Though the mine ceased operation in the late 1990s, the site was designated a United Nations Educational, Scientific and Cultural Organization (UNESCO) World Heritage Cultural site in 1978 and now operates as a tourist attraction.

The mine consists of nine levels, more than 120 miles of tunnels, and more than 2,000 chambers. At its deepest, it rests 1,073 feet below the surface. Visitors to the site travel a two-mile route that winds through three levels of the mine. On display are several chapels, life-size statues, and scenes replicating famous pieces of art, including Leonardo da Vinci's *Last Supper*—all carved out of salt. A sanatorium and museum complex are also housed underground.

JOHN HANSON,
REAL FIRST PRESIDENT?

*You've had it ingrained into your brain since early childhood that
George Washington was the first president of the United States.
Care to make a little wager on that?*

You're sitting in a bar minding your own business
when some guy comes up to you and says, "Did
you know that John Hanson was the *real* first
president of the United States?"

Aside from the fact that you've never even
heard of John Hanson, you look at the guy
and say, "Are you nuts? Everyone knows
George Washington was the first president."

Your new acquaintance smiles and replies, "I'll bet you a pint of
this establishment's finest ale that I can prove that John Hanson
was indeed America's first president."

You quickly pull out the crumpled one-dollar bill in your pocket
and gaze at the stately, powdered-wig portrait of George Washington. And knowing a sure thing when you see it, you accept his
challenge.

Much to your surprise, amusement, or chagrin (depending on
how many ales *you've* had), he pulls out a musty, dog-eared copy
of a book by Seymour Wemyss Smith entitled, *John Hanson, Our
First President.*

Suddenly, your sure thing doesn't seem so sure anymore.

HIS CASE, PART 1

Your antagonist begins his argument with a brief dissertation on
the Continental Congress, the Articles of Confederation, and
those heady first years after America's declaration of independence from Britain.

He tells you that from 1776 to 1777, the representatives from the 13 states gathered in the Congress to hammer out the details of the new American nation's first governing charter, the Articles of Confederation.

He adds that by 1779, all the states except for Maryland had ratified the Articles of Confederation. Maryland was holding out until New York and Virginia ceded their western lands to reduce their territorial size and, consequently, their clout in the new union. Unanimous ratification was required to bring the Articles into force.

HIS CASE, PART 2

Then, opening Smith's book, he begins to enlighten you about John Hanson.

Hanson, he says, was a highly respected scholar and politician who had served in the Maryland assembly since 1757. He had been an early and raucous proponent of independence and was recognized by his peers as one of the movement's leading lights.

Hanson, he continues, was elected to the Congress in 1779, and once there did more than just fill a seat. He worked diligently to get his home state to accept the Articles of Confederation, arguing that the diplomatic recognition the new country desperately needed would only be given if the Articles were ratified. His efforts were rewarded in March 1781 when Maryland finally signed on, thus making the Articles of Confederation a done deal.

HIS CASE, PART THREE

Now, he says, comes the clincher.

He points out that Congress members, grateful for Hanson's efforts, unanimously elected him as president of the United States in Congress Assembled in November 1781. Hanson, he says, was the first person to hold that office under the ratified Articles of Confederation, and as such, was *the* first president of the United States.

To bolster his case, he offers a list of precedent-setting initiatives presided over by Hanson during his one-year term in office. Among these were the founding of a national census and postal service, expanding America's foreign relations, negotiating foreign loans, and establishing the Thanksgiving holiday—all of which were continued under the presidency of George Washington.

Finally, he adds one more little tidbit. Washington, he contends, was actually the *eighth* president of the United States—there were six successors to Hanson before Washington took office.

"Pay up," he says.

HOW YOU WIN

Before you start crying in your beer, here's a counter-argument that will win you the bet.

Yes, Hanson was the first president of the United States in Congress Assembled. But in this capacity, Hanson's primary function was to preside over the Continental Congress, which was a legislative body responsible for establishing the structure of the nascent American nation in accordance with the Articles of Confederation. Hanson's role then was similar to what today might be called the House chair or speaker of the Parliament.

The Articles emphasized state sovereignty over a strong national or central government. They made no provision for a federal government as exists today or an executive branch or a chief executive—in other words, no office of president of the United States.

The 13 states did empower the Congress to carry out several specific functions on their behalf, such as territorial defense, foreign relations, coinage and currency, and a postal service. As president of the United States in Congress Assembled, Hanson did preside over these "national" operations.

But when the flaws of the Articles of Confederation became apparent (namely, no effective way for the Congress to raise an army for defense or taxes to fund its assigned tasks), Congress members set about writing a more balanced governing charter.

The result was the creation of the Constitution in 1787–1788, which established a robust federal government and a chief executive office formally called the "president of the United States of America."

And the first person to hold that office was none other than George Washington—not John Hanson, who, though a hero in his time, is mostly forgotten today—a victim of both bad historical timing and constitutional semantics.

Enjoy your beer.

What's in a Name: Presidents

There have been six presidents named James, five Johns, four Williams, three Georges, and two Andrews, Franklins, and Thomases.

There have been two Adamses, two Bushes, two Harrisons, two Johnsons, and two Roosevelts. All of the pairs except the Johnsons were related to each other.

Rutherford is the longest presidential first name at 10 letters.

Seventeen of the forty-two presidents to date have no known middle name.

Several presidential middle names were originally surnames: Baines, Birchard, Delano, Fitzgerald, Walker, Knox, Milhous, Quincy, and Simpson. Most of these were the president's mother's maiden name.

George Herbert Walker Bush is the only president with two middle names.

There are no duplicate presidential middle names, with the partial exception of Herbert Walker and Walker.

Three presidents used their middle name as their given name: Calvin Coolidge, Grover Cleveland, and Woodrow Wilson.

Only three of the ten most common surnames in the United States (Smith, Johnson, Williams, Jones, Brown, Davis, Miller, Wilson, Moore, and Taylor) have been the surnames of presidents (Andrew and Lyndon Johnson, Woodrow Wilson, and Zachary Taylor).

THE ORIGINAL DEMOLITION MAN

With a single spark from his torch, Guy Fawkes could have killed dozens and changed the course of British history.

It happens each year after nightfall on November 5 in England and in former British colonies such as Australia: Rowdy groups of people gather around blazing bonfires to dance, chant, and set off fireworks. At a climactic moment, a straw effigy of a man—the "Guy"—is tossed into the flames, while the revelers shout a poem that begins, *"Remember, remember the fifth of November/The gunpowder treason and plot/I know of no reason why the gunpowder treason/Should ever be forgot."*

Today, "Bonfire Night" is a lighthearted social event. It's likely that many of the revelers who are bathed in firelight and swept up in the noise of celebration have only the vaguest idea of the origins of this uniquely British tradition. But Bonfire Night grew out of one of the most dramatic episodes in English history—the Gunpowder Plot of 1605.

A CHURCH UNDER FIRE

In 1534, King Henry VIII broke with the Roman Catholic Church to set up the Church of England, touching off decades of religious and political strife. Most of the common folk ultimately accepted the "New Faith" (Protestantism). A minority remained loyal to Rome, although English Catholics faced discrimination and repression—especially after King James I ascended the throne in 1603. For years, some English Catholics had hoped that Spain would conquer England and restore the nation to Rome. By the turn of the 17th century that prospect looked unlikely, as Spain was preoccupied with fighting various wars on continental Europe. So a small group of Catholic plotters, led by the wealthy Robert Catesby, turned to terrorism. Catesby and his fellow conspirators decided to attempt what modern military commanders would call a "Decapitation Strike": They intended to take out all of England's leadership by blowing up London's House of Lords during the state opening of Parliament on November 5, 1605—an event that would be attended by the king, most of his family, and the leading nobles of the land. But they needed an expert with explosives, which in those days meant gunpowder. So they turned to Guy Fawkes.

"A PENNY FOR THE OLD GUY…"

Fawkes was born in York, England, in 1570. Raised a Protestant, he converted to Catholicism in his teens and later went off to fight for Spain in its war against Protestant rebels in the Netherlands. Guy—or Guido, as he now styled himself—gained a reputation for coolness in combat and skill with explosives. In the spring of 1604, Robert Catesby sent an agent to the Netherlands to recruit Fawkes, who agreed to help the plotters, though he probably didn't learn the details of the plan until he arrived back in England.

At first the plotters intended to reach the House of Lords from below, via a tunnel, but when the task of disposing the dirt proved too troublesome, they simply rented cellar storage space and, under Fawkes's direction, packed it with 36 barrels of gunpowder—about a ton of the stuff. Realizing that some Catholic aristocrats would also be in the building on November 5, however, one of the plotters sent a warning to one of his co-religionists. Despite the fact that the scheme had been compromised, the plotters went ahead. However, word of the plan reached the government via an anonymous letter, and in a scene reminiscent of a Hollywood thriller, the authorities raided the cellar just in time to pounce on Fawkes as he was lowering a torch to set off the fuse. (Or so some official accounts have it—the real circumstances may never be known.)

Furious at the assassination attempt "not only… [on] my person, nor of my wife and posterity also, but of the whole body of the State in general," King James authorized the use of torture in Fawkes's interrogation. Fawkes grimly held out for several days and didn't name names until he was subjected to the rack—a vicious instrument that stretched a victim's limbs until they popped from their sockets. Even then, Fawkes only gave up the names of plotters who'd already been arrested.

A brief trial in January 1606 ended with guilty verdicts for Fawkes and the others. He was sentenced to the traditional punishment for treason—to be "hung, drawn, and quartered." This meant he was to be hanged until not quite dead, then taken down from the gallows so that his organs could be torn from his body. After that (!), he'd be beheaded and his body would be chopped into four parts. Fawkes managed to escape this awful fate by jumping from the gallows and breaking his neck.

Protestant England rejoiced at the country's "deliverance" from the plot and developed the Bonfire Night tradition over the next few years. Included among the participants were children who begged for "a penny for the Old Guy." (The penny was to buy fireworks.) And eventually "guy" entered the English language as a slang term for any male.

- *The heads of Guy Fawkes and the other plotters were placed on stakes as a warning to others.*

- *In January 1606, Parliament met to pass the Thanksgiving Act, which marked November 5 as a day of remembrance for the foiled plot. Early celebrations included sermons, ringing church bells, and fireworks displays.*

- *In early celebrations of Guy Fawkes Day, revellers would burn effigies of the pope and the devil, rather than of Guy Fawkes.*

THE FATE OF THE PASSENGER PIGEON

When Europeans first visited North America, the passenger pigeon was easily the most numerous bird on the continent. But by the early 1900s, it was extinct. What led to this incredible change in fortune?

PIGEONS ON THE WING

From the first written description of the passenger pigeon in 1534, eyewitnesses struggled with how to describe what they saw. Flights of the 16-inch-long birds were staggeringly, almost mind-numbingly big; flocks were measured in the millions, if not billions, and could be heard coming for miles. When passing overhead, a flight could block out the sun to the point that chickens would come in to roost. Passenger pigeons flew at around 60 miles an hour—one nickname dubbed the bird the "blue meteor"—but even so, a group sighted by Cotton Mather was a mile long and took hours to pass overhead. At least one explorer hesitated to detail what he had seen, for fear that the entirety of his report would be dismissed as mere exaggeration.

Settlers viewed the pigeons with trepidation. A passing flock could wreak havoc on crops, stripping fields bare and leading to famine. A flight passing overhead or roosting on your land would leave everything covered with noxious bird droppings—a situation that would lead to more fertile soil in following years but did little to endear the creatures to farmers at that moment.

PIGEONS ON THE TABLE

With such vast numbers, what could possibly have led to the extinction of the passenger pigeon? There are a number of theories, but the most likely answer seems to be the most obvious:

People hunted them out of existence. Native Americans had long used the pigeons as a food source, and the Europeans followed suit, developing a systematic approach to harvesting the birds that simply outstripped their ability to reproduce. At first, the practice was an exercise in survival—a case of explorers feeding themselves on the frontier or settlers eating pigeon meat in place of the crops the birds had destroyed. However, necessity soon evolved into a matter of convenience and simple economy—the birds were cheap to put on the table.

Killing the birds in bulk was almost a trivial exercise. Initially, settlers could walk up under trees of nesting birds and simply knock them down using oars. As the birds became more wary, firearms were a natural choice for hunters; flocks were so dense, one report gives a count of 132 birds blasted out of the sky with a single shot. Nets were strung across fields, easily yanking the birds from the air as they flew. Perhaps most infamously, a captive bird would be tied to a platform that was raised and then suddenly dropped; as the pigeon fluttered to the ground, other pigeons would think the decoy was alighting to feed and would fly down to join him—a practice that became the origin for the English term "stool pigeon." Hunters would catch the birds in nets, then kill them by crushing their heads between thumb and forefinger.

PIGEONS ON DISPLAY

By 1860, flocks had declined noticeably, and by the 1890s calls went out for a moratorium on hunting the animals—but to no avail. Conservation experts tried breeding the birds in captivity to little effect; it seemed the pigeons longed for the company of their enormous flocks and could not reproduce reliably without them. By the time experts realized this, the flocks no longer existed.

Sightings of passenger pigeons in the wild stopped by the early 1900s. A few survivors remained in captivity, dying one by one as ornithologists looked on helplessly. The last surviving pigeon, a female named Martha, died at the Cincinnati Zoological Garden on September 1, 1914. Her body was frozen in ice and shipped to the Smithsonian Institution, a testament to the downfall of a species.

Fast Facts

- *Isaac Newton, a notoriously distracted man, claimed that upon arising some mornings he would sit motionless for hours upon the edge of his bed as new thoughts, presumably freed by the night's sleep, occurred to him.*

- *Half of the world's present calorie consumption comes from a small variety of wheat and barley grains first cultivated in the Middle East around 8000 B.C.*

- *The oldest known furnace for copper smelting was discovered at Timna in southern Israel. The furnace dated to approximately 4200 B.C. and was simply a small hole in the ground that could be covered with a flat rock.*

- *As late as the 19th century, aborigines in Tasmania and rustics in Germany believed that touching the exposed wood on a tree struck by lightning would bring bad luck.*

- *The 365-day calendar has its origin in ancient Egypt.*

- *Ancient Egyptian families mourned the death of a pet cat by shaving off their eyebrows.*

- *Around 4000 B.C., scholars in the Mesopotamian city of Ur began breaking down their pictorial form of writing to represent the syllables of the word they were depicting. This move constitutes what many historians believe to be the single most important event in the history of writing.*

- *Around 700 B.C., warriors from the city of Nineveh destroyed rival Babylon by breaking the walls of a dam and diverting the torrent of water into the city. Less than 100 years later, an army of Babylonians destroyed Nineveh in exactly the same fashion.*

- *Until the invention of the steamship, no country could maintain a navy without an ample supply of flax—the key component of the strong material used to make sails.*

History of the Weird
FOUNDING FATHER WITH ODD HABITS

Benjamin Franklin was an unsurpassed diplomat, writer, and inventor. He may also have been the most eccentric, and funniest, of the founding fathers.

In the early 1760s, early-rising Londoners passing the apartment of the noted representative from the American colonies would get quite a surprise. Each morning, stout Benjamin Franklin would step naked through his rooms, opening up the windows to let in the fresh air he found so invigorating. If the weather was mild, Franklin would step outside and peruse the morning's newspaper outside his digs, a gentle breeze lapping at his bare body.

The famous printer and scientist urged others to try his scanty approach to apparel, but he was less encouraging to strangers who crowded around his property. Interlopers pressing against the iron fence of one domicile were shocked, literally, by an electric charge sent coursing through the metal by the discoverer of electricity.

FRANKLIN ON THE HUMAN BODY

As his displays of nudity might attest, Franklin was very comfortable with his body. He was evidently also proud of his bodily functions. He penned an essay dubbed "Fart Proudly," in which he proposed to:

"Discover some Drug wholesome & not disagreeable, to be mixed with our common Food, or Sauces, that shall render the natural Discharges of Wind from our Bodies, not only inoffensive, but agreeable as Perfumes."

With regard to another key physical function, Franklin urged a friend, who was having trouble landing a young wife, to take an elderly woman as his mistress. He counseled:

"Because in every animal that walks upright, the Deficiency of the Fluids that fill the Muscles appears first in the highest Part: the Face first grows lank and wrinkled; then the Neck; then the Breast and Arms; the lower Parts continuing to the last as plump as ever: So that covering all above with a Basket, and regarding only what is below the Girdle, it is impossible of two Women to know an old from a young one.

And as in the dark all Cats are grey, the Pleasure of corporal Enjoyment with an Old Woman is at least equal, and frequently superior."

FRANKLIN ON RELIGION

Franklin also had distinctive religious views, often skeptical, sometimes more traditional. He anonymously copublished an *Abridgment of the Book of Common Prayer,* which shortened funeral services to six minutes to better "preserve the health and lives of the living."

In the run-up to the American Revolution, Franklin's Committee of Safety—a sort of state provisional government—was deadlocked over whether Episcopal priests should pray for King George. Franklin told the committee:

"The Episcopal clergy, to my certain knowledge, have been constantly praying, these twenty years, that 'God would give the King and his Council wisdom,' and we all know that not the least notice has ever been taken of that prayer."

The prayers were canceled.

Yet, Franklin believed religion had a salutary effect on society and men's morals. In a letter to pamphleteer Thomas Paine, a decided agnostic, he wrote: "If men are so wicked with religion, what would they be if without it?" Asked to design the Great Seal of the United States, Franklin submitted a sketch of Moses and the Israelites drowning the Pharaoh's army in the Red Sea, with the motto: "Rebellion Against Tyrants is Obedience to God."

On ultimate questions of faith—the afterlife, the nature of God—Franklin was sometimes droll:

"As to Jesus of Nazareth...I think the System of Morals and his Religion... the best the world ever saw or is likely to see; but I apprehend it has received various corrupt changes, and I have, with most of the present Dissenters in England, some Doubts as to his divinity; tho' it is a question I do not dogmatize upon...when I expect soon an Opportunity of knowing the Truth with less Trouble."

THE END

In 1785, a Frenchman wrote a satire of Franklin's famous literary character Poor Richard in which the notoriously frugal Richard bequeathed a small amount of money, whose accumulating interest was not to be touched for 500 years. Franklin wrote the satirist, thanking him for a "great idea," and proceeded to bequeath 1,000 pounds each to his home and adopted towns, Philadelphia and Boston, to be placed in trust for 200 years. By 1990, the amount in the Philadelphia fund had reached $2 million and was dispensed as loans to townspeople and scholarships for students. The other trust tallied closed to $5 million, paying for a trade school that blossomed into the Franklin Institute of Boston.

Lastly, the eccentric, sharp-witted founder composed his own epitaph. It read:

"The Body of B. Franklin Printer; Like the Cover of an old Book, Its Contents torn out, And stript of its Lettering and Gilding, Lies here, Food for Worms. But the Work shall not be wholly lost: For it will, as he believ'd, appear once more, In a new & more perfect Edition, Corrected and Amended By the Author."

Timeline

Continued from page 266.

1260
Kublai Khan, grandson of Mongol leader Ghengis Khan, becomes the first foreigner to rule China as emperor, founding the Yuan Dynasty.

1271
Spaghetti Eastern. Marco Polo visits China; he is happy to sample local pasta dishes, which Italians have enjoyed for generations. On his return, Polo's writings spark Western interest in trade that continues through the early 20th century.

1337–1453
The Hundred Years War drains England and France. France wins by a nose, although England holds on to a bit of the French coastline around Calais.

1346–1351
Aw, Rats! The Black Death sweeps across western Europe, killing an estimated 25 million people; about a third of Europe's population is wiped out (60 percent of Venice died within 18 months). No one makes the connection with the hordes of flea-laden rats that infest European cities.

1368
Rebellion in China leads to the eventual overthrow of Mongol rule. The Ming Dynasty, which would rule China until 1644, leads China into a period of scientific, military, and cultural enlightenment.

1370
For 35 years, Samarkand noble Timur-i Lang cuts a bloody swath of conquest from Syria to India.

The dreaded Tamerlane, as he is known in Europe, dies before he can begin his conquest of China. Eight years later, Mongolian rule in China collapses as the Ming emperors take power for the next three centuries.

1378–1413
The Roman Catholic papacy is torn by influences from France and the Holy Roman Empire. The Great Schism, in which competing popes claimed the throne of Saint Peter, weakens the influence of the pope.

c. 1380
Geoffrey Chaucer begins work on *The Canterbury Tales,* a monumental work that takes nearly 20 years to complete.

1440
"Start the Presses!" German inventor Johannes Gutenberg changes the world with the invention of the printing press, making written knowledge available to the masses.

1453
It's Getting Late. The Ottoman capture of Constantinople marks the end of the Middle Ages. The Orthodox church moves to Moscow, and Greek scholars head west to start a humanist movement that flowers into the Renaissance.

1455
Pruning Flowers. The three-decade Wars of the Roses begins when England's House of York (symbolized by a white rose) rises up against the House of Lancaster (symbolized by a red rose) over the succession of King Henry VI, a Lancastrian noble.

Timeline

1461
Wallachia's Prince Vlad Tepes turns back an Ottoman force at Tirgoviste by treating the invaders to the sight of some 20,000 prisoners impaled on sharp stakes before his castle walls. Some 430 years later, author Bram Stoker will turn Vlad the Impaler into one of Western literature's most enduring villains: the vampire Dracula.

1475
Good Fences Make Good Neighbors. Leaders of China's Ming dynasty bulk up the Great Wall to some 4,100 miles of walls and watchtowers to guard against Mongol incursions.

1478
"Nobody Expects the Spanish Inquisition!" To solidify their Catholic kingdom, Spain's King Ferdinand and Queen Isabella begin a program of religious persecution that becomes the Spanish Inquisition, a tool of repression to persecute Jews and Protestants. Some 2,000 Spaniards would be executed under the administration of Inquisitor-General Tomas de Torquemada.

1485
"My Kingdom for a Horse." At the Battle of Bosworth Field, England's Henry Tudor defeats King Richard III and claims the English throne. He inaugurates the Tudor Dynasty, which rules England for the next 118 years.

1489
Italian genius Leonardo da Vinci begins detailed drawings of the human skull, building a body of work that makes him history's best-known "Renaissance Man."

1492
Under the Spanish flag, Christopher Columbus crosses the Atlantic Ocean to land at San Salvador in the New World. If sailors had known how to calculate longitude back then, American natives would not have been called "Indians."

1497–1499
Out of Africa. Portuguese explorer Vasco da Gama circumnavigates Africa to reach the lucrative Asian trade market.

1508–1512
Italian painter Michelangelo paints the ceiling of the Vatican's Sistine Chapel.

1512
"What Goes Around . . . " Polish astronomer Nicolai Copernicus begins popularizing the theory of heliocentrism, arguing that the world revolves around the sun. Scientists scoff at what is obviously an incorrect theory.

1517
Irascible Catholic monk Martin Luther nails his famous "95 Theses" to the door of Wittenberg, Germany's Castle Church, calling for an end to established papal practices such as the sale of indulgences. His crusade to reform the Catholic Church sparks the Reformation, as well as the eventual splintering of Western Christians into various Protestant denominations.

Wondering what happened next? Turn to page 360 to find out!

HIGH PRIESTESS OF THE CULT OF *PERONISMO*

Long before cinema and media drama brought her back into North American eyes, the woman many called "Santa Evita" was a legend in her native land. Her memory now casts a shadow larger than life, which makes it hard to believe that she held influence for less than ten years and didn't live to be 35.

Is it "Eva" or "Evita"?

Eva liked the familiar version, which translates roughly to "Evie." It's like calling Lady Diana "Di."

What do we know about Evita's origin?

Eva María Ibarguren breathed her first on May 7, 1919, in Los Toldos, Argentina. Her mother, Juana, was involved with married estate manager Juan Duarte. Juana adopted Juan's last name for herself and her kids, but he soon went back to his wife in another town. When he died, Juana insisted on attending his funeral—scandalous, but the move hints at the origin of Evita's own strength and bravery. Juana's family endured small-town whispers, breeding in young Eva much contempt for the stratified Argentine social order.

How did Eva find her way to greater things?

Early on, Eva was a thin, quiet, often truant girl. Acting in a school play convinced her she wanted a career in show business, so she headed to Buenos Aires. She was a hit at theater, movies, and radio acting, making herself one of Argentina's best-paid actresses by 1943. Her stage presence and sense of public opinion would come in handy later in life.

Then came Juan Perón.

Argentina, theoretically democratic, was ruled by a series of oligarchies. Some were better, some worse, some in between. *El coronel* and widower Juan Domingo Perón was an influential soldier involved in politics, normal for the Argentine military of the day. In 1944, with Perón serving in the military government, an Andean earthquake devastated San Juan. Perón organized a benefit performance, and there he met Evita Duarte.

Fireworks?

For both. She soon moved in with him; their mutual love shows in all they did.

And that brought her into politics?

Evita left acting to lend her influential voice to *peronismo,* a cult-like mix of populism, nationalism, and authoritarianism. In effect, she became its high priestess.

So, Perón vaulted her into power?

Or perhaps Evita vaulted Perón into a position of power. Evita Duarte was influential independent of and before Juan Perón; he didn't make her. They were a mutually complementary political dream team.

When did Evita become Señora Dictator?

Perón's government enemies arrested him in October 1945. The *peronista* masses rallied, and the ruling junta yielded in time to save itself. Reunited with his jubilant partner, Juan planned to run for president. One problem: They were still living in sin. Eva Duarte became Señora Eva Duarte de Perón in a private civil ceremony. On June 4, 1946, Perón was elected president of Argentina.

Good deal for Evita?

Yes—but it also polarized perceptions of her. Argentina knew her well from Juan's campaign trail. To *peronistas,* Evita was the caring face of the movement. For anti-*peronistas* (now keeping low profiles), she was the upstart soap opera harlot, living high on the hog.

Which is more accurate?

The space between the extremes called her a "strong, smart woman." She did live far better than the impoverished *descamisados* ("shirtless") she championed. Monastic heads of state, or spouses of same, are rare anywhere. But she was wealthy and popular before *peronismo,* and her affinity for the downtrodden rings genuine given her upbringing. By building her husband's personality cult, she built her own. She held a political religion in the palm of her hand, and she learned to wield it with gutsy skill.

What else did she do?

Argentine women got the vote in 1947. *¿Coincidencia o Evita?*

In 1947, she also toured Europe, beginning with Franco's Spain. When the British didn't treat her visit as equal to one by Eleanor Roosevelt, Evita snubbed the U.K. *Peronistas* swelled with patriotism to see their defiant heroine on the world stage. Evita also founded a charity and a women's political party. By 1951, however, uterine cancer had begun to sap her strength.

Could the disease have been arrested if caught sooner?

Only Evita herself could tell us when she first felt something was wrong, but the physical impact is documented as early as 1950. By the time she underwent chemo and a radical hysterectomy, it was far too late. On July 26, 1952, Eva María Duarte de Perón, now anointed "Spiritual Leader of the Nation," passed from life to legend. Argentina wept bitter tears for her.

I heard that it didn't end with her death—some ghoulish story about embalming and a lost corpse. What really occurred?

Soon after she died, an embalmer did an outstanding job preserving Evita. She was supposed to be exhibited under glass in perpetuity, like Lenin. However, in 1955, a military coup booted Juan out of office—and out of Argentina. *Peronismo* was proscribed. Evita's body vanished.

Turns out she was interred in Milan, Italy, under an assumed name. In 1971, Evita was exhumed and sent to Juan's Spanish exile house, which in itself is a little macabre: "Excuse me, *Señor*, but that is my wife, not a coffee table." In 1973, Perón returned to Argentina to fan the *peronista* coals into a presidency. After his death in 1974, Evita Perón was reinterred in the securest possible crypt.

The heroine lay at last in the only true place that could give her rest: Argentina.

- *Perón's first wife also died of uterine cancer.*

- *So far as we know, Evita never said, "Don't cry for me, Argentina." Hollywood put the words in her mouth. Since Evita began as an actress and camouflaged her own history, it's fitting that Hollywood embossed her on American pop culture with a mythical line.*

- *Interesting linguistic twist:* evitar *can mean "to avoid," "to prevent," or "to shun."* Evita *could thus be read "she avoids." We see it in the English word "inevitable." It's amusing because the only thing Evita definitely avoided was letting the truth come out about her childhood. She even had her birth certificate removed from the records.*

- *Hollywood got it wrong; Evita didn't orchestrate the massive demonstrations for Perón's 1945 release. However, the swiftness and energy of the* peronista *demonstrations in Juan's favor owed plenty to Evita's past contributions to his image.*

- *In 1947,* Time *magazine alleged (correctly) that Evita was illegitimate. This act of* lèse-majesté *got* Time *banned from Argentina for months.*

THE GREAT SICKNESS

When Western explorers, traders, and settlers made their way into the Alaskan frontier in the 18th and 19th centuries, they brought with them diseases to which the natives had never before been exposed. Diseases such as measles, tuberculosis, and influenza wiped out entire communities, who had no natural immunity to such illnesses. So many natives died that it forever destabilized the traditional Alaskan culture. But not all stories had a tragic ending.

NORTH TO ALASKA

Almost nobody had heard of Nome, Alaska, before January 1925. Just two degrees south of the Arctic Circle on the Bering Sea, it was a small village isolated during the summer and inaccessible during the long Arctic winters.

Nome had one doctor, four nurses, a 24-bed hospital, and 8,000 units of expired diphtheria serum when it radioed for help on January 22, 1925. The doctor, Curtis Welch, desperately pleaded for 1.1 million units of serum to combat the diphtheria epidemic that threatened 10,000 lives. Without the serum, the mortality rate would be close to 100 percent.

Nome called for help, and the nation responded. The needed serum was quickly gathered and sent northward from Seattle by steamship. Meanwhile, 300,000 units—enough to treat 30 people—were found in Anchorage. Though not enough to control the epidemic, it was enough to contain it until the rest arrived.

But how to get the serum from Anchorage to Nome? An airlift was considered but was quickly abandoned. The local planes were too unreliable, and the weather was too poor for flying. The Bering Sea was already frozen over for the winter, making a delivery by water impossible. The only way to reach Nome, it was decided, was by dogsled.

In the years before the bush plane, the dogsled was the only reliable way to get around the interior of Alaska. Sled teams and their mushers traveled down the Iditarod Trail, among others, delivering mail and supplies and bringing out gold. This time, they were asked to deliver a more precious cargo.

THE GREAT RACE OF MERCY

The 20-pound package of serum was rushed by train from Anchorage northward to the town of Nenana. On January 27, 1925, at 9:00 P.M., "Wild Bill" Shannon and his team of 9 dogs were the first of 20 mushers and approximately 150 dogs to relay the serum 674 miles to Nome.

Known as the Great Race of Mercy, the mushers followed the Tanana River for 137 miles to the village of Tanana, where the Tanana and Yukon rivers meet. There, the route followed the Yukon for 230 miles to the village of Kaltag. From Kaltag, it was a 90-mile run to Unalakeet. There started the most dangerous leg of the relay: 208 miles over the Seward Peninsula completely exposed to the worst Arctic winter in 20 years (including −50-degree temperatures and gale-force winds). Once across the Peninsula, the last 42 miles to Nome were across the treacherous frozen ice of the Bering Sea.

At 3:00 A.M. on February 2, Gunnar Kaasen and his team of dogs, led by Balto, made it into Nome with the serum. Eventually, another run was made to deliver the rest of the much-needed medicine. Officially, the epidemic claimed between 5 to 7 lives, but there were probably 100 cases among the natives outside Nome, who buried their children without reporting their deaths.

The mushers and their dogs became instant celebrities. Everyone involved received letters of commendation from President Calvin Coolidge, gold medals, and the princely sum of $25 for their troubles. Many participants traveled the country recounting their trip to Nome, including Kassen and Balto, who toured the West Coast from 1925 to 1926. In 1925, a statue of Balto was placed in New York's Central Park. When Balto died in 1933, he was stuffed and put on display at the Cleveland Museum of Natural History.

EPITAPHS OF THE FAMOUS

OLIVER HARDY (OF LAUREL & HARDY):
A GENIUS OF COMEDY
HIS TALENT BROUGHT JOY AND
LAUGHTER TO ALL THE WORLD.

JAMES B. "WILD BILL" HICKOK (FRONTIER FIGURE):
Pard, we will meet again in the Happy Hunting Ground
To part no more, Goodbye

JESSE JAMES (ROBBER):
Murdered by a traitor and a coward whose name is not
worthy to appear here.

THOMAS JEFFERSON (THIRD PRESIDENT):
AUTHOR OF THE DECLARATION OF AMERICAN
INDEPENDENCE OF THE STATUTE OF VIRGINIA
FOR RELIGIOUS FREEDOM AND FATHER OF
THE UNIVERSITY OF VIRGINIA

CHARLES & ANNE LINDBERGH
(PIONEERING PILOT AND WIFE):
... If I take the wings of the morning
and
dwell in the uttermost parts of the sea. ...

JACK LONDON (AUTHOR):
The Stone the Builders Rejected
mebody Sometime

KARL MARX (POLITICAL THEORIST):
Workers of all lands unite.
The philosophers have only interpreted the world in various ways;
the point is to change it.

DRACULA IMPALES IN COMPARISON

*The origins of Dracula, the blood-sucking vampire of Bram
Stoker's novel (and countless movies, comics, and costumes) are
commonly traced to a 15th-century Romanian noble,
whose brutal and bloody exploits made him both
a national folk hero and an object of horror.*

THE REAL DRACULA

Vlad III Tepes (1431–1476) was born into the ruling family of
Wallachia, a principality precariously balanced between the Ottoman (Turkish and Muslim) and Holy Roman (Germanic and
Catholic) empires. His father, Vlad II, became known as *Dracul*
("Dragon") due to his initiation into the knightly Order of the
Dragon. As a part of Dracul's attempt to maintain Wallachia's
independence, he sent Vlad III and his brother Radu as hostages
to the Turks. When Dracul was assassinated in 1447 and a rival
branch of the family took the throne, the Turks helped Vlad III
to recapture it briefly as a puppet ruler before he was driven into
exile in Muldovia. Eight years later (1456), Vlad III, known as
Dracula, or "son of Dracul," regained the throne with Hungary's
backing and ruled for six years.

Dracula faced several obstacles to independence and control. The
Ottoman Empire and Hungary were the largest external threats.
There was also internal resistance from the *boyars* (regional
nobles), who kept Wallachia destabilized in their own interests, as
well as from the powerful Saxon merchants of Transylvania, who
resisted economic control. Lawlessness and disorder were also
prevalent.

Dracula's successes against these obstacles are the source of the
admiration that still pervades local folklore, in which there are
many tales of his exploits. Locally, he is portrayed as a strong,
cunning, and courageous leader who enforced order, suppressed

disloyalty, and defended Wallachia. Not only did Wallachia remain independent and Christian, but, as the story goes, Dracula could leave a golden cup by a spring for anyone to get a cool drink without it being stolen—no one was above the law.

His methods, however, are the source of his portrayal elsewhere as a sadistic despot who merited an alternate meaning of Dracula, namely "devil." He eliminated poverty and hunger by feasting the poor and sick and, after dinner, burning them alive in the hall. He eliminated disloyal boyars by inviting them to an Easter feast, after which he put them in chains and worked them to death building his fortress at Poenari. Ambassadors who refused to doff their caps had them nailed to their heads. Dishonest merchants and bands of gypsies suffered similarly grisly ends.

Vlad's favorite method of enforcement was impaling (a gruesome and purposefully drawn-out form of execution in which victims were pierced by a long wooden stake and hoisted aloft), though he also found creative ways of flaying, boiling, and hacking people to death. When the Turks cornered him at Tirgoviste in 1461, he created a "forest" of 20,000 impaled captive men, women, and children, which so horrified the Turks that they withdrew. They called him *kaziklu bey* ("the Impaler Prince"), and though Vlad himself did not use it, the epithet *Tepes* ("Impaler") stuck.

The Turks then backed Radu and besieged Vlad in Poenari. Dracula escaped to Hungary with the help of a secret tunnel and local villagers, but was imprisoned there. Dracula gradually ingratiated himself and, upon Radu's death, took back the throne in 1476. Just two months later, Dracula was killed in a forest battle against the Turks near Bucharest. Tradition has it that his head was put on display by the Turks and his body buried in the Snagov Monastery, but no grave has been found.

Bram Stoker, while researching for a vampire story about "Count Wampyr," discovered in a library book that "Dracula" could mean "devil" and changed his character's name. Connecting Stoker's Count to Vlad III has been popular in the press (starting with the 1958 *In Search of Dracula*) and in the tourist industry. However, Stoker's character probably has little basis in Vlad Dracula.

GREAT OBSCURE QUOTES

"There are two insults which no human being will endure: The assertion that he hasn't a sense of humor, and the doubly impertinent assertion that he has never known trouble."
—SINCLAIR LEWIS, AUTHOR

"God has a special providence for fools, drunks, and the United States of America."
—OTTO VON BISMARCK

"If wishes were horses, beggars would ride."
—J. KELLY, SCOTTISH PROVERBS, 1721

"If I see a murderous fellow sharpening a knife cleverly, I can borrow his way of sharpening the knife without borrowing his probable intention to commit murder with it."
—WOODROW WILSON, *The Study of Administration,* 1886

"There is only one antidote to mental suffering, and that is physical pain."
—KARL MARX, *Herr Vogt,* 1860

RASPUTIN:
DEPRAVED SEX FREAK OR
MALIGNED HOLY MAN?

*We know this much: Grigori Yefimovich Rasputin, a barely literate
Russian peasant, grew close to the last tsaritsa—
close enough to cost him his life. Incredibly lurid stories
ricocheted off the walls of the Winter Palace: drunken satyr,
faith healer, master manipulator. What's true?
And why does Rasputin fascinate us even today?*

The Rasputin saga began on January 22, 1869, in the grubby
peasant village of Pokrovskoe, Russia. Baby Rasputin was born on
the day of the Orthodox saint Grigori, and was thus named after
him. There wasn't much to distinguish little Grigori from tens of
millions of Russian peasant kids, and he grew up a rowdy drunk.
He married a peasant woman named Praskovia, who hung back in
Pokrovskoe raising their five kids in Rasputin's general absence.

At 28, Rasputin was born again, rural Russian style. He sobered
up—a small miracle in itself—and wandered between monasteries seeking knowledge. Evidently, he fell in with the *khlysti*—a
secretive, heretical Eastern Orthodox sect swirling with rumors
of orgies, flagellation, and the like. He gained a mystical aura, and
his behavior reflected a sincere spiritual search.

In 1903, he wandered to the capital, St. Petersburg, where he
impressed the local Orthodox clergy. Word spread. The ruling
Romanov family soon heard of Rasputin.

The Romanovs held a powerful yet precarious position. Ethni-
cally, they were more German than Russian, a hot-button topic
for the *bona fide* Slavs they ruled. Greedy flatterers and brutal
infighters made the corridors of power a steep slope with weak
rock and loose mud: As you climbed, your prestige and influence grew—but woe to you if you slipped (or were pushed). In

that event, the rest would step aside and let you fall—caring only to get out of your way. This was no safe place for a naive peasant—however spiritually inclined. Even the Romanovs lived in fear, for tsars tended to die violent deaths. They ruled a dirt-poor population that was seething with resentment. Tsaryevich ("tsar's son") Alexei, the heir apparent, was a fragile hemophiliac who could bleed out from a skinned knee, aptly symbolic of the blood in the political water in St. Petersburg in those final days of the last tsar, Nikolai II.

As the tsaritsa worried over gravely ill Alexei in 1906, she thought of Rasputin and his healing reputation. He answered her summons in person, blessed Alexei with an Orthodox *ikon* and left. Alexei improved, and Tsaritsa Aleksandra was hooked on Rasputin. She consulted him often, promoted him to her friends, and pulled him onto that treacherous slope of imperial favor. For his final ten years, Rasputin became a polarizing figure as he grew more influential. His small covey of upper-crust supporters (mostly female) hung on his every word, even as a growing legion of nobles, peasants, and clergy saw in Rasputin all that was wrong with the monarchy.

What few ask now is: What was Rasputin thinking? What was he feeling? His swift rise from muddy fields to the counsels of Russian power gave him an understandable ego trip. He was a peasant but not an idiot; he realized his rise would earn him jealous enemies. The sheer fury of their hatred seems to have surprised, frightened, and saddened him, for he wasn't a hateful man. He certainly felt duty-bound to the tsaritsa, whose unwavering favor deflected most of his enemies' blows. Rasputin's internal spiritual struggle (against sin, toward holiness) registers authentic, at least until his last year or so of life—but he made regular visits to prostitutes long before that. Defenders claim that he was only steeling himself against sexual temptation; you can imagine what his enemies said.

Life worsened for Rasputin in 1914, when he was stabbed by a former prostitute. He survived, but the experience shook him. After recuperating, he abandoned any restraint he'd ever exercised. Rasputin better acquainted himself with the bottoms of liquor bottles—and those of his visitors. Most likely he expected death and gave in to natural human desires: Cartoons portrayed him as a cancer infecting the monarchy, especially after Russia went to war with Germany. Military setbacks left Russians with much to mourn and resent. A wave of mandatory patriotism swept Russia, focusing discontent upon the royal family's Germanic ties.

In the end, clergy and nobility agreed with the media: down with Rasputin.

Led by a fabulously rich libertine named Felix Yusupov, a group of Rasputin's enemies lured him to a meeting on December 29, 1916. The popular story is that he scarfed a bunch of poisoned food and wine, somehow didn't die, was shot, got up, was beaten and shot some more, then was finally tied up and thrown alive through the ice of a frozen river. What is sure: Rasputin was shot, bound, and dumped into freezing water to die. Whether or not he was still alive when dumped and whether or not he actually partook of the cyanide munchies, he was found with at least one fatal bullet wound.

The tsaritsa buried her advisor on royal property. After the Romanovs fell, a mob dug up Rasputin and burned his corpse. To our knowledge, nothing remains of him.

Rasputin had predicted that if he were slain by the nobility, the Russian monarchy wouldn't long survive him. His prophecy came true: Less than a year after his death, the Russian Revolution deposed the tsar. The Reds would soon murder the entire royal family; had they captured Rasputin, it's hard to imagine him being spared. For the "Mad Monk" who was neither mad nor monastic, the muddy road of life had dead-ended in the treacherous forest of imperial favor.

Fast Facts

- Many believe that the first coins were minted on the island of Aegina around 470 B.C.

- While perfecting his craft, Demosthenes, Athens' greatest orator, once shaved half the hair from his head so he would not be tempted to leave his house. To overcome an inclination to stutter, he practiced sounding out words while holding a mouthful of pebbles.

- The first known use of the wheelbarrow was around 333 B.C. during the construction of a shrine at Eleusis in Greece. Nearly 1,500 years later, Christians brought the labor-saving device back with them from the second Crusade.

- The first translation of the Old Testament from Hebrew into Greek occurred in the city of Alexandria, Egypt, and was known as the Septuagint because it took more than 70 translators to complete.

- The lighthouse at Pharos, completed in 280 B.C., boasted a fire that burned at a height equal to a modern 25-story skyscraper and served as a beacon to ships approaching Alexandria, which lacked hills for such a purpose.

- The Macedonian Greeks who founded and ruled ancient Alexandria were so disdainful of the native Egyptian population that it was considered more honorable to marry one's own sister than to marry an Egyptian woman. In fact, the practice of marrying one's sibling was fairly common and had been borrowed from the royal families of Egypt.

- The stirrup was first used about 500 B.C. by mounted warriors on the steppes of southern Russia, where the horse was first domesticated around 2000 B.C.

- Ancient Chinese kings were buried in elaborate tombs filled with precious jade items. The bodies of the workers who had constructed the tomb were often buried with the king so that they could not tell others how to get inside.

THE RISE AND FALL
OF THE KNIGHTS TEMPLAR

*The Crusades, Christendom's quest to recover and hold
the Holy Land, saw the rise of several influential military orders.
Of these, the Knights Templar had perhaps the greatest
lasting influence—and took the hardest fall.*

July 15, 1099: On that day, the First Crusade stormed Jerusalem
and slaughtered everyone in sight—Jews, Muslims, Christians—
didn't matter. This unleashed a wave of pilgrimage, as European
Christians flocked to now-accessible Palestine and its holy sites.
Though Jerusalem's loss was a blow to Islam, it was a bonanza for
the region's thieves, from Saracens to lapsed Crusaders: a steady
stream of naive pilgrims to rob.

DEFENDING THE FAITHFUL

French knight Hugues de Payen, with eight chivalrous comrades,
swore to guard the travelers. In 1119, they gathered at the Church
of the Holy Sepulchre and pledged their lives to poverty, chastity,
and obedience before King Baldwin II of Jerusalem. The Order of
Poor Knights of the Temple of Solomon took up headquarters in
said Temple.

GOING MAINSTREAM

The Templars did their work well, and in 1127 Baldwin sent a
Templar embassy to Europe to secure a marriage that would
ensure the royal succession in Jerusalem. Not only did they suc-
ceed, they became rock stars of sorts. Influential nobles showered
the Order with money and real estate, the foundation of its future
wealth. With this growth came a formal code of rules. Some highlights include:

• Templars could not desert the battlefield or leave a castle by
stealth.

- They had to wear white habits, except for sergeants and squires who could wear black.
- They had to tonsure (shave) their crowns and wear beards.
- They had to dine in communal silence, broken only by Scriptural readings.
- They had to be chaste, except for married men joining with their wives' consent.

A LAW UNTO THEMSELVES—AND NEVER MIND THAT PESKY "POVERTY" PART

Now with offices in Europe to manage the Order's growing assets, the Templars returned to Palestine to join in the Kingdom's ongoing defense. In 1139, Pope Innocent II decreed the Order answerable only to the Holy See. Now exempt from the tithe, the Order was entitled to accept tithes! The Knights Templar had come far.

By the mid-1100s, the Templars had become a church within a church, a nation within a nation, and a major banking concern. Templar keeps were well-defended depositories, and the Order became financiers to the crowned heads of Europe—even to the Papacy. Their reputation for meticulous bookkeeping and secure transactions underpinned Europe's financial markets, even as their soldiers kept fighting for the faith in the Holy Land.

DOWNFALL

Templar prowess notwithstanding, the Crusaders couldn't hold the Holy Land. In 1187, Saladin the Kurd retook Jerusalem, martyring 230 captured Templars. Factional fighting between Christians sped the collapse as the 1200s wore on. In 1291, the last Crusader outpost at Acre fell to the Mamelukes of Egypt. Though the Templars had taken a hosing along with the other Christian forces, their troubles had just begun.

King Philip IV of France owed the Order a lot of money, and they made him more nervous at home than they did fighting in Palestine. In 1307, Philip ordered the arrest of all Templars in France. They stood accused of apostasy, devil worship, sodomy, desecration, and greed. Hideous torture produced piles of confessions, much like those of the later Inquisition. The Order was looted, shattered, and officially dissolved. In March 1314, Jacques de Molay, the last Grand Master of the Knights Templar, was burned at the stake.

WHITHER THE TEMPLARS?

Many Templar assets passed to the Knights Hospitallers. The Order survived in Portugal as the Order of Christ, where it exists to this day in form similar to British knightly orders. A Templar fleet escaped from La Rochelle and vanished; it may have reached Scotland. Swiss folktales suggest that some Templars took their loot and expertise to Switzerland, possibly laying the groundwork for what would one day become the Swiss banking industry.

Shroud of Turin: Real or Fake?

Measuring roughly 14 feet long by 3 feet wide, the Shroud of Turin features the front and back image of a man who was 5 feet, 9 inches tall. The man was bearded and had shoulder-length hair parted down the middle. Dark stains on the Shroud are consistent with blood from a crucifixion.

First publicly displayed in 1357, the Shroud of Turin has apparent ties to the Knights of Templar. At the time of its first showing, the Shroud was in the hands of of the family of Geoffrey de Charney, a Templar who had been burned at the stake in 1314 along with Jacques de Molay. Some accounts say it was the Knights who removed the cloth from Constantinople, where it was kept in the 13th century.

Some believe the Shroud of Turin is the cloth that Jesus was wrapped in after his death. All four gospels mention that the body of Jesus was covered in a linen cloth prior to the resurrection.

Others assert that the cloth shrouded Jacques de Molay after he was tortured by being nailed to a door.

Still others contend that the Shroud was the early photographic experiments of Leonardo da Vinci. He mentioned working with "optics" in some of his diaries and wrote his notes in a sort of mirrored handwriting style, some say, to keep his experiments secret from the church.

Is the Shroud of Turin authentic? In 1988, scientists using carbon-dating concluded that the material in the Shroud was from around A.D. 1260 to 1390, which seems to exclude the possibility that the Shroud bears the image of Jesus.

THE AMAZONS: MAN-EATERS OF THE ANCIENT WORLD

They were the ultimate feminists—powerful, independent women who formed female-only societies that had no use for men beyond procreation. They were the epitome of girl power, fierce mounted warriors who often emasculated the best male fighters from other societies. They were the Amazons— man-eaters of the ancient world.

The ancient Greeks were enthralled by the Amazons. Greek writers, like today's Hollywood gossip columnists, relished lurid tales of love affairs between Amazon queens and their Greek boy toys. Others wrote of epic battles between Amazon warriors and the greatest heroes of Greek mythology.

Given their prominent place in Greek lore, the story of the Amazons has generally been considered the stuff of legend. But recent archeological finds suggest that a race of these warrior über-women actually did exist.

THE AMAZONS ACCORDING TO THE GREEKS

History's first mention of the Amazons is found in Homer's *Iliad*, written in the 7th or 8th century B.C. Homer told of a group of women he called *Antianeira* ("those who fight like men"), who fought on the side of Troy against the Greeks. They were led by Penthesilea, who fought Achilles and was slain by him. According to some accounts, Achilles fell in love with her immediately afterward. Achilles was highly skilled in the art of warfare, but it seems he was sorely lacking in the intricacies of courtship.

From then on, the Amazons became forever linked with the ancient Greeks. Their very name is believed to derive from the Greek *a-mazos*, meaning "without a breast." This referred to the Amazon practice of removing the right breast of their young girls so that they would be unencumbered in the use of the bow and spear. Somewhat draconian, yes, but no one could accuse the Amazons of being anything less than hard-core. This may have made Greek, Roman, and European artists a bit squeamish because their depictions of Amazons showed them with two breasts, though the right breast was often covered or hidden.

According to Greek mythology, the Amazons were the offspring of Ares, god of war, who was the son of the mightiest of the Greek gods, Zeus. Though the Amazons may have had Greek roots, they didn't want anything to do with them. Like young adults eager to move from their parents' homes, the Amazons established their realm in a land called Pontus in modern-day northeastern Turkey, where they founded several important cities, including Smyrna.

The Greeks paint a picture of the Amazons as a female-dominated society of man-haters that banned men from living among them. In an odd dichotomy between chastity and promiscuity, sexual encounters with men were taboo except for once a year when the Amazons would choose male partners from the neighboring Gargareans strictly for the purposes of procreation. Female babies were kept; males were killed or sent back with their fathers. Females were raised to do everything a man could do—and to do it better.

SOAP OPERA ENCOUNTERS WITH GREEK HEROES

The Greeks and the Amazons interacted in a turbulent love-hate relationship resembling something from a Hollywood soap opera. Hercules, as one of his labors, had to obtain the girdle of the Amazon queen Hippolyte. He was accompanied in his task by Theseus, who stole Hippolyte's sister Antiope. This led to ongoing warfare between the Greeks and Amazons as well as several trysts between members of the two societies. One account has Theseus and Antiope falling in love, with her dying by his side during a battle against the Amazons. Another account has Theseus and Hippolyte becoming lovers. Stories of Hercules have him alternately wooing and warring with various Amazonian women.

Jason and the Argonauts met the Amazons on the island of Lemnos. Completely unaware of the true nature of the island's inhabitants, Jason queried the Amazons as to the whereabouts of their men. They told him their men were all killed in an earlier invasion. What the Argonauts didn't realize was that the Amazons themselves were the killers. The Amazons, anticipating another opportunity for manslaughter, invited the Argonauts to stay and become their husbands. But Jason and the boys, perhaps intimidated by the appearance of the Amazons in full battle dress, graciously declined and hightailed it off the island.

MORE THAN MYTH?

The Greek historian Herodotus perhaps provides the best connection of the Greeks to what may be the true race of Amazons. Writing in the 5th century B.C., Herodotus chronicles a group of warrior women who were defeated in battle by the Greeks. These *Androktones* ("killers of men"), as he called them, were put on a prison ship, where they happily went about killing the all-male Greek crew. Hellcats on land but hopeless on water, the women drifted to the north shores of the Black Sea to the land of the Scythians, a nomadic people of Iranian descent.

Here, says Herodotus, they intermarried with the Scythian men on the condition that they be allowed to keep their traditional warrior customs. They added a heartwarming social tenet that no woman could wed until she had killed a man in battle. Together, they migrated northeast across the Russian steppes, eventually evolving into the Sarmatian culture, which featured a prominent role for women hunting and fighting by the sides of their husbands. The men may have given their wives the loving pet name *ha-mazan,* the Iranian word for "warrior."

Though the Amazons are still mostly perceived as myth, recent archeological discoveries lend credence to Herodotus's account and help elevate the Amazons from the pages of Greek legend to historical fact. Excavations of Sarmatian burial grounds found the majority of those interred there were heavily armed women, all of whom got the very best spots in the site.

PANCHO VILLA:
THE MAN WITH TWO FACES

Hero or criminal? You decide.

The man the world knew as Pancho
Villa led a contradictory life that caused
some to venerate him as a saint and others to loathe him as a fiend. Certainly,
Pancho Villa was a man of bold action
with an uncanny sense of destiny whose
exploits—whether actual or mythical,
inherently good or evil—have become
the stuff of legend. Even in his own time,
he was celebrated as a living folk hero by
Mexicans and Americans alike. In fact, film companies sent crews
to revolutionary Mexico to chronicle his exploits—a circumstance
that pleased the wily Villa, if for no other reason than the gold
the directors brought with them. Journalists, novelists, friends,
and enemies all conspired to create the image of a man whose
true nature remained elusive. To the present day, the name of
Francisco "Pancho" Villa continues to inspire both admiration and
scorn with equal fervor... depending on whom you ask.

GENERAL PANCHO VILLA:
HERO OF THE PEOPLE

Pancho Villa was born Doroteo Arango in Durango, Mexico,
either in 1877 or 1879. As the son of a peasant family working for
a hacienda owner, he realized that he would eventually inherit
his father's debt and work the land until the day he died. At age
16, however, Doroteo returned home to find his sister fending
off the lecherous advances of a local don. Unable to countenance
the dishonoring of his beloved sister, Villa obtained a pistol, shot
and killed the offending "gentleman," and escaped to the hills.
For nearly ten years, he lived as a bandit, robbing from the rich
and giving to the poor men who joined him. With the start of the

Mexican Revolution, Villa came down from the mountains to form an army in support of the populist platform espoused by Francisco Madero.

As a general, Villa staged bold cavalry charges that overwhelmed his opponents even at great risk to his own life. General Villa was very popular with the ladies (purportedly marrying 26 times) and loved to dance. However, he did not drink and once famously choked on a dram of brandy offered him by fellow revolutionary General Emilano Zapata. As the Mexican Revolution ground through a series of corrupt leaders, Villa remained true to his populist ideology.

When his political rival, Venustiano Carranza, came to power, Villa became a wanted man again, this time in both Mexico and the United States. As in his youth, he took to the mountains, evading capture for several years until, weary of life on the run, he surrendered in 1920. Villa purchased a former hacienda known as La Purísima Concepción de El Canutillo and moved there with about 400 of his soldiers and their families. Rather than become like the wealthy landowners he despised, however, Villa used the hacienda to form an agricultural community that soon swelled to approximately 2,000 men, women, and children who received an education and shared in the profits.

PANCHO VILLA: MURDEROUS THUG

When American President Woodrow Wilson chose to support the presidency of Villa's rival Venustiano Carranza, Villa retaliated. On January 11, 1916, Villa and a group of his men stopped a train in Santa Ysabel, Mexico, and brutally killed 18 Texas businessmen. Murder and banditry were nothing new to Villa; as a young man he had made his living stealing cattle and was a murderer before he reached 20. As a revolutionary general, he ordered executions for specious reasons, robbed herds of cattle to sell north of the border, and shot merchants who refused to take the money he had printed for his army. His cattle thieving incensed powerful newspaper magnate Randolph Hearst who conducted a long-term smear campaign against the bandit, which, among other things, led to the criminalization of marijuana in the United States.

Pancho Villa's greatest moment of infamy, however, came at 2:30 A.M. on March 9, 1916, when he led a band of 500 horse-mounted followers against the 13th U.S. Cavalry and then into Columbus, New Mexico, where the bandits killed indiscriminately and destroyed property. When the Villistas departed at 7:00 A.M., 14 American soldiers, 10 civilians, and scores of bandits lay dead. President Wilson ordered Brigadier General John J. Pershing to lead a punitive cavalry expedition into Mexico to capture Villa but multiple, costly attempts to corner the cunning outlaw proved fruitless. Soon, the nuisance of Pancho Villa was replaced in the national consciousness by the United States' entry into the war raging in Europe.

THE END OF THE MAN,
THE START OF THE LEGEND

Pancho Villa was assassinated by unknown persons while visiting the village of Parral in 1923. After Villa's death, one of his officers allegedly opened his tomb in Parral and removed his head to sell to a Chicago millionaire who collected skulls. Villa's body was later moved to Mexico City and interred in the Tomb of the Illustrious, but many believe that it was simply a headless decoy and his true resting place remains in Northern Mexico. Thus, even the final resting place of Villa's body has become obscured by speculation and doubt.

- *Pershing's pursuit of Villa in Northern Mexico marks the last time that the U.S. Cavalry was deployed for military purposes.*

- División del Norte—*Soldier of fortune Captain Tracy Richardson, legendary journalist John Reed, a Californian bank robber called the "Dynamite Devil," and Sam "the Fighting Jew" Drebben, as well as a quartet of barnstorming pilots with their primitive aircraft, all served under Pancho Villa for a period of time as several of the many Americans who flocked to the revolutionary general's cause.*

Fast Facts

- Istanbul could vie for the mantle of "Most Besieged City." Persians, Macedonians, Lombards, Slavs, Avars, Bulgarians, Russians, Goths, Huns, Crusaders, and more all assailed it at some point in history.

- One of Baghdad's great Arab mathematicians, Al-Khwarizmi, pioneered algebra. The term comes from the book he wrote, Kitab al-Jabr.

- Lake-bound Tenochtitlan had floating gardens—bundles of twigs with mud on top called chinampas. A farmer could tow his garden around.

- Carthaginian family values: When King Agathocles of Syracuse besieged the city, the city leaders supposedly sacrificed 100 children to one of their grim gods.

- Although the most common image of Lawrence of Arabia is of a fighter crossing the desert on camel, he preferred riding to battle in his armored Rolls-Royce.

- Although Charles I was executed in 1649, his autopsy wasn't performed until 164 years later. The coffin was misplaced, and it wasn't until 1813 that the remains were rediscovered. Royal surgeon Sir Henry Halford performed the much-delayed autopsy. During the procedure, Halford removed a vertebra, using it at dinner parties as a salt holder until Queen Victoria ordered him to stop.

- In the 1820s, Anne Royall secured the first interview granted to a female reporter by a U.S. president by refusing to give John Quincy Adams his clothes after one of his regular nude swims in the Potomac.

- Benjamin Franklin thought the Boston Tea Party was "an act of violent injustice" and urged Massachusetts to repay the East India Company for the tea that had been destroyed.

ART ON TRIAL: THE CASE OF *MADAME BOVARY*

The publication of Gustave Flaubert's Madame Bovary *offended national sensibility and caused Flaubert to be charged with offending morality and religion.*

THE CASE

When *Madame Bovary* was first published serially in the *Revue de Paris* in 1851, the *Revue's* editor, Leon Laurent-Pichat; the work's author, Gustave Flaubert; and the publisher, Auguste-Alexis Pillet, were charged with "offenses to public morality and religion" by the conservative Restoration Government of Napoleon III. Many, including Flaubert, believed that his work was being singled out because of the regime's distaste for the notoriously liberal *Revue*. The prosecutor at the trial, Ernest Pinard based his case upon the premise that adultery must always be condemned as an affront to the sanctity of marriage and society at large. In this, Pinard had a point. The novel conspicuously lacks any voice reminding the reader that adultery is reprehensible and simply tells the tale of Emma Bovary's gradual but inevitable acceptance of her need for sexual satisfaction outside the confines of a provincial marriage. Other works of the period, notably the popular plays of Alexandre Dumas, commonly featured adulterous characters. But in these, there was a voice of reason reminding the audience that the character's actions were wrong and worthy of punishment. That *Madame Bovary* lacked such perspective was certainly unprecedented and—according to the government—worthy of censure.

THE DEFENSE

The defending attorney, Maitre Jules Sénard (a close friend of Flaubert's and one of the people to whom the work was dedicated) argued that literature must always be considered art for art's sake and that Flaubert, in particular, was a consummate artist whose intentions had nothing to do with affecting society at large.

Whether or not Flaubert intended to undermine any aspect of French society is debatable. As the son of a wealthy family, he could afford to sit in his ivory tower and decry what he perceived as the petty hypocrisies of the emerging middle class. Certainly, Gustave Flaubert was a perfectionist who spent weeks reworking single pages of prose. In *Madame Bovary*, he sought to create a novel that was stylistically beautiful above all else. To test his craft, Flaubert would shout passages out loud to test their rhythm. It took the author five years of solitary toil to complete the work. The literary elite, notably Sainte-Beuvue, Victor Hugo, and Charles-Pierre Baudelaire, immediately recognized the novel's genius, but the general public largely ignored the work when it was first published.

THE VERDICT

In the end, the judges agreed with Sénard and acquitted all of the accused but not before the sensational trial had sparked public interest in a work that might otherwise have gone unnoticed by the very society—the emerging middle class of France's provinces—the trial was meant to protect.

- Madame Bovary *was Flaubert's first published novel, and when it appeared in full, the author received a commensurate fee: 800 francs. The morality trial, however, boosted sales, and Flaubert estimated that he missed out on some 40,000 francs worth of income in the deal.*

- *Although it survived the trial, the influential* Revue de Paris *finally capitulated to political and financial pressure and stopped publication a year later.*

- Madame Bovary *was first published in book form in 1857.*

I, CLAUDIA, TROPHY WIFE

Upper-class women in ancient Rome weren't expected to do much during the course of an average day—just manage the house, oversee the slaves, educate their daughters, and allow themselves to be put on public display. The following is a fictionalized first-hand account of what a day in the life of an ancient Roman might have been like.

It is early morning in ancient Rome. Claudia, matron of her aristocratic household, finishes her breakfast: bread, cheese, dried fruit, and honey. Her husband, a Roman senator, has left for the day. She now assumes her daily role as the consummate 2nd century B.C. Roman wife.

Only 27, Claudia possesses the virtues esteemed Roman men most want in a wife—fertility, impeccable housewifery skills, and loyalty to her man and family. In 12 years of marriage, she has produced five children, and most importantly, three sons. She excels in household management, including supervising the slaves. And as a woman in a staunchly patriarchal society, she accepts her husband's legal and social control of her private life and obligingly dons her public persona as adoring trophy wife.

DEVELOPING FUTURE CLAUDIAS

During the day, Claudia manages the house and cares for the kids—being a working mom is forbidden for women of Republican Rome's elite. After checking on things and instructing the slaves, she summons her two young daughters. It's time to school the girls in the fine art of being Claudia.

Claudia's sons attend schools outside the home where they learn the classics and martial arts in preparation for political or military careers. The girls are trained at home in how to be the ideal housewife. Today, Claudia teaches them wool working—spinning, sewing, and weaving—skills necessary for every Roman woman.

Claudia takes her daughters' education very seriously. Their performance as wives will be one of the standards by which *her* success in life will be measured.

KEEPING UP APPEARANCES

After lessons and a light lunch—generally leftovers—Claudia readies herself for some personal time outside the home.

Even a casual stroll requires getting all dolled up. Claudia puts on an immaculate white *stolla,* the female version of the ubiquitous toga, which is usually cloaked by a *palla.* A slave styles her hair, elaborately raised, layered, and accented with cascading ringlets. She bedecks herself in ornate jewelry and accessories. She slips into her *calcei,* standard leather shoes that typically accompany the *stolla.*

Claudia leaves escorted by a slave who carries a parasol to shade her from the sun. Her first stop is the luxury goods market for a little shopping. Her slave then totes her purchases home as Claudia makes her way to visit a friend. From there, Claudia stops at the public baths to relax and gossip before heading home.

CLAUDIA ON DISPLAY

The baths reinvigorate Claudia for tonight's engagement—attendance with her husband at a grand banquet. As with any outing with her husband, Claudia will be on display as the perfect wife.

The banquet lasts for hours and becomes a gluttonous affair. A first course of eggs, salads, vegetables, and shellfish is followed by a main course featuring meat ranging from beef, lamb, and pork to wild goat, porpoise, and ostrich. Fruit, cake, and pudding are offered as dessert.

During dinner, Claudia's husband reclines on his left elbow while picking food off the table with his fingers. She remains upright. He downs goblets of wine. She abstains altogether. She is careful not to upstage him in any way.

Her acquiescence earns her the life reward she desires most— a place of reverence in ancient Roman society.

PORTRAIT OF A KILLER

*Though some argue that humans are the most dangerous
creatures on Earth, the distinction actually
belongs to a tiny insect.*

Diseases transmitted via mosquito bites have caused more death
and misery than the total number of casualties and deaths suffered in all of history's wars. The Roman Empire crumbled in the
3rd and 4th centuries when the Legions, decimated by malaria,
were unable to repel barbarian invaders. American planners took
control of the Panama Canal construction project when French
interests withdrew after losing more than 22,000 workers to mos-
quito-borne illnesses over an eight-year period.

More than 2,500 species of mosquito spread disease throughout
the world. The killers begin life as larvae, hatched in almost any
kind of water. Within one week, adults emerge to ply their deadly
trade.

As with other species, the female is the deadlier of the two sexes,
while the male concerns himself with nothing more than fertiliz-
ing eggs. Females need blood to nourish their eggs; the process of
collecting this food supply can wreak havoc on humans.

Mosquitoes can fly more than 20 miles from the water source in
which they were born. Sensory glands allow the insects to detect
carbon monoxide exhaled by their victims and lactic acid found in
perspiration. When a female mosquito dips her proboscis into an
unwilling victim, she transfers micro-organisms through her saliva
into her donor. These are responsible for some of the world's most
deadly and debilitating diseases, which include malaria; Yellow,
Dengue, and Rift Valley fevers; West Nile virus; and at least six
different forms of encephalitis.

According to the U.S. Department of Health and Human Sciences, more than 500 million cases of malaria are reported worldwide each year, resulting in an average of one million deaths.

HOLLYWOOD VERSUS HISTORY

You may not be surprised to learn that Hollywood doesn't always get history right.

Jack always appreciated a gal who could give a good back rub

PT 109 (1963)—This World War II adventure suggests that JFK's back problems began with a football injury and were aggravated when his PT boat was rammed by a Japanese destroyer—but Kennedy had a bad back for most of his life, and his father had to pull strings to even get him admitted into the service.

Would it be so hard to just stop at a gas station and pick up a new one?

Raiders of the Lost Ark (1981)—Indy studies a map that notes "Iran" when that country was still known as Persia. It also says "Thailand" when that nation was called Siam.

Are the drivers naked, too?

The Naked Prey (1966)—Although the film is set in 1915 Africa, modern cars are visible as they pass in the distance.

If not for this, the Best Picture award would have been in the bag

L.A. Confidential (1997)—The logo of *Hush-Hush* magazine is set in Helvetica Compressed, a typeface that wasn't created until the mid-1970s, some 20 years after the setting of this crime thriller.

I buy all my books on wormhole.com

Donnie Darko (2001)—A character in this story set in 1988 refers to Stephen Hawking's writings about wormholes—remarks that didn't appear until the 1998 tenth-anniversary reissue of Hawking's *A Brief History of Time.*

So long, suckers

Bonnie and Clyde (1967)—This biopic suggests depthless empathy, but neither Bonnie nor Clyde had a shred of sympathy for the Depression-era poor.

No wonder Jackie's always a step ahead of everybody else

Jackie Brown (1997)—Although the story is set in 1995, the calendar in Jackie's kitchen is for 1997.

No, it's just a botany poster for the science fair

You Can't Win 'em All (1970)—The modern, maple-leaf Canadian flag is seen in this movie set in 1922.

Blunderoso

Apocalypto (2006)—Mayan villages seen in this historical thriller set in the 16th century date from the 9th century, erroneously implying that Mayan civilization didn't change with the centuries.

How much did you pay for that sundial wristwatch?

Julius Caesar (1953)—Cassius casually makes mention of a striking clock, many centuries before there were such things.

Hippies *raus*!

Victory (1981)—In this soccer movie set inside a German-run POW camp during World War II, the playing field is overrun at the climax by people wearing flare pants.

Know whut I'm sayin'?

Bobby (2006)—Telephone operators in this biopic set in 1968 tell callers to "Have a nice day"—a phrase that wouldn't become annoyingly popular for nearly another 20 years.

For those long-distance ship-to-shore calls

Midway (1976)—During a long tracking shot of the Japanese carrier *Agaki* in the middle of the Pacific, the camera pans up to reveal power lines.

BATTING 1,000 IN THE IROQUOIS LEAGUE

Long before English settlers swarmed over the eastern coast of the "New World," Native Americans—the real original settlers— occupied the land around Lake Ontario now known as New York, as well as parts of New England, and parts of Canada. Sometime between the 14th and 16th centuries, the area became home to thousands of Indians in dozens of tribes.

THE HIGH FIVE

Five of these tribes experienced much intertribal fighting. According to legend, a wise sachem (chief) named Deganiwidah sought to make peace and foster goodwill among the nations through the efforts of another sachem named Hiawatha (no, not *the* Hiawatha). These five tribes—Seneca, Cayuga, Onondaga, Oneida, and Mohawk—sent 50 chiefs as a council and formed an alliance between 1500 and 1650 that came to be known as the "Five Nations of the Iroquois League." (A sixth nation, Tuscarora, joined in 1722.) Other names for this tribal organization were "the Woodland Democracy" and "the Iroquois Confederation."

Each tribe in the League had its own unique traits and qualities. The Seneca tribe—"People of the Great Hills"—was the largest, while the Cayuga, called "the Pipe People," was the smallest. The Onondaga were relatively peaceful and known as the "People of the Mountain." The Oneida—"People of the Standing Stone"— were pretty violent. The Mohawk, known as the "People of the Flint," were the fiercest of them all. Yet, the League had four moral principles to which they all agreed: a love of peace, respect for their laws, a sense of brotherhood, and a reverence for their ancestors.

A LONGHOUSE IS A HOME

Life in an Iroquois village was based on farming, even though the tribes did not have animals to help cultivate their fields. As such, many settlements were situated along rivers, where a spiral wooden fence surrounded the main buildings. These structures, known as "longhouses," could be anywhere from 30 to 350 feet long and were home for many, many families in individual living quarters under one roof (a somewhat primitive form of tenement housing). Several longhouses in an Iroquois village could house as few as 100 to as many as 3,000 people. A number of fires were kept burning in the middle of the longhouse, to provide heat in the winter months and allow cooking and baking year-round.

So strong was the concept of the longhouse in the Iroquois League, the tribes actually regarded their occupied land as one enormous longhouse. The Seneca considered themselves the "Keepers of the Western Door," and the Mohawk were the "Keepers of the Eastern Door" on the other end at the Atlantic Ocean. In between, the Onondaga were the "Keepers of the Fire," the Cayuga were the "Younger Brothers of Seneca," and the Oneida were the "Younger Brothers of Mohawk."

The social order of the League was matrilineal—women owned the longhouse, as well as garden plots and farming tools. They also set and maintained rules in the village and could appoint religious leaders. Women in the village were wholly responsible for daily life, as the men were seldom in camp. Their jobs—warfare, trading, trapping, and hunting—kept them away from the longhouse for months at a time.

MAKE WAR, NOT PEACE

Though the League claimed to have a "love of peace," they still engaged in many warlike activities. The Huron and Algonquin tribes were natural enemies of the League, and tribal warfare was an important component of Iroquois society. The Mohawk were known for swift "hit-and-run" techniques of attack, wielding heavy tomahawk axes to kill their enemies and pillage their goods. But the League avoided large-scale war, remaining satisfied with small skirmishes of 20 to 30 warriors. The League, as sophisticated as it may seem, lacked the social economics and organization to maintain standing armies and stage full-blown war with their enemies. Europeans joined the list of foes in the mid-1600s, as they landed in America and hunted beaver and other animals for pelts. As a result, the Iroquois were forced to move out into other territories for their prey, which increased their aggressive attacks.

Still, the Iroquois were masters of psychological warfare. They understood and exploited intimidation through kidnapping and torture, which instilled fear in others. Many captives were tortured, then assigned by the longhouse women as slaves to their families. Hideous instances of cannibalism were also common among the Iroquois. Jesuit priests like Jean de Brebeuf suffered such atrocities while attempting to minister their faith among the League nations.

THE DOCTOR IS IN

The Iroquois League held many religious beliefs, including the power of medicine men. One group, known as the "False Face Society," donned fearsome carved wooden masks. They danced, shook turtle shells, and sprinkled ashes to bring about a cure for illness. A similar curing group, called the "Huskface Society," wore cornhusks as masks.

WORKING WITH THE WHITE MAN

These seemingly savage people had much to offer in the way of operating a complex government body. The council of 50 sachems required that all decisions of the village had to be unanimous. If a sachem caused problems in the council, he was given three warnings. After that, he was ousted. Some historians believe that portions of the U.S. Constitution were based on the council of the Iroquois Confederacy. A curious visitor to many of the council meetings in the 1700s was a man named Benjamin Franklin. The Presidential Seal of America features an eagle holding 13 arrows—one for each original colony. Similarly, the Iroquois seal showed an eagle with five arrows in its talon—one for each nation. The Iroquois nations established peace and harmony with the United States, signing a treaty in 1794. Terms of the agreement endure to this day as, according to the 200-plus-year-old document, some nation members receive calico cloth as annual payment, while other tribes receive the handsome amount of $1,800 a year.

CROSSDRESSERS THROUGHOUT HISTORY

Clothes, the saying goes, make the man. For some men, clothes also make the woman. And vice versa.

A transvestite wears garments of the opposite sex and sometimes assumes alternate cross-gender identity as part of daily life. Women dress as men; men dress as women. For the record, transvestism, though less common than, say, Republicanism, is not a mental illness or a perversion. And transvestites are not usually transsexuals (men and women who undergo hormonal and/or surgical sex change); in fact, the typical transvestite is heterosexual and comfortable with his/her gender.

Transvestite activity traces back to the earliest days of recorded civilization and recurs throughout the span of human history, across all societies and walks of life. Although ordinarily a private inclination, transvestism has occasionally been very public.

SHE'S IN CHARGE HERE

More than 3,400 years ago, a woman named Hatshepsut ruled Egypt as a king. Her story is the first recorded instance of transvestism in history. Hatshepsut, part of the 18th royal dynasty of ancient Egypt, became pharaoh when her husband, Thutmose II, died and the heir to throne was only nine years old. So Hatshepsut initially ruled as regent, in her capacity as both aunt and stepmother to the true royal heir. But sometime between the second and seventh years of her reign (1477–72 B.C.), Hatshepsut assumed the trappings of manhood and kinghood. She was often depicted wearing a false beard and without apparent breasts. She commanded that she be addressed as "he" and changed her name to the masculine Hatshepsu.

Like Hatshepsut, many female-to-male crossdressers throughout history have donned male garb for the social, political, and even military opportunities they would never have had access to in the traditional roles of their gender. For instance, James Barry (1795–1865), a surgeon in the British Army, was a woman working as man and was unsuspected for years. It was only at Barry's death that attending physicians were astounded to discover that their comrade was a woman—or, according to some reports, a hermaphrodite (a person born with the complete or partial genitals of both sexes).

Less open to dispute are the lives of stagecoach driver Charlie Parkhurst (d. 1879) and New York political figure Murray Hall (1831–1901)—both of whom lived entire adult lives as men, only to be discovered at their deaths to have been women. And the female jazz musician Billy Tipton (1914–1989) pursued a life and career during which everyone, including her wife, thought her to be a man.

ROYAL SURPRISES

One of history's most popular examples of a woman in men's plumage came in 1429, when the 17-year-old peasant Joan d'Arc bravely presented herself to the court of French heir apparent Prince Charles as God's appointed ruler of the force that would overthrow occupying English forces. Her male attire, too, she said, was God's will. When Charles handed Joan command of the peasant army with which she would make history, the prince overlooked the capital crime that the Grand Inquisition, two years later, would not: "Condemn[ing herself] in being unwilling to wear the customary clothing of [the female] sex."

The French court also offers up a royal story of transvestism oriented in the other direction: King Henri III, who ruled from 1574–1589, was infamous for wearing gowns, makeup, earrings, and perfume. He sometimes commanded that he be referred to as "Her Majesty," and he kept a court of "mignons"—young male favorites whom the king dressed as ladies of the night.

The history of male-to-female crossdressing cuts through all social castes and sexual persuasions. The story of Henri III, married and evidently bisexual, splits the difference between heterosexual transvestites (such as the contemporary British comedian Eddie Izzard and the famed American B-movie director of the 1950s Edward D. Wood, Jr.) and the campier standards of generally gay drag queens, such as pop star RuPaul.

FUN IN THE NEW WORLD

Doomed to be outcasts according to American and European traditions, transvestites have held prominent roles in some non-Western cultures. Aboriginal nations across what is now North, Central, and South America treated crossdressing and cross-gender roleplaying as acceptable parts of society.

"Strange country this," wrote one Caucasian, circa 1850, about the Crow nation of the Yellowstone River Valley in North America, "where males assume the dress and perform the duties of females, while women turn men and mate with their own sex!"

Aboriginal women in what is today Brazil were often welcomed as male warriors and hunters—which in 1576 inspired the Portuguese explorer Pedro de Magalhaes to name the country's great river after the famous matriarchal society from Greek mythology, the Amazons.

A source of disquiet in some societies, and an invitation to prestige and respect in others, transvestism will be a part of human sexuality for as long as there are gender boundaries to be crossed and explored.

- *Other famous crossdressers include: the legendary Pope Joan, the female pope who outed herself during childbirth; Anne Bonny and Mary Read, 17th-century pirates; and George Sand, a 19th-century female novelist who wore men's clothing almost exclusively.*

THE BLOODY COUNTESS

In the early 1600s, villagers in the Carpathian region of Hungary whispered amongst themselves about a vampire living in the local castle. An investigation brought to light the brutal atrocities of Countess Elizabeth Bathory, who was accused of torturing hundreds of young girls to death and bathing in their blood.

THE BEST SORT OF PEOPLE

Elizabeth Bathory (born Erzsébet Báthory in 1560) was the daughter of one of the oldest and most influential bloodlines in Hungary. Her wedding in 1575 to Ferenc Nadasdy was enough of an event to warrant written approval and an expensive gift from the Holy Roman Emperor himself.

Of course, there were rumors that a streak of insanity ran in Elizabeth's family; some rumors hint that she may have been related to Vlad the Impaler. However, nobles of the time were given wide latitude when it came to eccentric behavior.

Ferenc would go on to become one of the greatest Hungarian military heroes of the age. He was a battle-hardened man, but even so, his own wife made him nervous. He was aware that she treated the servants even more harshly than he did—and he had no reservations when it came to punishing the help. He was known to place flaming oil-covered wicks between the toes of lazy servants. But Elizabeth's punishments far exceeded even this brutality. Ferenc saw evidence of this when he discovered a honey-covered servant, who had been tied to a tree and ravaged by ants as punishment for stealing food. Still, Ferenc spent a great deal of time away at war, and someone had to manage his castle.

Elizabeth took on the task willingly; in turn, he turned a deaf ear to complaints about her activities.

FROM PUNISHMENT TO ATROCITY

Initially, Elizabeth's punishments may have been no more harsh than those imposed by her contemporaries. However, with her husband's lengthy absences and eventual death, Elizabeth found that she had virtually no restrictions on her behavior. A series of lovers of both sexes occupied some of her time. She also dabbled in black magic, though this was not uncommon in an age when paganism and Christianity were contending for supremacy. She spent hours doing nothing more than gazing into a wraparound mirror of her own design, crafted to hold her upright so that she would not tire as she examined her own reflection. Always a vain woman, the exacting fashion of the day required Elizabeth to constantly worry over the angle of her collar or the style of her hair. She had a small army of body servants constantly by her side to help maintain her appearance. They were often required to attend to their mistress in the nude as an expression of subservience. If they failed in their duties, Elizabeth would strike out, pummeling them into the ground. On one notable occasion, a servant pulled too hard when combing Elizabeth's hair; Elizabeth struck the offender in the face hard enough to cause the girl's blood to spray and cover the countess. Initially furious, Elizabeth discovered she liked the sensation, believing her skin was softer, smoother, and more translucent after the experience.

A TASTE FOR BLOOD

The incident led to the legends, which cannot be confirmed, that Elizabeth Bathory took to bathing in the blood of virgins to maintain her youthful appearance. One rumor has her inviting 60 peasant girls for a banquet, only to lock them in a room and slaughter them one at a time, letting their blood run over her body. Though that incident may be apocryphal, it is certain that the countess began torturing girls without restraint. Aided by two trustworthy servants who recruited a never-ending supply of hopeful girls from the poor families of the area, she would beat her victims with a club until they were scarcely recognizable. When her arms grew tired, she had her two assistants continue the punishment as she watched. She had a spiked iron cage specially built and would place a girl within it, shaking the cage as the individual bounced from side to side and was impaled over and over on the spikes. She drove pins into lips and breasts, held flames to pubic regions, and once pulled a victim's mouth open so forcefully that the girl's cheeks split. Perhaps most chillingly, allegations of vampirism and cannibalism arose when Elizabeth began biting her victims, tearing off the flesh with her bare teeth. On one occasion, too sick to rise from her bed, the countess demanded that a peasant girl be brought to her. She roused herself long enough to bite chunks from the girl's face, shoulders, and nipples. Elizabeth's chambers had to be covered with fresh cinders daily to prevent the countess from slipping on the bloody floor.

JUSTICE FOR THE COUNTESS

Eventually, even the cloak of nobility couldn't hide Elizabeth's atrocities. The situation was compounded by the fact that she got sloppy, killing in such numbers that the local clergy refused to perform any more burials. Thereafter, she would throw bodies to the wolves in full view of local villagers, who naturally complained to the authorities. The final straw was when Elizabeth began to prey on the minor aristocracy as well as the peasants; the disappearance of people of higher birth could not be tolerated. The king decided that something had to be done, and in January 1611, a trial was held. Elizabeth was not allowed to testify, but her assistants were compelled to—condemning themselves to death in the process—and they provided eyewitness accounts of the terrible practices of the countess. Especially damning was the discovery of a list, in Elizabeth's own handwriting, describing more than 600 people she had tortured to death.

Elizabeth Bathory was convicted of perpetrating "horrifying cruelties" and was sentenced to be walled up alive in her own castle. She survived for nearly four years but was finally discovered dead on August 21, 1614, by one of her guards who had risked a peek through a tiny food slot. The countess was unrepentant to the end.

PETRA:
THE FABULOUS RED CITY
OF THE NABATAEANS

*In the wilds of southern Jordan lies one of antiquity's most
beautifully preserved sights: what survives of Petra,
the ancient Nabataean capital.*

Where exactly is Petra?

Petra lies within the Hashemite Kingdom of Jordan, perhaps
80 miles south of Amman in the Naqab Desert, about 15 miles
east of the Israeli border. It is a World Heritage Site and a Jorda-
nian national treasure, cared for accordingly.

Why settle out in the desert?

Petra was a key link in the trade chain connecting Egypt, Babylon,
Arabia, and the Mediterranean. It had water (if you knew how to
look) and was quite defensible.

When was it founded?

In 600 B.C., the narrow red sandstone canyon of Petra housed a
settlement of Edomites: seminomadic Semites said to descend
from Biblical Esau. Egypt was still rich but declining. Rome was a
young farming community dominated by its Etruscan kings. The
rise of classical Athens was decades away. Brutal Assyria had fallen
to Babylonian conquerors. With the rise of the incense trade,
Arab traders began pitching tents at what would become Petra.
We know them as the *Nabataeans*.

Did they speak Arabic?

The answer is as fluid as a Petra incense broker's sales pitch.
Nabataean history spanned a millennium. They showed up speaking early Arabic in a region where Aramaic was the business-
speak. The newcomers thus first wrote their Arabic in a variant

of the Aramaic script. But Petra's trade focus meant a need to adopt Aramaic as well, so Nabataeans did—many words crossed the Arabic/Aramaic linguistic fence at Petra. By the end (about 250 years before the rise of Islam), Nabataean "Arabaic" had evolved into classical (Koranic) Arabic.

What were these Nabataeans like?

The Swiss or Swedes of the Biblical world. They weren't expansionists, but defended their homeland with shrewd diplomacy and obstinate vigor. Despite great wealth, they had few slaves. Despite monarchical government, Petra's Nabataeans showed a pronounced democratic streak. Empires rose and fell around them; business was business.

The trade must have been lucrative indeed.

Vastly. The core commodity was incense from Arabia, but many raw materials and luxuries of antiquity also passed through Petra—notably bitumen (natural asphalt), useful in waterproofing and possibly in embalming.

Speaking of religion, were they religious?

Religious, yes; fanatical, no. Most Nabataeans were pagan, worshipping benevolent fertility and sun deities. Jews were welcome at Petra, as were Christians in its later days.

What of Nabataean women's roles?

Nabataean women held a respected position in society, including property and inheritance rights. While no major ancient Near Eastern culture was truly egalitarian, the women of Petra participated in its luxuriant prosperity.

Take me to Petra in its heyday. What do I experience?

It is 70 B.C., and you walk the streets of Petra, home to about 20,000 people. Ornate homes and public buildings rivaling Athenian and Roman artistry are carved into the high red sandstone walls of the canyon. A camel caravan arrives from Arabia loaded with goods; white-robed traders dismount with elegant gifts for their buying contacts. The wealthy aroma of frankincense constantly reminds your nostrils why Petra exists. Most people wear robes and cloaks, often colored by exotic dyes. Petra is luxurious without being licentious.

You overhear conversations in Aramaic and Arabic: A new cistern is under construction in the nearby hills. Workers are shoring up a building damaged by a recent earth tremor. Old-timers grouse that reigning King Aretas III wishes he were Greek. A modestly robed vendor walks past with dates for sale; you fish out a thick silver coin to offer her. Along with your bronze change and the delicious dates, she wishes you the favor of al-Uzza, the Nabataean goddess identified with Aphrodite and Venus.

You ask a passing water-bearer: Who's that guy in the outlandish robe draped over one shoulder, followed by servants? *A man of faraway Rome*, says she. You've heard of this Rome, a dynamic market for Petra's goods, with domains beginning to rival Alexander the Great's once-mighty empire. Only time will tell how Petra will reckon with this next tide of power.

No one lives at Petra now. When and why did it decline?

Petra's last king, Rabbel II, willed his realm to Rome. When he died in A.D. 106, Nabataea became the Roman province of Arabia Petraea. Again the Nabataeans adjusted—and kept up the trade. In the 2nd and 3rd centuries A.D., the caravans began using Palmyra (in modern Syria) as an alternate route, starting a long, slow decline at Petra. An earthquake in 363 delivered the knockout punch: damage to the intricate water system sustaining the city. By about 400, Petra was an Arabian ghost town.

How might I see this for myself?

Thousands do it daily. If you can travel to Jordan, you can travel to Petra—either with an organized tour booked through a travel agent or on your own if that's your style. Nearby hotels and restaurants offer modern accommodations. The site charges a daily entrance fee.

GREAT OBSCURE QUOTES

"The girl doesn't, it seems to me, have a special perception or feeling which would lift that book above the curiosity level."
—Rejection letter for *The Diary of Anne Frank*

"That was a long time ago. I am now old and my mind has changed. I would rather see my people living in houses and singing and dancing."
—Two Moon (Cheyenne chieftain who fought at the Battle of Little Big Horn), Explaining, in an interview with *McClure's Magazine*, why he no longer believes in war, September 1898

"It is better to be violent, if there is violence in our hearts, than to put on the cloak of nonviolence to cover impotence."
—Gandhi

"In certain trying circumstances, urgent circumstances, desperate circumstances, profanity furnishes a relief denied even to prayer."
—Mark Twain

"Engines of war have long since reached their limits, and I see no further hope of any improvement in the art."
—Frontinus, A.D. 90

Fast Facts

- Did you know that tug-of-war was once an Olympic event? The contest first appeared at the Games in 1900. But the event must not have had much "pull" with crowds—the 1920 Olympics were its last.

- Germany and the United States were ready to start shooting in 1889 over Samoa. A hurricane damaged both fleets, making battle impossible. Happily, cooler heads prevailed soon after.

- As late as the 1800s, the English had a unique means of divorce: auctioning off the wife. The husband took her to the public marketplace in a halter, then began his sales pitch. It might sound awful, except when you consider the wife's good fortune to be rid of such a creep.

- The award for longest-serving U.S. president goes to Franklin D. Roosevelt. He served for 12 years.

- Peter the Great's reign over Russia might have been a little less "hairy" than that of his predecessors—any Russian nobleman who chose to wear a beard had to pay a special beard tax.

- Sir Isaac Newton wrote in his journal about how he once inserted a needle into his eye socket to learn more about the eye's anatomy. On another occasion, he reportedly stared at the sun for as long as he could stand to find out how light and color were perceived. In both cases, the scientist sustained no permanent injury.

- At its height, the city of Rome held close to 900 public baths.

- The Republic of Rome was ruled by a pair of elected consuls who served for only a year and began their term by watching the sky at dusk on their first day in power. If they witnessed a flash of lightning to their left, it was taken as a good omen for their tenure.

THE REAL MANCHURIAN CANDIDATES

From the mid-1950s through at least the early 1970s, thousands of unwitting Americans and Canadians became part of a bizarre CIA research project codenamed MKULTRA. Participants were secretly "brainwashed"—drugged with LSD and other hallucinogens, subjected to electro-convulsive shock therapy, and manipulated with abusive mind-control techniques.

MKULTRA began in 1953 under the orders of CIA director Allen Dulles. The program, which was in direct violation of the human rights provisions of the Nuremberg Code that the United States helped establish after WWII, was developed in response to reports that U.S. prisoners of war in Korea were being subjected to Communist mind-control techniques.

CIA researchers hoped to find a "truth drug" that could be used on Soviet agents, as well as drugs that could be used against foreign leaders (one documented scheme involved an attempt in 1960 to dose Fidel Castro with LSD). They also aimed to develop means of mind control that would benefit U.S. intelligence, perhaps including the creation of so-called "Manchurian Candidates" to carry out assassinations. As part of MKULTRA, the CIA investigated parapsychology and such phenomena as hypnosis, telepathy, precognition, photokinesis, and "remote viewing."

MKULTRA was headed by Dr. Sidney Gottlieb, a military psychiatrist and chemist known as the "Black Sorcerer," who specialized in concocting deadly poisons. More than 30 universities and scientific institutes took part in MKULTRA. LSD and other mind-altering drugs including heroin, mescaline, psilocybin, scopolamine, marijuana, and sodium pentothal were given to CIA employees, military personnel, and other government workers, often without the subjects' knowledge or prior consent. To broaden their subject pool, researchers targeted unsuspecting civilians, often those in vulnerable or socially compromising situations. Prison inmates, prostitutes, and mentally ill hospital patients were often used. In a project codenamed Operation Midnight Climax, the CIA set up brothels in several U.S. cities to lure men as unwitting test subjects. Rooms were equipped with cameras that filmed the experiments behind one-way mirrors. Some civilian subjects who consented to participation were used for more extreme experimentation. One group of volunteers in Kentucky was given LSD for more than 70 straight days.

In the 1960s, Dr. Gottlieb also traveled to Vietnam and conducted mind-control experiments on Viet Cong prisoners of war being held by U.S. forces. During the same time period, an unknown number of Soviet agents died in U.S. custody in Europe after being given dual intravenous injections of barbiturates and amphetamine in the CIA's search for a truth serum.

MKULTRA experiments were also carried out in Montreal, Canada, between 1957 and 1964 by Dr. Donald Ewen Cameron, a researcher in Albany, New York, who also served as president of the World Psychiatric Association and the American and Canadian psychiatric associations. The CIA appears to have given him potentially deadly experiments to carry out at Canadian mental health institutes so U.S. citizens would not be involved. Cameron also experimented with paralytic drugs—in some cases inducing a coma in subjects for up to three months—as well as using electroconvulsive therapy at 30 times the normal voltage. The subjects were often women being treated for anxiety disorders and postpartum depression. Many suffered permanent damage. A lawsuit by victims of the experiments later uncovered that the Canadian government had also funded the project.

At least one American subject died in the experiments. Frank Olson, a U.S. army biological weapons researcher, was secretly given LSD in 1953. A week later, he fell from a hotel window in New York City following a severe psychotic episode. A CIA doctor assigned to monitor Olson claimed he jumped from the window, but an autopsy performed on Olson's exhumed remains in 1994 found that he had been knocked unconscious before the fall.

The U.S. army also conducted experiments with psycho-active drugs. A later investigation determined that nearly all army experiments involved soldiers and civilians who had given their informed consent, and that army researchers had largely followed scientific and safety protocols. Ken Kesey, who would later write *One Flew over the Cuckoo's Nest* and become one of the originators of the hippie movement, volunteered for LSD studies at an army research center in San Francisco in 1960. LSD stolen from the army lab by test subjects was some of the first in the world used "recreationally" by civilians. The army's high ethical standards, however, seem to have been absent in at least one case. Harold Blauer, a professional tennis player in New York City who was hospitalized for depression following his divorce, died from apparent cardiac arrest during an army experiment in 1952. Blauer had been secretly injected with massive doses of mescaline.

CIA researchers eventually concluded that the effects of LSD were too unpredictable to be useful, and the agency later acknowledged that their experiments made little scientific sense. Records on 150 MKULTRA research projects were destroyed in 1973 by order of CIA Director Richard Helms. A year later, the *New York Times* first reported about CIA experiments on U.S. citizens. In 1975, congressional hearings and a report by the Rockefeller Commission revealed details of the program. In 1976, President Gerald Ford issued an executive order prohibiting experimentation with drugs on human subjects without their informed consent. Ford and CIA Director William Colby also publicly apologized to Frank Olson's family, who received $750,000 by a special act of Congress.

Though no evidence exists that the CIA succeeded in its quest to find mind-control techniques, some conspiracy theories claim that the MKULTRA project was linked to the assassination of Robert F. Kennedy. Some have argued that Kennedy's assassin, Sirhan B. Sirhan, had been subjected to mind control. Sirhan claims that he has no recollection of shooting Kennedy, despite attempts by both government prosecutors and his defense lawyers to use hypnosis to recover his memories.

Timeline

Continued from page 311.

1519
Rude House Guests. Spanish conquistador Hernando Cortes visits the Aztec capital of Tenoch-titlán and repays the courteous welcome of King Moctezuma by taking the king hostage and extorting gold and silver from his subjects—a true "king's ransom." That same year, Portuguese navigator Ferdinand Magellan sets sail with five ships and 270 men to circumnavigate the globe. When his sole surviving ship returns to Spain three years later, Magellan is not among the sailors left to tell the tale.

1520
Suleiman the Magnificent presides over the zenith of the Ottoman Empire, ruling territory from the Persian Gulf to the Polish frontier.

1526
The Apple Doesn't Fall Far from the Tree. Babar, a descendant of Ghengis Khan and Tamerlane, marches southwest into India and declares himself emperor of Hindu-stan after defeating the Sultans of Delhi and Bengal.

1533
Spanish conquistador Francisco Pizarro captures the Inca king, murders him after receiving a ransom, and loots the Inca capital at Cuzco. One Old World gift to the Inca peoples, smallpox, kills some-where between 70 to 94 percent of the native population.

1534
Messy Divorce. England's King Henry VIII splits with the Roman church over political and personal issues. The Act of Supremacy makes Henry the head of the Church of England, and his king-dom becomes the rallying point in the Protestant struggle against Catholicism.

1552
Russia's Ivan IV defeats the Tatars in southeastern Russia and expands the Muscovite Empire deep into Crimean, Caspian, and Siberian lands.

1571
The Battle of Lepanto, the last naval battle between galleys, halts the tide of Ottoman conquest in central and southern Europe.

1582
Mark Your Calendars. Pope Gregory junks the Julian Calendar for the more accurate "Gregorian" version, and Gregory declares October 4, 1582, to be October 15, 1582. Orthodox coun-tries will continue to use Julius Caesar's old system, resulting in major confusion on occasion.

1588
Bad weather and crafty English seamanship combine to defeat the Spanish Armada. Britannia begins her ascension to the title of World's Greatest Maritime Power.

c. 1590
No Cliff Notes Here. Shakespeare pens *Henry VI*, his first play. *Henry VI* will be followed by 37 other major plays, topping off the Bard's writing credits, which include 154 sonnets and two long poems.

Timeline

1592
Japan's Hideyoshi Toyotomi invades Korea. Impressive Japanese gains are offset when China comes to Korea's aid.

1595
Dutch lens maker Zacharias Janssen develops the compound microscope, paving the way for advances in medicine and microbiology.

1600
Victory at the Battle of Sekigahara concentrates Japanese military and political power in the hands of *shogun* Tokugawa Ieyasu and his successors. The Tokugawa Shogunate will last until 1868, and during much of that time the *shogun* rules Japan as emperor in all but name.

1605
Tilting at Windmills. Miguel de Cervantes, a veteran of the Battle of Lepanto, publishes the first part of his novel *Don Quixote,* one of Western literature's great tales of misguided chivalry.

1606
Dutch explorer Willem Janzsoon discovers New Holland, a continent that will later be known as Australia.

1607
English colonists land at Jamestown, Virginia. Another band of colonists, at Plymouth, Massachusetts, will set up shop 13 years later.

1608
The East India Company sets up shop in India under a royal charter, leading the way to British domination of India that lasts until 1947.

1613
Tsar Mikhail Romanov founds Russia's longest-running dynasty, one that will last until revolution topples the monarchy in 1917.

1618
Catholics and Protestants go at each other's throats during the Thirty Years War. By the time the Peace of Westphalia settles matters in 1648, about a third of present-day Germany and Czechoslovakia is killed off in bitter fighting.

1641
"I Think, Therefore I Am." René Descartes publishes his *Meditations on First Philosophy,* setting forth some of the questions over which future philosophers will wrestle.

1642–1649
The first and second English Civil Wars pit King Charles I against Parliament. Charles loses more than just his throne in 1649 when an executioner's axe gives him a close shave.

1672
A Bit over the Top. France's King Louis XIV moves his court into his fantastic new palace at Versailles, outside Paris. While the palace was a stunning achievement, its cost to the nation and the in-your-face opulence set the stage for revolution just over a century later.

Wondering what happened next? Turn to page 434 to find out!

FRANZ MESMER
TRANSFIXES EUROPE

*The Age of Enlightenment saw the explosion of new ideas. One of
these was the possibility of tapping into a person's subconscious,
causing them to enter a dreamlike state where they might find
relief from various ailments, whether through actual effect or
merely by the power of a hypnotist's suggestion.
One early practitioner of this technique became so famous that
his very name became synonymous with the ability to send his
patients into a trance—the art of mesmerism.*

Franz Anton Mesmer was a late bloomer.
Born in Germany in 1734, Mesmer had
difficulty finding a direction in life. He first
studied for the priesthood, then drifted into
astronomy and law before finally graduating
at age 32 from the University of Vienna with
a degree in medicine. He set up practice
in Vienna and married a well-to-do widow,
becoming a doctor to the rich and famous
and using his connections to cater to an
upper-crust clientele. He lived comfortably
on a Viennese estate and counted among his friends Wolfgang
Amadeus Mozart, who wrote a piece for Mesmer to play on the
glass harmonica, an instrument lately arrived from America.

At first, Mesmer's medical prescriptions were unremarkable;
bleeding and purgatives were the order of the day, and Mesmer
followed accepted medical convention. But Mesmer's attention was also drawn to the practice of using magnets to induce
responses in patients, a technique much in vogue at the time.
Mesmer experimented with magnets to some effect and came
to believe that he was successfully manipulating tides, or energy
flows, within the human body. He theorized that illness was
caused by the disruption of these flows, and health could be

restored by a practitioner who could put them back in order. He also decided that the magnets themselves were an unnecessary prop and that he was performing the manipulation of the tides himself, because of what he termed his animal magnetism—the word "animal" merely stemming from the Latin term for "breath" or "soul." He would stir the tides by sitting in a chair opposite a patient, knees touching, gazing unblinkingly into their eyes, making passes with his hands, and massaging the areas of complaint, often continuing the treatment for hours until the patient felt the magnetic flows moving inside their body.

EUROPE BECOMES MESMERIZED

Mesmer gained notoriety as a healer, his fame growing to the point where he was invited to give his opinion in other famous cases of the day. He investigated claims of unusual cures and traveled around Switzerland and Germany, holding demonstrations at which he was able to induce symptoms and their subsequent cures by merely pointing at people, much to the amazement of his audience. He also took on more challenging cases as a doctor, but a scandal involving his treatment of a blind piano player—he temporarily restored her sight, only to have her lose her audiences because the novelty of watching her play was now gone—caused Mesmer to decide that 1777 was an opportune year to move to Paris.

France would prove to be a fertile ground for Mesmer. He resumed seeing patients, while at the same time seeking approval from the scientific community of Paris for his techniques. The respect and acknowledgment he felt he deserved from his peers was never to come, but his popular reputation soared; Marie Antoinette herself wrote Mesmer and begged him to reconsider when he once announced that he intended to give up his practice. His services were in such demand that he could no longer treat patients individually; he resorted to treating groups of patients with a device he called a *baquet,* a wooden tub bristling with iron rods around which patients would hold hands and collectively seek to manipulate their magnetic tides. Mesmer himself would stride back and forth through the incense-laden room, reaching out and tapping patients with a staff or finger. For a complete cure, Mesmer believed the patients needed to undergo a convulsive crisis—literally an experience wherein they would enter a trancelike state, shake and moan uncontrollably, and be carried to a special padded chamber until they had come back to their senses. The treatment proved particularly popular with women, who outnumbered men 8–1 as patients of Mesmer. This statistic did not go unnoticed by the monitors of public decency, who drew the obvious conclusion that something immoral was taking place, though they were unable to produce much more than innuendo in support of their accusations.

WHEN I SNAP MY FINGERS...

Unfortunately, Mesmer's incredible popularity also made him an easy target for detractors. Mesmerism became such a fad that the wealthy even set up baquets in their own homes. But, as with many trends, once over they are held up for popular ridicule. As a result, Mesmer saw his client base decline and even found himself mocked in popular theater.

Copycats emerged to the extent that in 1784, the king set up a commission—including representatives from both the Faculty of Medicine and the Royal Academy of Science—to investigate all claims of healing involving animal magnetism. Benjamin Franklin, in Paris as an ambassador at the time, was one of the investigators. In the end, the commission determined that any treatment benefits derived from Mesmerism were imagined. This rejection by the scientific community combined with the erosion of his medical practice drove Mesmer from Paris in 1785. He kept an understandably low profile after that, spending some time in Switzerland, where he wrote and kept in touch with a few patients. He died in 1815.

Mesmer's legacy remains unresolved. Some still view him as a charlatan of the first order. Others see in his techniques the foundation of modern hypnotherapy, which has become a well-recognized practice in modern psychiatry. Regardless, it is indisputable that Franz Anton Mesmer's personal animal magnetism continues to capture our imagination even today.

FIRST AMERICAN NOVEL

*Steeped in controversy, the plot of the first American novel—
with its themes of seduction, incest, and suicide—
would be more readily accepted in today's culture than it was
in late 18th-century America.*

William Hill Brown wrote *The Power of Sympathy*, the first
American novel, in 1789. Printer Isaiah Thomas was contracted
to publish a limited run of the book and to sell it through his two
bookshops. In an ironic twist—given the historical significance the
book later assumed—*The Power of Sympathy* was presented as
the work of an anonymous author.

Even if the book had been properly credited at the outset, few
readers outside of upper-crust Boston would have been familiar
with the author. When *The Power of Sympathy* appeared, William
Hill Brown was a reasonably prolific but little-known playwright;
he later wrote a comic opera, poetry, essays, and two more novels.

The son of a respected clockmaker, Brown was born in Boston
in November 1765. He attended the Boston Boy's School, where
he pursued creative writing, a craft encouraged by his step-aunt.
Brown spent his formative years in an upper-class Boston neighborhood, living across the street from a married, politically active
lawyer named Perez Morton.

A STORY BORN IN SCANDAL

In 1788, rumors of a romantic scandal involving Morton and his
sister-in-law, Frances Apthorp, circulated among Boston's elite.
The rumor turned out to be true, and rather than face public
ridicule, the mortified Frances committed suicide. Perez, on the
other hand, continued with his life as though nothing had happened. The public apparently went along with this tactic; Morton
was later elected speaker of the lower house in the General
Court of Massachusetts in 1806 and was named attorney general
in 1810.

Writer (and former neighbor) William Brown was naturally well aware of the Morton-Apthorp scandal and published his book just a year later.

Following a novelistic style popular during the period, *The Power of Sympathy* unfolds via letters exchanged by central and secondary characters. The stinger is that the protagonists, Thomas Harrington and Harriot Fawcett, are about to unknowingly embark on an incestuous relationship.

In the novel, Harriot is Thomas's half-sister, born out of wedlock to a mistress of Thomas's father. For obvious reasons of propriety, the pregnancy and birth had been kept secret from the community and the rest of the family. When Harriot discovers the truth, she commits suicide. The facts soon become clear to Thomas as well, and he elects to follow his half-sister in suicide.

CREDIT WHERE CREDIT IS DUE

Pressure from the Morton and Apthorp families, as well as from other prominent citizens, forced Brown to remove his book from circulation. Many copies were subsequently destroyed, and few exist today. In an odd twist, when the novel was reissued in the 19th century—nearly 100 years later—it was attributed to a deceased, once-popular Boston poet named Sarah Apthorp Morton, who happened to be the wife of Perez Morton—the man whose indiscretion helped inspire the novel in the first place! A correction issued by William Brown's aged niece not long after the book's republication led to proper attribution at last. Brown would finally be recognized as the author of the first novel written and published in America.

FAMOUS LAST WORDS

"Love is more pleasant than marriage for the same reason that novels are more amusing than history."
—Chamfort, French playwright, 1741-1794

BROTHERS KILLING BROTHERS

*The ancient Greeks had two philosophies of war. A "blood war"
was a nasty thing, with no good reason at its source.
A "just war," however, was considered to be necessary and fair.
The War Between the States might be considered the ultimate
"just war," as it lead the United States through its growing pains
and into adulthood. The conflict, which raged between 1861 and
1865, brought carnage and death to levels seldom
seen in the annals of world history.*

More than 623,000 Americans lost their lives in the Civil War. Yet
only a third of that number actually died in battle. The rest succumbed to poor and ineffective medical care and massive outbreaks of contagious diseases, such as dysentery. Another 400,000
were wounded but survived.

New and more efficient weapons increased the death toll. Mus-
kets with grooved bores, using a technique called "rifling" to
give the bullet more spin, were much more accurate than the
previously smooth-bored guns. Artillery shells delivered deadly
payloads of 75 to 80 musket balls, and impact shells detonated
with ten pounds of black powder upon landing. Canister shells
exploded like giant shotgun shells, shooting 25 to 50 small iron
balls in all directions. These munitions supported a revolutionary
concept in war strategy: The main focus of weapons moved from
destroying property to killing people.

THE DEADLIEST OF AMERICAN WARS

The number of soldiers, both Union and Confederate, killed in
the Civil War is higher than those of the American Revolutionary
War, World War I, World War II, the Korean War, and the Vietnam War combined. The Battle of Antietam on September 17,
1862, was the single-bloodiest day in American history, as more
than 23,000 soldiers were left dead or wounded in the aftermath.

Fast Facts

- *Rock, Paper, Scissors, Dyamite is a variation on the classic game Rock, Paper, Scissors. In it, dynamite beats rock and paper, but scissors beat dynamite (by cutting the wick).*

- *According to the Book of Acts, the city of Antioch, now Antakya in southern Turkey, was the first place where converts to the teachings of Jesus began calling themselves "Christians" and permitted non-Jews to become members of the fledgling church.*

- *When Mohammed, the founder of Islam, conquered Mecca in A.D. 630, his forces were augmented by several nomadic tribes of Abyssinian Christians.*

- *According to some scholars, two of Africa's staple foods, the banana and the yam, are not indigenous to the continent. They were carried there by Indonesian explorers and settlers around A.D. 400.*

- *The first minimum wage, started in 1938, was 25 cents an hour.*

- *Early Mongolian herders would gallop their horses across ice-covered pastures to reveal the brown grass lying beneath and thus provide sustenance to their animals in the dead of winter.*

- *Upon besieging a town, the Mongol ruler Genghis Khan offered his enemy a choice: surrender one-tenth of their wealth and one-tenth of their citizens to be slaves or face complete annihilation.*

- *The Chinese were the first people to use toothbrushes and toothpaste. Early Chinese toothbrushes were made from long hair embedded into bone.*

- *In A.D. 1045, Chinese physicians made incisions in the stomachs of 56 prisoners so they could examine the anatomy of a still-living body.*

- *Early Scandinavians used ammonia manufactured from cow's urine to clean their clothing.*

EUROPE FALLS FOR CHOCOLATE

Ancient South Americans considered it no less than a gift from heaven, but in 1500, chocolate was still unknown to Europeans. The great age of exploration would soon change that, and a hundred years later the "food of the gods" had conquered Old World taste buds, inciting a culinary obsession that continues to this day.

Humankind's taste for chocolate predates the dawn of recorded history. According to one Aztec legend, the seeds of the cacao tree, from which chocolate is made, were given to the Aztecs' ancestors by the god Quetzalcoatl. Regardless of origin, chocolate was held in high regard not only by the Aztecs, but also by the Olmecs, Mayans, and other indigenous peoples of South America. Several cultures used cacao beans as currency. In fact, the seeds held as prominent a place in Montezuma's treasury as did gold, and a slave could be had for the price of 100 pods. Cacao seeds were so valuable that an industry of counterfeiters trafficked in fake beans made of clay.

Some cultures reserved chocolate for consumption exclusively by royalty as an expression of power and wealth—after all, to eat it would be nothing less than swallowing money. So great were the perceived benefits of chocolate that it became a staple in the diets of some armies. In Mayan tradition, couples exchanged cacao seeds at their weddings as an expression of commitment.

Christopher Columbus was probably the first European to encounter the cacao bean; he captured a number of the seeds from a Mayan trading canoe on his fourth voyage in 1501. However, the significance of the find was overlooked in the expedition's zealous quest for gold and silver, and it was left to later Spanish visitors to recognize and capitalize on the potential of chocolate.

AN ACQUIRED TASTE

For most of its history, chocolate has been consumed primarily in the form of a beverage rather than as the solid candy we know today. It was in the liquid form that Europeans became acquainted with its use. However, chocolate was not at all pleasing to the European palate when first encountered; in its purest form, chocolate is a bitter, alkaloid substance, and the native custom of spicing it with chili peppers and other exotic herbs did nothing to endear it to the Spanish. Early encounters described it as being an obnoxious "drink for pigs," rather than a treat for people.

Though it may not have initially been seen as a food, chocolate gained a reputation as a wonder medicine. It was said to be good for treating any number of ailments—from tired livers to flagging libidos—a reputation modern confectioners encourage us to remember every Valentine's Day.

Europeans were soon adding cane sugar, cinnamon, vanilla, and other flavors to make chocolate not just tolerable, but desirable. One addition of particular importance was milk, which made for a lighter, smoother treat, and created the taste that's still the most popular flavor of chocolate today.

CHOCOLATE CHICANERY

As chocolate became more pleasing to European tastes, it spread from the Spanish explorers—and the Franciscan clergy that accompanied them—to the monasteries of Spain. There its production was kept a secret for years, causing a minor religious schism along the way, as theologians debated whether or not drinking chocolate violated mandatory periods of fasting.

Monks introduced chocolate to the Spanish nobility, who enjoyed it at pastimes as diverse as official court functions and bullfights. In a macabre twist, it was even served as refreshment for spectators viewing the infamous punishments of the Spanish Inquisition of the 16th century.

European aristocracy of the time was a very close group, and the fashion in one country was sure to spread to another. Such was the case with the drinking of chocolate. During the 17th century, the practice spread from Spain to Italy, and via Italian chefs to the palace of the Sun King, Louis XIV of France, who restricted its consumption to the nobility and served it at receptions three times a week. He also established a new position on the royal court: Royal Chocolate Maker to the King.

CHOCOLATE FOR EVERYONE

The drink also gained favor as a tool in court intrigues when chocolate's strong taste was found to be an effective mask of poison. This sinister use aside, there was no keeping chocolate a secret, and when an expatriate Frenchman opened the first chocolate house in London in 1657, chocolate was finally available to the masses—at least any of the masses that could afford the 50–75 pence per pound.

The chocolate craze has never left us. Though its place as a dominant drink was largely overtaken by coffee and tea, consumption of solid chocolate and use of it as a flavoring began to soar. Today, Americans spend about $13 billion a year on chocolate—and yet our per capita consumption is only robust enough to rank us 11th on the global list (Switzerland, Austria, and Ireland are 1–2–3). But the United States beats Swizerland in chocolate production. Chocolate is truly a worldwide obsession. Montezuma would be proud.

- *Milton Hershey established his soon-to-be-famous chocolate company in 1871 at the tender age of 19.*

- *You can thank the U.S. government for the familiar Hershey Milk Chocolate Bar. It was developed—by government request—for soldier ration kits during World War II.*

THE STORY OF ANESTHESIA

*In the middle of the 19th century, three intoxicating solvents
with bad reputations became the first crude "switches"
that could turn consciousness off and on—paving the way for
the revolution of painless surgical medicine.*

On March 30, 1842, a doctor from rural Georgia laid an ether-soaked towel across the mouth and nose of a young patient with two cysts on the back of his neck. The physician, Crawford Williamson Long, excised one of the growths while his patient was under. In the process, he made medical and scientific history. Long was perhaps the first doctor to use what is today called a "general anesthetic"—a substance that reduces or eliminates conscious awareness in a patient, allowing a doctor to perform incisions, sutures, and all other surgical procedures in between.

The "general"—which means complete or near-complete unconsciousness—is quite different from the targeted "local" anesthetic, an invention with origins shrouded in mystery. (Some ancient Inca trepanation rituals involved drilling a hole in the patient's skull to allow evil spirits to escape; to reduce the literally mind-numbing pain, the Incan shaman chewed leaves of the narcotic coca plant and spat the paste into the subject's wound.)

Unfortunately for Georgia's Dr. Long, the awards and acclaim that should have accompanied his medical milestone went to a dentist from Boston, who used ether four years later to knock out a patient in order to remove a tooth. Because this procedure was performed at the world-renowned Massachusetts General Hospital—and not at a backroads country practice in the Deep South—the fame of the Massachusetts innovator, William T. G. Morton, was practically assured. Within two months of Morton's tooth extraction, doctors across Europe were toasting the Yankee who had invented pain-free surgery.

The story of the stolen spotlight, however, can't entirely be blamed on the prejudice of urban versus rural or North versus South. Long, who was known to enjoy the occasional "ether frolic," didn't publicize his use of ether as a general anesthetic until 1849, seven years after his initial use of it, and three years after Morton's world-acclaimed surgery.

WAKE UP, MR. GREEN. MR. GREEN?

By 1849, a London physician, John Snow, had invented a specialized ether inhaler to better administer a safe but effective dose of the painless surgical gas. Snow was responding to the need for more scientific care in the fledgling field of anesthesiology. Lethal doses of ether had already been administered in some botched surgeries, and Snow eventually championed chloroform, which, he would later write is "almost impossible...[to cause] a death... in the hands of a medical man who is applying it with ordinary intelligence and attention."

Chloroform and ether each had their downsides, though. Chloroform could damage the liver and occasionally even cause cardiac arrest, but ether required more time for the patient to both enter and exit the anesthetized state.

NOTHING TO LAUGH ABOUT

Some American practitioners championed a third popular early anesthetic: nitrous oxide or "laughing gas," although its reputation suffered when not enough of it was administered in an early demonstration during a tooth extraction at Harvard Medical School. When the patient cried out in pain, the dentist, Horace Wells, was booed out of the room. In a turn of tragic irony, Wells later became a chloroform addict and committed suicide in 1848, just three years after the Harvard fiasco.

By the 1860s and '70s, many surgeons had given up advocating one gas over another, preferring instead to use a mixture—either chloroform or nitrous to induce anesthesia, followed by ether to keep the patient in an unconscious state.

PEACE CHURCHES: ANABAPTISTS AND QUAKERS

The Protestant Reformation of the 1500s sent chunks of Christianity, such as Lutherans and Calvinists, flying in all directions. The Anabaptists (Brethren, Mennonite, Hutterite, and Amish) and Friends (Quakers) represented some of the more radical trends in late medieval Christian thought. Both branches have nourished their core faiths into modern times.

ANABAPTISTS

"Anabaptist" means "rebaptizer." In January 1525, a group of young Swiss Christians agreed that Christian faith should be an informed adult decision, not something imposed upon an infant. Anabaptists baptized one another and planned not to baptize their children until they were of age.

Anabaptism spread swiftly throughout German-speaking Europe and the Netherlands, and many of its adherents paid the ultimate price for their "heresy." Amid gruesome persecution and martyrdom, they began to scatter, forming the sects described as follows.

MENNONITES

Father Menno Simons, a Dutch Catholic priest, became an Anabaptist in 1536. Soon, his followers began to call themselves Mennonites, and most eventually moved to Prussia and Russia. In the 1870s, they joined the great waves of immigration to the United States. Today, there are some 350,000 Mennonites in the world, two-thirds of them in the United States. They range from communal groups (who practice with varying degrees of strictness) to mainstream urban dwellers who simply happen to attend a Mennonite church.

AMISH

By 1693, some Mennonites in Alsace (modern France) felt the movement had lost its way. Under the leadership of Jakob Ammann, they separated to form their own communities removed from worldly influence and corruption. During the following century, Amish groups (along with a few Mennonites and Brethren) started migrating to the Americas. Nearly all of today's approximately 100,000 Amish live in the United States. Their strict communities are the most conservative of all Anabaptist groups.

BRETHREN

The story of the German Baptist Brethren begins (not surprisingly) in Germany in 1708 with Alexander Mack. Sr. Mack's congregants embraced many Anabaptist beliefs and found themselves mockingly called "Dunkers" by the general public for their pratice of adult baptism by immersion. By 1740, nearly all had moved to what would soon become the United States; today, there are some 215,000 North American Brethren, mostly in the United States. Some Brethren subgroups are very conservative, others less so.

HUTTERITES

In 1528, one group of Anabaptists fled to Moravia, taking their name from leader Jakob Hutter. Their efforts to live in communal peace came to naught in Moravia; Hutter himself was burned alive in 1535. In 1770, the small Hutterite remnant fled to Russia. One hundred years after that, the group began a migration to North America, particularly to Canada. Today, they number approximately 24,000. About 70 percent live in Canada's western provinces, pursuing a communal farming lifestyle. As dedicated pacifists, they refuse to fight in any war.

Most Anabaptists today live in North America. Anabaptist diversity is nearly as great as the general diversity of Christianity itself. Less conservative Anabaptists accept government benefits and serve in the military; members of stricter groups do neither (though all pay taxes). Although some use technology in business and agriculture, the conservative *Swartzentruber* Amish have gone to jail rather than affix modern reflectors to their buggies.

FRIENDS

In the early 1650s, some 60 independent-thinking English Puritans reached a radical conclusion for the day: direct experience of the light of Christ was universally possible regardless of clergy, sacrament, or church. Founded by George Fox, they soon organized as the Religious Society of Friends. Their worship was centered on the Meeting (congregation), where silent prayer was combined with preaching and testimony. Outsiders began calling them Quakers due to their emotional way of trembling when giving their testimony of faith. They believed in pacifism, which they practiced by refusing to cooperate with warlike actions or with leaders who encouraged them.

While the Friends were originally mocked as "Quakers," most today have embraced the term. Oliver Cromwell's Puritans, not known for their warm tolerance or rollicking sense of fun, threw many Friends in jail. From that prison experience stems the long-time Quaker sympathy with inhumane jail conditions—a tradition of social activism that would become, after worship, a second *raison d'être* of the Quaker faith.

By 1656, Friends had begun moving to North America. Unfortunately for them, the Massachusetts Bay Colony, like England, was in Puritan hands. Many Friends were jailed and abused. Most moved to less hostile Colonial areas: Rhode Island, New Jersey, Delaware, Maryland, and especially Pennsylvania. It didn't take long for the plight of the slaves to trouble the collective Quaker conscience, and Friends were early rejectors of the "peculiar institution." They wouldn't have countenanced war to free slaves, but from the Quaker standpoint, if ever a wrong spawned a right, it was the Civil War, which led to the abolition of slavery.

Most of today's 350,000 Quakers live in the United States and England. Unlike many Anabaptists, Quakers don't live apart from society. You'll find them active in all professions and volunteering in numerous organizations that promote peace and human rights.

Fast Facts

- *The first clocks were produced in 14th-century Italy and were massive metal structures. Due to the similarity of manufacture, many early clockmakers were also gunmakers.*

- *Until the advent of the printing press in the 15th century, most churches in Europe could not afford to have a copy of the Bible.*

- *Until the Flemish artist Jan Van Eyck began using oil to prepare his paints in the 15th century, European artists used liquid egg yolks (called tempura) as a coagulant.*

- *Columbus landed in the West Indies instead of Florida due to a flock of southwesterly birds he chose to follow during the Atlantic crossing.*

- *The first horses to arrive on the North American continent were 16 war horses attached to Hernando Cortes's 1519 expedition to conquer the Aztecs.*

- *When the Cortes expedition reached the Aztec capital of Tenochtitlán, the city had a population of about 200,000—making it one of the world's largest cities at the time.*

- *Thanks to an intricate and well-maintained system of roads and runner relay stations, the Incans were able to send a message as far as 149 miles in a single day.*

- *Incan women existed on par with men and were able to own property and serve as soldiers.*

- *There is strong evidence to suggest that Incan doctors successfully performed blood transfusions and brain surgery long before Europeans mastered the same techniques.*

- *Incan women prepared beer by chewing grains and fruits; their saliva served to break down the sugars and begin the fermentation process.*

- *In 1707, an outbreak of smallpox in Iceland killed one out of four people.*

THE GREAT HUNGER

When the Irish potato crop failed in 1845, it caused a tragedy that devastated the nation for generations.

The Ireland of 1845 was a British colony where many of the people labored as tenant farmers for English landlords, raising grain and grazing cattle for export. To feed themselves, the Irish cultivated potatoes on tiny plots of land. Some historians assert that by the 1840s, half of Ireland's population of eight million ate *nothing* but potatoes. Then an unwelcome visitor—a mold called *Phytophthora infestans*—arrived from America. This "potato 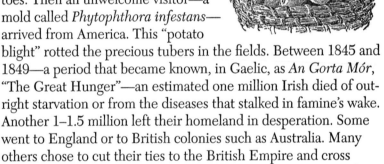 blight" rotted the precious tubers in the fields. Between 1845 and 1849—a period that became known, in Gaelic, as *An Gorta Mór*, "The Great Hunger"—an estimated one million Irish died of outright starvation or from the diseases that stalked in famine's wake. Another 1–1.5 million left their homeland in desperation. Some went to England or to British colonies such as Australia. Many others chose to cut their ties to the British Empire and cross the Atlantic to settle in the United States—where they played a crucial role in building America. Seventy years after the famine ended, Ireland's population was only about half of what it had been in 1845.

The British government organized some relief efforts, but the effort was a classic case of too little, too late. Worse was the fact that even at the height of the famine, the Emerald Isle still teemed with food—for export to England! The fiercely independent, mostly Catholic Irish had long resented British domination of their island, but the timid British response to the famine fueled a new spirit of rebellion that culminated in Ireland's full independence in 1937.

IDENTITIES LOST: THE DRUIDS AND THE PICTS

What do you know about the Druids? How about the Picts?
Chances are, what you know (or think you know) is wrong.
These two "lost" peoples are saddled with serious cases
of mistaken identity.

Most contemporary perceptions of the Druids and Picts tend to be derived from legend and lore. As such, our conceptions of these peoples range from erroneous and unlikely to just plain foolish.

Let's start with the Druids. They are often credited with the building of Stonehenge, the great stone megalith believed to be their sacred temple, as well as their arena for savage human sacrifice rituals. True or False?

False. First of all, Stonehenge was built around 2000 B.C.—1,400 years before the Druids emerged. Second, though we know admittedly little of Druidic practice, it seemed to be traditional and conservative. The Druids did have specific divinity-related beliefs, but it is not known whether they actually carried out human sacrifices.

What about the Picts? Although often reduced to a mythical race of magical fairies, the Picts actually ruled Scotland before the Scots.

So who were the Druids and the Picts?

THE DRUIDS—THE PRIESTLY CLASS

As the priestly class of Celtic society, the Druids served as the Celts' spiritual leaders—repositories of knowledge about the world and the universe, as well as authorities on Celtic history, law, religion, and culture. In short, they were the preservers of the Celtic way of life.

The Druids provided the Celts with a connection to their gods, the universe, and the natural order. They preached of the power and authority of the deities and taught the immortality of the soul and reincarnation. They were experts in astronomy and the natural world. They also had an innate connection to all things living: They preferred holding great rituals among natural shrines provided by the forests, springs, and groves.

To become a Druid, one had to survive extensive training. Druid wannabes and Druid-trained minstrels and bards had to endure as many as 20 years of oral education and memorization.

MORE POWERFUL THAN CELTIC CHIEFTAINS

In terms of power, the Druids took a backseat to no one. Even the Celtic chieftains, well-versed in power politics, recognized the overarching authority of the Druids. Celtic society had well-defined power and social structures and territories and property rights. The Druids were deemed the ultimate arbiters in all matters relating to such. If there was a legal or financial dispute between two parties, it was unequivocally settled in special Druid-presided courts. Armed conflicts were immediately ended by Druid rulings. Their word was final.

In the end, however, there were two forces to which even the Druids had to succumb—the Romans and Christianity. With the Roman invasion of Britain in A.D. 43, Emperor Claudius decreed that Druidism throughout the Roman Empire was to be outlawed. The Romans destroyed the last vestiges of official Druidism in Britain with the annihilation of the Druid stronghold of Anglesey in A.D. 61. Surviving Druids fled to unconquered Ireland and Scotland, only to become completely marginalized by the influence of Christianity within a few centuries.

Stripped of power and status, the Druids of ancient Celtic society disappeared. They morphed into wandering poets and storytellers with no connection to their once illustrious past.

THE PICTS—THE PAINTED PEOPLE

The Picts were, in simplest terms, the people who inhabited ancient Scotland before the Scots. Their origins are unknown, but some scholars believe that the Picts were descendents of the Caledonians or other Iron Age tribes who invaded Britain.

No one knows what the Picts called themselves; the origin of their name comes from other sources and probably derives from the Pictish custom of tattooing or painting their bodies. The Irish called them *Cruithni*, meaning "the people of the designs." The Romans called them *Picti*, which is Latin for "painted people"; however, the Romans probably used the term as a general moniker for all the untamed peoples living north of Hadrian's Wall.

A SECOND-HAND HISTORY

The Picts themselves left no written records. All descriptions of their history and culture come from second-hand accounts. The earliest of these is a Roman account from A.D. 297 stating that the Picti and the Hiberni (Irish) were already well-established enemies of the Britons to the south.

The Picts were also well-established enemies of each other. Before the arrival of the Romans, the Picts spent most of their time fighting amongst themselves. The threat posed by the Roman conquest of Britain forced the squabbling Pict kingdoms to come together and eventually evolve into the nation-state of Pictland. The united Picts were strong enough not only to resist conquest by the Romans, but also to launch periodic raids on Roman-occupied Britain.

Having defied the Romans, the Picts later succumbed to a more benevolent invasion launched by Irish Christian missionaries. Arriving in Pictland in the late 6th century, they succeeded in converting the polytheistic Pict elite within two decades. Much of the written history of the Picts comes from the Irish Christian annals. If not for the writings of the Romans and the Irish missionaries, we might not have knowledge of the Picts today.

Despite the existence of an established Pict state, Pictland disappeared with the changing of its name to the Kingdom of Alba in A.D. 843, a move signifying the rise of the Gaels as the dominant people in Scotland. By the 11th century, virtually all vestiges of them had vanished.

ARE YOU RELATED TO GENGHIS KHAN?

Your DNA may carry the stuff you need to conquer the world.

FROM RICHES TO RAGS TO RICHES

Genghis Khan was one of the first self-made men in history. He was born to a tribal chief in 1162, probably at Dadal Sum, in the Hentii region of what is now Mongolia. At age 9, Genghis was sent packing after a rival tribe poisoned his father. For three years, Genghis and the remainder of his family wandered the land living from hand to mouth.

Genghis was down, but not out. After convincing some of his tribesmen to follow him, he eventually became one of the most successful political and military leaders in history, uniting the nomadic Mongol tribes into a vast sphere of influence. The Mongol Empire lasted from 1206 to 1368 and was the largest contiguous dominion in world history, stretching from the Caspian Sea to the Sea of Japan. At the empire's peak, it encompassed more than 700 tribes and cities.

A UNITER, NOT A DIVIDER

Genghis gave his people more than just land. He introduced a writing system that is still in use today, wrote the first laws to govern all Mongols, regulated hunting to make sure everybody had food, and created a judicial system that guaranteed fair trials. His determination to create unity swept old tribal rivalries aside and made everyone feel like a single people, the "Mongols."

Today, Genghis Khan is seen as one of the founding fathers of Mongolia. However, he is not so fondly remembered in Asia, the

Middle East, and Europe, where he is regarded as a ruthless and bloodthirsty conqueror.

WHO'S YOUR DADDY?

It seems that Genghis was father of more than the Mongol nation. Recently, an international team of geneticists determined that one in every 200 men now living is a relative of the great Mongol ruler. More than 16 million men in central Asia have been identified as carrying the same Y chromosome as Genghis Khan.

A key reason is this: Genghis's sons and other male descendants had many children by many women; one son, Tushi, may have had 40 sons of his own, and one of Genghis's grandsons, Chinese dynastic ruler Kublai Khan, fathered 22 sons with recognized wives and an unknown number with the scores of women he kept as concubines.

Genetically speaking, Genghis continues to "live on" because the male chromosome is passed directly from father to son, with no change other than random mutations (which are typically insignificant). When geneticists identify those mutations, called "markers," they can chart the course of male descendants through centuries.

Is the world large enough for 16 million personal empires? Time—and genetics—will reveal the answer.

"I am the punishment of God.... If you had not committed great sins, God would not have sent a punishment like me upon you."

"The greatest happiness is to vanquish your enemies, to chase them before you, to rob them of their wealth, to see those dear bathed in tears, to clasp to your bosom their wives and daughters."

—QUOTES FROM GENGHIS KHAN

STEALING HISTORY

*Move over, Indiana Jones—the theft of priceless artifacts
has been going on for centuries.*

It's like something out of a James Bond movie: An international
collector pays big bucks to organized criminals to steal priceless
antiquities and smuggle them over international borders. National
treasures have been purloined for centuries—taken to distant
lands to bring prestige and value to museums, treasuries, and
private collections.

A THIEF IN THE NIGHT

Sometimes, looters go straight to the source. Since the days of the
earliest pharaohs, Egyptian rulers lived in fear of tomb robbers
and went to great lengths to protect the possessions they intended
to take into the hereafter.

But thieves were not always cloaked peasants who dug into pyramids in the dark of night; sometimes even Egyptian kings entered
the graves of their predecessors to "borrow" goodies for use in
the afterlife. King Tutankhamen's tomb included a second inner
coffin, four miniature coffins, and some gold bands that had been
removed from the tomb of his older brother, Smenkare. The tomb
of Pharaoh Pinudjem I included "recycled" sarcophagi from the
tomb of Thothmosis I, Egypt's ruler from three dynasties earlier.
(Perhaps this sort of grave robbing was simply considered "borrowing from Peter to pay Peter," since every Egyptian king was, in
theory, a reincarnation of the falcon god Horus.)

More recently, archaeological sites in the western United States
have suffered a rash of thefts by shovel-toting bandits intent on
digging up Native and Central American artifacts to sell in thriving legitimate and gray-market art and collectibles markets. In
2003, for instance, one Vanderbilt University professor worked
with Guatemalan police, villagers, and even local drug lords to
track down a stolen 1,200-year-old monument to a Mayan king.

MUSEUMS ROBBED AND LOOTED

Museum robberies have become a huge problem, especially for institutions that cannot afford state-of-the-art security systems. In 2001, for example, Russia's Culture Ministry stated that, on average, one Russian museum was victimized by theft each month. In Iraq in April 2003, during the chaos of the U.S.-led invasion of Iraq, some 170,000 items were looted or destroyed in the Iraqi National Museum; many of these artifacts subsequently made their way into private hands.

Authorities are slowly stirring themselves to crack down on a burgeoning traffic in stolen artifacts. In 2005, an Italian court sentenced a Roman antiquities dealer to ten years in prison for receiving and exporting stolen artifacts. The dealer's company sold 110 items through the prestigious auction house Sotheby's and sold another 96 artifacts to ten museums around the world before the operation was shut down.

GOVERNMENT THEFT

Conquest and colonization have provided other supply sources for collections. The Israelite temple in Jerusalem was looted by invading armies at least twice: by Babylonian King Nebuchadnezzar around 586 B.C., and again by Roman Emperor Vespasian in A.D. 70. In 480 B.C., when the Persian army sacked Athens, artifacts in the wooden Acropolis temple were carted off to Persepolis as war booty, and during his 1798–99 expedition to Egypt, Napoleon's army uncovered one of the most famous spoils of war, the Rosetta Stone—which was in turn captured by Britain in 1801. Equally famous are the "Elgin Marbles," relief statues from Greece's Parthenon that were brought to London's British Museum in 1816 by the British ambassador to Turkey.

During World War II, the Nazi regime took the pastime of art collecting to a new level. Thousands of priceless paintings, drawings, and sculptures were removed from museums in France and Russia at the behest of senior Nazi leaders. After Europe was liberated in 1945, many works of art were recovered, but others, such as Russia's fabled Amber Room panels, were never recovered at all.

FRANCISCO PIZARRO AND THE RANSOM OF AN EMPEROR

In 1532, Spanish explorer Francisco Pizarro—already a veteran of several expeditions to the New World—set out to conquer Peru. Through a combination of good luck and sheer hubris, Pizarro and his men met with astounding success. The most notable victim of their conquest was the Incan Emperor Atahualpa, who sought to bargain for his freedom by playing on Spanish greed.

FORTUNE FAVORS THE BOLD

The morning of November 16, 1532, found Francisco Pizarro in a dodgy position. The would-be conqueror of Peru and his 150 men were camped in the village of Cajamarca to await the arrival of Atahualpa, emperor of the Inca. Atahualpa had agreed to come and meet the strangers—and he was bringing his army with him. The approach of the Inca—80,000 strong—could be seen for miles. The disparity in numbers caused no small amount of worry among the Spanish soldiers; some terrified men wet themselves as they stood at their posts.

Pizarro, however, was made of sterner stuff. Hernando Cortes had conquered the Mexican Aztecs scarcely a dozen years earlier against similar odds, and Pizarro was determined to do no less. Regardless of the risks, Pizarro would go through with the meeting, promising to receive Atahualpa as a "friend and brother." If the emperor proved too strong, the ruse would be kept up; if not, the audacious plan was to demand political submission. And if Atahualpa refused, he would be taken hostage.

THE CONQUISTADOR VERSUS THE LIVING GOD

The emperor entered town as the sun was setting, leaving most of his army to camp half a mile away. However, he was still personally accompanied by a retinue that numbered in the thousands. Atahualpa himself, bedecked in emeralds and wearing a crown and parrot feathers, rode ensconced on a gold-plated litter carried high by 80 finely dressed Incan nobles. When he momentarily halted, he was greeted by Vincente de Valverde, a Dominican friar accompanying the Spanish expedition. Valverde invited Atahualpa to dine with Pizarro—possibly a trick designed to separate the emperor from his men. When the invitation was declined, Valverde extended a crucifix and Bible, asking the Incan ruler to embrace the Christian faith and acknowledge himself a vassal of the Holy Roman Emperor. Predictably enough, Atahualpa did not look favorably on the friar's suggestion and slapped the book into the dirt. And just to be certain his mood hadn't been misunderstood, Atahualpa demanded that the Spanish return all that they had stolen since arriving in his lands.

Tempers flared, and the Spanish opened fire. Concealed cannons tore into the massed Incan party, and Spanish horsemen cut through the crowd like a scythe. The sudden eruption of fire and noise, combined with the strange sight of mounted troops, threw the native force into a panic. After just minutes, the Incas were unable to mount an effective defense. They trampled each other underfoot, and many suffocated from the mass of their own numbers. The emperor's bearers continued to physically support him as long as they lived, some trying to carry him on their shoulders after their hands were severed by Spanish swords. But escape proved impossible, and the emperor was captured. Pizarro himself saved Atahualpa's life by parrying a blow from a Spanish soldier intent on killing the Incan leader. The clash was nothing less than a slaughter. Incan estimates put the number of local troops killed at 10,000 in less than two hours.

BUSINESS AS USUAL

After the bloody encounter, Atahualpa quickly adopted a pragmatic outlook, dismissing the episode as "the fortune of war" as he dined that night with Pizarro from seats overlooking a courtyard still littered with fallen men. By the emperor's own admission, the outcome was his fault for underestimating the Spaniards. Aware of the European thirst for treasure, Atahualpa immediately sought to buy his freedom, promising to fill a room measuring 22 feet by 17 feet by 8 feet high with gold in exchange for his release. Pizarro agreed, and a cooperative Atahualpa continued to manage his empire from captivity. His first order of business was to instruct his people to collect the ransom.

Pizarro was certainly interested in Atahualpa's gold, but he was in no particular hurry to see the process of collection finished. Atahualpa's word was the equivalent of divine law to the Incan people—a very useful resource for an outnumbered invader trying to control an entire country. However, as the treasure accumulated and Spanish reinforcements arrived, Atahualpa became progressively less important to the Spanish. The situation climaxed in August 1533, when Atahualpa was led forth to be executed by burning at the stake—a sentence that was generously reduced to death by garrote when the emperor requested baptism into the Christian faith at the last moment. After asking Pizarro to care for his children, Atahualpa was strangled to death as the assembled Spaniards offered prayers for his soul.

THE SOLDIER GETS A TONGUE-LASHING

The massacre of the Incas was largely seen as inconsequential at the time—a mere product of the way war was conducted. Indeed, the Incan leader himself said had their positions been reversed, he would have sacrificed some of the Spanish to the sun god while castrating the rest and using them to guard his concubines. However, many in Spain saw the execution of Atahualpa, a captive under Spanish protection, as murder and a scandal. Perhaps most notably, Holy Roman Emperor Charles V regarded the execution of a monarch by a common soldier as a bad precedent. Charles officially reprimanded Pizarro—another blow to the prestige of the fortune-hunting soldier.

European guilt notwithstanding, there is no record of the millions of pesos Pizarro sent back to Spain being anything but welcome.

A GAY TIME IN
THE OVAL OFFICE?

*Before he became U.S. president, the unmarried James Buchanan
enjoyed a long, close association with his housemate, William R.
King—so close that unconfirmed speculation about the pair still
swirls after more than 150 years. Was Buchanan—the nation's
only bachelor chief executive—also its first homosexual president?*

The year 1834 was a momentous one for
42-year-old James Buchanan. Already a veteran political leader and diplomat, Buchanan
won a seat in the U.S. Senate and formed a
friendship with the man who would be his
dearest companion for the next two decades.

Buchanan and his chum, William Rufus de
Vane King, a U.S. senator from Alabama,
became virtually inseparable. They shared
quarters in Washington, D.C., for 15 years. Capitol wits referred
to the partners—who attended social events together—as "the
Siamese twins."

Buchanan's bond with Senator King was so close that the future
president described it as a "communion." In praising his friend as
"among the best, purest, and most consistent public men I have
ever known," Buchanan added that King was a "very gay, elegant-
looking fellow." The adjective "gay," however, didn't mean "homosexual" back then. It commonly meant "merry."

It's also useful to understand that it was not unusual for educated
men to wax rhapsodic about other men during the 19th century.
Admiring rather than sexual, this sort of language signified shared
values and deep respect.

Historians rightly point out a lack of evidence that either of the
bachelors found men sexually attractive. They note that when

Buchanan was younger, he asked a Pennsylvania heiress to marry him. (She broke off the engagement.) Later, he was known to flirt with fashionable women.

BUCHANAN'S "WIFE"

Whatever the nature of his relationship with Buchanan, King seemed to consider it something more than casual. After the Alabaman became U.S. minister to France in 1844, he wrote home from Paris, expressing his worry that Buchanan would "procure an associate who will cause you to feel no regret at our separation."

Buchanan did not find such a replacement, but it was apparently not for want of trying. He wrote to another friend of his attempts to ease the loneliness caused by King's absence: "I have gone a wooing to several gentlemen, but have not succeeded with any one of them. . . ."

Sometimes the pair drew derisive jibes from their peers. The jokes often targeted King, a bit of a dandy with a fondness for silk scarves. In a private letter, Tennessee Congressman Aaron V. Brown used the pronoun "she" to refer to the senator, and called him Buchanan's "wife." President Andrew Jackson mocked King as "Miss Nancy" and "Aunt Fancy."

HIGH-FLYING CAREERS DERAILED

Despite the childish jokes, both Buchanan and King advanced to ever-more-important federal posts. President James K. Polk selected Buchanan as his secretary of state in 1845. King won the office of U.S. vice president (running on a ticket with Franklin Pierce) in 1852. Voters elected Buchanan to the White House four years later.

Unfortunately, neither of the friends distinguished himself in the highest office he reached. King fell ill and died less than a month after taking the oath as vice president.

Erupting conflicts over slavery and states' rights marred Buchanan's single term in the Oval Office. Historians give him failing marks for his lack of leadership as the Civil War loomed. The pro-slavery chief executive (he was a Pennsylvania Democrat) opposed secession of the Southern states but argued that the federal government had no authority to use force to stop it. As a result, Buchanan made no effort to save the Union, leaving that task to his successor, Abraham Lincoln.

WHAT'S SEX GOT TO DO WITH IT?

Would Buchanan have risen to the highest office in the land if his peers honestly believed he was homosexual? It's hard to say. Today's perception is that 19th-century Americans were more homophobic than their 21st-century descendents. Yet in an era when sexuality stayed tucked beneath Victorian wraps, there was a de facto "don't ask, don't tell" policy for virtually any profession. Whatever their private proclivities, Buchanan and King clearly excelled in their public lives—at least until Buchanan got into the White House. Based on what little evidence history provides, neither man's sexual orientation had much, if any, bearing on what he accomplished, or failed to accomplish, in his career.

FAMOUS LAST WORDS

"What is right and what is predicatable are two different things."

"I like the noise of democracy."

"The test of leadership is not to put greatness into humanity, but to elicit it, for the greatness is already there."

"The ballot box is the surest arbiter of disputes among free men."
—QUOTES FROM JAMES BUCHANAN

OH THE CALAMITY!

You probably know her from the HBO series Deadwood.
But what's the real story behind Wild Bill Hickok's gal pal?
And how did she get that nickname?

She swore. She drank. She was an expert rider and was handy with a gun. She scouted for the army. She mined for gold. She wore *pants*. She did just about everything that 19th-century American women weren't supposed to do. But Calamity Jane got away with it—and became a Wild West legend.

As with most of the legendary figures of the Wild West, it's hard to separate fact from fiction when it comes to Calamity Jane. We don't even know her real birthdate. What we do know is that she was born Martha Jane Canary (or Cannary) in Missouri, probably in 1852. Orphaned not long after her family left Missouri for the Montana Territory, teenage Martha turned to prostitution—a trade she'd ply occasionally throughout her life. Over the next decade or so, Martha drifted through the mining camps and army posts of the West, where she earned the respect of her masculine peers by showing that she could do anything a man could do—and in some cases, do it better. A heavy drinker, Calamity was thrown into various frontier jails for disturbing the peace.

She first started wearing men's clothes while scouting and carrying messages for the army during the Indian campaigns of the early 1870s. She won the name "Calamity Jane" when she rode to the rescue of an officer caught in an ambush—he declared that she'd saved him from "a calamity." (Though some say her moniker came from her threat that if any man messed with her, "it would be a calamity" for him.)

WELCOME TO DEADWOOD

Around 1876, Calamity landed in Deadwood, South Dakota, where she developed a serious crush on the handsome gunslinger Wild Bill Hickok. Later in life, she claimed they'd been married and had a child together, but they were probably just "friends." She stayed in Deadwood after Hickok caught a bullet during a poker game. A couple of years later, tough Calamity showed her tender side by nursing victims of a smallpox epidemic that swept the town.

By then, word of this crossdressing hell-raiser had reached the publishers back East who were busy churning out "dime novels" to satisfy the public's taste for tales of Western derring-do. Calamity Jane quickly became a recurring character in these outlandish fictions. She was usually described as a beautiful woman; in illustrations, her baggy trousers mysteriously turned into skin-tight leggings. Photographs of Calamity don't exactly bear out this image.

It was all downhill from there for Calamity. She resumed drifting around the West, married briefly, and in the 1890s she toured the country with Buffalo Bill's famous Wild West Show. She got fired for drinking and ultimately died in poverty in 1903. But she gets to spend eternity with Wild Bill; as per her deathbed request, she's buried next to him in Deadwood's cemetery.

- *During her brief stint as a married woman, Calamity Jane gave birth to a daughter, who was raised in a convent.*

- *Calamity Jane allegedly penned an autobiography,* The Life and Adventures of Calamity Jane, *in 1896. Some sources speculate that the book was actually written by a ghostwriter.*

Fast Facts

- The backlash against Protestant incursion into France was intense. On St. Bartholomew's Day in 1572, approximately 20,000 Parisian Protestants were killed.

- The Russian Orthodox Church so discouraged literacy that many of its priests could not read the Bible and simply recited passages from memory. The first full-text edition of the Bible in Russian was not available in that country until 1876.

- The turkey was the only source of meat indigenous to the Americas to find popularity on European tables.

- The Portuguese settlement of Brazil was inspired by a large demand for the logwood tree, which was valued for the brilliant dyes that could be produced from its wood and was highly esteemed by European dye-makers.

- Gabriele Fallopio, a 16th-century Italian anatomist, was the first to discover the tubes that connect the ovaries to the uterus, and was also the first to develop an effective condom, which he fashioned from pig intestines.

- By the late 13th century, the city of Venice was esteemed as the center of glass-making in Europe. So numerous were the glassmaker's shops that they posed a serious fire hazard, and in 1291, the city government moved them all to the island of Murano.

- The Venetian glassmakers were the first to produce lucid mirrors, which contributed to the city's reputation for beauty and vanity. The secret by which these mirrors were manufactured, a backing of mixed mercury and tin, was jealously guarded for nearly 150 years.

- One of the telescope's first uses was to spot returning cargo ships before they were visible to the naked eye. The bearer of such knowledge could often profit handsomely in the fiercely competitive European commodities market.

THE UNITED FRUIT COMPANY

A tale of dramatic leaps, octopuses, railroads, corruption, contrition, and...bananas.

On Monday, February 3, 1975, corporate raider Eli M. Black stood before the glass window of his office on the 44th floor of the Pan American Building in New York City. As Black stood looking at the Manhattan skyline, it is possible he thought of the Honduran banana plantations that had recently been wiped out by Hurricane Fifi. Or perhaps he thought of the devalued United Fruit Company shares that were dragging down the market viability of his newly created United Brands Company.

Unfortunately, nobody will ever know exactly what Eli M. Black's thoughts were the moment he sent his briefcase sailing through Pan American's glass wall and dove after it, plunging to his death on the Park Avenue pavement far below.

BEFORE THE FALL

Seven years prior, Black had purchased enough shares to become the majority stockholder of the United Fruit Company—a powerful corporation that had molded Central and South American politics for nearly a century. Eli M. Black had the distinction of presiding over the final days of the United Fruit Company. The corporation, which ended so dismally, had an equally rough beginning. In 1871, railroad speculator Henry Mieggs secured a contract with the government of Costa Rica to develop the young country's railroad system. Unfortunately, the Costa Ricans ran out of money, and the railroad remained unfinished upon Mieggs's death. His nephew, Minor C. Keith, realized that the true value of the railroad lay not in its ability to transport people, but in its ability to transport the bananas that grew plentifully along its tracks. Keith borrowed money from London banks and private investors to finish the railroad. He then acquired tax-free rights to the land adjacent to the rails and earned exclusive trading status at the country's seaports. His banana empire thus secured, Keith joined his operation with Boston Fruit's Lorenzo Dow Baker and Andrew W. Preston. This merger brought substantial financial backing as well as one of the world's largest private holdings of transport ships, known as "The Great White Fleet." With control of the railroads and shipping, the newly created United Fruit Company soon came to dominate the region's trade.

BANANA REPUBLIC

In 1901, the Guatemalan government hired the United Fruit Company to handle the country's postal service. Keith realized that Guatemala, with its right-wing dictator and ample supply of cheap labor, represented the "ideal investment climate." United Fruit soon lorded over every aspect of the Guatemalan economy. It established a base of operations in its own town, Bananera, and was able to procure extremely favorable terms from a succession of pliant governments. And with that, the "banana republic" was born.

As a key tactic, United Fruit extracted rights for vast tracts of property under the premise that the region's unpredictable weather necessitated backup plantations. The result: Large amounts of land lay fallow. Unable to farm, the majority of the populace, mostly Indian, struggled to subsist on the company's meager wages or simply had no work at all. Apologists for United Fruit cited the growth of infrastructure as well as the relatively high wages for its permanent employees, but for the average citizen, United Fruit's regional monopoly meant curtailed opportunity. Beginning in the 1920s, the company dominated life in the region so completely that locals began calling it *El Pulpo*—The Octopus.

The first real test of the company's power came in 1944 when Guatemalans overthrew their oppressive dictator, Jorge Ubico, and elected reformer Dr. Juan Jose Arevalo Bermej, who was peacefully and democratically succeeded by Jacobo Arbenz. Besides building schools and improving the circumstances of the average citizen, these men (Arbenz in particular) promised to break up the vast tracks of land held by private firms and redistribute it to the populace. As it was, 90 percent of the people had access to only 10 percent of the land. United Fruit Company, the primary land-holder in the region, appealed to the United States to overthrow the democratic Guatemalan government, claiming that Arbenz was allied with the Soviet Union. In 1954, a CIA-backed coup ousted Arbenz and installed a repressive right-wing dictatorial government, sparking a civil war that lasted 36 years and resulted in the deaths of hundreds of thousands of people. Many died as a result of being on a list of "dissidents" compiled by the CIA at the behest of the United Fruit Company.

In 1968, Eli M. Black bought his ill-fated shares in United Fruit. He later merged the company with his own—a move that created the United Brands Company. Financial problems, coupled with Black's mismanagement of the company, led to serious debt for the United Brands. A 1974 hurricane, which destroyed huge crops of bananas, was perhaps the final straw for Eli Black and may have been a factor in his 1975 suicide.

In 1999, three years after the end of the Guatemalan civil war, U.S. President Bill Clinton visited the region, and during a brief stop in Guatemala City, delivered a speech in which he expressed regret for the United States' role in the country's civil war, stating that Washington "was wrong" to have supported Guatemalan security forces during its "dark and painful" period. By the time President Clinton made these comments, the United Fruit Company had undergone its own "dark and painful" period but currently survives as Chiquita Brands International Corporation, which acquired the deceased Eli M. Black's United Brands in 1984.

- *A fictionalized account of the Santa Marta Massacre, in which tens of thousands of striking United Fruit workers in Columbia were assaulted by government forces, forms the basis of Gabriel Garcia Márquez's novel* One Hundred Years of Solitude.

A SHORT HISTORY OF THE SHORTEST WAR

The British proved that it only takes 38 minutes to destroy a palace, depose a king, sink a navy, and burn a harem.

NO FRIEND OF THE QUEEN

On the morning of August 27th, 1896, the new Sultan of Zanzibar, Khalid bin Barghash, a 29-year-old who had been sultan for a mere 48 hours, awoke to the sight of five British warships anchored in the harbor just outside his palace's windows.

Things were not going well for young Khalid. Although he enjoyed the support of his people and had a legitimate claim to the throne, the British favored another successor. In a clearly worded communication to Queen Victoria, Khalid had expressed his hope that friendly relations could continue between his country and England but stated he could not abandon the "house of his fathers." Meanwhile, the British felt they could not tolerate the rule of a man they considered far too traditional.

AN UNEVEN CONTEST

To convince Khalid that he should abdicate the throne, the British hastily assembled a fleet that, though small in number, boasted the largest concentration of artillery ever deployed in East Africa at the time. The Zanzibari navy, on the other hand, consisted of a showpiece called the *Glasgow*, a wooden steam vessel equipped with ancient, muzzle-loading cannons. Nevertheless, the crew of the *Glasgow* affirmed their allegiance to Khalid—as did almost 3,000 Zanzibari soldiers and loyalists who occupied the palace—and prepared for a siege. They didn't have to wait long. Just before the deadline hour of 9:00 A.M., the captain of the *Glasgow* was rowed to his ship, which was anchored amongst the formidable British vessels. The British took this as a sign that Khalid would not capitulate without a lesson.

A SHORT LESSON

At exactly 9:05 A.M., the British warships opened fire. The *Glasgow* bravely returned fire but was soon sinking in the harbor's shallow water. The barrage on the palace was intense. By some estimates, more than a thousand shells were fired by the British ships that morning. Finally, the smoke obscuring the target and the complete cessation of return fire caused the British to stop their bombardment. The royal harem next to the palace was fiercely ablaze, and the palace itself had been reduced to ruins. The war was over—less than 40 minutes after it had begun.

AFTERMATH

Khalid survived the bombardment and fled to the German embassy where he was given sanctuary for several weeks before escaping to Dar el Salaam. The royal palace was utterly destroyed and never rebuilt. The harem, however, was soon replaced. Khalid's British-supported successor, Hamoud bin Mohammed, made good on his promise to begin the modernization of his country— his first step was to outlaw slavery; for this he was decorated by Queen Victoria.

- *Zanzabari succession practices were once described as the crown falling to the eligible candidate with "the longest sword."*

- *Some believe that Zanzibar was originally a 1st-century outpost of the Queen of Sheba.*

- *After the destruction of the palace, Khalid never again set foot upon British soil. Instead he stepped directly from the German embassy, where he had sought sanctuary, onto a boat.*

- *The world's longest war is commonly considered to be that which existed between the Netherlands and Isles of Scilly off the Cornish Coast. War was declared by the Netherlands during the confusing years of the English Civil War (1642–1651), and the proclamation was forgotten until 1985. Officially, the war lasted 335 years.*

YO HO HO AND ALL THAT: A FEW FAMOUS PIRATES

During the late 17th and early 18th centuries—a time often called the Golden Age of Piracy—daring men (and a few women) lived outside the law and struck fear into merchants whose ships plied the Caribbean and Atlantic. Thousands of pirates sailed and died in obscurity, but a few became legends. Here's a brief look at some of their stories.

Henry Morgan (active 1663–1674) Captain Morgan was one of the most successful pirate leaders, as well as one of the few who managed to retire with his fortune intact. Ostensibly acting under authority given him by the British crown to make war against Spain, Morgan's actions frequently exceeded the bounds of a privateer's commission, not to mention human decency. Remarkable in that many of his successful raids targeted towns rather than ships, Henry Morgan showed a ruthlessness that respected little but the pursuit of treasure. On one occasion, he locked captured enemy soldiers in houses, then blew up the buildings with gunpowder. He would routinely torture prominent residents of captured towns, looking for treasure whether it existed or not.

Most infamously, during an attack in Panama, Morgan took advantage of the Catholic beliefs of his foes by forcing priests and nuns to the front of the assault, ensuring that the Spanish could not fire on his troops without killing the clergy.

Morgan made a fortune during the course of his career, sacking Puerto Principe, Portobelo, Maracaibo, the coast of Cuba, Panama City, and other hapless targets. He pocketed more than 100 million dollars, but when Morgan's actions became so egregious that they threatened a peace treaty between England and Spain, he was briefly arrested by his benefactors. The British had no real wish to punish Morgan, however, and he was released and knighted, after which he retired from the sea. The British government eventually saw to his appointment as Lieutenant Governor of Jamaica. Morgan died in 1688 of natural causes exacerbated by a life of hard drinking. Ironically, a fanciful version of his image lives on as the mascot of a popular brand of rum.

William Kidd (active 1695–1701) The famous Captain Kidd may have been the most misunderstood pirate of all time. A prominent citizen of New York, Kidd was on friendly terms with several colonial governors. In 1695, he was commissioned to hunt down some of the more well-known pirates of the day. Kidd dutifully outfitted a ship, the *Adventure Galley*, and set out for the pirate haven of Madagascar. Shortly after his voyage began, however, many of his handpicked crew were pressed into service by a British naval ship, and Kidd was forced to replace them with common criminals and ex-pirates. Discipline immediately suffered, and Kidd struggled to maintain control over his men, eventually killing one in a heated argument. With no luck at finding pirates, the *Adventure Galley* took a number of merchant ships as prizes over the protest of Kidd himself, who finally acceded to his crew's demands for plunder.

On encountering their first pirate ship, the *Adventure Galley* crew mutinied and joined the outlaw vessel, leaving Kidd and 13 loyal men to make their way back to the Americas, where Kidd was astonished to find that he was wanted as a pirate. He was charged with murder and the illegal seizure of English ships. Captured and sent back to England for trial, Kidd was found guilty and sentenced to be hanged. More ignominy was in store: The executioner's rope broke on the first drop and required a second, successful attempt. Subsequently, Kidd's corpse dangled from a gibbet over the River Thames for several years, as a warning to other pirates.

Edward Teach (active 1713–1718) More infamously known as Blackbeard, Edward Teach was a privateer turned pirate whose success and reputation for cruelty made him a legend across the Caribbean. From his ship, *Queen Anne's Revenge,* Blackbeard terrorized the commercial lanes and coastal waters of the West Indies and the American Atlantic coast for four years. Never one to run from a fight, Teach gained immense fame among his fellow pirates by successfully fighting off a Royal Navy ship, an encounter that he could have, and that most other pirate captains *would* have, completely avoided.

Blackbeard was well aware that his public image of wickedness was a key to his success, and he took pains to cultivate the impression. Before battle, he embedded match cord in his beard and set it alight, wreathing his head in smoke and giving his enemies the impression that he had arisen from the depths of hell. His unfortunate crews sometimes bore the brunt of his attempts to reinforce his image; on one occasion Teach shot his chief gunner, crippling the man for life. When asked his reason, Blackbeard replied that if he didn't kill one of his men now and then, they would forget who he was. Despite this capriciousness, Teach's achievements in plunder and his seeming invincibility made men eager to sail with him. Aware that he was being sought for capture, Blackbeard briefly retired in January 1718 and was pardoned by the governor of North Carolina, a man to whom Teach paid a number of bribes. However, Edward Teach wasn't temperamentally suited to retirement, and soon returned to his old ways.

Blackbeard's career came to an end in November 1718, when two Royal Navy sloops commanded by Lieutenant Robert Maynard came athwart of the outlaw. Although outnumbered by more than two to one, Blackbeard and his crew chose to give battle to their pursuers, fighting hand to hand on the deck of *Queen Anne's Revenge*. Teach had snapped Maynard's sword and was on the verge of killing the British officer when one of Maynard's men slashed his throat. Teach continued to fight viciously until his body succumbed to blood loss. Maynard decapitated the famous pirate and hung his head from the bowsprit—the spar that projected from the bow of *Queen Anne's Revenge*—for all to see.

Anne Bonny and Mary Read (active c. 1720) Piracy was largely a man's trade, but two remarkable women earned their places in the annals of the profession. Coincidentally, both were found on the same ship, the *Revenge*, captained by Calico Jack Rackham. Bonny was the daughter of a wealthy Charleston planter, and had a reputation as something of a wild child. At 13, she was rumored to have stabbed a servant girl with a table knife. She eventually left decent society behind to run away with the dashing Calico Jack. Though she may have initially tried to conceal her gender, secrets were hard to keep on a small ship.

Mary Read had a long history of crossdressing, having posed as a boy to trick a relative out of an inheritance and also serving as a man in the British military. Read was on board a ship that was taken by Calico Jack and was pressed into service with his crew. One day, Anne Bonny happened to walk in on Read while she was undressing, and Mary's secret was out. The two naturally gravitated to each other and lived openly as women accepted by the crew, donning men's clothes only in times of battle.

Pirate hunters seized the *Revenge* in 1720. Accounts of the capture say that Bonny and Read fought ferociously with cutlasses and pistols while the men of the ship cowered below decks. Tried and sentenced to hang, the two women achieved a nine-month reprieve by "pleading their bellies"—both were pregnant. Mary Read eventually died in prison, possibly in childbirth. Anne Bonny disappears from the history books; one popular legend claims she escaped justice through the auspices of her estranged father, who bought her freedom before she could be executed.

Bartholomew "Black Bart" Roberts (active 1719–1722) The "Great Pyrate Roberts" was a man of contradictions. Although initially reluctant to sail under the black flag, he was forced into the role when brigands captured the vessel he was on.

Bartholomew Roberts had one of the greatest careers in history, capturing an estimated 400 ships and pocketing treasure beyond reckoning. Black Bart's reputation was such that many authorities refused to tangle with him, but his success ended in 1722 when pirate hunters surprised his ship, the *Royal Fortune,* as its crew lay drunk from celebrating the capture of a prize the day before. Roberts died in the battle, his throat ripped open by grapeshot as he defiantly stared down his enemies from astride a gun carriage during the exchange of cannon fire—a pirate to the end.

A Day in the Life
WORKING FOR THE MAN IN OLDE ENGLAND

An average day for a serf in medieval England involved working land allotted to him by his master, the manor lord. But although his lord giveth, his lord also taketh away, thus relegating him to a life of servitude and poverty. In the following account, we take a look at what a "day in the life" may have been like.

It's not yet daybreak, but Thomas is getting ready for the workday. Flickering rush-lights illuminate his tiny wood-frame, mud-walled cottage, which is topped with a straw thatched roof—much like the other dwellings in the small, mid-14th century English village Thomas calls home.

Thomas has a bit of oatmeal porridge and his usual breakfast drink—tepid ale poured from an earthenware jug. The same brew will quench Thomas's thirst throughout the day.

At sun up, Thomas, along with his wife and children, trudge to the plots of land allotted to him by the lord of the manor on which Thomas's village is located. Ostensibly, Thomas works the land for himself, but in reality most of the fruits of his labor go to his lord. It's medieval England's version of working for The Man.

Thomas, like more than half of his fellow citizens, is a serf. He is socially and legally indentured to his lord for life, unless he can buy his freedom or his lord grants it.

SLOGGING AWAY IN FIELDS OF DREAMS

The latter isn't likely to happen. So Thomas works his own fields of dreams hoping that his toiling will earn him a ticket to freedom.

Thomas dresses for the hard work ahead: a tattered shirt tucked into well-worn wool breeches; a ragged knee-length hooded coat;

thick-soled leather shoes. It is standard serf garb, and Thomas wears it pretty much every day.

First task is weeding and watering the onions, cabbages, beans, leeks, and herbs sprouting in the gardens near the cottage. The two hogs in the cottage-side sty are thrown scraps and waste. The rooster, hens, and geese are fed while eggs are collected.

Next it's off to scratch out a living from the ten half-acre strips of land Thomas holds outside the village. Today, wheat and rye are harvested from the first strip. Thomas cuts the sheaves by hand with a sickle while his wife and children gather them onto an ox-pulled wooden cart that carries the crop home.

STICKING IT TO THE MAN

After harvesting, Thomas uses the little remaining daylight to surreptitiously procure some necessities at the expense of his lord.

First, he forages for dung, an activity done on the sly since all droppings on manor grounds are the exclusive property of his lord. Then he treks to the woods to poach his lord's forests and streams. Poaching usually involves late-night fishing for eels or salmon, but today Thomas goes to a well-hidden rabbit snare where tonight's dinner struggles vainly to get free. It's his lucky day—meat at supper is an infrequent treat.

REFUGE AT THE ALE HOUSE

After dinner, Thomas walks to the village alehouse to escape the monotony of his dreary daily existence. There he spends the evening quaffing ales, socializing, singing, and gambling.

Thomas chats with a mate about the prospect, however bleak, of buying his freedom. What Thomas doesn't know is that freedom will come shortly, but at a terrible cost. The approaching scourge of the Black Plague will quickly wipe out a third of England's population and suddenly make Thomas's labor an extremely valuable commodity.

Thomas will soon have the economic leverage he needs to get out from under his lord's thumb.

EMILIANO ZAPATA AND THE MEXICAN LAND REFORM MOVEMENT

Most people know Emiliano Zapata as the revolutionary leader of southern Mexico who, along with Poncho Villa in the North, fought in the Mexican Revolution. Some also know him as the subject of the film Viva Zapata!*, starring Marlon Brando, for which John Steinbeck wrote a masterful screenplay. Few, however, know him as the spiritual and intellectual father of Mexico's land reform movement. But Emiliano Zapata, who loved nothing more than the lifestyle of the agrarian village in which he was raised, was a passionate proponent of land-use rights for Mexico's farmers.*

LAND AND LIBERTY

At the start of the 20th century, Mexico's small farmers were becoming increasingly disenfranchised by the powerful *hacienda* owners who sought to supplant the native corn crop with the more internationally valuable sugarcane plant. Through intimidation, violence, and indentured servitude, the *hacienda* owners—and the government that backed them—steadily encroached upon land that had been farmed by peasant families for generations.

In 1909, the village of Anenecuilco, in the small central-Mexico state of Morelos, elected Emiliano Zapata to the traditional post of defender of the village's interests. The orphaned son of a prosperous but humble local mestizo family whose ancestors had fought against the Spanish and the French, Zapata was a perfect fit for the position. He worked to establish land rights for farmers through ancient title deeds and petitioned the government to recognize the farmers' rightful ownership of their lands. Sometimes he was able to settle land disputes through diplomacy, but the lack of government support increasingly frustrated him.

In 1910, just a year after Zapata's election, the Mexican Revolution began. Zapata, who counseled the villagers to farm with rifles over their shoulders, joined the forces of Francisco Madero, a revolutionary who planned to overthrow Mexican President Porfirio Díaz. Zapata became a general of the Liberation Army of the South and aided Madero to success. Díaz was overthrown, and Francisco Madero became the new president of Mexico. Unfortunately, Zapata was soon disappointed by the slow pace of land reform under Madero, and relations between the two former allies broke down.

By this time, Zapata had become a popular leader, whose soft-spoken but passionate dedication to the peasants' cause attracted thousands of people willing to fight for the right to farm their own land as they pleased. Through a succession of corrupt leaders and broken promises, Zapata maintained his agrarian ideals and his rallying slogan of *Tierra y Libertad* (Land and Liberty).

THE "LIBERAL-BOURGEOIS" REVOLUTIONARY

Zapata's ideology found its fruition in the Plan de Ayala, a radical document that outlined a plan for land reform that Zapata wrote with his former teacher and mentor, Otilio Montaño Sanchez, in 1911. Though awkwardly worded, full of misspellings, and rife with redundancies, the land reform proposed by the Plan de Ayala was incendiary and galvanized support around Zapata's movement. Though Zapata admired Communist ideas, he considered Marxism impractical and instead simply sought to return the land to those from whom it had been taken.

When the Plan de Ayala was first printed, the intellectual elite in Mexico City considered the poorly written work a joke. Zapata's old enemy, President Francisco Madero, gave the editor of the *Diario del Hogar* permission to reprint the Plan de Ayala, reportedly saying, "Publish it so that everybody will know how crazy Zapata is." The plan backfired, and the Plan de Ayala received enthusiastic support that eventually led to Madero's ousting.

In the Plan de Ayala, Zapata did not seek to destroy the *hacienda* system, but rather to place legal checks upon its powers to seize and hold land. Under the Plan de Ayala, *ejidas*, or communally held lands, would be re-established in the villages that chose such a system. Alternately, the farmers could elect to establish individual plots. Zapata's ideology has since been labeled "liberal-bourgeois" or "bourgeois democratic," as it was truly an inclusionary, practical system that maintained as its primary goal peasant enfranchisement without recourse to completely subverting the existing capitalistic system.

LIFE AFTER DEATH

The corrupt revolutionary leader Venustiano Carranza (who took over the reins of power from President Madero) consolidated his power by ordering his followers to assassinate Zapata in 1919. After Zapata was killed, the government forces took pictures of his face while shining a flashlight upon it to prove he was dead.

The agrarian leader's ideas were not so easily dispatched, however. Soon after Zapata's murder, men who had been sympathetic to Zapata's philosophy ousted Carranza and began to institute the land reform policies championed by their fallen leader. Today's Zapatistas, the spiritual descendents of Emiliano, have departed markedly from the specifics of the Plan de Ayala, but they retain the goal of uplifting the peasant class by striving against social injustice and government interference.

FAMOUS LAST WORDS

"I am determined to fight against anything and anyone with nothing more than the confidence and support of my people."

"It is better to die on your feet than to live on your knees."

—QUOTES FROM EMILIANO ZAPATA

GREAT OBSCURE QUOTES

"A few decades hence, energy may be free, just like unmetered air."
—JOHN VON NEUMANN, PHYSICIST, TOP MEMBER OF THE MANHATTAN PROJECT, 1956

"Aeroplanes are interesting toys but of no military value."
—MARSHAL FERDINAND FOCH, FRENCH MILITARY STRATEGIST, 1911

"Ours has been the first, and doubtless to be the last, to visit this profitless locality."
—LT. JOSEPH IVES, AFTER VISITING THE GRAND CANYON, 1861

"With over 50 foreign cars already on sale here, the Japanese auto industry isn't likely to carve out a big slice of the U.S. market."
—BUSINESS WEEK MAGAZINE, 1968

"It will be years—not in my time—before a woman will become Prime Minister."
—MARGARET THATCHER, 1974

✧✧✧

"No matter what happens, the U.S. Navy is not going to be caught napping."
—U.S. SECRETARY OF NAVY, DECEMBER 4, 1941

THE FIRST WORLD'S FAIR: A SMASHING SUCCESS

England's hugely popular 19th-century exhibition set the standard by which all subsequent World's Fairs would be measured.

In her diary on May 1, 1851, Queen Victoria could barely contain herself: "This day is one of the greatest and most glorious in our lives," she gushed. England's monarch wasn't referring to a glorious military triumph, but to the opening of the awkwardly named "Great Exhibition of the Works of Industry of all Nations," or, as it later came to be identified, the first World's Fair.

Who could blame Victoria for such lavish overstatement? Her husband, Prince Albert, was in charge of the great event. No doubt influenced by the successful French Industrial Exposition of 1844, the prince formed the Royal Commission for the Exhibition of 1851 to look into ways of bringing a similar event to England.

Held at the height of the Industrial Revolution, the Great Exhibition's objective was to demonstrate the leading manufacturing and engineering achievements of the day and to display the top arts and crafts that the world had to offer. Some contemporary cynics—including philosopher Karl Marx—sneered at the event, dismissing the inaugural Expo as a thinly disguised attempt for England to show off its economic, industrial, and military might.

And show off it did. On the premises of London's Hyde Park rose the event's centerpiece, the famous Crystal Palace, which would be imitated at subsequent World's Fairs. The structure, made of iron and glass and resembling a massive greenhouse, housed more than one million exhibits from England, its 15 colonies, and 25 other countries around the globe.

On opening day, 300,000 visitors paid their shilling entrance fee and eagerly made their way through the Expo, marveling at such displays as the world's largest organ, a knife with 80 blades, a pro-totype for a submarine, and the world's first life-size re-creations of dinosaurs.

The U.S. exhibits included such diverse offerings as furniture made out of coal, a Colt revolver, modern kitchen appliances, a model of Niagara Falls, and an astounding envelope machine that could process 60 pieces of mail per minute.

The event was popular right from the start and became an over-whelming success when organizers dropped the price to a penny to allow working families to take part in the festivities. Special train services were set up to run from all parts of England to Lon-don. When the doors finally closed in October 1851, more than six million people had filed through the Crystal Palace—almost a third of England's population.

Curiously, the contraption that drew the most attention and proved to have lasting value wasn't even an official exhibit. Public flush toilets made their debut at London's Expo: a brilliant innova-tion for which fair-goers ever since have been truly grateful.

- *The Crystal Palace was so popular that it was relocated after the fair so it could be made permanent. It was subsequently lost in a 1936 fire.*

- *The 1893 World's Fair, hosted by Chicago, introduced the Ferris Wheel for the first time.*

- *The 1904 World's Fair in St. Louis, Missouri, marked the debut of iced tea.*

- *Franklin Delano Roosevelt made history at the 1939 World's Fair in New York when he became the first president ever to appear on television.*

- *The Space Needle, located in Seattle, Washington, was built for the 1962 World's Fair.*

SEND ME TO TIMBUKTU?

*The city of Timbuktu lives in modern English vocabulary
as a somewhat mythical place remembered for its unique, lyrical
name. If someone were actually to travel to Timbuktu,
what (if anything) would they find there?*

The real Timbuktu is a small city in northwestern Africa. It is located in central Mali about 500 miles from the Atlantic coast on the Niger River. Its roughly 30,000 inhabitants are mostly of Tuareg, Songhai, Fulani, or Moorish heritage. Most of Timbuktu's residents are Sunni Muslims.

THE NAME

The Tuaregs, a nomadic Berber people of the Sahara region, founded Timbuktu sometime around A.D. 1000. The story goes that a well-respected elderly lady named Buktu lived near a well ("tin" in Tuareg). Nomads who needed to leave things behind for safekeeping entrusted them to Buktu and said they had left their possessions at "Tin Buktu." Ms. Buktu is long gone, but her name has endured through Timbuktu. Even today, there is a well in Timbuktu, said to be that of Buktu herself.

THE PLACE

Timbuktu began as an encampment and grew into a town, becoming an important stop on the trans-Saharan trade route. Salt mined from the Sahara went south and west; slaves and gold went north toward the Mediterranean. Even though Timbuktu changed hands among African empires, it developed into a prestigious Islamic cultural and religious center.

In its peak era beginning in about 1330, Timbuktu had 100,000 residents, including an astonishing 25,000 students. The prized turban of a Timbuktu scholar proclaimed its wearer to be a devout Muslim steeped in Islamic learning. In order to receive the lowest of four degrees conferred in Timbuktu, the student had to memorize the entire Koran. Learned scholars coming to Timbuktu from afar required extra teaching to bring their knowledge up to Timbuktu standards. In terms of prestige, it might be fair to call Timbuktu the Oxford or Harvard of the medieval Islamic world.

The golden era ended in 1591, when Moroccans armed with the latest gunpowder weapons conquered the Songhai Empire. The Moroccan conquest didn't kill Timbuktu, but the city was mortally wounded as trade routes shifted after the year 1600. Carrying goods across the sea became safer and faster than hauling everything across the Sahara. The city became somewhat of a backwater, yet remained an important destination for dedicated students seeking immersion in Islam.

By the 1800s, Timbuktu was only known as a legend to Europeans. A French exploration society offered a handsome bounty to anyone who visited Timbuktu and returned to describe it. At least one explorer perished in the attempt to locate Timbuktu, but an intrepid Frenchman named René-Auguste Caillé finally returned with an account of the contemporary city. His report would have made a lousy tourist brochure, as he found only a collection of mud huts threatened by the rising sands of the Sahara. The only remarkable aspects of Timbuktu, Caillé said, were its centers of Islamic learning.

The French captured Timbuktu in 1893, incorporating it into their immense West African domain. In 1960, the Republic of Mali achieved independence. At that time Timbuktu hadn't changed a lot since Caillé's visit. However, Timbuktu's prominence has risen in subsequent years. Today, Timbuktu is sometimes called "The Mecca of Africa" for the prestigious Islamic study courses offered at the city's Sankore Mosque. Additionally, hundreds of thousands of priceless historical documents can still be found in Timbuktu. Refusing to be erased and forgotten again, the city has even successfully managed to keep the Sahara's drifting sands at bay.

HENRY VIII IS EXCOMMUNICATED

On April 20, 1534, a taut rope on the Tyburn gallows in Westminster, England, strangled the life out of a popular and charismatic 28-year-old nun. Elizabeth Barton, the "Holy Maid of Kent"—a veritable, homegrown, Joan of Arc—had become an unlikely public spokesperson against King Henry VIII. God, she said, had told her in a series of holy visions that he would visit his vengeance upon the middle-aged king for defiling a divinely consecrated marriage. The king responded as he would to others who stood in his way (such as Sir Thomas More, author of Utopia, *the following year): Their opposition made them traitors, and therefore they had to die.*

The previous year, Henry had, in defiance of the pope, divorced his first wife Catherine of Aragon to marry one of Catherine's ladies-in-waiting, the charming and sophisticated (and pregnant!) Anne Boleyn. To marry Anne, Henry had not only to contravene the reigning Catholic Church's prohibition against divorce, he also had to face actual excommunication. The Church of England— aka the Anglican faith—was the phoenix that ultimately rose from the ashes.

Although some accounts of Henry VIII's break with Rome portray the split as "King Marries Temptress, Starts Own Church," the historical reality is slightly more complex.

On one hand, Henry was undeniably enraptured with Anne. Seventeen of his love letters to her—nine of them in French, a language in which both were fluent but precious few other Englishmen were—can be perused today at the Vatican Library in Rome. Henry tells his mistress in one missive that "for more than a year, [I've been] struck with the dart of love." Elsewhere he implores her to give "body and heart to me, who will be, and has been, your most loyal servant."

On the other hand, Henry's extramarital love life wasn't happening in a historical vacuum either. In 1529, what historians now call "the Reformation Parliament" clapped economic and political shackles upon the operation of the Catholic Church in England—regulating excessive fees the church had levied for burials, reducing clergy's ability to make money on the side, and eliminating their de facto above-the-law status by subjecting church officials to the same secular courts as any English commoner.

THE CHUCH OF ENGLAND IS BORN

What momentum Parliament had established was compounded by the rise of two reformist members of Henry's court in the early 1530s: Thomas Cranmer (made Archbishop of Canterbury, the highest ecclesiastical position in the nation, in 1533) and Thomas Cromwell (Henry VIII's chief advisor and principal minister). The two Thomases provided the political and theological muscle to establish an independent church body and, with it, put the squeeze on the Catholic Church in England. In 1533, Cranmer ensured swift approval by his bishops of the annulment of King Henry's first marriage, while at the same time Cromwell's Act in Restraint of Appeals effectively set forth the English monarch as ruler of the British Empire, rendering the papacy irrelevant by deriving a monarch's authority directly from God. The pope, thanks to Cromwell's legislative strong-arm, suddenly had no claim over true English subjects.

Naturally, Pope Clement VII did not take this news lightly, and after three months of threats, excommunicated Henry VIII from the Catholic Church in September 1533. Though true theological reform of the fledgling Anglican Church into a bona fide Protestant sect would have to wait for the brief but outsized reign of Henry's only son, Edward VI (reign 1547–53), there was no turning back. The Church of England had been born.

THE FALLOUT

Both the inspiration and the instigators of the break with Rome eventually met with gruesome deaths: Boleyn lasted all of three years as her king's wife before Henry, in concert with Cromwell, rounded up four courtiers and servants to Boleyn who were all variously charged with luring Boleyn away from the marriage bed. Boleyn was swiftly tried for adultery and beheaded in May 1536. Cromwell lasted only four more years before he too became victim to the capricious whims of his monarch. For proposing a disastrous fourth marriage to Anne of Cleves, Cromwell faced a rigged jury, was found guilty of treason and, at the king's behest, faced the further brutality of an inexperienced executioner. Three unsuccessful ax blows drew out Cromell's pain before a fourth severed his head, which was then boiled and placed on a pike on London Bridge.

Cranmer outlived his king and his king's son, only to face the furies of the brutally anti-Protestant queen "Bloody" Mary Tudor (reign 1553–58).

Yet perhaps it was Anne Boleyn herself who bequeathed the greatest legacy in the form of her daughter, who took the reigns of power at Queen Mary's death. The frail young princess, not expected to survive any longer than her siblings, instead enjoyed a prosperous 45 years on the throne as perhaps England's greatest monarch, Queen Elizabeth I. Under Elizabeth, the Church of England established itself as the ecclesiastical force that underpinned the rise of a true global empire—on whose influence, to this day, the sun never sets.

- *In total, Henry VIII married six times: Catherine of Aragon, Anne Boleyn, Jane Seymour, Anne of Cleves, Kathryn Howard, and Katherine Parr.*

- *Henry had two of his six wives executed (Anne Boleyn and Kathryn Howard). He divorced two (Catherine of Aragon and Anne of Cleves). Jane Seymour died and was the only one of Henry's wives to be buried with him. Katharine Parr was widowed after four years of marriage.*

Fast Facts

- Europeans discovered Australia's hospitable east coast on April 20, 1770, as a secondary directive of an unsuccessful expedition to observe a Venutian eclipse of the sun from the island of Tahiti.

- Sailors aboard explorer James Cook's ship benefited from their captain's belief that fresh vegetables would help prevent many of the sicknesses common to sailors in the 18th century. A beer brewed from cabbage-palm hearts and spruce leaves from New Zealand proved particularly effective at curbing illness.

- Beer was considered a vital component of a meal for young and old in 18th-century Europe. Pupils at London boarding schools breakfasted upon bread and beer, and workhouse residents received a daily ration of brew.

- Bread was so important to the European diet for many centuries that a rise or fall in its price served as an indicator of economic well-being, and a baker who attempted to sell an underweight loaf could be hanged.

- A massive earthquake in northern China in 1557 killed an estimated 830,000 people.

- In 1788, Emperor Joseph II banned the use of coffins. He did so, in part, to draw attention to the growing scarcity of wood as forests succumbed to the demands of a rapidly increasing population.

- Due to rampant smuggling to avoid import duties in the mid-18th century, the average colonist in the American colonies paid $\frac{1}{26}$ the amount of taxes that a citizen living in England paid.

- The British soldiers who held New York at the conclusion of the American War of Independence remained garrisoned there for many years afterward.

MURDER IN THE VATICAN

As head of the Catholic Church, they serve as the Vicar of Christ and are among the world's most respected leaders. Yet over the centuries, this hasn't always been the case for the popes of Rome. Dozens have met untimely fates at the hands of pagan oppressors, rivals to their papal throne, scheming cardinals, plotting aristocrats, and outraged husbands.

Many of the first 25 popes are believed to have been martyred by the Romans. Pontian (230–235) is the first pope recorded by history as having been murdered for his Christian beliefs. Arrested under the orders of Emperor Maximinus Thrax, Pontian was exiled to Sardinia—then known as the "island of death"—where he is believed to have died from starvation and exposure. Sixtus II (257–258) was another early martyr, killed in the persecutions of Emperor Valerian, who condemned all Christian priests, bishops, and deacons to death. Sixtus was arrested by Roman soldiers while giving a sermon and may have been beheaded on the spot. Martin I (649–653) began his papacy on bad terms with Emperor Constans II, who refused to recognize his election. Martin made matters worse by condemning the doctrines of the Monothelite heretics, whose tenets were followed by many powerful Roman officials, including Constans II. Ordered to Constantinople, Martin I was sentenced to death and exiled to the Crimea, where he died of starvation.

The martyrdom of popes passed into history with the fall of the Roman Empire, but the ascendancy of the Catholic Church was accompanied by endless papal intrigues. From the 9th to the 20th centuries—when popes served not only as head of the church but as rulers of the Papal State, a substantial kingdom in central Italy—rumors abounded that many had been murdered.

Most documented murders occurred during the Middle Ages, particularly between 867 and 964, the so-called Iron Age of the Papacy, when the politically powerful families of Rome had pontiffs elected, deposed, and killed to advance their own ambitions. Seven popes died by violence during this period.

The first to receive this dubious honor was Pope John VIII (872–882), who was so concerned about plots swirling around him that he had several powerful bishops and cardinals excommunicated. Unknown conspirators convinced a relative to poison his drink. When the poison failed to kill him, he was clubbed to death by his own aides. According to some accounts, however, Pope John was actually Pope Joan—a female pope who was erased from the historical record when her true identity was uncovered. Though some historians believe Pope Joan is a myth, others point to an obscure Church ritual that began in the late 9th century, in which a papal candidate sat in an elevated chair with his genitals exposed, prompting passing cardinals to exclaim in Latin, "He has testicles, and they hang well!" Lacking a similar endowment, Pope Joan may have paid with her life.

Stephen VI (896–897) was the "mad pope" who placed his rival, the late Pope Formosus, on trial nine months after his death. The dead pope had enraged Stephen by crowning one of the illegitimate heirs of Charlemagne as emperor, after having performed the same rite for Stephen's favorite candidate. Formosus's corpse was disinterred, placed on a throne in the council chambers, and provided with legal council. When Stephen VI had finished hurling abuse at the corpse, it was thrown from a balcony to a waiting mob and dumped into the Tiber River. All ordinations performed by Formosus were annulled. In the tumult that followed among the Roman aristocracy, Stephen was imprisoned and ultimately strangled to death, making way for a saner pontiff.

The papal carnage continued over the next few hundred years. Adrian III (884–885) was allegedly poisoned. Leo V (903) was allegedly strangled. John X (914–928) may have been smothered with a pillow. Both Stephen VII (928–931) and Stephen VIII (939–942) met similar untimely ends due to palace intrigues.

John XII (955–964) was only 18 years old when elected pope. A notorious womanizer, he turned the papal palace into something resembling a brothel. He either suffered a heart attack while with a mistress or was murdered by a cuckolded husband. Pope Benedict V (964–966) raped a young girl and fled to Constantinople with the papal treasury, only to return to Rome when his coffers were empty. He was killed by a jealous husband, his corpse bearing a hundred dagger wounds as it was dragged through the streets.

Benedict VI (973–974) and John XIV (983–984) had strangely parallel fates. Intriguers rebelled against Benedict VI after the death of his protector, Emperor Otto the Great. Benedict VI was strangled by a priest on the orders of Crescentius, brother of the late Pope John XIII. Boniface Franco, a deacon who supported Crescentius, became Pope Boniface VII but fled Rome due to the peoples' outrage over Benedict's murder, becoming Antipope Boniface. John XIV was chosen as a replacement by Emperor Otto II without consultation of the Church. When Otto suddenly died, another new pope was left without allies. Antipope Boniface returned and had John XIV thrown in prison, where he starved to death.

Popes Gregory V (996–999), Sergius IV (1009–1012), Clement II (1046–1047), and Damasus II (1048) were all allegedly poisoned or met otherwise convenient ends. Boniface VIII (1294–1303) died from beatings by his French captors while held prisoner in Anagni. Benedict XI (1304–1305) may have also been poisoned.

Officially, no pope has been murdered in the modern age, though rumors held that Pope Clement XIV was poisoned in 1771, following his disbandment of the Jesuits. Two hundred years passed before such allegations arose again in 1978 with the sudden death of Pope John Paul I, who had planned such reforms as ordaining women as priests and welcoming gays into the church. In both cases, coroners and investigators found no evidence of foul play. John Paul's successor, John Paul II, was nearly murdered in St. Peter's Square in 1981 by Mehmet Ali Agca, a Turkish gunman who was part of a conspiracy involving the KGB and Bulgarian secret police.

A DISCOVERY OF BIBLICAL PROPORTIONS

While rounding up a stray animal near Qumran, Israel, in early 1947, Bedouin shepherd Mohammed el-Hamed stumbled across several pottery jars containing scrolls written in Hebrew. It turned out to be the find of a lifetime.

News of the exciting discovery of ancient artifacts spurred archaeologists to scour the area of the original find for additional material. Over a period of nine years, the remains of approximately 900 documents were recovered from 11 caves near the ruins of Qumran, a plateau community on the northwest shore of the Dead Sea. The documents have come to be known as the Dead Sea Scrolls.

Tests indicate that all but one of the documents were created between the middle of the 2nd century B.C. and the 1st century A.D. Nearly all were written in one of three Hebrew dialects. The majority of the documents were written on animal hide.

The scrolls represent the earliest surviving copies of Biblical documents. Approximately 30 percent of the material is from the Hebrew Bible. Every book of the Old Testament is represented with the exception of the Book of Esther and the Book of Nehemiah. Another 30 percent of the scrolls contain essays on subjects including blessings, war, community rule, and the membership requirements of a Jewish sect. About 25 percent of the material refers to Israelite religious texts not contained in the Hebrew Bible, while 15 percent of the data has yet to be identified.

Since their discovery, debate about the meaning of the scrolls has been intense. One widely held theory subscribes to the belief that the scrolls were created at the village of Qumran and then hidden by the inhabitants. According to this theory, a Jewish sect known as the Essenes wrote the scrolls. Those subscribing to this theory have concluded that the Essenes hid the scrolls in nearby caves during the Jewish Revolt in A.D. 66, shortly before they were massacred by Roman troops.

A second major theory, put forward by Norman Golb, Professor of Jewish History at the University of Chicago, speculates that the scrolls were originally housed in various Jerusalem-area libraries and were spirited out of the city when the Romans besieged the capital in A.D. 68–70. Golb believes that the treasures documented on the so-called Copper Scroll could only have been held in Jerusalem. Golb also alleges that the variety of conflicting ideas found in the scrolls indicates that the documents are facsimiles of literary texts.

The documents were catalogued according to which cave they were found in and have been categorized into Biblical and non-Biblical works. Of the eleven caves, numbers 1 and 11 yielded the most intact documents, while number 4 held the most material—an astounding 15,000 fragments representing 40 percent of the total material found. Multiple copies of the Hebrew Bible have been identified, including 19 copies of the Book of Isaiah, 30 copies of Psalms, and 25 copies of Deuteronomy. Also found were previously unknown psalms attributed to King David, and stories about Abraham and Noah.

Most of the fragments appeared in print between 1950 and 1965, with the exception of the material from Cave 4. Publication of the manuscripts was entrusted to an international group led by Father Roland de Vaux of the Dominican Order in Jerusalem.

Access to the material was governed by a "secrecy rule"—only members of the international team were allowed to see them. In late 1971, 17 documents were published, followed by the release of a complete set of images of all the Cave 4 material. The secrecy rule was eventually lifted, and copies of all documents were in print by 1995.

Many of the documents are now housed in the Shrine of the Book, a wing of the Israel Museum located in Western Jerusalem. The scrolls on display are rotated every three to six months.

TYPHOID MARY— THE MOST DANGEROUS WOMAN IN AMERICA?

There were hundreds, if not thousands, of typhoid carriers in New York at the turn of the 20th century. Only one of them, however, was labeled a menace to society and banished to an island for life.

The popular image of Typhoid Mary in the early 1900s—an image enthusiastically promoted by the tabloids of the day—was of a woman stalking the streets of New York, infecting and killing hundreds of hapless victims. In truth, Mary Mallon, the woman who came to be recognized as Typhoid Mary, is known to have infected 47 people, 3 of whom died.

Mary Mallon immigrated to the United States from Ireland in 1883 at age 15. For a time, she lived with an aunt in New York City, but soon began working as a domestic servant, one of the few avenues of gainful employment open to a poor young woman of the day. Sometime before the turn of the century, she must have contracted and then recovered from a mild case of typhoid. Since a mild case of typhoid can mimic the symptoms of the flu, it is quite possible that she never even knew she had contracted the disease.

Mallon, an excellent cook, was working in the kitchens of the city's wealthiest families. In August 1906, she was hired by banker Charles Warren to cook for his family at their rented summer home on Long Island. After 6 of the 11 people in the house fell ill with typhoid, George Soper, a sanitary engineer, was hired by Charles Warren's landlord to pinpoint the source of the outbreak. Soper's attention eventually focused on the cook. After months of tracing Mary Mallon's job history, Soper discovered that typhoid had struck seven of the eight families for whom she'd cooked.

In March 1907, Mallon was working at a home on Park Avenue when George Soper paid a visit. Soper told Mary that she was a possible typhoid carrier and requested samples of her blood, urine, and feces for testing.

The idea that a healthy person could pass a disease on to others was barely understood by the general public at the time. For someone like Mary Mallon, who prided herself on never being sick, Soper's requests seemed particularly outrageous. Believing herself falsely accused, she picked up a carving fork and angrily forced Soper out of the house.

Because Mallon refused to submit voluntarily to testing, the New York Health Department called in the police. Officers dragged her into an ambulance and, with the city health inspector sitting on top of her, took her kicking and screaming to the Willard Parker Hospital. Tests revealed high concentrations of typhoid bacilli in her blood.

QUARANTINE

Declaring her a public menace, the health department moved Mallon to an isolation cottage on the grounds of the Riverside Hospital on North Brother Island in the East River. She had broken no laws and had not been given a trial, but she remained in quarantine for nearly three years.

In 1909, Mallon sued the health department for her freedom, insisting that she was healthy and that her banishment was illegal and unjustified. The judge ruled against Mallon, and she was sent back to Brother Island. In 1910, a new health department inspector freed her on the condition that she never work as a cook again. Mallon kept her promise for a time, but eventually returned to the only profession she knew that could offer her a decent income.

A 1915 typhoid outbreak at Sloane Maternity Hospital in New York City killed 2 people and infected 25 others. An investigation revealed that a recently hired cook named "Mary Brown" was in fact Mary Mallon. Mallon was immediately returned to her lonely cottage on Brother Island, where she remained quarantined until her death in 1938.

Historians have debated why Mallon was treated so differently than hundreds of other typhoid carriers. At the time of her first arrest, there were 3,000–4,500 new cases of typhoid each year in New York City. Approximately three percent of typhoid fever victims became carriers, which translated to roughly 100 new carriers per year. The city would have gone bankrupt had it tried to quarantine even a handful of them as it did Mallon.

WHY MARY?

Typhoid Mary was not even the deadliest carrier. A man named Tony Labella was responsible for 122 cases and 5 deaths in the 1920s. Despite the fact that he handled food and was uncooperative with authorities, he was isolated for only two weeks and then released. A bakery and restaurant owner named Alphonse Cotils was also a carrier. In 1924, Cotils was arrested after officials discovered him inside his restaurant after being warned to stay away from food. Cotils was released after promising to conduct his business by phone.

So why was Mary Mallon forced into a life of quarantine when others were not? For one thing, Mallon was the first discovered healthy carrier of typhoid. At the time, Mallon, like most people, didn't understand that a healthy person could be a carrier of the disease, so she saw no reason to change her behavior. Mallon's use of an assumed name in the Sloane Maternity Hospital case was also seen by the public as a deliberate act, maliciously designed to put others at risk.

Some historians suspect that Mallon's fate was tied to the fact that she was a single female and an Irish immigrant. Prejudice against the Irish still ran high at the time, and it was considered unnatural—if not immoral—for a woman to remain single all her life. Another strike against Mary Mallon was her work as a domestic servant. Diseases like typhoid fever were associated with the unclean habits of the "lower classes." These factors combined to transform Mary Mallon from a simple woman into the menacing, legendary Typhoid Mary—a threat that had to be contained.

THE DAY KING TUT'S TOMB WAS OPENED

There was a time when archaeology was commissioned privately by wealthy individuals. Some of these benefactors desired to advance historical knowledge, while others simply hoped to enhance their personal collections of antiquities.
The much-heralded opening of the tomb of the Pharaoh Tutankhamun, better known today as "King Tut," represented one of the last hurrahs for these old days of archaeology.

Who was King Tut, anyway?

King Tut was an ancient Egyptian ruler, or pharaoh. His full name, Tutankhamun, meant to say that he was the living image of the sun god, Amun. Tut ruled Egypt from 1333 B.C. to 1324 B.C., during what is referred to as the New Kingdom period. Sometimes called "The Boy King," he became pharaoh when he was 9 years old and died at age 19. Researchers believe Tut died from an infection caused by a broken leg.

How was his tomb located?

Finding the tomb required scholarship, persistence, patience, and lots of digging. A wealthy Englishman, Lord Carnarvon, sponsored one of the day's brightest archaeologists, Howard Carter. With Carnarvon's backing, Carter poked around in Egypt between 1917 and 1922 with little luck. Then, in November 1922, just as Lord Carnarvon was ready to give up, Carter uncovered steps leading down to a tomb marked with Tut's royal seals. Carter dashed off a communiqué to Carnarvon, telling him to get to Egypt, and fast.

What happened next?

Carnarvon wasted no time, and once the sponsor reached the scene, Carter was ready to cut his way into the tomb. Workers soon exposed a sealed doorway bearing Tut's name. Those present would witness the unveiling of history as Carter peered into the tomb. However, thanks to the meticulous nature of archaeology, work on Tut's tomb could only happen at a slow pace. The entire process stretched across ten years.

What was in there?

The contents of the tomb were incredible. It was clear that ancient plunderers had twice raided the tomb for some smaller items. Although they did leave the place a mess, many amazing treasures remained. Carter and company catalogued piles of priceless artifacts, including gold statues and everything from sandals to chariots. Tut's mummified body had been placed in an ornate coffin, and canopic jars held his internal organs. In addition, two mummified premature babies, thought to be Tut's children, were found. Tut was also buried with everything he would need to be stylish in the afterlife, including ornate bows and gloves fit for a pharaoh. Scholars would spend years preserving and studying the artifacts in the tomb.

King Tut's tomb was the archaeological find of that decade—perhaps even the find of the 20th century.

- *Tut's famous mask actually covered the mummy's head. From the side, it looks like what could be an Egyptian deep-sea diver's helmet, contoured to fit the shoulders. This brilliant gold-and-blue glass item, along with the pyramids, remains one of the best-known symbols of ancient Egyptian glory.*

- *Amun, the Egyptian god that Tutankhamun was supposed to embody, was an ancient deity whose roles evolved over the centuries. However, his most celebrated duty was as a sun god.*

- *Why wasn't everything of value in Tut's tomb ripped off by the ancient tomb raiders? The holes hacked through the mortar and rock in antiquity weren't very big and nothing of any size could fit through.*

GHOSTS OF A MURDERED DYNASTY

The fate of Russia's imperial family remained shrouded in mystery for nearly a century.

THE END OF A DYNASTY

In the wake of Russia's 1917 uprisings, Tsar Nicholas II abdicated his shaky throne. He was succeeded by a provisional government, which included Nicholas and his family—his wife, Tsarina Alexandra; his four daughters, Grand Duchesses Olga, Tatiana, Marina, and Anastasia; and his 13-year-old son, Tsarevich Alexei—under house arrest.

When the radical Bolshevik party took power in October 1917, its soldiers seized the royal family and eventually moved them to the Ural Mountain town of Ekaterinburg, where they were held prisoner in the home of a wealthy metallurgist. As civil war waged between the "White" and "Red" factions in Russia, the Bolsheviks worried that the White Army might try to free the royal family and use its members as a rallying point. When White troops neared Ekaterinburg in July 1918, the local executive committee decided to kill Nicholas II and his family.

The bedraggled imperial family was rudely awakened by their captors in the middle of the night. The sounds of battle echoed not far from the spacious home that had become their makeshift prison, and the prisoners were ordered to take shelter in the basement. Outside the basement, a waiting truck revved its engine.

After a long wait, the head jailer reappeared, brandishing a pistol and backed by ten men armed with rifles and pistols. He declared, "Because your relatives in Europe carry on their war against Soviet Russia, the Executive Committee of the Ural has decided to execute you." Raising his revolver, he fired into Tsar Nicholas II's chest as his family watched in horror.

With that shot, the militia opened fire. Bullets ricocheted around the room as family members dove for cover, trying to escape the deadly fusillade. None made it. The wounded children who clung to life after the firing stopped were dragged into the open and set upon with rifle butts and bayonets until all lay quiet in the blood-splattered room. Tsar Nicholas II, the last of the Romanov emperors, died alongside his beloved family.

A BUNGLED BODY DISPOSAL

After the murders, the bodies were taken by truck into nearby woods, stripped, and thrown into an abandoned mine pit. The corpses were visible above the pit's shallow waterline. Fearing that the bodies would be discovered, the communist officials tried to burn them the following day. When that did not work, they decided to move the bodies to a deeper mine pit farther down the road. The truck got stuck in deep mud on the way to the mines, so the men dug a shallow grave in the mud, buried the bodies, and covered them with acid, lime, and wooden planks, where they remained untouched until their discovery in 1979.

In his official report, the lead executioner, Yakov Yurovsky, stated that two of the bodies were buried and burned separately, giving rise to speculation that one or two of the Romanov children escaped the massacre. Several pretenders came forth claiming to be Tsarevich Alexei, heir to the Russian throne, and his sister Grand Duchess Maria. But the most famous of the "undead Romanovs" was young Anastasia.

DID ANASTASIA SURVIVE?

Anastasia, the fourth daughter of Nicholas and Alexandra, was 17 at the time of the executions. At least ten women have stepped forward claiming to be the lost grand duchess. The most famous of these was the strange case of Anna Tchaikovsky.

In Berlin, two years after the murders, a woman named Anna Tchaikovsky, hospitalized for an attempted suicide, claimed to be Anastasia. She explained that she had been wounded but survived the slaughter with the help of a compassionate Red Army soldier, who smuggled her out of Russia through Romania.

Anna bore a striking physical resemblance to the missing Anastasia, enough to convince several surviving relatives that she was indeed the last of the imperial family. She also revealed details that would be hard for an impostor to know—for instance, she knew of a secret meeting between Anastasia's uncle, the grand duke of Hesse, and Nicholas II in 1916, when the two men's countries were at war.

Other relatives, however, rejected Anna's claim, noting, among other things, that Anna Tchaikovsky refused to speak Russian (although she understood the language and would respond to Russian questions in other languages). A drawn-out German court case Anna commenced in 1938 to claim her inheritance ended in 1970 with no firm conclusions.

Anna, later named Anna Anderson, died in 1984. It was not until DNA evidence became available in the 1990s that her claim to imperial lineage could finally be disproved.

THE ROMANOV GHOSTS

But what of the hidden remains?

After the location of the royal resting place was made public in 1979, nine skeletons were exhumed from the muddy pit. The bodies of the royal couple and three of their children—Olga and Tatiana, as well as one other daughter, whose identity has been disputed—were identified by DNA tests as Romanov family members. Their remains, as well as those of four servants who died with them, were interred in 1998 near Nicholas's imperial predecessors in St. Petersburg.

By all accounts, 11 people met their deaths that terrible night in July 1918. In late August 2007, two more bodies were found in a separate grave near Ekaterinburg. Though DNA tests are still pending, regional authorities believe the bodies were those of Tsarevich Alexei and the last of the four Romanov sisters. Should testing confirm their identities, the mystery of Anastasia will at last be solved.

Fast Facts

- China did not ban slavery until 1908; the African country of Mauritania did not ban it until 1980.

- By 1820, the United States had received slightly more African slaves than free European settlers. However, whites formed the majority population because they had a higher birth rate and lower death rate.

- Switzerland produced the first guidebook in the 19th century.

- Napoleon, employing the labor of 30,000 men, built the first road across the Alps.

- The word "timetable" was first used in 1838 in reference to the new train system developing in England. Before the advent of trains, the likelihood of a traveler arriving on time was so remote as to make the word unnecessary.

- In 1839, the first commercial telegraph lines were established by railway companies in England to ease the demands of the ever-increasing rail traffic. Only later did they begin allowing individuals to transmit personal messages.

- The first transatlantic telegraph line was completed in 1858 but only functioned for two weeks before it fell silent. Another laid in 1866 was successful.

- The first automatic telephone exchange capable of transmitting messages 24 hours a day was established in 1892 in the town of La Porte, Indiana.

- The first telephone cable across the North Atlantic was not laid until 1956.

- In 1860, London was the largest city in the world with a population of three million people.

- It was not until the German biologist Robert Koch's work with anthrax in the 1870s that bacteria were discovered to be the cause of disease.

WITCHES TO THE GALLOWS

In 1692, the quiet little town of Salem Village, Massachusetts, convulsed in the grip of witchcraft. The only way the town could save itself was to track down every last witch and hang them from the gallows. Or so the elders of Salem thought.

In the early 1690s, Salem Village, a small Massachusetts town on the Danvers River, was experiencing growing pains. It was making the rough move from farming community to mercantile center; a violent Indian war raged less than 100 miles away; and poor harvests and disease frequently threatened the Puritans who lived there. The community weathered a rough winter in early 1692, and as spring approached, odd behavior among some local children began to frighten the adults.

In February 1692, nine-year-old Betty Parris, the daughter of a local preacher brought in from Boston, began acting wildly. She ran about screaming, dove under furniture, contorted in pain, and complained of fever. There was no obvious medical explanation for Betty's condition, but a local minister named Cotton Mather thought he had found one: Betty was a victim of witchcraft. When two of Betty's playmates showed similar symptoms and local medicines failed to cure them, the townspeople drew the only logical conclusion: There was a witch in their midst.

Suspicion first fell on a Caribbean slave named Tituba, who worked in Betty's home. Tituba had been known to tell the children stories of West Indian voodoo, and when Tituba was caught trying to cure Betty by feeding a "devil cake" to a dog (dogs being common forms of demons), Tituba's guilt seemed assured.

The hunt for Salem's witches took a new turn when the afflicted girls, now seven in all, began accusing other local women of sending evil spirits against them. Tituba and two others were hauled into Ingersoll's Tavern on March 1 and examined by local magistrates. Thoroughly frightened, Tituba confessed to being a witch.

Tituba's confession lit a powder keg that would claim the lives of 19 men and women before it was over. Four more women, along with the four-year-old daughter of one of the accused, were collectively accused of sending spirits to torment their accusers. (The young daughter, jailed for eight months, watched as her mother was carted off to the gallows.) The young accusers grew more theatrical in their stories, and during the next several months, they and other witnesses identified some 200 townspeople as witches, all of whom were thrown into the colony's jail.

Panic spread. To get a handle on the growing alarm, Governor William Phips commissioned a seven-judge court to try the accused of witchcraft, a capital offense under Massachusetts law. At Reverend Mather's urging, the court admitted "spectral evidence"—testimony that an accuser had seen the ghostly specter of a witch—as well as evidence of "witch's teats," moles on a defendant's body on which a familiar spirit, such as a black cat, might suckle. The judges found the evidence persuasive, and when one jury failed to convict an accused woman, the court's chief justice, William Stoughton, instructed the jury to reconsider; it then returned with a verdict of guilt.

Armed with this compelling evidence, the court had no choice but to execute the newly discovered witches. Between June 10 and September 22, 19 men and women (one of whom was the village's ex-minister) were carted off to Gallows Hill and hanged. The 80-year-old husband of one witch, who refused to participate in his trial, was punished by pressing, a gruesome execution method in which the sheriff placed large stones on the man's chest until he expired. Four others died in prison, and two dogs were executed as accomplices to witchcraft.

By August, the town's mania began to subside. Better-educated villagers questioned the fantastic evidence against the accused, and in May 1693, Governor Phips shut down the proceedings and freed all remaining defendants. One judge made a public apology for sentencing so many to death, and several jurors admitted that they had been horribly misled by juvenile actors, hysterical townspeople, and fanatical judges.

Timeline

Continued from page 361.

1682
The Apple Still Doesn't Fall Far from the Tree. England's Isaac Newton publishes his *Principia*, a monumental work that defined human understanding of gravitation and mechanics until the early 20th century.

1692
Salem witch trials result in the hanging of 19 accused witches. The chief prosecutor, a hard-nosed witch hater, refuses to admit he was wrong and becomes the next governor of Massachusetts.

1701
Old World, New Wars. The War of Spanish Succession engulfs western Europe. Catholic France and Spain battle Protestant England and Holland on land and at sea over the religion of the to-be-named Spanish monarch. When the conflict ends in 1714, French hegemony over the western continent is sharply curtailed.

1707
The Acts of Union merges England, Wales, and Ireland with Scotland to create the Kingdom of Great Britain.

1709
Growing Bear. Russia's Peter the Great defeats Sweden's Charles XII at the Battle of Poltava, establishing Russia as the dominant kingdom in Eastern Europe and the Baltic region. Peter founds the city of St. Petersburg as his new administrative capital.

1740
The eight-year War of Austrian Succession pits Prussia, France, Spain, Sweden, and Bavaria against Austria, Britain, Holland, Saxony, and Russia. The war commences a rivalry between Prussia and Austria over dominance of the German-speaking lands.

c. 1750
The African slave trade reaches its peak, filling fields in the Caribbean and North America with kidnapped laborers.

1756–1763
The Seven Years War. Largely a struggle between Britain and France, this first "world war" sees Britain take control of New France (Canada).

1760s
Inventions like the water-powered spinning frame (for textiles) and an efficient steam engine lay the foundations for the Industrial Revolution—in which Britain takes an early lead.

1762
French philosopher Jean-Jacques Rousseau publishes *The Social Contract,* a key document of the Enlightenment—an intellectual movement skeptical of organized religion and favoring individual freedom.

1775–1783
Colonists in Britain's 13 North American colonies successfully throw off British rule after a long military struggle. The new United States of America draws up a con-

Timeline

stitution in 1787; George Washington is elected president in 1789.

1782–1801
Revolution spreads to the Caribbean and Latin America. A revolt against Spanish rule fails, but a former slave, Toussaint L'Ouverture, establishes Haiti's independence from France.

1789–1795
The storming of the Bastille prison in Paris begins the French Revolution. The movement descends into widespread bloodshed (including the execution of King Louis XVI and his queen, Marie Antoinette, in 1793).

1803–1848
Territorial expansion in the United States; the Louisiana Purchase (1803), war with Mexico (1846–1848), and other acquisitions see the nation expand to the Pacific coast.

1804
Napoleon Bonaparte declares himself emperor of France; over the next eight years, he conquers much of Europe.

1808–1830
Spain's South American colonies achieve independence after much struggle by leaders such as Simon Bolivar, Bernardo O'Higgins Riqueime, and Jose de San Martin.

1812–1815
Napoleon's European empire founders after a disastrous invasion of Russia and defeat at the hands of a British-led coalition at the Battle of Waterloo in Belgium.

1823–1854
Western nations led by Britain make inroads into China during the "Opium Wars"; the United States opens a reclusive Japan to international trade.

1848
A Year of Revolutions. Nationalist and democratic movements take to the streets in Prussia, Italy, France, and Hungary. Most are unsuccessful. Karl Marx and Friedrich Engels publish *The Communist Manifesto.*

1857–1858
Britain asserts control of the Indian subcontinent following a failed "rebellion." India becomes the "jewel in the crown" of a rapidly expanding British Empire.

1860–1871
Nationalist movements establish the modern states of Italy and Germany.

1861–1865
The American Civil War. After four years and 600,000 deaths, the Union defeats a confederacy of southern states and outlaws slavery in the United States.

1867–1868
Canada achieves dominion status within the British Empire. Japan begins to modernize under the rule of Emperor Meiji.

c. 1880–1900
The "Scramble for Africa"; by the end of the 19th century practically the entire continent is under European colonization.

Wondering what happened next? Turn to page 469 to find out!

PRESIDENTIAL NICKNAMES

Nicknames can be a measure of a president's notoriety or place in history. Few people remember the nicknames of lesser-known presidents such as James Buchanan ("Old Fogey") or Millard Fillmore ("The Wool-Carder President"). Yet other presidential nicknames have endured throughout history.

Theodore Roosevelt, deemed a great president by many, had quite a few memorable nicknames. Teddy Roosevelt was known as "The Trustbuster," who broke up giant corporations, and "The Rough Rider," whose wartime heroics in Cuba made him "The Hero of San Juan Hill." Yet Roosevelt was also cruelly dubbed "Old Four Eyes" for his pronounced myopia and "The Meddler" for his intervention in many sectors of society.

Abraham Lincoln was best known as "Honest Abe," but the 16th president had other monikers as well. His supporters hailed Father Abraham as "The Rail Splitter" and "The Great Emancipator." His detractors, playing on his long limbs, tagged him "The Illinois Ape." Abolitionists, who viewed him as weak on civil rights, called him "The Slave Hound from Illinois."

Two recent presidents, Bill Clinton and Ronald Reagan, had an array of nicknames both good and bad. Clinton has been called "The Comeback Kid," "Bubba," and "Slick Willie." Reagan was dubbed "The Great Communicator," "The Gipper," and "Bonzo"—the latter a reference to the chimp costar of one of the ex-actor's films. Reagan also had a nickname any politician would crave: "The Teflon President"—meaning that few criticisms stuck to him.

It seems odd that the longest-serving president, Franklin Delano Roosevelt, had no lasting nicknames except for his initials, FDR. Shortening Roosevelt's name to initials set a precedent for some future chief executives, namely JFK (John Fitzgerald Kennedy), and LBJ (Lyndon Baines Johnson).

Some nicknames fit the character like a well-measured shoe. Feisty Harry Truman was dubbed "Give 'Em Hell Harry" after voters' shouts of support during his 1948 whistle-stop campaign. And a presidential nickname may never have fit better than the one for tight-lipped Calvin Coolidge: "Silent Cal." At one state dinner, a guest told Coolidge she had wagered friends that she could get at least three words out of the Sphinx of the Potomac. Coolidge replied: "You lose."

Many nicknames were hard to live down. The guileful Richard Nixon was known as "Tricky Dick" and "The Trickster." And Chester A. Arthur was called "Prince Arthur" due to his weakness for fine clothes and accommodations. Grover Cleveland, who holds the record for most presidential vetoes, was dubbed "His Obstinacy." Worse, Cleveland was called "The Hangman of Buffalo" (while sheriff in Buffalo, New York, Cleveland personally slipped the noose around two felons). And the grandly named Rutherford B. Hayes was tagged "RutherFraud" after his disputed 1876 election.

Nicknames can be used for political advantage. Dwight Eisenhower used his for a catchy campaign slogan: "I Like Ike." (His college football moniker, "The Kansas Cyclone," was left on the sidelines.) George W. Bush used his mildly derisive nickname, "Dubya," to tweak opponent Al Gore's supposed invention of the Internet, noting that he himself was referred to as "Dubya, Dubya, Dubya," as in the World Wide Web.

One presidential nickname might have led to the most widely uttered phrase in English. Martin Van Buren, who hailed from Kinderhook, New York, was called "Old Kinderhook," which was then shortened to "OK." The name caught on.

Many recent nicknames, reflecting our less formal times, are simply shortened first names. Two notable examples are Bill Clinton and Jimmy Carter. Gerald Ford was often called Jerry. The more formal Ronald Reagan was never referred to as Ronnie—except by his wife, Nancy. And the name must suit the man: When Richard Nixon referred to himself as Dick, it came across as forced informality.

Some nicknames are stirring, especially those gained in the military. Zachary Taylor was called "Old Rough and Ready" for his spartan style of fighting the Mexican army. Andrew Jackson was named "Old Hickory" for leading a campaign against the Creek Indians while recovering from a dueling wound. William Henry Harrison was dubbed "Tippecanoe" to commemorate the name of his victorious battle in another Indian war. Ulysses S. Grant was known as "Unconditional Surrender" for his relentless leadership in the Civil War.

Yet some nicknames are deflating. As president of an often ineffective government, Ulysses S. Grant was derided as "Useless" Grant. John Tyler was called "His Accidency" when he took office after the untimely death of William Henry Harrison. Franklin Pierce was dubbed "The Fainting General" for having been knocked unconscious during a Mexican-American War battle when his saddle horn collided hard with his stomach. James Madison, best known as "The Father of the Constitution," was vilified as "The Fugitive President" for fleeing Washington, D.C., during the British invasion of 1814.

And when then-Vice President John Adams suggested that George Washington be referred to as "His Majesty," Adams's foes were so irked by the regal, undemocratic-sounding title that they responded by sticking the stout VP with his own honorific: "His Rotundity."

Presidential Nicknames: A Rundown

Here's a quick list of presidential nicknames, both good and bad, beginning with George Washington:

George Washington
His Excellency

John Adams
Old Sink or Swim
Your Superfluous Excellency

James Madison
Little Jemmy or His Little Majesty
(Madison was 5'4" tall)

James Monroe
The Last of the Cocked Hats

John Quincy Adams
Old Man Eloquent

Andrew Jackson
The Hero of New Orleans
King Andrew the First

Martin Van Buren
The Red Fox of Kinderhook
The Little Magician

William Henry Harrison
Granny Harrison
General Mum

John Tyler
The President Without a Party

James K. Polk
Young Hickory
Polk the Plodder

Zachary Taylor
The Hero of Buena Vista

Millard Fillmore
The Accidental President
The American Louis Philippe

Franklin Pierce
Handsome Frank

James Buchanan
Ten-Cent Jimmie
Old Buck

Abraham Lincoln
Honest Abe
The Rail-Splitter
The Uncommon Friend of the
Common Man

Andrew Johnson
Sir Veto

Ulysses S. Grant
The American Caesar

James A. Garfield
The Preacher President

Chester A. Arthur
The Dude President

Grover Cleveland
Uncle Jumbo
Grover the Good

Benjamin Harrison
Kid Gloves Harrison

William McKinley
Wobbly Willie

Theodore Roosevelt
Theodore the Meddler

Harry S. Truman
Haberdasher Harry

John Fitzgerald Kennedy
The King of Camelot

Richard Nixon
Richard the Chicken-Hearted
Iron Butt

Gerald Ford
Mr. Nice Guy
Jerry the Jerk

Ronald Reagan
Dutch
The Great Prevaricator

George H. W. Bush
Poppy
Bush 41, Bush the Elder, or Papa
Bush

Bill Clinton
Teflon Bill

George W. Bush
Bush 43, Bush the Younger, or
Bush II
Uncurious George or Incurious
George
The Decider or The Decider-In-
Chief
The Velcro President

HOW LONG WAS THE HUNDRED YEARS WAR?

Although a monumental medieval-era struggle between England and France lasted more than 100 years, the actual fighting took only a fraction of that period. So how long did the war really last? It depends how you do the math.

KING OF ENGLAND, KING OF FRANCE

The Hundred Years War started in 1337 when a legal dispute over the French crown turned violent. English nobles believed that their king, Edward III, was next in line to rule France because his mother was sister to French King Charles IV, who had no direct male heir. French nobles, uneasy at the idea of an English king of France, disagreed. Their choice was nobleman Philip of Valois, who claimed that his own lineage from a 13th-century French king—through his father—gave him the more legitimate claim to the throne.

Valois's ships raided English seaports, and Edward invaded French territory. The hostilities had begun. After Charles IV died in early 1328, Valois was crowned Philip VI. Philip attacked Edward's forces in Aquitaine, a French region long ruled by England. Many English invasions of France followed, with the English—whose claims to French lands dated to 1066—repeatedly gaining ground and the French repeatedly striking back.

PEACE BREAKS OUT

Although successive English kings steadfastly claimed the right to rule France, England lacked the resources to fight nonstop over many decades. It had other conflicts to deal with—military campaigns in Ireland, for example—and domestic strife such as the 1399 coup when Henry Bolingbroke stole the English crown from his cousin Richard II and became Henry IV.

France, meanwhile, fought other battles, too—including rebellious outbreaks by French nobles against the crown. Out of necessity, both sides agreed to long truces with one another. For example, peace erupted in 1360 and lasted nine placid years.

Sometimes the warring royal families cemented a truce with intermarriage. In 1396, England's Richard II married the child princess Isabelle, a daughter of French king Charles VI. Twenty-four years later, England's Henry V married Isabelle's little sister Catherine as part of a treaty he imposed on the French after his crushing victory at the battle of Agincourt in 1415 and after another successful campaign in 1417–1419.

THE CULMINATION

Although English invaders won major territorial concessions from the French over most of the war's duration, the tide turned in France's favor in 1429. That was when the peasant girl Joan of Arc rallied French forces and freed the city of Orléans from an English siege. The next 23 years saw the most intense fighting of the Hundred Years War, culminating with a French victory at the Battle of Castillon in 1453. England lost all of its lands on the European continent except for the port city of Calais.

The English didn't give up their claim to France for centuries—but with a civil conflict called the Wars of the Roses breaking out at home, they stopped attacking their continental neighbor. The Hundred Years War was over, after 116 years. It's correct to say that the war lasted well over a century. However, it's just about impossible to subtract all the lulls and truces with accuracy. If you could, you would come out with fewer than 100 years of war.

FAMOUS LAST WORDS

"We make war that we may live in peace."

—ARISTOTLE

GREAT OBSCURE QUOTES

*"If one morning I walked on top of the water across
the Potomac River, the headline that afternoon would read:
"President Can't Swim."*

—LYNDON B. JOHNSON

*"History is more or less bunk. It's tradition. We don't want
tradition. We want to live in the present and the only history that
is worth a tinker's damn is the history we make today."*

—HENRY FORD

"History is a set of lies agreed upon."

—NAPOLEON BONAPARTE

*"I hold that no man should ever put away a wife except for
adultery—not always even for that... I do not say that wives have
never been put away in our Church, but that I do not approve
of the practice."*

—BRIGHAM YOUNG, INTERVIEWED IN THE *NEW YORK TRIBUNE*, JULY 13, 1859

*"The U.S. Constitution doesn't guarantee happiness, only the
pursuit of it. You have to catch up with it yourself."*

—BENJAMIN FRANKLIN

FROM COTTON FIELD TO MANSION

*Born to former slaves and hit hard by fate,
this ambitious woman became a cosmetics queen and devoted
herself to African-American affairs.*

Decades before Oprah Winfrey arrived on the scene, an African-American woman built a business empire that made her immensely wealthy. Like Oprah, she used much of that wealth in the service of good causes. But Madame C. J. Walker did this at a time when segregation was the law of much of the land, and economic opportunities for African-Americans—let alone African-American women—were practically nonexistent.

"THERE IS NO ROYAL, FLOWER-STREWN ROAD TO SUCCESS"

A Louisiana native, Madame was born to former slaves in 1867 and named Sarah Breedlove. She had a crushingly hard early life, picking cotton as a little girl, and finding herself orphaned by the time she was seven. Sarah married at 14, and by 20 she was a widow with a young daughter.

Sarah moved to St. Louis, where she labored as a laundress and cook. A mysterious scalp ailment that left her bald inspired her to develop a restorative compound she dubbed "Madam Walker's Wonderful Hair Grower" (she'd taken the name "Madame C. J. Walker" after marrying a man named Charles Walker). A carefully recruited network of African-American saleswomen distributed the product door-to-door and helped make Madame's enterprise a huge success.

PHILANTHROPIST

In 1910, Walker established a factory in Indianapolis to manufacture the hair grower and other cosmetics. By 1917, Walker's company had assets of a million dollars—a huge sum at the time and an unprecedented achievement for someone of her background.

Walker built a townhouse in New York City's Harlem neighborhood and a magnificent estate, Villa Lewaro, in suburban Westchester County. But Madame Walker was a philanthropist as well as an entrepreneur. She gave generous financial support to organizations devoted to improving the lives of her fellow African-Americans—including the newly founded National Association for the Advancement of Colored People (NAACP).

Her influence went beyond just giving money: She traveled to the White House as part of a delegation protesting lynching in the South, and she regularly hosted the leading African-American intellectuals and activists of the day.

Madame Walker died on May 25, 1919. In her words, "There is no royal, flower-strewn road to success, and what success I have obtained is the result of many sleepless nights and real hard work."

FAMOUS LAST WORDS

"I am a woman who came from the cotton fields of the South. From there I was promoted to the washtub. From there I was promoted to the cook kitchen. And from there I promoted myself into the business of manufacturing hair goods and preparations.... I have built my own factory on my own ground."
—MADAM WALKER,
NATIONAL NEGRO BUSINESS LEAGUE CONVENTION, JULY 1912

Fast Facts

- The brown shirts worn by Hitler's early private army in the Nationalist Socialist German Workers' Party were purchased on the cheap because they had originally been intended for German soldiers defending colonies in East Africa.

- In 1938, Time *magazine named Adolf Hitler its Man of the Year. Of course,* Time's *selection was based on significance and influence—not on objective merit.*

- The first time the emperor of Japan's voice was broadcast on radio was when he announced his decision to surrender to the Allies at the conclusion of the Second World War.

- The European Union has its origins in a six-member free-trade zone established in 1952 for the exchange of coal, iron, and steel. By the 1970s, it had expanded to become the largest common market in history. In 1993, the scope grew beyond economics when the political alliance known as the European Union reached fruition.

- One-third of the world's people lived under European colonial rule at the start of the Second World War.

- Mahatma Gandhi learned the habit of fasting from his mother and practiced it himself while working as a lawyer in South Africa.

- In 1980, the state of Ohio contained more universities than the entire African continent.

- In 1666, the Great Fire destroyed 373 acres of London. It started when the King's baker, Thomas Farynor, forgot to extinguish his oven before retiring for the night.

- The death of the Chinese emperor in 74 B.C. was relayed more than 800 miles in less than 30 hours by the use of smoke signals.

- The rebellious forces of Hung Hsui-chuan during China's Taiping Rebellion contained 100,000 female soldiers led by his sister.

LORDS OF THE RISING SUN

*For nearly 800 years, they held the power of life and death in
the Heavenly Kingdom. The supreme lords of the samurai,
they were called shogun.*

THE RISE OF THE SHOGUN

Since ancient times, the title *sei-i taishogun*, or "great general
who subdues barbarians," had been awarded to the highest military officers recognized by Japan's imperial court at Kyoto. But in
A.D. 1184, the title took on a new, more powerful meaning. That
year, General Minamoto Yoritomo wrested power from the
emperor during a brutal civil war. Thus was born the *shogunate*,
a period in which the emperor retained formal power—as man-
dated by heaven—but where the real power lay with the shogun
(the short form of *sei-i taishogun*) and his administrators.

Two great houses nominally ruled a patchwork of warring feudal
provinces from 1192 to 1600, when one climactic battle settled
Japan's affairs for the next two and a half centuries. At the Battle
of Sekigahara, nearly 150,000 samurai, retainers, musketeers,
and men-at-arms viciously fought against one another in two rival
factions. In a bloody day of fighting, General Tokugawa Ieyasu
destroyed his rivals and emerged as master of Japan.

Tokugawa established the Tokugawa shogunate at Edo (now
called Tokyo) and began his reign by redistributing lands and
political power among his most loyal vassals. Two years after taking office, he abdicated, putting into practice the Japanese custom
of officially retiring, but sharing the governing of the country
with his son, Hidetada. Hidetada and his successors consolidated
the shogun's authority, and the Tokugawa dynasty survived as the
dominant Japanese government until 1868.

RULE BY THE SWORD

The Tokugawa ruled Japan with an iron fist. Its early governors
banned Christianity along with other Western influences. They

established a formal caste system that placed *samurai,* the warrior class akin to Western knights, at the top of the hierarchy, followed by farmers, artisans, and merchants. The great *han,* or provinces (akin to European duchies), were ruled by the *daimyo,* powerful nobles who were required to live at the Edo court every other year and keep their family members in Edo when they spent their alternating years at home.

In the late 1630s to early 1640s, the Tokugawa imposed sharp limitations on foreign business and immigration that created an insular kingdom, little known to the outside world until the turbulent 19th century. As a result of this strict control, Japan grew up in isolation, creating new forms of philosophy, poetry, and literature within its borders and promoting trade almost exclusively within the kingdom.

The shogunate system was efficient but inflexible and fostered a groundswell of local dissent that percolated under the surface during its 264-year reign. Lower classes chafed at the impossibility of advancement on merit, while the business class became frustrated by the shogun's monopoly on foreign trade.

BREAKING THE SWORD

In the mid-1800s, foreign powers pushed Japan into accepting the outside world. In 1853, Commodore Matthew Perry led a U.S. naval squadron into Tokyo Bay in a dramatic display of American military might, and the following year coerced the shogun into opening diplomatic relations with the United States. As foreign powers forced the shogunate to open its borders, Japanese liberals began pressing for a restoration of the emperor's powers. The last Tokugawa shogun abdicated his throne in November 1867, and civil war broke out between forces backing Emperor Meiji and those of the former shogun. The Boshin War, or "War of the Year of the Dragon," ended in early 1869 with the destruction of the emperor's foes, many of whom met their ends in the ancient suicide ritual of *seppuku.*

The age of the mighty shogun had ended.

PRESTON TUCKER: AUTOMOBILE DREAMS

An old adage of invention is that if you build a better mousetrap, the world will beat a path to your door. In the case of Preston Tucker, he built a better car... but the resulting knock at his door came from the federal government.

Preston Tucker couldn't leave things alone. In approximately 1919, at the young age of 16, he acquired an old car, fixed it up, and sold it—already demonstrating two of the skills that would occupy his life: building cars and selling them (or if not selling actual cars, at least selling the idea of them). Tucker's skills would lead him to fame, if not quite to fortune.

Tucker briefly had a job on a Ford assembly line; he also worked as a police officer, but was reprimanded for modifying his patrol car. He moved into car sales, tried his hand at modifying the engines of Indy race cars, and—after the onset of World War II—built gear for the military. His design for a combat car had an incredible top speed of around 120 miles an hour—well beyond the specifications provided by the military—and was rejected because it was too fast. However, the car's machine gun turret was quickly adopted by the navy and eventually saw service on B-17 and B-29 bombers as well.

Following the war, America's automobile industry moved quickly back into peacetime production. The easiest path for manufacturers was to recycle existing prewar designs with some cosmetic modification. In the booming postwar economy, demand was so high that cars essentially sold themselves. Preston Tucker had other ideas. A wealth of new knowledge had come out of the war, including aerodynamics, material science, and the craft of building high-performance engines. Tucker was sure that the American public would embrace a revolutionary automobile, and he set out to build "the car of the future."

"WHERE IS MY CAR?"

Tucker assembled a talented team of mechanics and other professionals, including designer Alex Tremulis, who had previously worked for automobile manufacturers Cord and Duesenberg. They went to work in the enormous Dodge Aircraft Engine Factory, a complex covering 475 acres in Cicero, Illinois, that had been used to build B-29 bombers during World War II. Tucker's car design was considerably advanced for the time: It was to have four-wheel disc brakes, fuel injection, magnesium wheels, and would be powered by an engine designed for an aircraft. Unfortunately, a number of the innovations were eventually cut in the interest of keeping the price of the car down. Still, their removal couldn't diminish the scope of Tucker's original vision.

The Tucker Torpedo, as it was called during design, was intended to be the safest car of the time: The windshield was designed to harmlessly pop out during a collision; the dashboard was padded; a center front headlight would swivel to match the driver's steering; and the instrument panel was designed not to injure the occupants of the car in the case of a collision. The design also included seat belts. Since no other car manufacturers were using them, company officials feared that their presence would give the impression that the Tucker Torpedo was unsafe. Tremulis was given six days to design the car and succeeded. Two clay models were also built, but the 51 cars in the production run were largely constructed using only Tremulis's sketches as a reference. The Tucker 48s, as the final model of the car was called, were all hand-built—the factory never got a full production line up and running.

TUCKER'S DEMISE

The years 1947 to 1949 marked the end of the Tucker Corporation and its remarkable car. Concern over Tucker's fund-raising techniques—the company sold accessories and even licenses for dealerships before any cars actually existed—caused the Securities and Exchange Commission to launch an investigation that effectively put the company out of business. Investigators questioned whether Tucker ever really intended to mass-produce a car, and if he did, whether the company was capable of meeting production demands. Preston Tucker believed that the investigation was an attempt by rival automakers to crush his efforts so they wouldn't have to compete with the innovative Tucker 48 in the marketplace. In 1950, a jury acquitted Preston Tucker of wrongdoing, but by then it was too late—the company was already out of business.

After the trial, Preston Tucker continued with plans to produce a sports car in Brazil, but he died in 1956 before his ideas could come to fruition. Of the Tucker 48s that were built, nearly all still remain in existence, and they have become legendary in automotive circles. They regularly sell at auction in the $400,000 range, with one example going for around $750,000—quite an increase over the original sticker price of $2,450. The vehicles themselves are proudly displayed in museums and at car shows around the world, and Preston Tucker's story was the subject of *Tucker: The Man and His Dream*, a 1988 movie by Francis Ford Coppola. While many of the features of the Tucker have found their way into the standard design of modern cars, none of these descendants can quite match the legend of the 1948 Tucker—an American original.

FAMOUS LAST WORDS

"That the automobile has practically reached the limit of its development is suggested by the fact that during the past year no improvements of a radical nature have been introduced."
—SCIENTIFIC AMERICAN, JANUARY 1909

HEY, IT'S THE FREEMASONS!

For many, talk of "Freemasonry" conjures up images of intricate handshakes, strange rituals, and harsh punishment for revealing secrets about either. In actuality, the roots of the order are brotherhood and generosity. Throughout the ages, Masons have been known to fiercely protect their members and the unique features of their society.

The fantastically named Most Ancient and Honorable Society of Free and Accepted Masons began like other guilds; it was a collection of artisans brought together by their common trade, in this case, stone cutting and crafting. (There are many speculations as to when the society first began. Some believe it dates back to when King Solomon's temple was built. Others believe the guild first formed in Scotland in the 16th century.) The Freemasons made the welfare of their members a priority. Group elders devised strict work regulations for masons, whose skills were always in demand and were sometimes taken advantage of.

Organized Freemasonry emerged in Great Britain in the mid-17th century with the firm establishment of Grand Lodges and smaller, local Lodges. (No one overarching body governs Freemasonry as a whole, though lodges worldwide are usually linked either to England or France.) In 1730, transplanted Englishmen established the first American Lodge in Virginia, followed in 1733 by the continent's first chartered and opened Grand Lodge in Massachusetts. Boasting early American members including George Washington, Benjamin Franklin, and John Hancock, Freemasonry played a part in the growth of the young nation in ways that gradually attracted curiosity, speculation, and concern.

The source of the organization's mysterious reputation lay partly in its secrecy: Masons were prohibited from revealing secrets (some believed Masons would be violently punished if they revealed secrets, though the Masons deny such rumors). The Masonic bond also emphasized a commitment to one another. Outsiders feared the exclusivity smacked of conspiracy and compromised the motives of Masons appointed to juries or elected to public office. And nonmembers wondered about the meanings of the Freemasons' peculiar traditions (such as code words and other secretive forms of recognition between members) and symbolism (often geometric shapes or tools, such as the square and compass). Design elements of the one-dollar bill, including the Great Seal and the "all-seeing eye," have been credited to founding fathers such as Charles Thomson and other Masons.

Freemasonry in the United States suffered a serious blow in September 1826 when New York Masons abducted a former "brother" named William Morgan. Morgan was about to publish a book of Masonic secrets, but before he could, he was instead ushered north to the Canadian border and, in all likelihood, thrown into the Niagara River. His disappearance led to the arrest and conviction of three men on kidnapping charges (Morgan's body was never found)—scant penalties, locals said, for crimes that surely included murder. The affair increased widespread suspicion of the brotherhood, spawning an American Anti-Mason movement and even a new political party dedicated to keeping Freemasons out of national office.

In the decades following the Civil War, men were again drawn to brotherhood and fellowship as they searched for answers in a changing age, and Freemasonry slowly regained popularity. Today, Freemasonry remains an order devoted to its own members, charitable causes, and the betterment of society. It has a worldwide membership of at least five million. Its members are traditionally male, though certain associations now permit women. Despite the name, most members are not stonemasons. They are, however, required to have faith in a supreme being, but not necessarily the Christian god (Mohammed, Buddha, and so forth are all acceptable).

OLD HICKORY'S BIG CHEESE

How America's first populist president traded 12 bottles of wine for the largest wheel of cheese he had ever seen.

In the early 19th century, Sandy Creek, New York, was a small farming community renowned for its dairy products, particularly its cheese. In 1835, one of the town's more colorful citizens, Colonel Thomas S. Meacham, conceived of a plan to deliver an enormous wheel of cheddar cheese to President Andrew Jackson in the name of the governor and the people of the State of New York. For five days, the colonel collected milk from 150 cows and piled the curd into an enormous cheese hoop and press he had constructed for the project. The resulting wheel of cheddar weighed in at half a ton, but this did not satisfy Meacham's lofty ambition. So, he enlarged the hoop and added more curds until the cheese reached a gargantuan 1,400 pounds. Judging his creation fit for the president he so admired, Meacham used a team of 48 horses to transport the cheese to Port Ontario, New York, and—amid firing cannons and cheering crowds—the cheese embarked on a water journey to Washington, D.C. Meacham accompanied his creation and delivered passionate orations to throngs of well-wishers at every stop. When the mammoth cheese was presented to President Jackson, the appreciative president, whose love of cheese was well known, gave Meacham a dozen bottles of wine and his hearty thanks.

At the order of the president, the cheese was allowed to age for two years in the White House lobby. Finally, on the occasion of Washington's birthday in 1837, Jackson determined that the cheese was ready for consumption and threw open the doors of the White House so the public could dine upon the cheddar.

It was common practice at the time for citizens to freely enter the White House during parties. In fact, the throng of revelers had grown so large during Jackson's first inauguration party that the new president escaped through a window and spent the night at the tavern where he had lodged before his election. The rumor of a giant, free wheel of cheese had a similar effect upon the populace, and scores of people pressed into the hall. Some even entered on walkways built to the windows to accommodate the large crowd. Among the notable people present at the cheese party were Vice President Martin Van Buren, Daniel Webster, Colonel Benton, and Colonel Trowbridge. The people carved huge chunks from the cheddar wheel and passed balls of cheese back to waiting guests. In the ensuing feeding frenzy, Meacham's entire creation was consumed in a scant two hours. All that remained of the mighty wheel were some curds, which had been trampled into the carpet during the rush. For years afterward, the lobby of the White House reeked of cheddar.

Van Buren, who succeeded Jackson as president soon afterward, also received cheese from Meacham (though it weighed in at a mere 700 pounds) and attempted to continue the cheese reception tradition. However, it soon ended when it became obvious that the White House finery could not bear the wear and tear of repeated cheese exposure.

Over the years, other U.S. presidents have received gifts of cheese as well:

• Thomas Jefferson enjoyed the 1,235-pound cheddar given to him by the citizens of Cheshire, Massachusetts. Jefferson first ordered that the cheese be served at the White House's New Year's Eve party, but the wheel lasted for several such occasions.

• Calvin Coolidge received a 147-pound Swiss cheese from the grateful citizens of Wisconsin, who approved of his heavy tariff on imports (including cheese) from Switzerland.

• George W. Bush, while campaigning in Wisconsin in 2004, stopped into a cheese factory in the town of Wilson. The surprised staff presented him with a platter of cheese curds. The resulting photos of the president, holding the curds and surrounded by hair-netted employees, made national news.

HOLLYWOOD VERSUS HISTORY

You may not be surprised to learn that Hollywood doesn't always get history right.

Today the place is a Motel 6

Interview with the Vampire (1994)—When Brad Pitt and Kirsten Dunst tour Bavaria in the 1790s, they visit the castle of King Ludwig, which wasn't built until about 90 years later.

And this is supposed to make the Bronx feel better?

Operation Crossbow (1965)—The Nazi "New York rocket" that's investigated by Allied agent George Peppard wasn't an intercontinental ballistic missile, as shown in the film, but a two-stage rocket with a winged second stage.

It's magic, leave it alone

Houdini (1953)—Houdini performs a Halloween stunt from inside a locked trunk that's been dumped into the frozen Detroit River. The problem? The river is never frozen at that early date.

They said "Spaniel"

Gladiator (2000)—Maximus's nickname is "Spaniard." Never mind that Spain did not yet exist.

And leave the trail-driving to us

The Comancheros (1966)—A Greyhound bus is briefly visible behind a hill in this 19th-century Western.

Grisly executions are so-o boring

Braveheart (1995)—As a crowd gathers to watch a disembowelment, a female extra loses mental focus and shoots glances at the camera.

Those subscriber-only perks are amazing

The Green Mile (1999)—Actor Michael Jeter relaxes with the November 1937 issue of *Weird Tales* in this story set in 1935.

CLEOPATRA: STRANGER THAN FICTION

In his work, Antony and Cleopatra, *the immortal William Shakespeare gave the Egyptian queen the following line: "Be it known that we, the greatest, are misthought." These "misthoughts" could be the myths, untruths, and fallacies that seem to surround Cleopatra. Though movies and the media tend to focus on these misconceptions, the true stories are equally fascinating.*

MYTH: Cleopatra was Egyptian.

FACT: Cleopatra may have been the queen of Egypt, but she was actually Greek. Though her family had called Egypt home for hundreds of years, their lineage was linked to a general in Alexander the Great's army named Ptolemy who had come from Macedonia, an area in present-day Greece.

MYTH: Cleopatra was a vision of beauty.

FACT: Beauty, of course, is in the eye of the beholder. In ancient times, there were no cameras, but a person of Cleopatra's stature and wealth could have their likeness sculpted. If the image on an ancient Roman coin is believed to be accurate, then Cleopatra was endowed with a large, hooked nose and was as cheeky as a chipmunk.

MYTH: Cleopatra dissolved a pearl earring in a glass of vinegar and drank it. As the story goes, upon meeting Marc Antony, Cleopatra held a series of lavish feasts. On the eve of the final gala, Cleopatra bet Antony that she could arrange for the costliest meal in the world. As the banquet came to a close, she supposedly removed an enormous pearl from her ear, dropped it into a goblet of wine vinegar, then drank it down, with Antony admitting defeat.

FACT: Scientifically speaking, calcium carbonate—the mineral of which pearls are composed—will dissolve in an acid such as vinegar. However, based on the description of the pearl in question, it is likely that the short dip in vinegar resulted in nothing more than a soggy gem, as it would have taken a very long time for that amount of calcium carbonate to dissolve.

MYTH: Julius Caesar allowed Cleopatra to remain queen of Egypt because he loved her.

FACT: Though not married, Cleopatra did bear Caesar a son, Caesarion. However, that was hardly reason enough to hand over an entire country to her. Most likely, Caesar felt that any male ruler would pose a formidable threat to his empire, whereas Cleopatra was a safer alternative to rule Egypt.

MYTH: Cleopatra died from the bite of an asp after learning of Marc Antony's death.

FACT: It's unknown exactly how or why Cleopatra committed suicide. According to legend, after hearing of the death of her lover, she had two poisonous asps brought to her in a basket of figs. The person who found the expired Cleopatra noted two small marks on her arm, but the snakes in question were never located. Cleopatra may very well have been distraught about her lover's demise, but it is more likely that rumors she was about to be captured, chained, and exhibited in the streets of Rome drove her to suicide.

- *Before marrying Marc Antony, Cleopatra was married to two of her brothers. But not at the same time! She married one brother, Ptolemy XIII, when he was 11. When he died, she married her other brother, Ptolemy XIV. He died not long after they were married.*

Fast Facts

- Following the American War of Independence, the British retained ownership of Florida, which became a haven for British loyalists. These same loyalists were forced to flee, however, when the British agreed to give Florida to Spain in order to retain their harbor at Gibraltar.

- The White House wasn't always a secure fortress. Warren G. Harding (president 1921–23) sometimes answered the front door himself.

- Confucius holds the distinction of being the secular thinker whose ideas have remained influential for the longest period of time—more than 2,500 years and counting!

- Benjamin Franklin reckoned that a 1739 open-air oratory delivered by English evangelist and master elocutionist George Whitefield in Philadelphia was heard by more than 30,000 people.

- The early Protestant sect of the Anabaptists was widely persecuted by both Catholics and other Protestants. In 1535, 12 Anabaptists, 5 women and 7 men, were executed in Amsterdam for running naked through the streets shouting their message of God's wrath. In the following ten years, some 30,000 additional Anabaptists were put to death in Holland alone.

- Countess Margaret Pole, sentenced to die for treason in 1541 by Henry VIII, refused to lie down for the killing blow. The executioner's clumsy first blow hit her on the shoulder. She then jumped up and ran for her life. The executioner chased her around the scaffold, gashing her 11 times before she finally died.

- George I, King of England from 1714–1727, was fluent in German and French but spoke almost no English.

- Herbert Hoover, Dolley Madison, Lyndon LaRouche, Annie Oakley, Daniel Boone, Joan Baez, Susan B. Anthony, and

PHILOSOPHY OF PEACE

Followers of this ancient religion wouldn't hurt a fly—literally.

Jainism is one of India's three ancient religions, along with Buddhism and Hinduism. Despite the fact that it has only a few million adherents and is confined almost entirely to Southern India, its philosophy of nonviolence has spread throughout the world.

PEACE AND UNDERSTANDING

To Jainists, the world is divided into the living (or the soul) and the nonliving. They believe that the soul is invaded by karmic matter, or negative passions, that can dominate people's lives. These include violence, greed, anger, and self-indulgence. This karma bonds to the soul and impedes the search for perfect understanding and peace. To reach the heavenly stage, Jainists must stop the inflow of bad karma and shed the karmic matter that has already bonded to their souls. Once this has been accomplished, they reach *moksha*—a level of pure understanding where the soul is liberated from all earthly matter.

Achieving this heavenly stage is quite an ordeal. An individual must spend 12 years as a Jainist monk and go through 8 reincarnations in order to get there. Along the way, each must also adhere to the Three Jewels of Right Faith, Right Knowledge, and Right Conduct. More extreme worshippers deny themselves even the most basic of life's pleasures by fasting and wearing only the simplest clothing.

WATCH YOUR STEP

Jainism's most famous principle is that all life—whether plant, animal, or human—is sacred. For this reason, Jainist followers go to great lengths to refrain from harming any living creature. Besides practicing strict vegetarianism, white-robed Jainist monks often carry a broom to sweep insects out of the way of their footsteps to avoid inadvertently taking a life. Some actually refuse to brush away mosquitoes, even if it means being bitten.

THE JUDITH COPLON CASE

*How one beautiful American spied for the Russians
and used promiscuity, patience, and the U.S. Constitution
to best the FBI at the start of the Cold War.*

A MOTHER'S SORROW

In the spring of 1949, Mrs. Rebecca Coplon sat
in a New York courtroom sobbing into a handkerchief. The cause of Mrs. Coplon's grief: her
beautiful and talented 27-year-old daughter
Judith was on trial for international espionage.

Judith Coplon had come from a respectable
family in upstate New York. Her father, a retired
toy merchant, was known as the "Santa Claus
of the Adirondacks" for his yuletide generosity to needy children.
Judith herself had shown great promise at New York City's
Barnard College and, more recently, as an analyst for the Department of Justice in Washington, D.C.

Sadly, Mr. Coplon died of a cerebral hemorrhage shortly after
hearing of his daughter's arrest. Mrs. Coplon was completely
unnerved by both her daughter's arrest and her husband's sudden demise. She could only sit sadly on the sidelines of one of the
most sensational trials of the 20th century.

A SLOPPY ARREST

Judith Coplon had been arrested in New York City, ostensibly
on her way to visit her family. In her possession were confidential documents that had been fed to her by FBI agents. The
FBI suspected that Russian engineer and U.N. liaison Valentin
Gubitchev, whom Coplon met with regularly, was more than he
appeared to be. In fact, Coplon began gathering information for
the Soviet Union in her college days, with Gubitchev acting as her
case manager in the newly formed New York bureau of the KGB.
Moreover, Coplon and Gubitchev were lovers.

The FBI already knew all of this. Following information gleaned from a secret decryption project codenamed "Verona," they conducted extensive wiretapping and surveillance of the pair to gain further information. However, the FBI arrested Coplon before she had actually handed the confidential documents to Gubitchev. What's more, they failed to obtain a warrant for her arrest, despite having had ample time to do so.

A BURLESQUE TRIAL

For her trial in Washington, D.C., Coplon hired the first lawyer she could find who agreed to work *pro bono*—the inexperienced, comedic, and essentially inept Archie Palmer. Despite his professional shortcomings, Archie turned out to be a genius at creating an aura of sensational wrongdoing and soon won public sympathy for Coplon's cause. The FBI alleged that, in addition to Gubitchev, Coplon was involved in a sexual relationship with a lawyer (who would end up serving as one the prosecutors in a second trial in New York). However, Palmer's courtroom clowning and Coplon's hedged denials effectively downplayed the issue. Palmer sneered, laughed, and sarcastically poked holes in the FBI's case. He argued that the "confidential source" named by the FBI was nothing more than an illegal wiretap, which was true. One FBI agent even admitted that the details of the meeting between Coplon and Gubitchev were only known because of tapped phone conversations.

AMERICA'S EVIL DARLING

The lurid details of Coplon's promiscuous and traitorous life made their way to the front pages and gossip columns of newspapers and magazines across the United States. The public was entranced by stories of the so-called "sexy spy," who giggled throughout her trial, and by the antics of her sensationalistic lawyer. Nevertheless, the juries in both the Washington, D.C., and New York trials found Coplon guilty. Both cases were appealed. The dubious legality of the wiretaps and the lack of an arrest warrant created a legal quagmire. As a result, Coplon never served a day in jail and lived to see both cases against her dismissed.

CAPTAIN BLIGH AND THE LOSS OF THE *BOUNTY*

*In 1787, the Bounty was a ship on the simplest of missions—
an easy trip to collect samples of the Tahitian breadfruit tree for
use as a food source on the slave plantations of the West Indies.
Instead, it would become famous for an act of mutiny that
continues to fascinate today.*

A BENEVOLENT BLIGH?

William Bligh was a mariner of no small experience. Having gone
to sea at 15, he was later praised by the legendary James Cook
for his work as sailing master of the *Resolution* on Cook's third
voyage. Bligh, in turn, learned a great deal from Cook and put a
number of the famed explorer's techniques into practice when he
became captain of the *Bounty*. He set about readying his new ship
for the voyage: the mundane task of loading supplies and oversee-
ing the construction of a greenhouse designed to safely transport
their botanical cargo. In a prescient move, he also demanded
that the ship's boats be replaced with more suitable vessels—a
request that would later save his own life. Along with the physical preparations, Bligh instituted many shipboard practices that
were perhaps avant-garde for the time—new ideas were always
met with suspicion by the tradition-bound British navy—but that
were clearly designed for the direct benefit of the crew. Bligh
changed the ship's routine to give the men a full eight hours of
rest each night, rather than the traditional four. He took particular
care to provide for cleanliness and prevent disease among his men
through rigorous enforcement of bathing and dietary regulations.
During the *Bounty*'s time in Tahiti, he even permitted the men to
bring the island women on board overnight.

A DISGRUNTLED SAILOR

Of course, Bligh was not without his faults. He was witheringly
sarcastic—not above publicly humiliating his men in front of

their shipmates if they did something incorrectly. In fact, he was described as having a "wonderful capacity for breeding rebellion." Unfortunately, the *Bounty* was a small ship, about 90 feet in length by a scant 25 feet wide, and there was no escaping Bligh's invective once a sailor had attracted his wrath. One man in particular, Fletcher Christian, came to bear the brunt of Bligh's assaults. Christian was popular with shipmates and island ladies alike but was known to suffer quick and sudden bouts of depression, stalking around the ship in a black silence. He also had a melodramatic streak, describing his existence as "hell." He planned to throw himself overboard if his call to mutiny failed.

The life-threatening voyage to Tahiti, followed by months of easy discipline on the island, created a powder keg when normal shipboard life resumed on the return trip. In the meantime, the personalities of Bligh and Christian combined to produce the explosive spark. Bligh's temper was on edge; he had recently discovered that his crew had allowed sails to rot and had neglected to wind the ship's chronometer—cardinal sins on any sailing ship. Shortly after leaving Tahiti, Bligh came to believe that someone was pilfering coconuts from the ship's supplies and publicly accused Fletcher Christian of being the thief. The altercation proved to be the breaking point for Christian, and he led the crew in seizing Bligh as he slept and setting him adrift in a small boat to face almost certain death in the Pacific.

AFTERMATH AND LEGACY

Bligh's seamanship proved equal to the task. He led his remaining men to safety on an incredible 41-day journey of survival in a boat that would doubtless be judged unfit for passengers by modern Coast Guard standards. British naval regulations of the time demanded a court martial on the loss of any vessel, but the proceeding found Bligh blameless, the soundness of his actions reinforced by the presence of the loyal sailors who had risked their lives to join him adrift rather than taking their ease in the islands.

Captain Bligh was promoted and given a new command. He went on to attain the rank of admiral. Fletcher Christian was murdered in his island paradise as his mutineers clashed with natives.

GREAT OBSCURE QUOTES

"Stocks have reached what looks like a permanently high plateau."
—IRVING FISHER, PROFESSOR OF ECONOMICS, YALE UNIVERSITY, 1929

"A severe depression like that of 1920–1921 is outside the range of probability."
—THE HARVARD ECONOMIC SOCIETY, 1929

"Not of any commercial value."
—THOMAS EDISON, ON THE PHONOGRAPH, 1880

"[There is] a world market for maybe five computers at most."
—THOMAS J. WATSON, CHAIRMAN OF IBM, 1943

"Computers in the future may have only 1,000 vacuum tubes and weigh no more than 1.5 tons."
—*POPULAR MECHANICS* MAGAZINE, 1949

"Louis Pasteur's theory of germs is ridiculous fiction."
PIERRE PACHET, PROFESSOR OF PHYSIOLOGY AT TOULOUSE, 1872

WORTH THE PAPER IT'S PRINTED ON: THE HISTORY OF PAPER

Three cheers for Ts'ai Lun! Without him, there would be no daily
gazette. Without him, there would be no dollar bills.
Without him, nobody could let their fingers walk through the local
phone directory. Without him, no one could read this very book.
Thanks to this gentleman from Lei-Yang, China,
the world enjoys the gift of paper.

WHERE'S THE PAPER, BOY?

Ts'ai Lun's invention of paper dates to A.D. 105. However, paperlike papyrus had been produced in Egypt for more than 3,000 years prior. The word "paper" is even derived from "papyrus." Ancient Egyptians developed it by hammering strips of the papyrus plant into a unified sheet for writing. They even sold it to the Greeks and Romans until around 300 B.C. With their papyrus supply cut off, Greeks and Romans turned to parchment, made from the skins of a variety of animals.

PAPER ON A ROLL

Ts'ai Lun was a member of the imperial court who became fascinated with the way wasps made their nests. Using that knowledge as a starting point, he took a mash of wood pulp and spread it across a coarse cloth screen. The dried fibers formed a sheet of pliable paper that could be peeled off and written on.

The new material quickly became a staple for official government business, for wrapping, and for envelopes. By the 7th century A.D., the Chinese had even invented toilet paper. A Chinese scholar at the time showed good judgment, observing, "Paper on which there are quotations or...the names of sages, I dare not use for toilet purposes."

PAPER GOES INTERNATIONAL

The art of papermaking remained in Asia for several centuries, spreading to Korea and Japan. Around A.D. 1000, papermaking reached the Middle East. Arabians used linen fibers in place of wood pulp, creating a higher quality paper. These superior products were in high demand, and exports increased. In this way, the art of papermaking reached Europe and flourished—particularly in Italy—by the 13th century.

The Italians took their papermaking very seriously, using machinery and standardized processes to turn out large amounts of top-notch paper. They used water power to run paper mills, created higher-quality drying screens, and improved the sizing process. A new coating was also developed to improve paper strength and reduce water absorbancy.

(DON'T) STOP THE PRESSES!

When a German named Johannes Gutenberg developed the movable type printing press in the mid-1400s, the world of papermaking was changed forever. Books that were once hand-copied were now available in a mass-produced format. As the appetite for new books grew, so did the need for paper.

The New World was introduced to papermaking in the late 1600s, when the first paper mill was built in Mexico. A German immigrant named William Rittenhouse started the first paper plant in the British colonies in Philadelphia in 1690. In less than a century, 20 mills were producing paper in the colonies.

ALL THE NEWS(PAPER) THAT'S FIT TO PRINT

Much of the paper being produced in the mills was made from old rags, clothing, and other textiles, making a thick paper. Around 1840, a Canadian named Charles Fenerty used a fine wood pulp to create a thin, inexpensive paper known as "newsprint." However, he didn't pursue a patent for his work and his claim of invention was lost to others. Still, Fenerty's invention enabled newspapers to be printed more frequently.

IT'S IN THE BAG

Paper has proved to be a versatile material in uses that go far beyond writing and printing. Following the Civil War, veteran Charles Stilwell returned to his home in Ohio and became a mechanical engineer. He noticed that paper bags used to carry groceries were not well made and wouldn't stand up on their own. He solved the problem, patenting a machine in 1883 that made paper grocery bags with a flat bottom and pleated sides. The style remains largely unchanged in the paper bags used today.

If Ts'ai Lun were still alive, he would most likely be amazed by how widespread his humble invention has become. In the modern world, it is virtually impossible to pass a day without picking up a book, a newspaper, an envelope, or a paper bag. Readers, writers, and even shoppers owe him a debt of gratitude for making their world an easier place in which to live.

- *By 1995, worldwide sales of toilet paper had reached $3.5 billion.*

- *In 1999, the United States used approximately 800 pounds of paper per person.*

- *The world's largest producers of paper and paper products are Canada and the United States.*

- *Recycling just one ton of paper saves 17 trees.*

Fast Facts

- Benjamin Franklin is credited with popularizing the game of chess in America.

- Communist leader Karl Marx was a reporter for the New York Tribune.

- The smallest U.S. president was James Madison; he was 5'4" tall and weighed approximately 98 pounds.

- St. Patrick, patron saint of Ireland, was not Irish.

- In 16th-century Turkey, drinking coffee was a crime punishable by death.

- There are 132 rooms, 35 bathrooms, and 6 levels in the White House. There are also 412 doors, 147 windows, 28 fireplaces, 8 staircases, and 3 elevators.

- Ice cream was introduced to the United States by Thomas Jefferson.

- Arnold Schoenberg, famous Austrian composer, suffered from triskaidekaphobia, the fear of the number 13. He died 13 minutes from midnight on Friday the 13th, 1951.

- Doc Holliday, known for his involvement in the shootout at O.K. Corral, was a dentist.

- At the moment of Pablo Picasso's birth, the midwife mistook him for a stillborn. However, his uncle, who was known to smoke cigars, revived him with a gust of air into his lungs.

- The House of David sponsored a team of bearded basketball players. In the early 1950s, they regularly played the Harlem Globetrotters.

- To conserve metal during World War II, the Academy Awards (known as the "Oscars") were made of wood.

Timeline

Continued from page 435.

1884
The first automobile goes on sale in Germany—just one invention in a century that sees the introduction of the telegraph, photography, the telephone, recorded sound, the electric light, radio, and motion pictures.

1900–1914
Austrian doctor Sigmund Freud publishes *The Interpretation of Dreams.* Henry Ford produces the Model T automobile. Anti-Western revolutionaries in China launch the "Boxer Rebellion." Japan defeats Russia in a 1904–1905 war.

1914–1918
World War I sweeps Europe and then the world. It ends with an Allied victory, the fall of the German and Austro-Hungarian empires, and the establishment of Bolshevik (Communist) rule in Russia.

1927
Height of the "Roaring '20s" in the United States. Charles Lindbergh makes the first solo flight across the Atlantic; Italian-American radicals Sacco and Vanzetti are executed; and *The Jazz Singer* is the first successful "Talkie" movie.

c. 1920–1940
Various forms of totalitarian government emerge in Europe—Fascism in Benito Mussolini's Italy, Nazism in Adolf Hitler's Germany, and Josef Stalin's regime in the Soviet Union.

1929–1939
The stock exchange crash in October 1929 and international financial jitters plunge much of the world into the Great Depression.

1936–1939
Civil war in Spain serves as a dress rehearsal for upcoming World War II. Japanese forces push deep into China. Stalin executes and imprisons millions in the Soviet Union.

1939–1941
World War II begins with a joint German–Soviet invasion of Poland. Most of continental Europe comes under German domination. Britain fights on alone.

1941–1945
Germany attacks the Soviet Union in June 1941. The United States enters the war after a Japanese attack on Pearl Harbor, Hawaii, on December 7, 1941. Germany surrenders in May 1945, and the Japanese surrender after the atomic bombings of Hiroshima and Nagasaki in August 1945. Worldwide death toll: 50–60 million.

1946–1953
Start of the Cold War between the West and the Soviet Union. India achieves independence, and the nation of Israel comes into existence. People's Republic of China is established in 1949. The Cold War turns hot in Korea in 1950.

1954
Communist Vietminh rebels defeat French colonial forces in Vietnam. The U.S. Supreme Court overturns segregation in public education

Timeline

sparking the movement for civil rights for African-Americans.

1957–1961
"Space Race" begins with the Soviet Union's launch of the first satellite, *Sputnik*. Yuri Gagarin of the Soviet Union becomes the first man in space.

1962–1963
The Cold War almost boils over when the Soviet Union installs nuclear missiles in Cuba. U.S. President John F. Kennedy is assassinated on November 22, 1963.

1968
A Year of Worldwide Unrest: Students riot in Paris; the "Cultural Revolution" rages in China; civil-rights leader Martin Luther King, Jr., and presidential candidate Robert Kennedy are assassinated in the United States; and Soviet forces crush a pro-democracy uprising in Czechoslovakia.

1969
The U.S. *Apollo 11* space mission lands men on the moon.

1973–1974
The United States withdraws from the Vietnam War and President Richard Nixon resigns in disgrace following the Watergate Scandal.

1979–1981
U.S. diplomatic personnel are held hostage in Tehran, Iran, for 444 days. The Soviet Union invades Afghanistan. China inches closer to capitalism following the death of communist dictator Mao Zedong.

1985–1991
Endgame in the Cold War: Soviet leader Mikhail Gorbachev liberalizes Communist rule in the Soviet Union; the Berlin Wall falls in 1989, ending Soviet domination of eastern Europe.

1991–1992
A multinational coalition led by the United States drives occupying Iraqi forces from Kuwait.

1991
British computer scientist Tim Berners-Lee develops the World Wide Web, fuelling the massive growth of the Internet.

1994
Former political prisoner Nelson Mandela is elected president of South Africa in the country's first multiracial elections after nearly 50 years of apartheid (official segregation).

2001
On September 11, Islamic fundamentalist terrorists attack New York City and Washington, D.C., killing nearly 3,000 people. The U.S. government announces a "war on terror."

2003
Claiming Iraq possesses "weapons of mass destruction," the United States invades the country and topple Saddam Hussein's regime, leading to a controversial and costly occupation of the country.

CASTRATI: GOING UNDER THE KNIFE TO HIT THE HIGH NOTES

"Mutilated for their art" is how one period writer praised the castrati, male sopranos and alto-sopranos whose manhood was intentionally removed before puberty to keep their voices "sweet."

Putting young boys under the knife to create a corps of eunuchs had been done since antiquity in many cultures. While the practice was applied by the Byzantine, Ottoman, and Chinese to create castes of priests, civil servants, and harem guards, the Italians of the 16th century used it to populate their church choirs.

Young boys can hit high notes for only so long before hormones kick in and thicken the vocal chords, turning altos into tenors and sopranos into baritones, bass-baritones, or big men who sing bass. Italians of the late Renaissance, with the blessing of a Papal Bull from 1589, preempted this progression of nature. Priests and choirmasters recruited boys, and parents sold or even volunteered their sons—often as young as eight years old—to undergo castration. The removal of their testicles ensured that the boys would keep their sweet, high, angelic voices—voices which, as they grew into men would become stronger and louder and more powerful without dropping in tone and timbre. Castrati had the "chest of man and the voice of a woman," as one enthusiastic supporter of the practice observed.

The Italians were not the first to introduce prepubescent emasculation in the name of art. Byzantine Empress Eudoxia first sanctioned this practice in A.D. 400 at the urging of her choirmaster, Brison, but the practice soon fell out of favor. Even so, as the Renaissance and the golden age of church music dawned, the castration of young boys began to occur with regularity throughout

Europe, particularly in Germany. It was in Italy, however, where it became something of a mania and where it continued for the longest amount of time.

By the late 18th century, as many as 4,000 boys a year were inducted into the ranks of the castrati in Italy alone—an especially staggering statistic considering the almost complete lack of anesthesia and the crude medical practices of the era. All of this was done "in the name of divine service" and was meant as a way to praise the Lord.

Castrati also appeared in plays, taking female roles at a time when women were still banned from performing in public. Although most castrati never left the choir, the popularization and proliferation of opera in the 17th, 18th, and 19th centuries gave them a new stage on which to showcase their talents. Opera castrati were the superstars of their era; noted composers wrote lead roles for them. Prized for the power and pitch of their angelic voices, the best of them were the toast of Europe, courted by kings, praised by artists, and sought after by rich women, partly as ornaments, partly as sexual curiosities.

The French, Industrial, and other revolutions that rocked Europe eventually turned public opinion against this practice. At first only frowned upon, it was soon banned by law. Italy, in 1870, was the last of the European countries to enact such legislation. The Catholic Church, however, continued to welcome castrati into church choirs until 1902, and it was not until the following year that Pope Leo XIII revoked the Papal Bull of 1589.

Even as their ranks thinned, cries of *eviva il coltello* or "long live the knife" continued to resound for these aging stars when they performed. Castrati hit the high notes right up until the eve of the First World War. Alessandro Moreschi, who retired in 1913, was the last, and by some accounts, the greatest of these physically flawed artists. His angelic falsetto has been preserved in a rare recording made in 1902.

Great Museums

TREASURES OF AN EMPIRE

A product of the Age of Enlightenment, London's British Museum
carved a new path in the diffusion of human knowledge
when it opened to the public in 1759.

It took the death of an obscure British physician, Sir Henry Sloane, to launch the world's first public museum. In his will, Sloane left a collection of some 71,000 natural and historical objects to the United Kingdom in return for a £20,000 stipend for his heirs.

Britain's King George II expressed little interest in the purchase of oddities and miscellanea, but far-sighted members of Parliament were moved to accept Sloane's posthumous deal. An Act of Parliament dated June 7, 1753, accepted the bequest and established a lottery to raise funds for the purchase and maintenance of the Sloane collection, as well as other items left to the king and country by wealthy collectors.

The collection originally consisted of three groups: Printed Books, Manuscripts (including medals), and "Natural and Artificial Productions," which included everything else. It slowly grew as George II contributed the Old Royal Library—rare works owned by Britannia's sovereigns. But the British Museum's place in world history was secured on January 15, 1759, when the museum opened its doors to "all studious and curious Persons" free of charge. Great Britain had founded the world's first public museum.

As the sun rose over the British Empire, the museum naturally benefited from exotic artifacts acquired from other lands by explorers, merchants, and generals. Classical sculptures from long-gone civilizations became a central feature of the growing museum, and before long, the 17th-century mansion in which the collection was housed had to make way for a larger building.

Between 1823 and 1857, the space around the old museum was rebuilt to accommodate a growing collection, as well as the throngs of ordinary citizens who came to see what the empire had collected.

In the early 19th century, the British Museum's curators embarked on a project that today would be called "public outreach." They scheduled public lectures, improved displays for visitors, and published a *Synopsis,* or museum guidebook, that ran to 60 editions before the end of the century. The museum also sponsored excavation projects abroad, and many treasures uncovered in these digs were sent to the museum.

The August 1939 Nazi-Soviet pact shook up British authorities, who decided to disperse much of the museum's collection amongst safer locations. Their precautions were warranted, as the museum was damaged by German incendiary bombs during the Blitz of London. Fortunately, Britain's most important treasures remained untouched and were repatriated when the war ended.

The postwar years marked a renewed effort to make the museum's holdings accessible and enjoyable to the public. The 1972 exhibition "Treasures of Tutankhamun" drew more than 1.6 million visitors to the museum and became the museum's most successful exhibit of all time. Since then, the museum has promoted temporary exhibits, as well as traveling exhibitions spanning the globe.

Today, some five million visitors tour the astonishingly varied collection of art and artifacts annually, which totals some 13 million objects. At the British Museum, tourists can find highlights of the collection, such as the Rosetta Stone; the Elgin Marbles, ancient statues that graced the pediments of the Athenian Parthenon; Michelangelo's sketch *The Fall of Phaeton;* the earliest surviving copy of *Beowulf;* and a colossal bust of Egyptian Pharaoh Ramses II. The world's first public museum is a fitting capstone to the empire that built it.

The Rest of the Best

Any list of the world's greatest museums is necessarily subjective. But beyond the Smithsonian (see p. 91), the Louvre (p. 206) and the British Museum (p. 475), one could round out a list of the world's top museums with the following:

1. Vatican Museums (Vatican City). *The world's smallest independent state boasts one of the world's largest collections of art and treasure. Founded in 1503 by Pope Julius II, the Vatican Museums showcase a huge collection of art, sculpture, tapestry, decorative works, and literature. Moreover, the walls, ceilings, and architecture of the buildings housing these treasures are themselves works of art; frescoes such as Rafael's* School of Athens *and the ceiling of the 15th-century Sistine Chapel provide a dramatic backdrop to one of the world's greatest assemblies of masterpieces. Little wonder that some three million visitors annually tour the museum's splendid halls.*

2. The Hermitage (St. Petersburg). *Built in a city that symbolized the emerging Russian empire of the 1700s, the Romanov dynasty's Winter Palace and its associated buildings house a massive collection of more than three million works of art assembled by Russian tsars, prerevolutionary bourgeois, and Communist-era benefactors. Ranging from a 7th-century B.C. Scythian gold statue to one of the world's greatest collections of impressionist art, the Hermitage has become one of Europe's most popular tourist attractions, drawing some two and a half million visitors annually. Taken together with its Moscow counterpart, the Kremlin Armory (home to the tsarist crown jewels and a magnificent collection of diamonds), the Hermitage ranks high on the list for any connoisseur of art treasures.*

3. Metropolitan Museum of Art (New York City). *Founded in 1870, the Met boasts a permanent collection of more than two million works of art covering some 5,000 years of human expression. Highlights of its American art collection include Emmanuel Leutz's* Washington Crossing the Delaware. *The museum boasts an equally impressive collection of Asian and Islamic art. The Met now draws about 4.5 million visitors annually, making it one of the world's most-visited museums.*

4. National Museum of China (Beijing). *China's ancient culture is on display at Beijing's National Museum, a gem of a museum that dates back to 1912. Some 610,000 pieces of archeological and artistic works from China's past are housed at the museum, giving the public a glimpse into China's 5,000-year history.*

5. Egyptian Museum (Cairo). *Although the museum's 120,000-piece collection runs from prehistoric times to the Greco-Roman period, the highlights are naturally found in its immense collection of Egyptian artifacts. Since its founding in 1835, the Egyptian Museum has grown to encompass the great works of the Pharonic eras, from ornate sarcophagus lids to golden statues of Egyptian gods and goddesses.*

6. J. Paul Getty Museum (Los Angeles). *Financed by oil magnate J. Paul Getty, the museum complex spreads out over some 750 acres in the foothills of the Santa Monica Mountains. Its highlights include Greco-Roman statues, illuminated monastic manuscripts, and some 450 European paintings dating from 1300 to the impressionist period. The Getty Museum arguably holds the world's finest private art collection.*

7. Museo Nacional del Prado (Madrid). *Situated in downtown Madrid, the Prado Museum has bragging rights to more than just Spanish masters such as Goya, Velázquez, El Greco, and Picasso. Like the Hermitage, the Louvre, and the Vatican, the Prado benefits from the global reach of Spain's pre-Renaissance empire. In 1868, the collection, which was the property of the Spanish crown, was nationalized for the benefit of its citizens, and each year some 2.5 million visitors view its collection of 7,600 paintings (plus another 11,700 drawings, prints, numismatics, sculptures, and objets d'art), which includes works by famed French, Italian, Flemish, Dutch, and German artists.*

FAMOUS LAST WORDS

"Museums are the cemeteries of the arts."
—Alphonse de Lamartine, French Poet, Writer, and Statesman, 1790–1869

"Give me a museum and I'll fill it."

—Pablo Picasso

THE WHACKED-OUT WORLD OF SIR GEORGE SITWELL

Fancy a breakfast of meat eggs? Does the history of the fork fascinate you? Do you like being ignored? If so, you'd get along famously with Sir George Sitwell.

The Sitwells, a gentrified English clan, were one of the most celebrated literary families of the 20th century. Dame Edith Sitwell (1887–1964) was an acclaimed author, poet, and literary critic. Her brothers, Sir Osbert Sitwell (1892–1969) and Sir Sacheverell Sitwell (1897–1988), made their marks in the literary world as an author and art critic, respectively. All three were noted for the frivolity, intelligence, and sophistication of their written works.

The literary accomplishments of the Sitwell siblings may seem remarkable when you consider that they were the offspring of Sir George Reresby Sitwell (1860–1943), an "out there" member of the English gentry of his day.

Sir George, like his progeny, made a name for himself, but not through literary greatness. Instead, he earned a more dubious reputation by penning scholarly tomes on inane topics, inventing thoroughly useless things, and exhibiting eccentric behavior that often left acquaintances wondering from what planet he originated.

IDLE HANDS, BUSY MIND

Sir George, it should be noted, never worked a day in his life. He became master of Renishaw Hall and Lord Manor of Eckington at a young age, allowing him to live off the income from his family estates as an English gentleman. He enjoyed the lifestyle of the idly rich, perhaps fostering the disconnection with the real world that he blithely displayed his whole life.

Sir George's idle hands were offset by a highly active mind—though he was certainly strange, he was definitely no dummy.

He was a renowned antiquarian and genealogist and was highly knowledgeable about medieval society. His research filled seven studies within Renishaw Hall and spawned numerous manuscripts, including such gripping treatises as "Wool-Gathering in Medieval Times and Since," "Domestic Manners in Sheffield in the Year 1250," and "Acorns as an Article of Medieval Diet." Sir George was also keenly interested in garden design, and in 1909 published a successful book entitled, *On the Making of Gardens*.

Sir George fancied himself a Renaissance man who possessed wisdom that extended well beyond medieval history and gardening. His extracurricular intellectual endeavors, however, revealed his true inner wackiness, suggesting something entirely different.

BOOKS NOBODY READ, INVENTIONS NOBODY WANTED

Sir George wrote a number of erudite works that demonstrated his skewed perspective as to what made for compelling reading. Included in these were densely worded dissertations such as, "The History of the Fork" and "The History of the Cold." To Sir George's dismay, none of his writings made it to the printing press. He also provided parenting expertise in a volume entitled "The Errors of Modern Parents," though his own parenting skills were questionable. During a short spell as a gentleman farmer, Sir George once tried to pay Sacheverell's Eton College fees in produce, and gave Osbert an allowance of the same amount that a previous Lord Manor of Eckington had given his eldest son 500 years earlier.

Sir George also tried his hand at inventing. One of his creations was an "egg" that featured a yolk of smoked meat, a white of compressed rice, and an ersatz lime shell. Sir George viewed his egg as a handy, nutritious snack for travelers. He was so convinced of its potential that he presented it to a prestigious London publicity firm announcing, "I am Sir George Sitwell and I have brought my egg with me." It didn't go over well, and Sir George never spoke of his egg again.

Undaunted, he later invented a tiny pistol designed specifically for shooting wasps, as well as an oversize toothbrush that played music.

A SOCIABLE ANTISOCIAL

It was while in the company of others that Sir George's detachment from reality was most vividly displayed. Guests invited to Renishaw Hall were greeted with a notice that read: "I must ask anyone entering the house never to contradict me in any way, as it interferes with the functioning of the gastric juices and prevents my sleeping at night." Usually he would eat alone, well before his guests sat down to dine, and would mingle only when approached. In typical Sir George illogic, he once lamented, "I never know anybody in this house."

His indifference to new acquaintances sometimes got him into sticky situations. On one occasion, he offered up a long and harsh critique of the writings of Rupert Brooke, completely unaware that amongst those listening to him was the young poet's mother. When delicately apprised of this, Sir George gave her a puzzled look and simply stopped talking.

Usually though, Sir George just didn't understand other people. He once went into a prolonged snit over the "bad behavior" of an acquaintance who failed to deliver him a piece of jewelry as promised. The person, hoping to arrange another meeting with Sir George, had told him in passing that he would give him a "ring" next Thursday.

Yes, Sir George was an odd duck. Daughter Edith would later publish a book entitled *English Eccentrics,* but, perhaps out of respect for her father, she made only a passing reference to him in it.

Make no mistake, however. Edith could easily have dedicated a whole chapter to Sir George.

THE ANCIENT PEDIGREE OF BIOLOGICAL AND CHEMICAL WARFARE

Considered the pinnacle of military know-how, biological and chemical warfare has actually been around for millennia.

CHINA'S DEADLY FOG

Inventors of gunpowder and rockets, the Chinese were also among the first to use biological and chemical agents. Fumigation to purge homes of vermin in the 7th century B.C. likely inspired the employment of poisonous smoke during war. Ancient Chinese military writings contain hundreds of recipes for such things as "soul-hunting fog," containing arsenic, and "five-league fog," which was laced with wolf dung. When a besieging army burrowed under a city's walls, defenders struck back. They burned piles of mustard in ovens, then operated bellows to blow the noxious gas at the subterranean attackers. In the 2nd century A.D., authorities dispersed hordes of rebellious peasants with a kind of tear gas made from chopped bits of lime.

ANCIENT GREEK POISONS

The ancient Greeks were also experienced with biological and chemical weapons. Herodotus wrote in the 5th century B.C. about the Scythian archers, who were barbarian warriors dwelling near Greek colonies along the Black Sea. By his account, Scythian bowmen could accurately fire an arrow 500 yards every three seconds. Their arrows were dipped in a mixture of dung, human blood, and the venom of adders. These ingredients were mixed and buried in jars until they reached the desired state of putrefaction. These poison arrows paralyzed the lungs, inducing asphyxiation.

A bioweapon figured prominently in the First Sacred War. Around 590 B.C., fighters from the city of Kirrha attacked travelers on their way to the Oracle of Delphi and seized Delphic territories.

Enraged at the sacrilege, several Greek city-states formed the League of Delphi and laid siege to Kirrha. For a time, the town's stout defenses stymied the attackers. However, according to the ancient writer Thessalos, a horse stepped through a piece of a buried pipe that brought water into the city. A medicine man named Nebros convinced the Greeks to ply the water with the plant hellebore, a strong purgative. The defenders, devastated by diarrhea, were rendered too weak to fight, and the Greeks captured the town and killed every inhabitant.

FLYING CORPSES SPREAD THE BLACK PLAGUE

In 1340, during the siege of a French town during the Hundred Years War, it was reported that catapults "...cast in deed horses, and beestes stynking...the ayre was hote as in the myddes of somer: the stynke and ayre was so abominable." Vlad the Impaler, the 15th-century Romanian warlord and real-life model for Dracula, used a similar method against his Turkish foes.

Scholars believe that this ghastly biological warfare tactic played a big role in spreading the worst plague in human history, the bubonic plague, better known as the Black Death. In 1346, merchants from Genoa set up a trading outpost in Crimea, which was attacked by Tartars, a warlike horde of Muslim Turks. However, during the siege, the attacking forces were decimated by the plague. To even the score, the Tartars catapulted the corpses of plague victims over the walls of the Genoan fortress.

Horrified, the Genoan merchants set sail for home. In October 1347, their galleys, carrying rats and fleas infested with the Black Death, pulled into Genoa's harbor. Within several years, the plague would spread from Italy to the rest of Europe, felling more than a third of its population.

A POX ON ALL THEIR HOUSES

In America, biological warfare darkened the French and Indian War. In 1763, during the vast rebellion of Native Americans under Chief Pontiac, the Delaware tribe allied with the French and attacked the British at Fort Pitt. Following the deaths of 400 soldiers and 2,000 settlers, the fort's defenders turned to desperate means.

William Trent, the commander of Fort Pitt's militia, knew that a smallpox epidemic had been ravaging the area, and he concocted a plan. He then made a sinister "peace offering" to the attackers. Trent wrote in his journal, "We gave them two Blankets and an Handkerchief out of the Small Pox Hospital. I hope it will have the desired effect." It did. Afflicted with the disease, the Delaware died in droves, and the fort held.

Trent's idea caught on. Soon after the Fort Pitt incident, Lord Jeffrey Amherst, the British military commander in North America, wrote to Colonel Henry Bouquet, "Could it not be contrived to send the Small Pox among those disaffected tribes of Indians? We must on this occasion use every stratagem in our power to reduce them." Amherst, for whom Amherst, Massachusetts, is named, added, "Try every other method that can serve to Extirpate this Execrable Race."

THE DA VINCI FORMULA

Even one of history's best and brightest minds, Leonardo da Vinci, dabbled with chemical weapons. The artist, and sometime inventor of war machines, proposed to "throw poison in the form of powder upon galleys." He stated, "Chalk, fine sulfide of arsenic, and powdered verdigris [toxic copper acetate] may be thrown among enemy ships by means of small mangonels [single-arm catapults], and all those who, as they breathe, inhale the powder into their lungs will become asphyxiated." Ever ahead of his time, the inveterate inventor even sketched out a diagram for a simple gas mask.

FAMOUS LAST WORDS

"Just as courage imperils life, fear protects it."

—Leonardo da Vinci

INDEX

Aristotle, 122
Armadillos, 68, 71
Armendáriz, Pedro, 108, 109
Around the World in 80 Days (1956), 29
Arthur, Chester A., 437
Arthur, King, 237
Articles of Confederation, 297, 298, 299
Asia
    emigration to U.S., 262
    Islamic influence, 265
    papermaking, 466
    symbols, 246
Astor, John Jacob, 295
Atahualpa, Emperor, 386–88
Athens
    animal trials, 219
    artistry, 353
    destruction and wars, 162, 214
    growth, 35
    laws, 161
    orators, 325
    sacking, 385
    society, 214
Attakullakulla, Chief, 172
Attila, king of Huns, 237
Augustus Caesar, 153, 236, 282
Aurelian, Emperor, 124, 137
Australia, 117, 281, 282, 361, 378, 417
Australopithecus anamensis, 68
Austria, 434
Austro-Hungarian Empire, 469
Aviator, The, (2004), 29
Avis Rent-A-Car, 269
Aztec Empire, 96
Aztecs, 128, 266, 280, 360, 369, 377, 386

B

Ba'al, 203, 204
Babar, 360
Babylon, 35, 86, 89, 161–62, 306
Bacon, Francis, 106–7
Bacon, Roger, 14
Bader, Douglas, 56
Baghdad, Iraq, 36
Baker, Lorenzo Dow, 396
Balboa, Vasco Núñez de, 143
Baldwin, Henry, 283–84
Baldwin II of Jerusalem, 326
Baldwin Locomotive Works, 79
Balkans, Alexander the Great's conquest of, 162
Balto, 317
Bananas, 368, 395, 397
Barbed wire, 240–42
Barbiturates, 358
Baroque art, 22–23, 222
Barry, James, 250, 347
Barton, Clara, epitaph, 216
Barton, Elizabeth, 414
Baseball, 291, 292
Basic Problems of Phenomenology, 231
Bastille prison, storming of, 435

Bathing, 105–7
Bathory, Countess Elizabeth, 349–51
Baudelaire, Charles-Pierre, 337
Beal, Mattie, 156
Beecher, Henry Ward, 112
Beijing, China, 102
Being and Time, 231
Beirut, Lebanon, 203
Bell, Alexander Graham, 242
Benedict, Maryland, 209
Benedict III, Pope, 263
Benedict V, Pope, 420
Benedict VI, Pope, 420
Benedict XI, Pope, 420
Ben-Hur (1959), 287
Bennett, Hugh Hammond, 199
Benton, Colonel, 454
Benton Harbor, Michigan, 290, 291, 292
Beowulf, 474
Berger, Ernest Peter, 176, 177
Bering Sea, 316
Berlin, Irving, 189
Berlin Wall, 186, 226–27, 470
Bernays, Minna, 148
Berners-Lee, Tim, 470
Bernini, Lorenzo, 222
Bible, 69, 93, 394, 421–22
Bible, The, (1966), 235
Big Brawl (1980), 29
Billy the Kid
    birthplace, 96
    epitaph, 65
Biological warfare, 480–82
Birdzell, Donald, 53
Birth of Tragedy, 230
Black, Eli M., 395, 397
Blackbeard, Edward Teach, 401–2
Black Death, 58, 146–47, 173, 187, 310, 405, 481
Blackfoot Indians, 185
Black Sunday, 197, 198–99
Bladensburg, Battle of, 209
Blanc, Mel, epitaph, 65
Blauer, Harold, 359
Bligh, William, 65, 462–63
Blood, James, 112, 113
Bobby (2006), 342
Boccaccio, 147
Boer War, 247–49
Bolingbroke, Henry. *See* Henry IV of England.
Bolivar, Simon, 435
Bolling, Edith. *See* Wilson, Edith.
Bolshevik party, 428, 469
Bonaparte, Elise, 63
Bones, Helen, 76
Bonfire Night, 301, 303
Boniface VII, Pope, 420
Boniface VIII, Pope, 420
Bonney, William H., epitaph, 65
Bonnie and Clyde (1967), 342
Bonny, Anne, 348, 402–3
Book of Mormon, 163

Totalitarianism, 469
Tours, Battle of, 223
Tower of Babel, 36
Trafalgar, 56
Trail of Tears, 171
Trains, 18, 160, 431
Transatlantic telegraph line, first, 431
Transvestites, 346–48, 392–93, 403
Tremulis, Alex, 449
Trent, William, 482
Triborough Bridge, 212
Trojan Horse, 213
Trojan War, 213
Trowbridge, Colonel, 454
Troy, 161, 213–14, 246, 329
Truman, Harry
    assassination attempt, 52–53
    as Freemason, 295
    nicknames, 437
Tsabar (Khan general), 102–3
Ts'ai Lun, 465, 467
Tsarskoye Selo, 20, 21, 23
Tubman, Harriet, 275
Tucker 48, 449–50
Tucker, Preston, 448–50
Tudor, Henry, Earl of Richmond. *See* Henry VII
    of England.
Tudor Dynasty, 233, 256, 311
Tuileries, 206, 207
tulip, 118–20
Tunguska blast, Siberia, 250
Tunis, Tunisia, 36, 215
Turkey, 87, 468
Tuscarora Indians, 39, 343
Tutankhamen, 281, 384, 426–27
Twain, Mark, 18, 110, 205, 295, 355
Tweed, William "Boss," 191–92
Twilight of the Idols, 230
Two Treaties on Civil Government, 229
Tyler, John, 438
Typhoid Mary, 423–25

U

U-202, 175–76
Ubico, Jorge, 396
Ulbricht, Walter, 226
Underground Railroad, 274–76
United Brands Company, 395, 397
United Fruit Company, 395–97
United Nations Educational Scientific and
    Cultural Organization (UNESCO) World
    Heritage Cultural site, 296
United States
    British occupation, 417
    German invasion, 175–77
    immigration, 260–62
    independence, 434–35
    invasion of Russia, 217
    quotes concerning, 321
    taxation, 95
    territorial expansion, 435

Ur, Iraq, 35, 36, 115, 306
Urban II, Pope, 200, 201, 202, 266
U.S. Constitution, 230, 300, 345, 434–35, 460
U.S. presidents
    deaths, 84
    elections, 75, 84
    first, 297–300, 435
    firsts, 267, 411
    interviews, 335
    longest–serving, 356
    names and nicknames, 300, 436–39
U.S. Supreme Court, 283–86, 295, 470
Ushiku Amida Buddha, 132
Utah Territory, 163, 165
Utah War, 164–65
Utopia, 414

V

Valdivia, Ecuador, 116–17
Valerian, Emperor, 418
Valverde, Vincente de, 387
Van Buren, Martin, 437, 454
Vanderbilt, Cornelius, 112
Vasilyevich, Anastasia, 193
Vasilyevich, Dmitri, 193
Vatican Museums, Vatican City, 475, 476
Vendetta (1950), 108
Vereeniging, Treaty of, 249
Versailles, France, 206, 217, 361
Versailles, Treaty of, 77, 78
Vespasian, Roman Emperor, 385
Vesuvius, Mount, eruption of, 237
Vichy French regime, 187
Victoria, Queen of Britain, 31, 48, 104, 257, 335,
    398, 399, 410
Victoria Eugénie of Battenberg, Princess, 30–31
Victoria Falls, 46, 89
Victory (1981), 342
Vienna, Siege of, 100
Vietnam War, 367, 469, 470
Vikings, 116, 128, 129, 138, 265, 266, 267, 280
Vila Nova de Ourém, Portugal, 133–34
Villa, Francisco Pancho, 332–34, 406
Visigoths, 237
Vlad II "Dracul," 319
Vlad III Tepes "the Impaler," 311, 319–20, 349,
    481
Vladimir I, of Kiev and Novgorod, 266
Voltaire, 194, 205, 295
Von Däniken, Erich, 54–55
Voynich manuscript, 13–15
Vulcan, 180

W

Walker, Madame C. J., 443–44
Wallachia, 311, 319, 320
War
    longest, 399
    quotes concerning, 51, 231, 355
    shortest, 398–99
Ward, Stephen, 270–72

AUTHOR CREDITS

Mark K. Anderson is a journalist, author, and lecturer who covers science, technology, and history for numerous publications. His most recent book is *"Shakespeare" By Another Name.*

Robert Bullington earned his master's in English from the University of Virginia and currently makes his home in Richmond, where he spends his time writing, raising a family, and performing with Nettwerk Recording Artists the Hackensaw Boys.

William W. David lives in Jacksonville, Florida. He is an IT professional by day and writes in his spare time. He hopes that some day the order of the two activities will be reversed.

Tom DeMichael has authored several books on American history and holds a degree in the subject. He also has published books and magazine articles on the subjects of American film and collectible toys. A native of the Midwest, he lives in the Chicagoland area with his wife and two sons.

Eric Ethier is a freelance writer and contributing editor for *America in WWII* magazine. He has also served as an editor on the staffs of both *American History* magazine and *Civil War Times Illustrated.* He is the coauthor of the *Insiders' Guide to Civil War Sites in the Eastern Theater,* Third Edition.

R.G.W. Griffin lives in Glen Burnie, Maryland. A technical writer by day, he spends his spare time writing more interesting things.

Peter Haugen has written such books as *Was Napoléon Poisoned? And Other Unsolved Mysteries of Royal History* and *World History for Dummies.* He is among the gang of writers responsible for *Condensed Knowledge* and its evil twin, *Forbidden Knowledge.* He lives in Wisconsin.

Jonathan W. Jordan is the author of numerous articles on military history as well as the books *Lone Star Navy: Texas, the Fight for the Gulf of Mexico* and *The Shaping of the American West.* He is currently researching a book on the American high command in World War II.

J. K. Kelley has a B.A. in history from the University of Washington in Seattle. Thus far, he has contributed to three Armchair Reader™ books. He resides in the sagebrush of eastern Washington with his wife Deb, his parrot Alex, and Fabius the Labrador Retriever.

David Lesjak has been interested in history since he was a teenager. He currently maintains an Internet site that explores the history of the Walt Disney Studio during World War II.

J. David Markham is a noted historian and award-winning author who has written five books (including *Napoleon for Dummies*). He has also contributed to four books and five encyclopedias. Markham has been featured on the History, Discovery, and Learning Channels, and his podcasts have thousands of listeners worldwide.

Bill Martin is a freelance writer whose diverse portfolio of work includes creative, media, and business writing. He holds a B.A. in history and political science from the University of Toronto and lives in Toronto with his wife Marianna and three daughters, Samantha, Paige, and Erica.

Michael Martin is a former editor at *Reminisce* magazine. He has written more than 30 nonfiction books for children as well as numerous historical articles for publications. He lives in La Crosse, Wisconsin.

Mark McLaughlin is a freelance journalist, political ghostwriter, board-game designer, and computer-game columnist. He has authored two books on military history and has contributed articles to several anthologies. Mark's next games, both on the Napoleonic era, will be published in the spring of 2008. He lives in Connecticut with his wife and two children.

Ed Moser is a former presidential speechwriter and was also a writer for *The Tonight Show.* He authored *The Politically Correct Guide to American History.* He currently works as an editorial consultant in IT and biotech.

Peter Muggeridge is a freelance writer based in Toronto, Ontario. He derives great pleasure and interest in the lighter side of history.

Eric D. Nelson teaches classics and writing at Pacific Lutheran University. He writes broadly on the ancient world, from academic works to *The Complete Idiot's Guide* series. He has appeared in and consulted on episodes of the History Channel's *Engineering an Empire* series and other programs.

Jean L. S. Patrick is an accomplished author, storyteller, columnist, and speaker. She has written five books and more than 100 magazine and newspaper articles. Her most recent book is *Who Carved the Mountain? The Story of Mount Rushmore.*

Bill Sasser is a freelance writer and journalist based in New Orleans. He writes for *Salon.com* and *The Christian Science Monitor,* among other publications.

Chuck Wills is a writer, editor, and consultant specializing in history, technology, and popular culture. He has written or contributed to more than 20 books, including *Grateful Dead: The Illustrated Trip, Destination America* (a companion volume to the PBS series), *America's Presidents,* and *Lincoln: The Presidential Archives.* He lives in New York City.